Business
Plans
Handbook

Business Plans

A COMPILATION
OF BUSINESS
PLANS DEVELOPED
BY INDIVIDUALS
THROUGHOUT
NORTH AMERICA

Plans

Handbook

VOLUME

28

Sonya D. Hill,
Project Editor

GALE
CENGAGE Learning®

Detroit • New York • San Francisco • New Haven, Conn • Waterville, Maine • London

GALE
CENGAGE Learning®

Business Plans Handbook, Volume 28

Project Editor: Sonya D. Hill

Product Manager: Michele LaMeau

Product Design: Jennifer Wahi

Composition and Electronic Prepress: Evi Seoud

Manufacturing: Rita Wimberley

Printed in Mexico
1 2 3 4 5 6 7 18 17 16 15 14 13

Contents

CONTENTS

Highlights

Business Plans Handbook, Volume 28 (*BPH-28*) is a collection of business plans compiled by entrepreneurs seeking funding for small businesses throughout North America. For those looking for examples of how to approach, structure, and compose their own business plans, BPH-28 presents 20 sample plans, including plans for the following businesses:

- Accounting Firm
- Alcohol-free Entertainment Center
- Arcade
- Bicycle Repair Business
- Chiropractic Office
- Custom Jewelry/Gift Box Business
- Educational Consulting Firm
- Event Planner
- Food, Diet, & Nutrition Company
- Gardening Consulting Business
- Health and Wellness Coaching Business
- In-Home Senior Adult Services
- Internet Cafe
- Landscape Contractor
- Marketing Consultant
- Martial Arts School
- Medical Billing Service
- Motel
- Plumbing Service
- Vending Machine Business

FEATURES AND BENEFITS

BPH-28 offers many features not provided by other business planning references including:

- Twenty business plans, each of which represent an attempt at clarifying (for themselves and others) the reasons that the business should exist or expand and why a lender should fund the enterprise.
- Two fictional plans that are used by business counselors at a prominent small business development organization as examples for their clients. (You will find these in the Business Plan Template Appendix.)

- A directory section that includes listings for venture capital and finance companies, which specialize in funding start-up and second-stage small business ventures, and a comprehensive listing of Service Corps of Retired Executives (SCORE) offices. In addition, the Appendix also contains updated listings of all Small Business Development Centers (SBDCs); associations of interest to entrepreneurs; Small Business Administration (SBA) Regional Offices; and consultants specializing in small business planning and advice. It is strongly advised that you consult supporting organizations while planning your business, as they can provide a wealth of useful information.

- A Small Business Term Glossary to help you decipher the sometimes confusing terminology used by lenders and others in the financial and small business communities.

- A cumulative index, outlining each plan profiled in the complete Business Plans Handbook series.

- A Business Plan Template which serves as a model to help you construct your own business plan. This generic outline lists all the essential elements of a complete business plan and their components, including the Summary, Business History and Industry Outlook, Market Examination, Competition, Marketing, Administration and Management, Financial Information, and other key sections. Use this guide as a starting point for compiling your plan.

- Extensive financial documentation required to solicit funding from small business lenders. You will find examples of Cash Flows, Balance Sheets, Income Projections, and other financial information included with the textual portions of the plan.

Introduction

Perhaps the most important aspect of business planning is simply doing it. More and more business owners are beginning to compile business plans even if they don't need a bank loan. Others discover the value of planning when they must provide a business plan for the bank. The sheer act of putting thoughts on paper seems to clarify priorities and provide focus. Sometimes business owners completely change strategies when compiling their plan, deciding on a different product mix or advertising scheme after finding that their assumptions were incorrect. This kind of healthy thinking and re-thinking via business planning is becoming the norm. The editors of *Business Plans Handbook, Volume 28* (*BPH-28*) sincerely hope that this latest addition to the series is a helpful tool in the successful completion of your business plan, no matter what the reason for creating it.

This twenty-eighth volume, like each volume in the series, offers business plans used and created by real people. *BPH-28* provides 20 business plans. The business and personal names and addresses and general locations have been changed to protect the privacy of the plan authors.

NEW BUSINESS OPPORTUNITIES

As in other volumes in the series, *BPH-28* finds entrepreneurs engaged in a wide variety of creative endeavors. Examples include a proposal for a Dance Studio, a Landscaping Business, and Concierge Service. In addition, several other plans are provided, including a Produce and Flower Market, a Digital Asset Management Consultant, and a Massage Therapist, among others.

Comprehensive financial documentation has become increasingly important as today's entrepreneurs compete for the finite resources of business lenders. Our plans illustrate the financial data generally required of loan applicants, including Income Statements, Financial Projections, Cash Flows, and Balance Sheets.

ENHANCED APPENDIXES

In an effort to provide the most relevant and valuable information for our readers, we have updated the coverage of small business resources. For instance, you will find a directory section, which includes listings of all of the Service Corps of Retired Executives (SCORE) offices; an informative glossary, which includes small business terms; and a cumulative index, outlining each plan profiled in the complete *Business Plans Handbook* series. In addition we have updated the list of Small Business Development Centers (SBDCs); Small Business Administration Regional Offices; venture capital and finance companies, which specialize in funding start-up and second-stage small business enterprises; associations of interest to entrepreneurs; and consultants, specializing in small business advice and planning. For your reference, we have also reprinted the business plan template, which provides a comprehensive overview of the essential components of a business plan and two fictional plans used by small business counselors.

SERIES INFORMATION

If you already have the first twenty-seven volumes of *BPH*, with this twenty-eighth volume, you will now have a collection of over 558 business plans (not including the updated plans); contact information for hundreds of organizations and agencies offering business expertise; a helpful business plan template; more than 1,500 citations to valuable small business development material; and a comprehensive glossary of terms to help the business planner navigate the sometimes confusing language of entrepreneurship.

ACKNOWLEDGEMENTS

The Editors wish to sincerely thank the contributors to *BPH-28*, including:

- BizPlanDB.com
- Fran Fletcher
- Paul Greenland
- Brenda Kubiac
- Claire Moore
- Zuzu Enterprises

COMMENTS WELCOME

Your comments on *Business Plans Handbook* are appreciated. Please direct all correspondence, suggestions for future volumes of *BPH*, and other recommendations to the following:

Managing Editor, Business Product
Business Plans Handbook
Gale, a part of Cengage Learning
27500 Drake Rd.
Farmington Hills, MI 48331-3535
Phone: (248)699-4253
Fax: (248)699-8052
Toll-Free: 800-347-GALE
E-mail: BusinessProducts@gale.com

Accounting Firm

Militello Accounting

PO Box 12345
Brooklyn, NY 11221

BizPlanDB.com

Militello Accounting will provide accounting services such as bookkeeping, tax preparation, and consulting to individuals and small businesses. The Company will earn a substantial amount of revenue during the tax season from filing tax returns from individuals and businesses within the target market. Mr. Militello will hire an associate CPA and a bookkeeper to assist with running the day to day operations of the business.

1.0 EXECUTIVE SUMMARY

The purpose of this business plan is to raise $150,000 for the development of an accounting firm while showcasing the expected financials and operations over the next three years. Militello Accounting, Inc.is a New York based corporation that will provide accounting, consulting, and tax services to customers in its targeted market. The Company was founded by Patrick Militello.

1.1 The Services

Militello Accounting will provide accounting services such as bookkeeping, tax preparation, and consulting to individuals and small businesses. The Company will earn a substantial amount of revenue during the tax season from filing tax returns from individuals and businesses within the target market. Mr. Militello will hire an associate CPA and a bookkeeper to assist with running the day to day operations of the business.

During tax season, the Company will hire 3 tax preparers.

The third section of the business plan will further describe the services offered by Militello Accounting.

1.2 Financing

Mr. Militello is seeking to raise $150,000 from as a bank loan. The interest rate and loan agreement are to be further discussed during negotiation. This business plan assumes that the business will receive a 10 year loan with a 9% fixed interest rate. The financing will be used for the following:

- Development of the Company's office.

- Financing for the first six months of operation.

- Capital to purchase a company vehicle.

Mr. Militello will contribute $25,000 to the venture.

1.3 Mission Statement

Militello Accounting's mission is to become the recognized leader in its targeted market for accounting services.

1.4 Management Team

The Company was founded by Patrick Militello. Mr. Militello has more than 10 years of experience in the accounting industry. Through his expertise, he will be able to bring the operations of the business to profitability within its first year of operations.

1.5 Sales Forecasts

Mr. Militello expects a strong rate of growth at the start of operations. Below are the expected financials over the next three years.

Proforma profit and loss (yearly)

Year	1	2	3
Sales	$655,290	$714,266	$778,550
Operating costs	$377,526	$391,666	$424,768
EBITDA	$212,235	$251,173	$275,927
Taxes, interest, and depreciation	$ 99,649	$108,901	$117,691
Net profit	$112,586	$148,165	$164,129

Sales, operating costs, and profit forecast

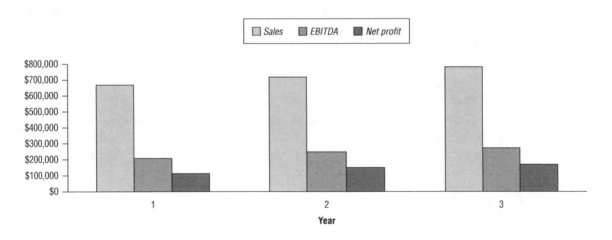

1.6 Expansion Plan

The Founder expects that the business will aggressively expand during the first three years of operation. Mr. Militello intends to implement marketing campaigns that will effectively target small businesses and individuals within the target market.

2.0 COMPANY AND FINANCING SUMMARY

2.1 Registered Name and Corporate Structure

The Company is registered as a corporation in the State of New York.

2.2 Required Funds

At this time, Militello Accounting requires $150,000 of debt funds. Below is a breakdown of how these funds will be used:

Projected startup costs

Initial lease payments and deposits	$ 25,000
Working capital	$ 65,000
FF&E	$ 25,000
Leasehold improvements	$ 10,000
Security deposits	$ 2,500
Opening supplies	$ 10,000
Company vehicle and lease deposits	$ 20,000
Marketing budget	$ 10,000
Miscellaneous and unforeseen costs	$ 7,500
Total startup costs	**$175,000**

Use of funds

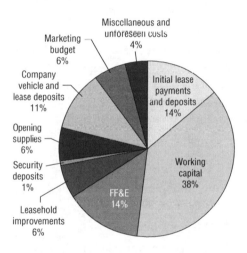

2.3 Investor Equity

Mr. Militello is not seeking an investment from a third party at this time.

2.4 Management Equity

Patrick Militello owns 100% of Militello Accounting, Inc.

2.5 Exit Strategy

If the Accounting is very successful, Mr. Militello may seek to sell the business to a third party for a significant earnings multiple. Most likely, the Company will hire a qualified business broker to sell the business on behalf of Militello Accounting. Based on historical numbers, the business could fetch a sales premium of up to 4 times earnings.

3.0 PRODUCTS AND SERVICES

Below is a description of the tax and accounting services offered by Militello Accounting.

3.1 Accounting and Consulting Services

The primary source of income for Militello Accounting will be accounting services that are provided to the general public. This section of the business will provide bookkeeping to individuals and small businesses within the target market. Each month, the Company will bill a client on a per hour basis. Expected hourly fees for bookkeeping will be $20 to $40 per hour based on the complexity of the work.

Mr. Militello, a licensed CPA, will also provide consulting advice directly to clients for $100 per hour.

3.2 Tax Services

Seasonally, Militello Accounting will make a substantial amount of money for filing tax returns for businesses. Each tax return will generate $300 to $1,000 depending on the complexity and the amount of paperwork to file.

4.0 STRATEGIC AND MARKET ANALYSIS

4.1 Economic Outlook

This section of the analysis will detail the economic climate, the accounting industry, the customer profile, and the competition that the business will face as it progresses through its business operations.

Currently, the economic market condition in the United States is moderate. The meltdown of the sub prime mortgage market coupled with increasing gas prices has led many people to believe that the US might be on the cusp of a double dip recession. This slowdown in the economy has also greatly impacted real estate sales, which has halted to historical lows. However, accounting firms are generally immune from changes in the economy as most people cannot effectively file their own tax returns.

4.2 Industry Analysis

The accounting industry is a highly fragmented group of individual practitioners, small firms, and large auditing institutions. There are over 621,000 accountants in the United States. The industry generates over $38 billion dollars a year, and employs over 390,000 Americans.

The demand for accounting services is expected to increase as the number of businesses and the complication of tax issues increase. With the advent of the Sarbanes-Oxley Act, businesses that have passive investors must comply with the myriad of laws stated throughout the Act.

4.3 Customer Profile

Militello Accounting's average client will be middle to upper middle income earners or a small to medium size business. The clients will seek professional advice to help them solve their accounting and tax issues. Common traits among clients will include:

- Annual household income exceeding $50,000

- Owns a small business or is involved in a profession

- Lives or works no more than 15 miles from the Company's location.

- Will spend $100 to $1,000 with Militello Accounting

4.4 Competition

There are a number of CPAs, enrolled agents, and tax preparation firms that operate within the Company's market of the greater New York metropolitan area. However, Mr. Militello, as a CPA, has substantial experience as it relates to handling all matters relating to individuals and businesses tax planning, estate planning, and other financial issues, His expertise will allow the firm to grow and thrive from the onset of operations.

5.0 MARKETING PLAN

Militello Accounting intends to maintain an extensive marketing campaign that will ensure maximum visibility for the business in its targeted market. Below is an overview of the marketing strategies and objectives of Militello Accounting.

5.1 Marketing Objectives

- Develop an online presence by developing a website and placing the Company's name and contact information with online directories.

- Implement a local campaign with the Company's targeted market via the use of flyers, local newspaper advertisements, and word of mouth advertising.

- Establish relationships with attorneys and accountants within the targeted market.

5.2 Marketing Strategies

Mr. Militello intends on using a number of marketing strategies that will allow Militello Accounting to easily target small businesses and individuals within the target market. These strategies include traditional print advertisements and ads placed on search engines on the Internet. Below is a description of how the business intends to market its services to the general public.

Militello Accounting will also maintain a large scale website that showcases the experience of Mr. Militello (as a CPA) as well as associate accountants. This website will be search engine optimized so that individuals seeking an accounting firm can quickly find the business when they conduct queries on major search engines. This will ensure that the business is able to generate a substantial amount of traffic from the onset of operations.

The Company will maintain a sizable amount of print and traditional advertisements among local circulars. Additionally, the business will establish relationships with local real estate agents (for people that have recently moved to the area) as a method for obtaining referrals for accounting services.

5.3 Pricing

For bookkeeping services the Company will charge $20 to $40 per hour depending on the complexity of the bookkeeping work. Mr. Militello will charge clients $100 per hour for providing tax advice and consulting services to the general public.

6.0 ORGANIZATIONAL PLAN AND PERSONNEL SUMMARY

6.1 Corporate Organization

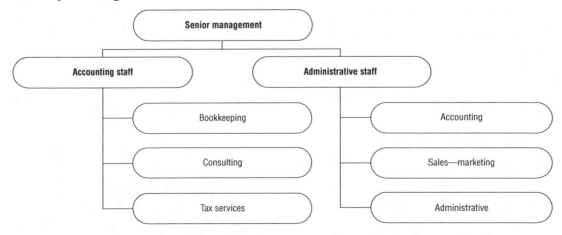

6.2 Organizational Budget

Personnel plan—yearly

Year	1	2	3
Owners	$ 65,000	$ 66,950	$ 68,959
Associate CPA	$ 50,000	$ 51,500	$ 53,045
Bookkeeper	$ 58,000	$ 59,740	$ 61,532
Tax staff (seasonal)	$ 45,000	$ 46,350	$ 63,654
Administrative staff	$ 25,000	$ 25,750	$ 26,523
Total	**$243,000**	**$250,290**	**$273,712**

Numbers of personnel

Owners	1	1	1
Associate CPA	1	1	1
Bookkeeper	2	2	2
Tax staff (seasonal)	3	3	4
Administrative staff	1	1	1
Totals	**8**	**8**	**9**

Personnel expense breakdown

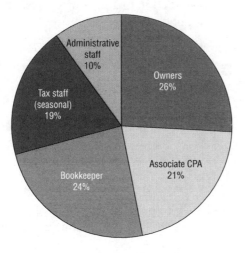

6.3 Management Biographies

Mr. Patrick Militello is a highly experienced CPA with more than 10 years in the industry. Since beginning his career as an accountant, Mr. Militello has acquired his CPA license, and he is now ready to launch his own firm. John's skill set includes:

• The ability to oversee agents and employees

• A complete understanding of accounting

• Licensure to operate as a CPA

7.0 FINANCIAL PLAN

7.1 Underlying Assumptions

The Company has based its proforma financial statements on the following:

• Militello Accounting will have an annual revenue growth rate of 9% per year.

• The Owner will acquire $150,000 of debt funds to develop the business.

• The loan will have a 10 year term with a 9% interest rate.

7.2 Sensitivity Analysis

In the event of an economic downturn, the business may have a decline in its revenues. However, accounting services are demanded by businesses and individuals due to the complexity of completing tax forms. As such, only a severe economic downturn would result in a decline in revenues.

7.3 Source of Funds

Financing

Equity contributions	
Management investment	$ 25,000.00
Total equity financing	**$ 25,000.00**
Banks and lenders	
Banks and lenders	$150,000.00
Total debt financing	**$150,000.00**
Total financing	**$175,000.00**

7.4 General Assumptions

General assumptions

Year	1	2	3
Short term interest rate	9.5%	9.5%	9.5%
Long term interest rate	10.0%	10.0%	10.0%
Federal tax rate	33.0%	33.0%	33.0%
State tax rate	5.0%	5.0%	5.0%
Personnel taxes	15.0%	15.0%	15.0%

7.5 Profit and Loss Statements

Proforma profit and loss (yearly)

Year	1	2	3
Sales	**$655,290**	**$714,266**	**$778,550**
Cost of goods sold	$ 65,529	$ 71,427	$ 77,855
Gross margin	90.00%	90.00%	90.00%
Operating income	**$589,761**	**$642,839**	**$700,695**
Expenses			
Payroll	$243,000	$250,290	$273,712
General and administrative	$ 14,400	$ 14,976	$ 15,575
Marketing expenses	$ 13,761	$ 15,000	$ 16,350
Professional fees and licensure	$ 25,000	$ 25,750	$ 26,523
Insurance costs	$ 7,500	$ 7,875	$ 8,269
Travel and vehicle costs	$ 15,000	$ 16,500	$ 18,150
Rent and utilities	$ 17,500	$ 18,375	$ 19,294
Miscellaneous costs	$ 4,915	$ 5,357	$ 5,839
Payroll taxes	$ 36,450	$ 37,544	$ 41,057
Total operating costs	**$377,526**	**$391,666**	**$424,768**
EBITDA	**$212,235**	**$251,173**	**$275,927**
Federal income tax	$ 70,038	$ 78,862	$ 87,359
State income tax	$ 10,612	$ 11,949	$ 13,236
Interest expense	$ 13,107	$ 12,197	$ 11,202
Depreciation expenses	$ 5,893	$ 5,893	$ 5,893
Net profit	**$112,586**	**$148,165**	**$164,129**
Profit margin	**17.18%**	**20.74%**	**21.08%**

Sales, operating costs, and profit forecast

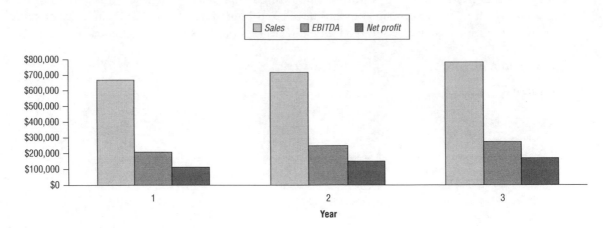

7.6 Cash Flow Analysis

Proforma cash flow analysis—yearly

Year	1	2	3
Cash from operations	$118,479	$154,058	$170,022
Cash from receivables	$ 0	$ 0	$ 0
Operating cash inflow	**$118,479**	**$154,058**	**$170,022**
Other cash inflows			
Equity investment	$ 25,000	$ 0	$ 0
Increased borrowings	$150,000	$ 0	$ 0
Sales of business assets	$ 0	$ 0	$ 0
A/P increases	$ 37,902	$ 43,587	$ 50,125
Total other cash inflows	**$212,902**	**$ 43,587**	**$ 50,125**
Total cash inflow	**$331,381**	**$197,645**	**$220,148**
Cash outflows			
Repayment of principal	$ 9,695	$ 10,605	$ 11,599
A/P decreases	$ 24,897	$ 29,876	$ 35,852
A/R increases	$ 0	$ 0	$ 0
Asset purchases	$ 82,500	$ 15,406	$ 17,002
Dividends	$ 94,783	$123,247	$136,018
Total cash outflows	**$211,876**	**$179,133**	**$200,471**
Net cash flow	**$119,506**	**$ 18,512**	**$ 19,677**
Cash balance	**$119,506**	**$138,018**	**$157,695**

Proforma cash flow (yearly)

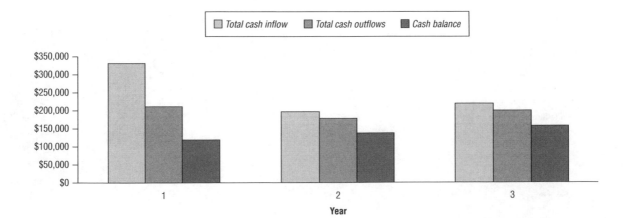

7.7 Balance Sheet

Proforma balance sheet—yearly

Year	1	2	3
Assets			
Cash	$119,506	$138,018	$157,695
Amortized expansion costs	$ 45,000	$ 46,541	$ 48,241
Opening supplies	$ 2,500	$ 5,581	$ 8,982
FF&E	$ 15,000	$ 18,851	$ 23,102
Company vehicles and lease deposits	$ 20,000	$ 28,473	$ 37,824
Accumulated depreciation	($ 5,893)	($ 11,786)	($ 17,679)
Total assets	**$196,113**	**$225,679**	**$258,165**
Liabilities and equity			
Accounts payable	$ 13,005	$ 26,716	$ 40,990
Long term liabilities	$140,305	$129,700	$119,096
Other liabilities	$ 0	$ 0	$ 0
Total liabilities	**$153,310**	**$156,416**	**$160,085**
Net worth	**$ 42,803**	**$ 69,262**	**$ 98,079**
Total liabilities and equity	**$196,113**	**$225,679**	**$258,165**

Proforma balance sheet

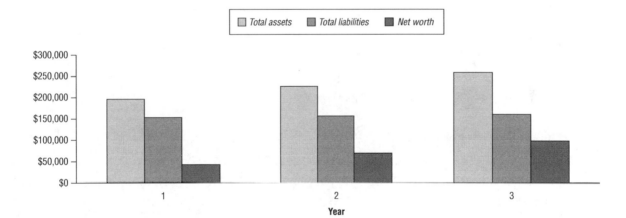

7.8 Breakeven Analysis

Monthly break even analysis

Year	1	2	3
Monthly revenue	$ 34,956	$ 36,265	$ 39,330
Yearly revenue	$419,473	$435,185	$471,964

Break even analysis

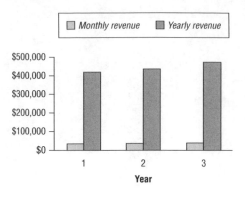

7.9 Business Ratios

Business ratios—yearly

Year	1	2	3
Sales			
Sales growth	0.00%	9.00%	9.00%
Gross margin	90.00%	90.00%	90.00%
Financials			
Profit margin	17.18%	20.74%	21.08%
Assets to liabilities	1.28	1.44	1.61
Equity to liabilities	0.28	0.44	0.61
Assets to equity	4.58	3.26	2.63
Liquidity			
Acid test	0.78	0.88	0.99
Cash to assets	0.61	0.61	0.61

7.10 Three Year Profit and Loss Statement

Profit and loss statement (first year)

Months	1	2	3	4	5	6	7
Sales	$67,375	$67,550	$67,725	$67,900	$44,735	$44,850	$44,965
Cost of goods sold	$ 6,738	$ 6,755	$ 6,773	$ 6,790	$ 4,474	$ 4,485	$ 4,497
Gross margin	90.00%	90.00%	90.00%	90.00%	90.00%	90.00%	90.00%
Operating income	$60,638	$60,795	$60,953	$61,110	$40,262	$40,365	$40,469
Expenses							
Payroll	$ 20,250	$ 20,250	$ 20,250	$ 20,250	$ 20,250	$ 20,250	$ 20,250
General and administrative	$ 1,200	$ 1,200	$ 1,200	$ 1,200	$ 1,200	$ 1,200	$ 1,200
Marketing expenses	$ 1,147	$ 1,147	$ 1,147	$ 1,147	$ 1,147	$ 1,147	$ 1,147
Professional fees and licensure	$ 2,083	$ 2,083	$ 2,083	$ 2,083	$ 2,083	$ 2,083	$ 2,083
Insurance costs	$ 625	$ 625	$ 625	$ 625	$ 625	$ 625	$ 625
Travel and vehicle costs	$ 1,250	$ 1,250	$ 1,250	$ 1,250	$ 1,250	$ 1,250	$ 1,250
Rent and utilities	$ 1,458	$ 1,458	$ 1,458	$ 1,458	$ 1,458	$ 1,458	$ 1,458
Miscellaneous costs	$ 410	$ 410	$ 410	$ 410	$ 410	$ 410	$ 410
Payroll taxes	$ 3,038	$ 3,038	$ 3,038	$ 3,038	$ 3,038	$ 3,038	$ 3,038
Total operating costs	$31,460	$31,460	$31,460	$31,460	$31,460	$31,460	$31,460
EBITDA	$29,177	$29,335	$29,492	$29,650	$ 8,801	$ 8,905	$ 9,008
Federal income tax	$ 7,201	$ 7,220	$ 7,238	$ 7,257	$ 4,781	$ 4,794	$ 4,806
State income tax	$ 1,091	$ 1,094	$ 1,097	$ 1,100	$ 724	$ 726	$ 728
Interest expense	$ 1,125	$ 1,119	$ 1,113	$ 1,107	$ 1,101	$ 1,095	$ 1,089
Depreciation expense	$ 491	$ 491	$ 491	$ 491	$ 491	$ 491	$ 491
Net profit	$ 19,269	$ 19,411	$ 19,552	$ 19,694	$ 1,703	$ 1,798	$ 1,893

Profit and loss statement (first year cont.)

Month	8	9	10	11	12	1
Sales	$45,080	$45,195	$68,950	$45,425	$45,540	$655,290
Cost of goods sold	$ 4,508	$ 4,520	$ 6,895	$ 4,543	$ 4,554	$ 65,529
Gross margin	90.00%	90.00%	90.00%	90.00%	90.00%	90.00%
Operating income	$40,572	$40,676	$62,055	$40,883	$40,986	$589,761
Expenses						
Payroll	$20,250	$20,250	$20,250	$20,250	$20,250	$243,000
General and administrative	$ 1,200	$ 1,200	$ 1,200	$ 1,200	$ 1,200	$ 14,400
Marketing expenses	$ 1,147	$ 1,147	$ 1,147	$ 1,147	$ 1,147	$ 13,761
Professional fees and licensure	$ 2,083	$ 2,083	$ 2,083	$ 2,083	$ 2,083	$ 25,000
Insurance costs	$ 625	$ 625	$ 625	$ 625	$ 625	$ 7,500
Travel and vehicle costs	$ 1,250	$ 1,250	$ 1,250	$ 1,250	$ 1,250	$ 15,000
Rent and utilities	$ 1,458	$ 1,458	$ 1,458	$ 1,458	$ 1,458	$ 17,500
Miscellaneous costs	$ 410	$ 410	$ 410	$ 410	$ 410	$ 4,915
Payroll taxes	$ 3,038	$ 3,038	$ 3,038	$ 3,038	$ 3,038	$ 36,450
Total operating costs	$31,460	$31,460	$31,460	$31,460	$31,460	$377,526
EBITDA	$ 9,112	$ 9,215	$30,595	$ 9,422	$ 9,526	$212,235
Federal income tax	$ 4,818	$ 4,830	$ 7,369	$ 4,855	$ 4,867	$ 70,038
State income tax	$ 730	$ 732	$ 1,117	$ 736	$ 737	$ 10,612
Interest expense	$ 1,083	$ 1,077	$ 1,071	$ 1,065	$ 1,059	$ 13,107
Depreciation expense	$ 491	$ 491	$ 491	$ 491	$ 491	$ 5,893
Net profit	$ 1,989	$ 2,084	$20,546	$ 2,275	$ 2,371	$112,586

Profit and loss statement (second year)

Quarter	Q1	2 Q2	Q3	Q4	2
Sales	$142,853	$178,567	$192,852	$199,995	$714,266
Cost of goods sold	$ 14,285	$ 17,857	$ 19,285	$ 19,999	$ 71,427
Gross margin	90.00%	90.00%	90.00%	90.00%	90.00%
Operating income	$128,568	$160,710	$173,567	$179,995	$642,839
Expenses					
Payroll	$ 50,058	$ 62,573	$ 67,578	$ 70,081	$250,290
General and administrative	$ 2,995	$ 3,744	$ 4,044	$ 4,193	$ 14,976
Marketing expenses	$ 3,000	$ 3,750	$ 4,050	$ 4,200	$ 15,000
Professional fees and licensure	$ 5,150	$ 6,438	$ 6,953	$ 7,210	$ 25,750
Insurance costs	$ 1,575	$ 1,969	$ 2,126	$ 2,205	$ 7,875
Travel and vehicle costs	$ 3,300	$ 4,125	$ 4,455	$ 4,620	$ 16,500
Rent and utilities	$ 3,675	$ 4,594	$ 4,961	$ 5,145	$ 18,375
Miscellaneous costs	$ 1,071	$ 1,339	$ 1,446	$ 1,500	$ 5,357
Payroll taxes	$ 7,509	$ 9,386	$ 10,137	$ 10,512	$ 37,544
Total operating costs	$ 78,333	$ 97,917	$105,750	$109,667	$391,666
EBITDA	$ 50,235	$ 62,793	$ 67,817	$ 70,329	$251,173
Federal income tax	$ 15,772	$ 19,716	$ 21,293	$ 22,081	$ 78,862
State income tax	$ 2,390	$ 2,987	$ 3,226	$ 3,346	$ 11,949
Interest expense	$ 3,138	$ 3,080	$ 3,020	$ 2,959	$ 12,197
Depreciation expense	$ 1,473	$ 1,473	$ 1,473	$ 1,473	$ 5,893
Net profit	$ 27,462	$ 35,538	$ 38,804	$ 40,469	$142,272

Profit and loss statement (third year)

Quarter	Q1	3 Q2	Q3	Q4	3
Sales	$155,710	$194,638	$210,209	$217,994	$778,550
Cost of goods sold	$ 15,571	$ 19,464	$ 21,021	$ 21,799	$ 77,855
Gross margin	0.0%	0.0%	0.0%	0.0%	0.0%
Operating income	$140,139	$175,174	$189,188	$196,195	$700,695
Expenses					
Payroll	$ 54,742	$ 68,428	$ 73,902	$ 76,639	$273,712
General and administrative	$ 3,115	$ 3,894	$ 4,205	$ 4,361	$ 15,575
Marketing expenses	$ 3,270	$ 4,087	$ 4,414	$ 4,578	$ 16,350
Professional fees and licensure	$ 5,305	$ 6,631	$ 7,161	$ 7,426	$ 26,523
Insurance costs	$ 1,654	$ 2,067	$ 2,233	$ 2,315	$ 8,269
Travel and vehicle costs	$ 3,630	$ 4,538	$ 4,901	$ 5,082	$ 18,150
Rent and utilities	$ 3,859	$ 4,823	$ 5,209	$ 5,402	$ 19,294
Miscellaneous costs	$ 1,168	$ 1,460	$ 1,577	$ 1,635	$ 5,839
Payroll taxes	$ 8,211	$ 10,264	$ 11,085	$ 11,496	$ 41,057
Total operating costs	$ 84,954	$106,192	$114,687	$118,935	$424,768
EBITDA	$ 55,185	$ 68,982	$ 74,500	$ 77,260	$275,927
Federal income tax	$ 17,472	$ 21,840	$ 23,587	$ 24,461	$ 87,359
State income tax	$ 2,647	$ 3,309	$ 3,574	$ 3,706	$ 13,236
Interest expense	$ 2,897	$ 2,834	$ 2,769	$ 2,702	$ 11,202
Depreciation expense	$ 1,473	$ 1,473	$ 1,473	$ 1,473	$ 5,893
Net profit	$ 30,696	$ 39,526	$ 43,098	$ 44,917	$158,237

7.11 Three Year Cash Flow Analysis

Cash flow analysis (first year)

Month	1	2	3	4	5	6	7
Cash from operations	$ 19,760	$ 19,902	$ 20,043	$ 20,185	$ 2,194	$ 2,289	$ 2,385
Cash from receivables	$ 0	$ 0	$ 0	$ 0	$ 0	$ 0	$ 0
Operating cash inflow	$ 19,760	$ 19,902	$ 20,043	$ 20,185	$ 2,194	$ 2,289	$ 2,385
Other cash inflows							
Equity investment	$ 25,000	$ 0	$ 0	$ 0	$ 0	$ 0	$ 0
Increased borrowings	$150,000	$ 0	$ 0	$ 0	$ 0	$ 0	$ 0
Sales of business assets	$ 0	$ 0	$ 0	$ 0	$ 0	$ 0	$ 0
A/P increases	$ 3,159	$ 3,159	$ 3,159	$ 3,159	$ 3,159	$ 3,159	$ 3,159
Total other cash inflows	$178,159	$ 3,159	$ 3,159	$ 3,159	$ 3,159	$ 3,159	$ 3,159
Total cash inflow	$197,918	$ 23,060	$ 23,202	$ 23,344	$ 5,352	$ 5,448	$ 5,543
Cash outflows							
Repayment of principal	$ 775	$ 781	$ 787	$ 793	$ 799	$ 805	$ 811
A/P decreases	$ 2,075	$ 2,075	$ 2,075	$ 2,075	$ 2,075	$ 2,075	$ 2,075
A/R increases	$ 0	$ 0	$ 0	$ 0	$ 0	$ 0	$ 0
Asset purchases	$ 82,500	$ 0	$ 0	$ 0	$ 0	$ 0	$ 0
Dividends	$ 0	$ 0	$ 0	$ 0	$ 0	$ 0	$ 0
Total cash outflows	$ 85,350	$ 2,856	$ 2,862	$ 2,867	$ 2,873	$ 2,879	$ 2,885
Net cash flow	$112,568	$ 20,204	$ 20,340	$ 20,476	$ 2,479	$ 2,568	$ 2,658
Cash balance	$112,568	$132,773	$153,113	$173,590	$176,069	$178,637	$181,295

Cash flow analysis (first year cont.)

Month	8	9	10	11	12	1
Cash from operations	$ 2,480	$ 2,575	$ 21,037	$ 2,767	$ 2,862	$118,479
Cash from receivables	$ 0	$ 0	$ 0	$ 0	$ 0	$ 0
Operating cash inflow	**$ 2,480**	**$ 2,575**	**$ 21,037**	**$ 2,767**	**$ 2,862**	**$118,479**
Other cash inflows						
Equity investment	$ 0	$ 0	$ 0	$ 0	$ 0	$ 25,000
Increased borrowings	$ 0	$ 0	$ 0	$ 0	$ 0	$150,000
Sales of business assets	$ 0	$ 0	$ 0	$ 0	$ 0	$ 0
A/P increases	$ 3,159	$ 3,159	$ 3,159	$ 3,159	$ 3,159	$ 37,902
Total other cash inflows	**$ 3,159**	**$ 3,159**	**$ 3,159**	**$ 3,159**	**$ 3,159**	**$212,902**
Total cash inflow	**$ 5,638**	**$ 5,734**	**$ 24,196**	**$ 5,925**	**$ 6,021**	**$331,381**
Cash outflows						
Repayment of principal	$ 817	$ 823	$ 829	$ 835	$ 842	$ 9,695
A/P decreases	$ 2,075	$ 2,075	$ 2,075	$ 2,075	$ 2,075	$ 24,897
A/R increases	$ 0	$ 0	$ 0	$ 0	$ 0	$ 0
Asset purchases	$ 0	$ 0	$ 0	$ 0	$ 0	$ 82,500
Dividends	$ 0	$ 0	$ 0	$ 0	$ 94,783	$ 94,783
Total cash outflows	**$ 2,892**	**$ 2,898**	**$ 2,904**	**$ 2,910**	**$ 97,699**	**$211,876**
Net cash flow	**$ 2,747**	**$ 2,836**	**$ 21,292**	**$ 3,015**	**−$ 91,679**	**$119,506**
Cash balance	**$184,041**	**$186,878**	**$208,170**	**$211,185**	**$119,506**	**$119,506**

Cash flow analysis (second year)

Quarter	Q1	2 Q2	Q3	Q4	2
Cash from operations	$ 30,812	$ 38,515	$ 41,596	$ 43,136	$154,058
Cash from receivables	$ 0	$ 0	$ 0	$ 0	$ 0
Operating cash inflow	**$ 30,812**	**$ 38,515**	**$ 41,596**	**$ 43,136**	**$154,058**
Other cash inflows					
Equity investment	$ 0	$ 0	$ 0	$ 0	$ 0
Increased borrowings	$ 0	$ 0	$ 0	$ 0	$ 0
Sales of business assets	$ 0	$ 0	$ 0	$ 0	$ 0
A/P increases	$ 8,717	$ 10,897	$ 11,769	$ 12,204	$ 43,587
Total other cash inflows	**$ 8,717**	**$ 10,897**	**$ 11,769**	**$ 12,204**	**$ 43,587**
Total cash inflow	**$ 39,529**	**$ 49,411**	**$ 53,364**	**$ 55,341**	**$197,645**
Cash outflows					
Repayment of principal	$ 2,563	$ 2,621	$ 2,680	$ 2,741	$ 10,605
A/P decreases	$ 5,975	$ 7,469	$ 8,067	$ 8,365	$ 29,876
A/R increases	$ 0	$ 0	$ 0	$ 0	$ 0
Asset purchases	$ 3,081	$ 3,851	$ 4,160	$ 4,314	$ 15,406
Dividends	$ 24,649	$ 30,812	$ 33,277	$ 34,509	$123,247
Total cash outflows	**$ 36,268**	**$ 44,753**	**$ 48,183**	**$ 49,929**	**$179,133**
Net cash flow	**$ 3,261**	**$ 4,658**	**$ 5,181**	**$ 5,412**	**$ 18,512**
Cash balance	**$122,766**	**$127,425**	**$132,606**	**$138,018**	**$138,018**

Cash flow analysis (third year)

Quarter	Q1	Q2	Q3	Q4	3
		3			
Cash from operations	$ 34,004	$ 42,506	$ 45,906	$ 47,606	$170,022
Cash from receivables	$ 0	$ 0	$ 0	$ 0	$ 0
Operating cash inflow	**$ 34,004**	**$ 42,506**	**$ 45,906**	**$ 47,606**	**$170,022**
Other cash inflows					
Equity investment	$ 0	$ 0	$ 0	$ 0	$ 0
Increased borrowings	$ 0	$ 0	$ 0	$ 0	$ 0
Sales of business assets	$ 0	$ 0	$ 0	$ 0	$ 0
A/P increases	$ 10,025	$ 12,531	$ 13,534	$ 14,035	$ 50,125
Total other cash inflows	**$ 10,025**	**$ 12,531**	**$ 13,534**	**$ 14,035**	**$ 50,125**
Total cash inflow	**$ 44,030**	**$ 55,037**	**$ 59,440**	**$ 61,641**	**$220,148**
Cash outflows					
Repayment of principal	$ 2,803	$ 2,867	$ 2,932	$ 2,998	$ 11,599
A/P decreases	$ 7,170	$ 8,963	$ 9,680	$ 10,038	$ 35,852
A/R increases	$ 0	$ 0	$ 0	$ 0	$ 0
Asset purchases	$ 3,400	$ 4,251	$ 4,591	$ 4,761	$ 17,002
Dividends	$ 27,204	$ 34,004	$ 36,725	$ 38,085	$136,018
Total cash outflows	**$ 40,577**	**$ 50,085**	**$ 53,927**	**$ 55,882**	**$200,471**
Net cash flow	**$ 3,452**	**$ 4,952**	**$ 5,513**	**$ 5,759**	**$ 19,677**
Cash balance	**$141,470**	**$146,422**	**$151,935**	**$157,695**	**$157,695**

Alcohol-free Entertainment Center

The Clean Slate Inc.

4360 Main St.
Center City, OH 43333

Paul Greeland

The Clean Slate is an entertainment destination for non-drinkers and individuals recovering from addictions who need a supportive environment for socialization and entertainment.

EXECUTIVE SUMMARY

The Clean Slate is an entertainment destination for non-drinkers and individuals recovering from addictions who need a supportive environment for socialization and entertainment. Much like a traditional bar or nightclub, The Clean Slate offers live entertainment; arcade games; amusements like billiards and darts; big-screen TVs showcasing live sports; special events; and food/beverages. The only difference is the absence of alcohol, offering non-drinkers a place to gather or have a substance-free night on the town.

The Clean Slate is the brainchild of John Emery, a former drug user who has been clean for five years. In partnership with Peter Falstaff, an experienced restaurant owner, and accountant Judith Braun, Emery is opening The Clean Slate in Center City, Ohio.

MARKET ANALYSIS

"Sober events" planners and alcohol-free social establishments were growing in popularity by 2013. Establishments and gatherings such as these were gaining traction in large cities such as Los Angeles and Chicago. Based on their success in those markets, continued growth is anticipated in other cities nationwide.

Target Markets
Although the business will certainly appeal to those recovering from addictions, The Clean Slate will have a much broader appeal. The destination will be of interest to non-drinkers, music enthusiasts (attracted to the live entertainment), churchgoers, and teens (over the age of 17), and young adults. In its marketing efforts, The Clean Slate will concentrate on this broader appeal.

Marketing initiatives will be targeted toward the following:

* Christian Singles & Couples Groups

* Young Adult Groups (local churches)

* Substance Abuse Counselors

* Center City Community College

* Local & Regional Performing Artists

Statistics

Data regarding illicit drug use in Ohio suggests strong market potential for The Clean Slate, which will be located in one of the state's largest cities. According to the Substance Abuse & Mental Health Services Administration's *2010-2011 National Surveys on Drug Use and Health State Estimates of Substance Use and Mental Disorders,* when surveyed, 725,000 individuals (8.36%) over the age of 18 reported engaging in illicit drug use in the past month. In addition, 24.88% indicated binge alcohol use (five or more drinks on the same occasion) within the last month.

These problems are not limited to those over the age of 18. For example, 90,000 individuals between the ages of 12 and 17 (9.77%) indicated illicit drug use in the past month, while 67,000 (7.22%) reported binge alcohol use. A greater percentage of this age category (13.48%, or 125,000 individuals) reported using alcohol within the past month. The Clean Slate will provide older teens (ages 17 and up), who arguably are at a greater risk for this type of behavior, with an alternative to environments where drug or alcohol experimentation is likely to occur.

Competition

Currently, several churches and community organizations host special events with "clean and sober" themes, but The Clean Slate will be unique in the local and regional marketplace, in that it is the only permanent physical destination of its kind. Although others may follow, The Clean Slate will have an advantage by being first in the market and establishing a loyal customer base.

PERSONNEL

John Emery (President/Owner)

The Clean Slate is the brainchild of John Emery, a former drug user who has been clean for five years. Emery's substance abuse issues began at an early age, when he began experimenting with marijuana and alcohol at the age of 15. Ultimately, this led to harder drugs, culminating with a cocaine addiction in his early 20s.

After completing a rehab program at the age of 25, Emery attended community college, and ultimately earned a business administration degree from the Ohio State University. At age 30, he is ready to utilize his formal business education, entrepreneurial spirit, and substance abuse experience to meet a market need, while also serving a greater social purpose.

In addition to overall responsibility for managing the business, Emery will specialize in growing and overseeing the entertainment and amusement aspect of The Clean Slate. In this regard, he will draw on his own experience as a local musician, and connections with those involved in the local and regional entertainment scene. Emery is seeking a business loan in the amount of $37,500 to cover a portion of his 51 percent ownership stake. In addition, he also will provide $22,500 in cash from personal savings and investments.

Peter Falstaff (Vice President/Co-Owner)

Emery's inspiration to establish The Clean Slate originated at Falstaff's Diner, a popular local eatery owned by Peter Falstaff, where individuals would congregate following 12-step meetings. Peter would open the diner, typically open for only breakfast and lunch, so that the group could have a safe place to socialize and unwind for a few hours. Peter's commitment to helping those in recovery originates from his son's struggles with substance abuse. He has agreed to invest $30,000 in the business in exchange for a 24.5 percent ownership stake. He will draw a small, $15,000 salary, and will be involved in operations on a part-time basis, providing assistance and guidance with the management, food, and beverage aspects of the business.

Judith Braun (Treasurer/Co-Owner)

Judith Braun is a local accountant whose late husband struggled for many years with alcoholism. Committed to helping others with addiction, she learned about plans for The Clean Slate from Falstaff, to whom she provides accounting services. Her accounting firm, Judith Braun & Associates LLC, has operated in Center City for more than 20 years, and is well-known in the business community. Braun has agreed to invest $30,000 in the business in exchange for a 24.5 percent ownership stake. In addition, she will draw a small, $15,000 salary. Her involvement in operations will be limited to the provision of accounting and tax services.

Support Staff

The Clean Slate also will employ support staff, including a full-time chef, two part-time cooks, bar staff, a dishwasher, and wait staff. During the first year of operations, salaries will be as follows:

Pres. & co-owner	$ 45,000
Treas. & co-owner	$ 15,000
VP & co-owner	$ 15,000
1 full-time chef	$ 28,500
2 part-time cooks	$ 20,000
2 full-time bar staff	$ 25,000
2 part-time bar staff	$ 20,000
1 full-time dishwasher	$ 20,000
5 part-time wait staff	$ 37,500
	$226,000

Professional and Advisory Support

The Clean Slate has established a commercial checking account with Mainland Bank, which also will provide a merchant account for accepting credit card and debit card payments. Legal services will be provided by Smith & Hampton Partners.

BUSINESS STRATEGY

The Clean Slate will commence operations in the spring of 2014. The business will focus its first three years of operations on generating awareness and establishing a loyal customer base.

The owners have prepared conservative financial projections (see Financial Analysis section). Following a net loss of $55,054 during the first year, the business will generate a modest profit during the second year, followed by $47,358 in the third year.

Based on the success of The Clean Slate during its first three years, the owners will consider establishing an additional location in another Ohio city, such as Columbus, Cincinnati, or Toledo. This may be accomplished via a franchising model.

SERVICES

The Clean Slate offers many of the same amenities as a traditional bar or nightclub, including:

- Live Entertainment
- Arcade Games
- Amusements (billiards, darts, shuffleboard, etc.)
- Big-Screen TVs
- Special Events
- Food/Beverages

The main difference is that these amenities are provided in an alcohol-free environment.

The Clean Slate will differentiate itself by offering more than typical "bar food." Our experienced chef and cook staff will provide mouthwatering selections that will make The Clean Slate a competitor to traditional restaurants. Our complete menu is available upon request, but will include everything from burgers and sandwiches to seafood and steaks. In addition to energy and soft drinks, our bartenders will prepare delicious non-alcoholic drinks, including proprietary selections not available anywhere else in the city.

The owners anticipate that the food and beverage category will account for 50 percent of sales, followed by live entertainment (30%), and amusements (20%).

Sales by category

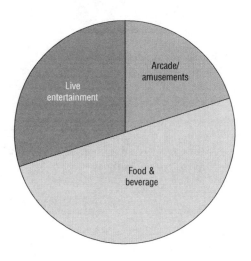

Live entertainment will be another differentiator for The Clean Slate in the local marketplace. Local bands should account for 60 percent of our entertainment offerings, followed by regional bands (20%), comedy acts (15%), and special acts such as magicians, etc. (5%).

Live entertainment

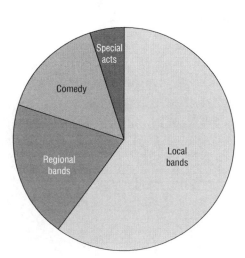

The Clean Slate also will offer special events, including singles nights, speed dating events, trivia contests, karaoke, and "open mic" nights for local poets and performers.

MARKETING & SALES

A marketing plan has been developed for The Clean Slate that includes these main tactics:

1. *Social Media:* Guests will be able to follow our business on Facebook and Twitter, and take advantage of exclusive specials.

2. *Web Site:* A site that lists information about our destination will be developed. The site will include information about our menu selections, location, hours, special discounts, and upcoming entertainment acts and special events.

3. Membership in the local Chamber of Commerce.

4. *Direct-mail:* A four-color postcard will be developed in partnership with a local digital printer. This will include space to showcase upcoming entertainment acts. Using variable data technology, these postcards can be personalized to people on our mailing lists, and sent out with the click of a button. Another aspect of our direct mail strategy will include letters to the target markets mentioned in the Market Analysis section of this plan (e.g., churches, substance abuse counselors, etc.), recommending The Clean Slate as a social and entertainment option for non-drinkers. Mailing lists for the latter mailing will be obtained from Peterson Schofield, a local list broker, as well as the Chamber of Commerce.

5. *Print & Online Advertising:* In order to establish The Clean Slate in the marketplace, a regular advertising presence will be maintained. Cost-effective advertisements will be placed in *The Center City Times,* a free local newspaper that is popular among music enthusiasts. We also will advertise online with a popular Christian singles service, and on Facebook (which allows us to target advertising based on geography and keywords).

6. *Sales Promotion:* Each month, John Emery will make at least four presentations to local substance abuse support groups, church groups, and counselors, promoting The Clean Slate. Passes for complementary beverages and half-price entrées will be distributed as incentives.

7. *Media Relations:* Because of the unique nature of The Clean Slate, there likely will be media attention surrounding the business. The owners will capitalize on this by being proactive with media, reaching out to them with press releases to tell their story and generate positive word-of-mouth among prospective customers and members of the community.

The Clean Slate will evaluate its marketing plan on a semi-annual basis during the first year of operations, and annually thereafter.

OPERATIONS

Location

The Clean Slate will operate from 4360 Main St. in Center City, Ohio, in an area known as the River District. The area is growing in popularity, thanks to ongoing economic revitalization efforts in downtown Center City. Other nightclubs and theaters have opened in recent years, along with a popular Riverwalk and an outdoor City Market (during the summer months) that draws local merchants, artists, etc.

The business will be located in a former electrical supply warehouse, which will be leased from AHC Property Management LLC. The property owners have agreed to perform renovations needed to bring the facility up to code for public access. In addition, $75,000 in equipment purchases and facility improvements (e.g., tables, chairs, bar, staging, sound system, telecommunications, lighting, kitchen appliances, etc.) will be needed to convert the space into an entertainment establishment. These improvements will be funded by The Clean Slate's owners. A detailed improvements breakdown is available upon request.

Hours of Operation

The Clean Slate will be open as follows:

- Monday—Thursday: 5 PM—11 PM

- Friday & Saturday: 4 PM—2 AM

- Sunday: 5 PM—9 PM

FINANCIAL ANALYSIS

The owners have prepared conservative financial projections for the first year of operations. Following a net loss of $55,054 during the first year, the business will generate a modest profit $6,325 during the second year, followed by $47,358 in the third year. In addition to the following information, detailed financial statements have been prepared, and are available upon request.

	2014	2015	2016
Sales			
Food & beverage	$159,900	$183,885	$211,468
Live entertainment	$ 95,940	$110,331	$126,881
Arcade	$ 63,960	$ 73,554	$ 84,587
	$319,800	$367,770	$422,936
Cost of goods sold	($ 31,980)	($ 36,777)	($ 42,294)
Gross margin	10%	10%	10%
	$287,820	$330,993	$380,642
Expenses			
Advertising & marketing	$ 7,500	$ 5,000	$ 5,000
General/administrative	$ 1,000	$ 1,000	$ 1,000
Legal	$ 1,500	$ 750	$ 750
Office supplies	$ 750	$ 500	$ 500
Computers/peripherals	$ 2,500	$ 500	$ 500
Business insurance	$ 3,750	$ 3,750	$ 3,750
Payroll	$226,000	$232,780	$239,763
Payroll taxes	$ 33,590	$ 34,598	$ 35,636
Lease	$ 14,400	$ 14,400	$ 14,400
Postage	$ 500	$ 500	$ 500
Utilities	$ 11,500	$ 12,000	$ 12,500
Telecommunications	$ 1,800	$ 1,890	$ 1,985
Startup loan	$ 12,500	$ 12,500	$ 12,500
Equipment	$ 25,584	$ 4,500	$ 4,500
Total expenses	**($ 55,054)**	**$ 6,325**	**$ 47,358**
Net income	**$ 34,241**	**$ 59,398**	**$ 53,427**

Arcade

The Fun Center

6788 Jefferson Ave.
Bronx, NY 10463

BizPlanDB.com

The Fun Center is a New York based corporation that will provide arcade games, limited food/beverage services, and event hosting to customers in its targeted market. The Company was founded by Brett Townsend.

1.0 EXECUTIVE SUMMARY

The purpose of this business plan is to raise $125,000 for the development of an arcade while showcasing the expected financials and operations over the next three years. The Fun Center is a New York based corporation that will provide arcade games, limited food/beverage services, and event hosting to customers in its targeted market. The Company was founded by Brett Townsend.

1.1 The Services

Management intends to develop an extensive retail location that will provide customers with the latest in arcade game technology. The Company intends to have 30 to 40 arcade game machines within the location.

Additionally, The Fun Center will offer a limited food and beverage service which will include candy, hotdogs, small sandwiches, coffee, and fountain drinks. This aspect of the business is very important because it will provide an additional stream of revenue for the business while concurrently allowing parents of children to stay at the facility longer.

Finally, the business will generate revenue streams from hosting birthday parties and other events within the arcade facility.

The third section of the business plan will further describe the services offered by The Fun Center.

1.2 Financing

Mr. Townsend is seeking to raise $125,000 from as a bank loan. The interest rate and loan agreement are to be further discussed during negotiation. This business plan assumes that the business will receive a 10 year loan with a 9% fixed interest rate. The financing will be used for the following:

- Development of the Company's location.

- Financing for the first six months of operation.

- Capital to purchase the Company's arcade game inventory

Mr. Townsend will contribute $25,000 to the venture.

1.3 Mission Statement

The Fun Center is designed to provide customers with an exciting array of arcade style video games while concurrently providing a safe and enjoyable environment. The business is also committed to providing quality birthday party and event hosting services so that children can have a memorable birthday at The Fun Center's location.

1.4 Management Team

The Company was founded by Brett Townsend. Mr. Townsend has more than 10 years of experience in the retail management industry. Through his expertise, he will be able to bring the operations of the business to profitability within its first year of operations.

1.5 Sales Forecasts

Mr. Townsend expects a strong rate of growth at the start of operations. Below are the expected financials over the next three years.

Proforma profit and loss (yearly)

Year	1	2	3
Sales	$451,278	$541,534	$633,594
Operating costs	$226,374	$235,578	$245,122
EBITDA	$151,171	$217,476	$284,951
Taxes, interest, and depreciation	$ 75,688	$ 96,264	$121,391
Net profit	$ 75,482	$121,212	$163,560

Sales, operating costs, and profit forecast

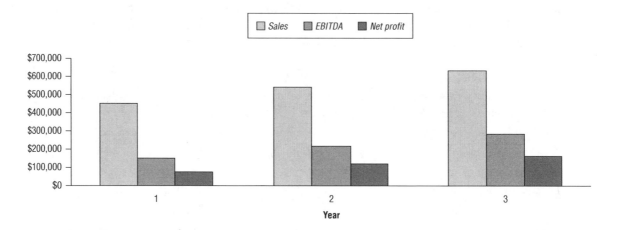

1.6 Expansion Plan

The Founder expects that the business will aggressively expand during the first three years of operation. Mr. Townsend intends to implement marketing campaigns that will effectively target young individuals within the target market.

2.0 COMPANY AND FINANCING SUMMARY

2.1 Registered Name and Corporate Structure

The Company is registered as a corporation in the State of New York.

2.2 Required Funds

At this time, The Fun Center requires $125,000 of debt funds. Below is a breakdown of how these funds will be used:

Projected startup costs

Initial lease payments and deposits	$ 15,000
Working capital	$ 30,000
FF&E	$ 20,000
Leasehold improvements	$ 15,000
Security deposits	$ 10,000
Insurance	$ 5,000
Arcade game inventory	$ 30,000
Marketing budget	$ 17,500
Miscellaneous and unforeseen costs	$ 7,500
Total startup costs	**$150,000**

Use of funds

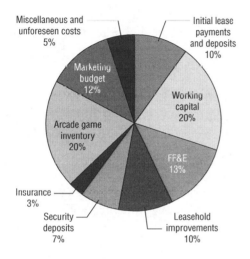

2.3 Investor Equity

Mr. Townsend is not seeking an investment from a third party at this time.

2.4 Management Equity

Brett Townsend owns 100% of The Fun Center, Inc.

2.5 Exit Strategy

If the business is very successful, Mr. Townsend may seek to sell the business to a third party for a significant earnings multiple. Most likely, the Company will hire a qualified business broker to sell the business on behalf of The Fun Center. Based on historical numbers, the business could fetch a sales premium of up to 4 times earnings.

3.0 PRODUCTS AND SERVICES

Below is a description of the arcade and entertainment services offered by The Fun Center.

3.1 Arcade Game Usage

The primary revenue center for the business will be the ongoing usage of arcade games among the Company's patrons. At any given time, Management anticipates that the business will have thirty to forty arcade game stations available for patron use. Each play of an arcade game will generate $.25 to $1.00 in revenue for the business. These machines will only accept The Fun Center-branded tokens, which will be used in lieu of direct cash. Tokens will be provided from specialized change machines that will dispense these coins. This practice is common among modern day arcade facilities. The games that management will rent or buy from arcade machine wholesalers will be popular in demand games that are well-known among the Company's target market of young children and adult arcade enthusiasts.

The Company will also have several arcade games that provide customers with tickets for redemption at The Fun Center's prize counter. These machines are often carnival style games that provide a certain number of tickets based on the score or outcome of each play. The Company will provide items such as small toys, candy, and other items enjoyed by children which can be obtained by redeeming tickets. This aspect of the business is specifically geared towards the children's section of the arcade.

3.2 Food and Beverage Service

The business will also maintain an area of the retail facility that will provide limited food and beverage service. This revenue center is extremely important for the business because it will provide an additional stream of income for the business while providing parents of children using the arcade an incentive to stay at the arcade longer. This business model is akin to Barnes and Nobles installation of cafes in most of their bookstores.

3.3 Event Hosting

The final revenue center for the business will be the hosting of birthday parties and other events (primarily for children ages 5 to 12) at The Fun Center facility. These parties are anticipated to generate approximately $150 to $200 from each event (with approximately 8 to 10 children). For these events, each child will be given enough tokens to play the arcade's games for 45 minutes to an hour.

From an advertising standpoint, this is an important aspect for the business as other children in attendance for a party may want to have their birthday party held at The Fun Center. These parties will also increase the visibility of the business among the Company's targeted demographic.

4.0 STRATEGIC AND MARKET ANALYSIS

4.1 Economic Outlook

This section of the analysis will detail the economic climate, the arcade and entertainment industry, the customer profile, and the competition that the business will face as it progresses through its business operations.

Currently, the economic market condition in the United States is moderate. The meltdown of the sub prime mortgage market coupled with increasing gas prices has led many people to believe that the US is on the cusp of a double dip economic recession. This slowdown in the economy has also greatly impacted real estate sales, which has halted to historical lows.

4.2 Industry Analysis

The arcade industry generates approximately $1.5 billion dollars a year among 2,700 companies that operate retail arcades. These revenue numbers does not include amusement parks, casinos, or resorts that provide arcade machines as a value added benefit to patrons. The industry employs more than 30,000 people and provides aggregate annual payrolls of $350 million dollars.

As stated earlier, the arcade industry is mature. The expected continued growth of these businesses is expected to mirror the general population growth plus the rate of inflation.

The key to thriving within this industry is to provide patrons with an extensive menu of arcade games available for use. The Fun Center will have the latest in gaming technology available for patrons coupled with a few classic arcade games which are popular among older arcade enthusiasts.

4.3 Customer Profile

The Fun Center's average client will be a middle to upper middle class man or woman with children living in the Company's target market. Common traits among clients will include:

- Annual household income exceeding $50,000

- Lives or works no more than 15 miles from the Company's location.

- Will spend $20 per visit to The Fun Center with their children.

4.4 Competition

Arcades have become less common over the past ten years as many individuals (especially among younger demographics) are able to play any game they wish via Wi-Fi enabled consoles. However, among all demographics people still enjoy going to arcades. Within the Company's target market, there are only a limited number of arcades still in operation. It is imperative that the business acquires old and new arcade machines in order to maintain a competitive advantage, The business intends maintain a strong competitive advantage over similar businesses by being able to cater to a very large demographic of younger people (who have not been exposed to a traditional arcade) as well as adults that want to experience the nostalgia of going to this type of business.

5.0 MARKETING PLAN

The Fun Center intends to maintain an extensive marketing campaign that will ensure maximum visibility for the business in its targeted market. Below is an overview of the marketing strategies and objectives of The Fun Center.

5.1 Marketing Objectives

- Develop an online presence by developing a website and placing the Company's name and contact information with online directories.

- Implement a local campaign with the Company's targeted market via the use of flyers, local newspaper advertisements, and word of mouth.

5.2 Marketing Strategies

Management intends on using a number of advertising and marketing channels to promote traffic to The Fun Center. The Company primarily intends to use a broad based advertising campaign that will raise the awareness of the retail location among the targeted young child and adolescent demographic.

To that end, Management will place a number of advertisements in locally based newspapers and advertisements from the onset of operations which may include discount coupons or coupons for free arcade tokens. This will create an immediate draw to The Fun Center's location.

Management also expects that the business will generate significant word of mouth advertising as the Company hosts events for children's birthday parties. As more and more children are invited to birthday parties at The Fun Center, these youngsters may have their parents host their next birthday party at the arcade. The Company anticipates that this type of advertising will take three to six months to become effective.

5.3 Pricing

In order to keep prices extremely affordable, the Company will charge approximately $0.50 for each game usage. Additionally, food and beverage costs will range from $1.50 to $3.00 for a beverage and $2.50 to $5.00 for food products. This will further provide a competitive advantage over other arcades in the greater New York metropolitan area.

6.0 ORGANIZATIONAL PLAN AND PERSONNEL SUMMARY

6.1 Corporate Organization

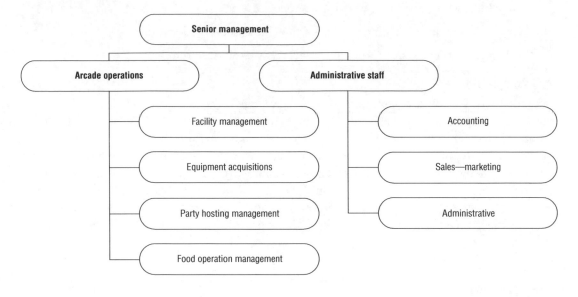

6.2 Organizational Budget

Personnel plan—yearly

Year	1	2	3
Owner	$ 40,000	$ 41,200	$ 42,436
Assistant manager	$ 29,000	$ 29,870	$ 30,766
Arcade employees	$ 48,000	$ 49,440	$ 50,923
Bookkeeper (P/T)	$ 9,000	$ 9,270	$ 9,548
Administrative (P/T)	$ 17,000	$ 17,510	$ 18,035
Total	**$143,000**	**$147,290**	**$151,709**

Numbers of personnel

Owner	1	1	1
Assistant manager	1	1	1
Arcade employees	3	3	3
Bookkeeper (P/T)	1	1	1
Administrative (P/T)	1	1	1
Totals	**7**	**7**	**7**

Personnel expense breakdown

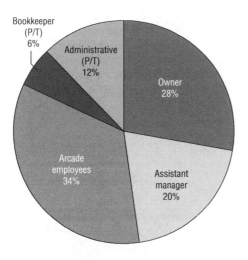

7.0 FINANCIAL PLAN

7.1 Underlying Assumptions

The Company has based its proforma financial statements on the following:

- The Fun Center will have an annual revenue growth rate of 16% per year.

- The Owner will acquire $125,000 of debt funds to develop the business.

- The loan will have a 10 year term with a 9% interest rate.

7.2 Sensitivity Analysis

The Fun Center's revenues are somewhat vulnerable to changes in the general economy. The Company is providing arcade games for use among customers, which are not a necessity. However, the pricing point for The Fun Centers' services is extremely low, and the general economy would need a serious recession before a revenue decline. The high margin revenue generated by the business will allow the Company to operate profitably despite negative economic climates.

7.3 Source of Funds

Financing

Equity contributions

Management investment	$ 25,000.00
Total equity financing	**$ 25,000.00**
Banks and lenders	
Banks and lenders	$ 125,000.00
Total debt financing	**$125,000.00**
Total financing	**$150,000.00**

7.4 General Assumptions

General assumptions

Year	1	2	3
Short term interest rate	9.5%	9.5%	9.5%
Long term interest rate	10.0%	10.0%	10.0%
Federal tax rate	33.0%	33.0%	33.0%
State tax rate	5.0%	5.0%	5.0%
Personnel taxes	15.0%	15.0%	15.0%

7.5 Profit and Loss Statements

Proforma profit and loss (yearly)

Year	1	2	3
Sales	**$451,278**	**$541,534**	**$633,594**
Cost of goods sold	$ 73,733	$ 88,480	$103,522
Gross margin	83.66%	83.66%	83.66%
Operating income	**$377,545**	**$453,054**	**$530,073**
Expenses			
Payroll	$143,000	$147,290	$151,709
General and administrative	$ 25,200	$ 26,208	$ 27,256
Marketing expenses	$ 2,256	$ 2,708	$ 3,168
Professional fees and licensure	$ 5,219	$ 5,376	$ 5,537
Insurance costs	$ 1,987	$ 2,086	$ 2,191
Travel and vehicle costs	$ 7,596	$ 8,356	$ 9,191
Rent and utilities	$ 14,250	$ 14,963	$ 15,711
Miscellaneous costs	$ 5,415	$ 6,498	$ 7,603
Payroll taxes	$ 21,450	$ 22,094	$ 22,756
Total operating costs	**$226,374**	**$235,578**	**$245,122**
EBITDA	**$151,171**	**$217,476**	**$284,951**
Federal income tax	$ 49,886	$ 68,413	$ 90,953
State income tax	$ 7,559	$ 10,366	$ 13,781
Interest expense	$ 10,922	$ 10,164	$ 9,335
Depreciation expenses	$ 7,321	$ 7,321	$ 7,321
Net profit	**$ 75,482**	**$121,212**	**$163,560**
Profit margin	**16.73%**	**22.38%**	**25.81%**

Sales, operating costs, and profit forecast

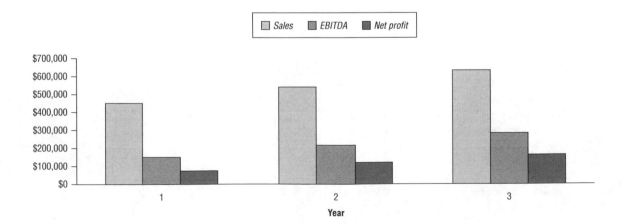

7.6 Cash Flow Analysis

Proforma cash flow analysis—yearly

Year	1	2	3
Cash from operations	$ 82,804	$128,533	$170,882
Cash from receivables	$ 0	$ 0	$ 0
Operating cash inflow	**$ 82,804**	**$128,533**	**$170,882**
Other cash inflows			
Equity investment	$ 25,000	$ 0	$ 0
Increased borrowings	$125,000	$ 0	$ 0
Sales of business assets	$ 0	$ 0	$ 0
A/P increases	$ 2,500	$ 2,875	$ 3,306
Total other cash inflows	**$152,500**	**$ 2,875**	**$ 3,306**
Total cash inflow	**$235,304**	**$131,408**	**$174,188**
Cash outflows			
Repayment of principal	$ 8,079	$ 8,837	$ 9,666
A/P decreases	$ 2,200	$ 2,640	$ 3,168
A/R increases	$ 0	$ 0	$ 0
Asset purchases	$102,500	$ 32,133	$ 42,720
Dividends	$ 57,963	$ 77,120	$102,529
Total cash outflows	**$170,742**	**$120,730**	**$158,084**
Net cash flow	**$ 64,562**	**$ 10,678**	**$ 16,104**
Cash balance	**$ 64,562**	**$ 75,240**	**$ 91,344**

Proforma cash flow (yearly)

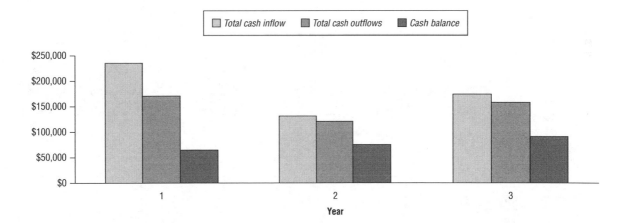

7.7 Balance Sheet

Proforma balance sheet—yearly

Year	1	2	3
Assets			
Cash	$ 64,562	$ 75,240	$ 91,344
Amortized development-expansion costs	$ 52,500	$ 55,713	$ 59,985
Arcade game inventory	$ 30,000	$ 54,100	$ 86,140
FF&E	$ 20,000	$ 24,820	$ 31,228
Accumulated depreciation	($ 7,321)	($ 14,643)	($ 21,964)
Total assets	**$159,740**	**$195,230**	**$246,734**
Liabilities and equity			
Accounts payable	$ 300	$ 535	$ 673
Long term liabilities	$116,921	$108,084	$ 99,247
Other liabilities	$ 0	$ 0	$ 0
Total liabilities	**$117,221**	**$108,619**	**$ 99,920**
Net worth	**$ 42,520**	**$ 86,612**	**$146,814**
Total liabilities and equity	**$159,740**	**$195,230**	**$246,734**

Proforma balance sheet

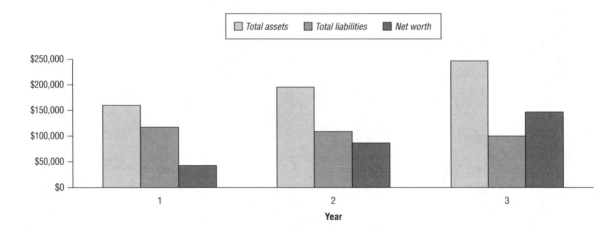

7.8 Breakeven Analysis

Monthly break even analysis

Year	1	2	3
Monthly revenue	$ 22,549	$ 23,465	$ 24,416
Yearly revenue	$270,584	$281,585	$292,993

Break even analysis

7.9 Business Ratios

Business ratios—yearly

Year	1	2	3
Sales			
Sales growth	0.00%	20.00%	17.00%
Gross margin	83.70%	83.70%	83.70%
Financials			
Profit margin	16.73%	22.38%	25.81%
Assets to liabilities	1.36	1.80	2.47
Equity to liabilities	0.36	0.80	1.47
Assets to equity	3.76	2.25	1.68
Liquidity			
Acid test	0.55	0.69	0.91
Cash to assets	0.40	0.39	0.37

7.10 Three Year Profit and Loss Statement

Profit and loss statement (first year)

Months	1	2	3	4	5	6	7
Sales	**$36,600**	**$36,783**	**$36,966**	**$37,149**	**$37,332**	**$37,515**	**$37,698**
Cost of goods sold	$ 5,980	$ 6,010	$ 6,040	$ 6,070	$ 6,100	$ 6,130	$ 6,159
Gross margin	83.70%	83.70%	83.70%	83.70%	83.70%	83.70%	83.70%
Operating income	**$30,620**	**$30,773**	**$30,926**	**$31,079**	**$31,232**	**$31,386**	**$31,539**
Expenses							
Payroll	$11,917	$11,917	$11,917	$11,917	$11,917	$11,917	$11,917
General and administrative	$ 2,100	$ 2,100	$ 2,100	$ 2,100	$ 2,100	$ 2,100	$ 2,100
Marketing expenses	$ 188	$ 188	$ 188	$ 188	$ 188	$ 188	$ 188
Professional fees and licensure	$ 435	$ 435	$ 435	$ 435	$ 435	$ 435	$ 435
Insurance costs	$ 166	$ 166	$ 166	$ 166	$ 166	$ 166	$ 166
Travel and vehicle costs	$ 633	$ 633	$ 633	$ 633	$ 633	$ 633	$ 633
Rent and utilities	$ 1,188	$ 1,188	$ 1,188	$ 1,188	$ 1,188	$ 1,188	$ 1,188
Miscellaneous costs	$ 451	$ 451	$ 451	$ 451	$ 451	$ 451	$ 451
Payroll taxes	$ 1,788	$ 1,788	$ 1,788	$ 1,788	$ 1,788	$ 1,788	$ 1,788
Total operating costs	**$18,864**	**$18,864**	**$18,864**	**$18,864**	**$18,864**	**$18,864**	**$18,864**
EBITDA	**$11,756**	**$11,909**	**$12,062**	**$12,215**	**$12,368**	**$12,521**	**$12,674**
Federal income tax	$ 4,046	$ 4,066	$ 4,086	$ 4,107	$ 4,127	$ 4,147	$ 4,167
State income tax	$ 613	$ 616	$ 619	$ 622	$ 625	$ 628	$ 631
Interest expense	$ 938	$ 933	$ 928	$ 923	$ 918	$ 913	$ 908
Depreciation expense	$ 610	$ 610	$ 610	$ 610	$ 610	$ 610	$ 610
Net profit	**$ 5,549**	**$ 5,684**	**$ 5,818**	**$ 5,953**	**$ 6,088**	**$ 6,223**	**$ 6,357**

Profit and loss statement (first year cont.)

Month	8	9	10	11	12	1
Sales	$37,881	$38,064	$38,247	$38,430	$38,613	$451,278
Cost of goods sold	$ 6,189	$ 6,219	$ 6,249	$ 6,279	$ 6,309	$ 73,733
Gross margin	83.70%	83.70%	83.70%	83.70%	83.70%	83.70%
Operating income	$31,692	$31,845	$31,998	$32,151	$32,304	$377,545
Expenses						
Payroll	$11,917	$11,917	$11,917	$11,917	$11,917	$143,000
General and administrative	$ 2,100	$ 2,100	$ 2,100	$ 2,100	$ 2,100	$ 25,200
Marketing expenses	$ 188	$ 188	$ 188	$ 188	$ 188	$ 2,256
Professional fees and licensure	$ 435	$ 435	$ 435	$ 435	$ 435	$ 5,219
Insurance costs	$ 166	$ 166	$ 166	$ 166	$ 166	$ 1,987
Travel and vehicle costs	$ 633	$ 633	$ 633	$ 633	$ 633	$ 7,596
Rent and utilities	$ 1,188	$ 1,188	$ 1,188	$ 1,188	$ 1,188	$ 14,250
Miscellaneous costs	$ 451	$ 451	$ 451	$ 451	$ 451	$ 5,415
Payroll taxes	$ 1,788	$ 1,788	$ 1,788	$ 1,788	$ 1,788	$ 21,450
Total operating costs	$18,864	$18,864	$18,864	$18,864	$18,864	$226,374
EBITDA	$12,827	$12,980	$13,133	$13,287	$13,440	$151,171
Federal income tax	$ 4,188	$ 4,208	$ 4,228	$ 4,248	$ 4,268	$ 49,886
State income tax	$ 634	$ 638	$ 641	$ 644	$ 647	$ 7,559
Interest expense	$ 903	$ 898	$ 893	$ 887	$ 882	$ 10,922
Depreciation expense	$ 610	$ 610	$ 610	$ 610	$ 610	$ 7,321
Net profit	$ 6,492	$ 6,627	$ 6,762	$ 6,897	$ 7,032	$ 75,482

Profit and loss statement (second year)

Quarter	Q1	2 — Q2	Q3	Q4	2
Sales	$108,307	$135,383	$146,214	$151,629	$541,534
Cost of goods sold	$ 17,696	$ 22,120	$ 23,890	$ 24,774	$ 88,480
Gross margin	83.70%	83.70%	83.70%	83.70%	83.70%
Operating income	$ 90,611	$113,263	$122,324	$126,855	$453,054
Expenses					
Payroll	$ 29,458	$ 36,823	$ 39,768	$ 41,241	$147,290
General and administrative	$ 5,242	$ 6,552	$ 7,076	$ 7,338	$ 26,208
Marketing expenses	$ 542	$ 677	$ 731	$ 758	$ 2,708
Professional fees and licensure	$ 1,075	$ 1,344	$ 1,451	$ 1,505	$ 5,376
Insurance costs	$ 417	$ 522	$ 563	$ 584	$ 2,086
Travel and vehicle costs	$ 1,671	$ 2,089	$ 2,256	$ 2,340	$ 8,356
Rent and utilities	$ 2,993	$ 3,741	$ 4,040	$ 4,190	$ 14,963
Miscellaneous costs	$ 1,300	$ 1,625	$ 1,755	$ 1,820	$ 6,498
Payroll taxes	$ 4,419	$ 5,523	$ 5,965	$ 6,186	$ 22,094
Total operating costs	$ 47,116	$ 58,894	$ 63,606	$ 65,962	$235,578
EBITDA	$ 43,495	$ 54,369	$ 58,719	$ 60,893	$217,476
Federal income tax	$ 13,683	$ 17,103	$ 18,471	$ 19,156	$ 68,413
State income tax	$ 2,073	$ 2,591	$ 2,799	$ 2,902	$ 10,366
Interest expense	$ 2,615	$ 2,566	$ 2,517	$ 2,466	$ 10,164
Depreciation expense	$ 1,830	$ 1,830	$ 1,830	$ 1,830	$ 7,321
Net profit	$ 23,294	$ 30,278	$ 33,101	$ 34,539	$121,212

Profit and loss statement (third year)

Quarter	Q1	3 Q2	Q3	Q4	3
Sales	**$126,719**	**$158,399**	**$171,070**	**$177,406**	**$633,594**
Cost of goods sold	$ 20,704	$ 25,880	$ 27,951	$ 28,986	$103,522
Gross margin	83.70%	83.70%	83.70%	83.70%	83.70%
Operating income	**$106,015**	**$132,518**	**$143,120**	**$148,420**	**$530,073**
Expenses					
Payroll	$ 30,342	$ 37,927	$ 40,961	$ 42,478	$151,709
General and administrative	$ 5,451	$ 6,814	$ 7,359	$ 7,632	$ 27,256
Marketing expenses	$ 634	$ 792	$ 855	$ 887	$ 3,168
Professional fees and licensure	$ 1,107	$ 1,384	$ 1,495	$ 1,550	$ 5,537
Insurance costs	$ 438	$ 548	$ 591	$ 613	$ 2,191
Travel and vehicle costs	$ 1,838	$ 2,298	$ 2,482	$ 2,574	$ 9,191
Rent and utilities	$ 3,142	$ 3,928	$ 4,242	$ 4,399	$ 15,711
Miscellaneous costs	$ 1,521	$ 1,901	$ 2,053	$ 2,129	$ 7,603
Payroll taxes	$ 4,551	$ 5,689	$ 6,144	$ 6,372	$ 22,756
Total operating costs	**$ 49,024**	**$ 61,280**	**$ 66,183**	**$ 68,634**	**$245,122**
EBITDA	**$ 56,990**	**$ 71,238**	**$ 76,937**	**$ 79,786**	**$284,951**
Federal income tax	$ 18,191	$ 22,738	$ 24,557	$ 25,467	$ 90,953
State income tax	$ 2,756	$ 3,445	$ 3,721	$ 3,859	$ 13,781
Interest expense	$ 2,414	$ 2,361	$ 2,307	$ 2,252	$ 9,335
Depreciation expense	$ 1,830	$ 1,830	$ 1,830	$ 1,830	$ 7,321
Net profit	**$ 31,799**	**$ 40,862**	**$ 44,521**	**$ 46,378**	**$163,560**

7.11 Three Year Cash Flow Analysis

Cash flow analysis (first year)

Month	1	2	3	4	5	6	7
Cash from operations	$ 6,159	$ 6,294	$ 6,428	$ 6,563	$ 6,698	$ 6,833	$ 6,968
Cash from receivables	$ 0	$ 0	$ 0	$ 0	$ 0	$ 0	$ 0
Operating cash inflow	**$ 6,159**	**$ 6,294**	**$ 6,428**	**$ 6,563**	**$ 6,698**	**$ 6,833**	**$ 6,968**
Other cash inflows							
Equity investment	$ 25,000	$ 0	$ 0	$ 0	$ 0	$ 0	$ 0
Increased borrowings	$125,000	$ 0	$ 0	$ 0	$ 0	$ 0	$ 0
Sales of business assets	$ 0	$ 0	$ 0	$ 0	$ 0	$ 0	$ 0
A/P increases	$ 208	$ 208	$ 208	$ 208	$ 208	$ 208	$ 208
Total other cash inflows	**$150,208**	**$ 208**	**$ 208**	**$ 208**	**$ 208**	**$ 208**	**$ 208**
Total cash inflow	**$156,367**	**$ 6,502**	**$ 6,637**	**$ 6,771**	**$ 6,906**	**$ 7,041**	**$ 7,176**
Cash outflows							
Repayment of principal	$ 646	$ 651	$ 656	$ 661	$ 666	$ 671	$ 676
A/P decreases	$ 183	$ 183	$ 183	$ 183	$ 183	$ 183	$ 183
A/R increases	$ 0	$ 0	$ 0	$ 0	$ 0	$ 0	$ 0
Asset purchases	$102,500	$ 0	$ 0	$ 0	$ 0	$ 0	$ 0
Dividends	$ 0	$ 0	$ 0	$ 0	$ 0	$ 0	$ 0
Total cash outflows	**$103,329**	**$ 834**	**$ 839**	**$ 844**	**$ 849**	**$ 854**	**$ 859**
Net cash flow	**$ 53,038**	**$ 5,668**	**$ 5,798**	**$ 5,928**	**$ 6,057**	**$ 6,187**	**$ 6,317**
Cash balance	**$ 53,038**	**$58,706**	**$64,504**	**$70,431**	**$76,489**	**$82,676**	**$88,993**

Cash flow analysis (first year cont.)

Month	8	9	10	11	12	1
Cash from operations	$ 7,102	$ 7,237	$ 7,372	$ 7,507	$ 7,642	$ 82,804
Cash from receivables	$ 0	$ 0	$ 0	$ 0	$ 0	$ 0
Operating cash inflow	**$ 7,102**	**$ 7,237**	**$ 7,372**	**$ 7,507**	**$ 7,642**	**$ 82,804**
Other cash inflows						
Equity investment	$ 0	$ 0	$ 0	$ 0	$ 0	$ 25,000
Increased borrowings	$ 0	$ 0	$ 0	$ 0	$ 0	$125,000
Sales of business assets	$ 0	$ 0	$ 0	$ 0	$ 0	$ 0
A/P increases	$ 208	$ 208	$ 208	$ 208	$ 208	$ 2,500
Total other cash inflows	**$ 208**	**$ 208**	**$ 208**	**$ 208**	**$ 208**	**$152,500**
Total cash inflow	**$ 7,311**	**$ 7,446**	**$ 7,581**	**$ 7,716**	**$ 7,851**	**$235,304**
Cash outflows						
Repayment of principal	$ 681	$ 686	$ 691	$ 696	$ 701	$ 8,079
A/P decreases	$ 183	$ 183	$ 183	$ 183	$ 183	$ 2,200
A/R increases	$ 0	$ 0	$ 0	$ 0	$ 0	$ 0
Asset purchases	$ 0	$ 0	$ 0	$ 0	$ 0	$102,500
Dividends	$ 0	$ 0	$ 0	$ 0	$ 57,963	$ 57,963
Total cash outflows	**$ 864**	**$ 869**	**$ 874**	**$ 879**	**$ 58,848**	**$170,742**
Net cash flow	**$ 6,447**	**$ 6,577**	**$ 6,706**	**$ 6,836**	**−$ 50,997**	**$ 64,562**
Cash balance	**$95,440**	**$102,016**	**$108,722**	**$115,559**	**$ 64,562**	**$ 64,562**

Cash flow analysis (second year)

Quarter	Q1	2			2
		Q2	Q3	Q4	
Cash from operations	$25,707	$32,133	$34,704	$35,989	$128,533
Cash from receivables	$ 0	$ 0	$ 0	$ 0	$ 0
Operating cash inflow	**$25,707**	**$32,133**	**$34,704**	**$35,989**	**$128,533**
Other cash inflows					
Equity investment	$ 0	$ 0	$ 0	$ 0	$ 0
Increased borrowings	$ 0	$ 0	$ 0	$ 0	$ 0
Sales of business assets	$ 0	$ 0	$ 0	$ 0	$ 0
A/P increases	$ 575	$ 719	$ 776	$ 805	$ 2,875
Total other cash inflows	**$ 575**	**$ 719**	**$ 776**	**$ 805**	**$ 2,875**
Total cash inflow	**$26,282**	**$32,852**	**$35,480**	**$36,794**	**$131,408**
Cash outflows					
Repayment of principal	$ 2,136	$ 2,184	$ 2,233	$ 2,284	$ 8,837
A/P decreases	$ 528	$ 660	$ 713	$ 739	$ 2,640
A/R increases	$ 0	$ 0	$ 0	$ 0	$ 0
Asset purchases	$ 6,427	$ 8,033	$ 8,676	$ 8,997	$ 32,133
Dividends	$15,424	$19,280	$20,822	$21,594	$ 77,120
Total cash outflows	**$24,514**	**$30,157**	**$32,445**	**$33,614**	**$120,730**
Net cash flow	**$ 1,767**	**$ 2,695**	**$ 3,036**	**$ 3,180**	**$ 10,678**
Cash balance	**$66,329**	**$69,024**	**$72,060**	**$75,240**	**$ 75,240**

Cash flow analysis (third year)

Quarter	Q1	3 Q2	Q3	Q4	3
Cash from operations	$34,176	$42,720	$46,138	$47,847	$170,882
Cash from receivables	$ 0	$ 0	$ 0	$ 0	$ 0
Operating cash inflow	**$34,176**	**$42,720**	**$46,138**	**$47,847**	**$170,882**
Other cash inflows					
Equity investment	$ 0	$ 0	$ 0	$ 0	$ 0
Increased borrowings	$ 0	$ 0	$ 0	$ 0	$ 0
Sales of business assets	$ 0	$ 0	$ 0	$ 0	$ 0
A/P increases	$ 661	$ 827	$ 893	$ 926	$ 3,306
Total other cash inflows	**$ 661**	**$ 827**	**$ 893**	**$ 926**	**$ 3,306**
Total cash inflow	**$34,838**	**$43,547**	**$47,031**	**$48,773**	**$174,188**
Cash outflows					
Repayment of principal	$ 2,336	$ 2,389	$ 2,443	$ 2,498	$ 9,666
A/P decreases	$ 634	$ 792	$ 855	$ 887	$ 3,168
A/R increases	$ 0	$ 0	$ 0	$ 0	$ 0
Asset purchases	$ 8,544	$10,680	$11,535	$11,962	$ 42,720
Dividends	$20,506	$25,632	$27,683	$28,708	$102,529
Total cash outflows	**$32,019**	**$39,493**	**$42,516**	**$44,055**	**$158,084**
Net cash flow	**$ 2,818**	**$ 4,054**	**$ 4,515**	**$ 4,717**	**$ 16,104**
Cash balance	**$78,058**	**$82,112**	**$86,627**	**$91,344**	**$ 91,344**

Bicycle Repair Business

Wheels On Wheels Inc.

45 Park Lane
Redwood City, IA 50300

Paul Greenland

Wheels On Wheels is a bicycle repair operation that is unique in the local marketplace. Unlike a traditional bicycle sales and service store, Wheels On Wheels primarily is a mobile business. Operating from a 6 x 12-foot trailer, Wheels On Wheels makes convenient house calls to people who need simple bicycle tune-ups and repairs. In addition, the business also offers a variety of bicycle safety, maintenance, and repair classes, and sells a limited inventory of used/reconditioned bicycles.

EXECUTIVE SUMMARY

Wheels On Wheels is a bicycle repair operation that is unique in the local marketplace. Unlike a traditional bicycle sales and service store, Wheels On Wheels primarily is a mobile business. Operating from a 6 x 12-foot trailer, Wheels On Wheels makes convenient house calls to people who need simple bicycle tune-ups and repairs. In addition, the business also offers a variety of bicycle safety, maintenance, and repair classes, and sells a limited inventory of used/reconditioned bicycles. Wheels On Wheels is being established by Peter Green, a long-time cycling enthusiast and former employee of Redwood City Cyclery.

MARKET ANALYSIS

Wheels On Wheels is located in Redwood City, Iowa, which was home to a population of approximately 150,000 people in 2013. The community has a sizable population of working professionals. This demographic is characterized by higher than average levels of household income, environmental responsibility, and health consciousness, boding well for a business such as Wheels On Wheels. Redwood City is home to numerous recreational bicycle trails (paved, gravel, and dirt), many of which are interconnected. Additionally, downtown streets and many surrounding roadways include a generous network of bicycle lanes, making the city a friendly place for bicycle-minded commuters.

SERVICES

Bicycle Maintenance & Repair
Wheels On Wheels will perform maintenance and repair services for $50 per hour. However, most services will be offered as one of the following cost-effective service packages:

Basic Tune-up ($40)

- Brake Adjustments
- Chain Lubrication
- Derailleur Adjustments
- Light Cleaning
- Tire Inflation

Deluxe Tune-up ($75)

- Bearing Adjustments
- Brake Adjustments
- Cable & Chain Lubrication
- Derailleur Adjustments
- Light Cleaning
- Tire Inflation
- Torque Nuts and Bolts
- True/Tension Wheels

The Max ($145)
*shop only; not available as a mobile service

This package is for bikes that need a great deal of work. Bicycles will be completely disassembled. All components are thoroughly cleaned and re-lubricated, and then the bicycle is reassembled. Repairs or new parts will incur additional charges.

Drive Train Cleaning ($45)
This package involves the removal and cleaning of the following parts:

- Cassette
- Chain Rings
- Clean and Lube Chain
- Front Derailleur
- Rear Derailleur is

Bike Assembly ($45)
This service involves the assembly of bicycles purchased online or via mail. It includes the same services provided in the basic tune-as up package.

Classes & Instruction

Wheels On Wheels also will offer a limited number of bicycle-related classes to the community. A minimum of 10 participants is required to schedule a course, which can be held at any location.

- Bicycle Safety Classes ($25/person; one session)
- Bicycle Maintenance Classes ($50/person; one session)
- Bicycle Repair Classes ($150/person; three sessions)

Bicycle Sales

Wheels On Wheels will sell a limited number of used and reconditioned bicycles, primarily at the beginning of each season. This will account for a very small portion of revenues. Although profit margins on used bicycles will not be very high, sales will provide an opportunity to establish new customers who may need bicycle maintenance services in the future.

OPERATIONS

Wheels On Wheels is largely a seasonal business, with the majority of activity occurring during the spring and summer months:

Seasonal Cycles:

- **Winter:** Focus on marketing/planning for the next season and reconditioning used bicycle inventory early spring & summer resale.

- **Spring:** Begin marketing used bicycle inventory through traditional, Web, and social media channels. Concentrate on repairs and bicycle courses.

- **Summer:** Concentrate on repairs and bicycle courses.

- **Fall:** Focus on collecting/purchasing used bicycles that can be reconditioned and resold next season.

Tools & Equipment

Although Peter Green already has all of the equipment and tools necessary to perform bicycle repair services, these will be utilized for work performed in his home garage (e.g., complete overhauls and reconditioning). An additional collection of tools and equipment must be purchased for the mobile operation, including:

- Adjustable Cup Tool
- Adjustable Wrench
- Axle Vise
- Bicycle Repair Stand
- Bottom Bracket Lock Ring Tool
- Cable Cutters
- Cartridge BB Tool
- Cassette/Freewheel Removers
- Chain Rivet Extractor
- Chain Wear Checker
- Combinations Wrenches
- Cone Wrench Set
- Crank Arm Pullers
- Derailleur Alignment Gauge
- Fixed Cup Tool
- Floor Pump
- Hammer (steel & rubber)

- Headset Locknut Wrench
- Headset Lower Race Wrench
- Hex Wrench Set
- Lock Ring Wrench
- Patch Kit
- Pedal Wrench
- Screwdriver Set (Phillips & Flathead)
- Shop Apron
- Socket & Bits (Standard & Metric)
- Spoke Ruler
- Spoke Tension Meter
- Spoke Wrenches
- Sprocket Removal Tool
- Tire Levers
- Torque Wrench
- Truing Stand
- Wheel Dishing Tool

Supplies & Parts

In addition, Wheels On Wheels must maintain an inventory of supplies and parts, including:

- Alcohol
- Bearing Grease
- Chain Lubricant
- Degreaser
- Gear Cables
- Hand Cleaner
- Polisher
- Rags
- Thread Locking Adhesives
- Tubes
- Zip Ties

Location

As a mobile bicycle repair business, the majority of Wheels On Wheels' operations occur on the road in a 6 × 12 cargo trailer. In addition to performing bicycle service on a mobile basis, a variety of administrative tasks will be performed from the road as well. Wheels On Wheels will handle customer communications (voice, text, and e-mail) via smartphone. In addition, a laptop and printer equipped with mobile Internet access will enable Peter Green to handle functions like appointment scheduling and invoicing from anywhere.

The trailer includes standard features such as:

- Rear Spring Assisted Ramp Door with Bar Locks for Security

- 16" O.C. Wall Studs

- 3/4" Heavy Duty Plywood Floors

- 3/8" Plywood Walls

- Interior Roof Vents

- 12 Volt Interior Trailer Dome Lights w/ Wall Switch

In addition, Peter has made several custom modifications to the trailer, in order to make it suitable for business operations.

These include:

- **Security System:** A simple vehicle alarm has been installed to prevent theft.

- **Promotional Graphics:** Custom semi-permanent graphics have been produced by a local large format printer, providing mobile advertising for Wheels On Wheels. These appear on the rear and sides of the trailer.

- **Generator:** A quiet generator provides up to 20 hours of power (3,000 watts/25 amps @ 120 volts) on 3.4 gallons of gas, providing enough energy for an RV air-conditioning unit, a space heater, and to meet other needs (recharging battery-powered tools, etc.). The generator features inverter technology that supplies safe power to sensitive equipment, including Peter's laptop computer and printer, when needed.

Although mobile operations will account for a significant portion of the business, Wheels On Wheels will utilize garage space, as well as an adjacent storage shed, at Peter Green's home to maintain its inventory of used bicycles, parts, and supplies. In addition, the physical garage location will provide workspace for performing extensive bicycle overhauls and repairs/reconditioning during the winter months.

Online Operations

Wheels On Wheels maintains a Web site and Facebook page where available reconditioned bicycles are featured.

PERSONNEL

Peter Green's passion for bicycles began at the age of three, when he received his first tricycle. During his youth, Peter became involved in BMX racing. Ultimately, his enthusiasm shifted to road and trail riding. Bicycles, in various states of repair and assembly, became permanent fixtures in his bedroom (and later his apartment). Along with riding, Peter's interests extended to the mechanical aspects of maintaining, repairing, upgrading, and tinkering with bicycles of all kinds.

Peter soon began working on bicycles for neighbors and friends, leading to a part-time job at a local bicycle store. After graduating from high school, Peter began working for the bicycle store on a full-time basis, learning important lessons in customer relations and small business management. These experiences fueled his desire to establish Wheels On Wheels.

MARKETING & SALES

Wheels On Wheels has developed a marketing plan that involves the following primary tactics:

1. Printed collateral describing the business.

2. A Yellow Page listing.

3. A Web site with complete details about the business and a listing of its used bicycle inventory.

4. An annual (early spring) direct mail campaign to recipients with household incomes of $50,000 and more. The mailer will include a newsletter providing information about bicycle care and Wheels On Wheels' services, as well as a promotional refrigerator magnet.

5. Flyers distributed at several large community events in Redwood City, including the Annual Air Show, Redwood City County Fair, and the Redwood City Rocks Festival.

6. A public relations campaign that involves the submission of news releases to local newspapers and TV stations when we host bicycle safety classes.

7. A customer loyalty program that provides a 10 percent discount to those referring a friend or family member to our business.

8. Mobile marketing (displaying the Wheels On Wheels name, Web site address, phone number, and tagline on the outside of our vehicle).

GROWTH STRATEGY

After covering start-up and operational costs, Peter Green anticipates that Wheels On Wheels will generate a net profit of almost $71,000 during the first year, providing capital needed to establish an additional mobile operation during the second year and leased space for truck/trailer storage, bicycle inventory, and reconditioning operations. In addition, at least one employee will need to be hired at that time. Based on the performance of the business during its first five years, Peter may consider expanding Wheels On Wheels to other markets, perhaps via a franchising model.

FINANCIAL ANALYSIS

Start-up Budget

Peter Green is anticipating $12,125 in start-up costs for Wheels On Wheels, which will be covered by his own cash savings:

- Tools & Equipment ($1,600)

- Initial Supplies & Parts Inventory ($375)

- 6 x 12 Cargo Trailer ($5,000)

- Security System ($200)

- Promotional Vehicle/Trailer Graphics ($750)

- Generator ($1,700)

- Laptop Computers/Peripherals ($2,500)

In addition, he is anticipating $87,572 in operational costs during the first year:

- Advertising & Marketing ($13,500)

- Fuel ($9,000)

- Miscellaneous Items ($500)

- Legal ($1,250)

- Accounting ($750)

- Office Supplies ($500)

- Insurance ($2,500)

- Salary ($55,000)

- Truck Loan Payments ($4,572)

The following sales projections have been developed for Wheels On Wheels' first year of operations:

	January	February	March	April	May	June
Bicycle safety classes ($25/person; one session)	$ 0	$ 0	$ 500	$ 1,000	$ 1,000	$ 1,000
Bicycle maintenance classes ($50/person; one session)	$ 0	$1,000	$ 2,000	$ 3,000	$ 4,000	$ 4,000
Bicycle repair classes ($150/person; three sessions)	$ 0	$ 0	$ 3,000	$ 6,000	$ 6,000	$ 6,000
Basic tune-up ($40)	$ 80	$ 80	$ 3,000	$ 4,880	$ 6,080	$ 6,080
Deluxe tune-up ($75)	$ 375	$ 375	$ 1,875	$ 3,150	$ 3,900	$ 3,900
The max ($145) *shop only; not available as a mobile service	$ 290	$ 290	$ 580	$ 870	$ 1,160	$ 1,160
Drive train cleaning ($45)	$ 180	$ 450	$ 2,340	$ 3,735	$ 4,680	$ 4,680
Bike assembly ($45)	$ 225	$ 450	$ 180	$ 270	$ 360	$ 360
Monthly total	**$1,150**	**$2,645**	**$13,475**	**$22,905**	**$27,180**	**$27,180**

	July	August	September	October	November	December
Bicycle safety classes ($25/person; one session)	$ 1,000	$ 750	$ 500	$ 0	$ 0	$ 0
Bicycle maintenance classes ($50/person; one session)	$ 3,000	$ 2,000	$ 1,000	$ 0	$ 0	$ 0
Bicycle repair classes ($150/person; three sessions)	$ 6,000	$ 4,500	$ 3,000	$ 0	$ 0	$ 0
Basic tune-up ($40)	$ 6,080	$ 4,880	$ 3,000	$2,440	$1,240	$ 600
Deluxe tune-up ($75)	$ 3,900	$ 3,150	$ 1,875	$1,575	$ 825	$ 375
The max ($145) *shop only; not available as a mobile service	$ 1,160	$ 870	$ 580	$ 435	$ 290	$ 290
Drive train cleaning ($45)	$ 4,680	$ 3,735	$ 2,340	$1,890	$ 945	$ 450
Bike assembly ($45)	$ 360	$ 270	$ 180	$ 135	$ 360	$ 450
Monthly total	**$26,180**	**$20,155**	**$12,475**	**$6,475**	**$3,660**	**$2,165**

Based on these monthly projections, the business' first-year annual revenues from bicycle classes, service, and repair will break down as follows:

Service	2014
Bicycle safety classes ($25/person; one session)	$ 5,750
Bicycle maintenance classes ($50/person; one session)	$ 20,000
Bicycle repair classes ($150/person; three sessions)	$ 34,500
Basic tune-up ($40)	$ 38,440
Deluxe tune-up ($75)	$ 25,275
The max ($145) *shop only; not available as a mobile service	$ 7,975
Drive train cleaning ($45)	$ 30,105
Bike assembly ($45)	$ 3,600
Annual total	**$165,645**

Used bicycle sales are expected to account for a very small portion of revenues initially. Although projections are difficult to compile, Peter Green is anticipating sales of approximately $5,000 in this category for the first year.

After covering start-up and operational costs, Peter Green anticipates that Wheels On Wheels will generate a net profit of almost $71,000 during the first year, providing capital needed for expansion, as outlined in the Growth Strategy section of this plan.

In order to provide initial working capital for the business, Peter Green has applied for a $20,000 commercial loan from Community Bank, as well as a line of credit.

SWOT ANALYSIS

- **Strengths:** As a mobile bicycle repair and resale business, we are unique in the local marketplace; no other bicycle repair shops are currently making house calls. This model provides the owner with considerable flexibility and significantly reduced overhead.

- **Weaknesses:** Under the mobile business model, Wheels On Wheels is limited in the number of repairs that can be performed on a mobile basis at one time. Expansion of the mobile service will require an additional trailer and employees.

- **Opportunities:** We are in a unique position to corner the market for busy bicycle owners and take advantage of "spontaneous customers" who see us performing repairs for their friends and neighbors.

- **Threats:** Because Peter Green will perform all services, the prospect of illness or injury is a potential threat. In addition, rising fuel costs and the risk of an accident (especially during unfavorable weather conditions) also are considerations.

Chiropractic Office

COLE'S CHIROPRACTIC

1450 East Wells Street
Madison, WI 53705

*This plan is balanced and economical, avoiding verbosity by dedicating only as much time as necessary for each section. Competence in Chiropractic Science is displayed and a brief description of the business operations is given, making the proposal focused and streamlined. Emphasized are the expenditures and startup costs, justifying the loan amount requested. This business plan appeared in **Business Plans Handbook, Volume 6**. It has been updated for this volume.*

PURPOSE

We are seeking to lease a 20/20 C-DR 1417 Sensor from Superior Radiographics, Ltd., approximate value $120,000, for use in the to be established Cole's Chiropractic Clinic.

The following prospectus will provide information concerning the profession of chiropractic, office description, specific expenditures, practice and marketing plans, and supporting documents. We expect to be open during June 2014 at 1450 East Wells Street, Madison, Wisconsin.

CHIROPRACTIC

Chiropractic is a profession that has been rapidly developing since its discovery in 1895 by D.D. Palmer. Today, there are approximately 52,600 doctors of chiropractic in the United States. Chiropractors are primary health care providers, licensed in all 50 states, and are participants in most major medical insurances.

Chiropractic is defined as the philosophy, science, and art of things natural, with the objective of locating, analyzing, and correcting the vertebral subluxation complex. The subluxation is the improper positioning of a vertebra from the ideal spinal model which causes interference of a nerve impulse from the brain to the body and back. We know that the central nervous system controls and regulates the entire body. If we have an interference of a nerve to a particular part of the body, this part has lost the necessary communication to function properly. The rest of the body is also adversely affected since no one part affected can NOT affect the whole body.

Doctors of chiropractic are the only professionals who are trained to locate, analyze, and correct the vertebral subluxation complex. Chiropractors adjust the vertebral subluxation complex by introducing a specific force in the direction that would thereby restore the biomechanical integrity, thus restoring the nerve impulse.

LOCATION

Cole's Chiropractic Clinic will be located at 1450 East Wells St. This office is centrally located in Madison, and allows for easy access both entering and exiting the parking area.

The office space is 1050 square feet, consisting of the following: 1 Reception Room, 1 Secretary Office, 1 X-ray Department, 1 Restroom, 2 Adjusting Rooms, and 1 private office.

MARKET

Cole's Chiropractic Clinic will primarily serve a population of over 75,000 in a ten-mile radius.

There are only 25 doctors of chiropractic in this ten-mile radius. The equipment that we will use in our office is the latest in chiropractic technology. The 20/20 C-DR 1417 digital X-ray unit in our office will be the only one within 150 miles of Madison. This machine is capable of directly capturing the image data and displaying it on a monitor within 10-12 seconds, thus eliminating darkroom film processing and associated costs while providing cleaner, artifact-free data. We will offer other doctors of chiropractic use of this equipment for a small fee so their patients can also benefit.

PROMOTION PLAN

Grand Opening: Personal invitations to family and friends. Invitations to residence and commercial establishments within 5 miles.

Advertisement: Newspaper and other publications press releases. Yellow pages in phone book. Large business sign in front of office. Online presence.

Public Relations: Continuous series of public health awareness seminars. Participation in local civic groups.

Patient Education: Quarterly newsletter, *Health Tracks: Chiropractic a New Beginning;* Office lending library.

Patient Relations: Systematic patient follow-up procedure. Special occasion and thank-you for referral mailings.

PATIENT MANAGEMENT

Daily Tasks

Day 1—Initial office visit
The first day of treatment will include the following tasks:

- Consultation

- Terms of acceptance

- Case History

- Comprehensive Examination

- Digital X-rays

- Patient Education

Day 2—Extended office visit

Day two of treatment will include:

- Report of findings

- Recommended program

- Instrumentation

- Spinal Examination and Adjustment

- Scheduling of next appointment

Future Office Visits

Future office visits will typically include:

- Instrumentation

- Spinal Examination and Adjustment if necessary

PROGRAM OF CARE

The program of care can broken down into three different groups, each with its own recommended care schedule. This includes:

Initial Care: (Acute) 3 visits per week

Reconstructive Care: (Subacute) 2 visits per week; (Chronic) 1—2 visits per month

Maintenance Care: 1—2 visits per month

DURATION OF CARE

The duration of care is dependent in the type of care being administered, including:

Initial Care: 3—6 weeks

Reconstructive Care: 4—8 weeks

Maintenance Care: Ongoing

FINANCIAL CONSIDERATIONS

FEE SCHEDULE 2014

Fee schedule, 2014

Initial care

Examination	$60
X-rays: cervical	$35/view
X-rays: lumbar/pelvic	$50/view
Cineradiography	$125/region

Reconstructive care

Office visit/adjustments	$45

Maintenance care

Office visit/adjustments	$45

CHIROPRACTIC OFFICE

FEE SCHEDULE 2018

Fee schedule, 2018

Initial care

Examination	$75
X-rays: cervical	$50/view
X-rays: lumbar/pelvic	$70/view
Cineradiography	$170/region

Reconstructive care

Office visit/adjustments	$55

Maintenance care

Office visit/adjustments	$55

PRE-OPERATING EXPENSES

Pre-operating expenses

Deposits

Lease (building)	$ 4,000
Insurances	500
Lease (X-ray)	8,500

Office supplies

Bookkeeping	$ 250
Letterhead	175
Filing cabinet	255
Business cards	50
Patient folders	85
Telephones (2)	175
Computer paper	50
Miscellaneous	350

Patient education

Health tracks	$ 100

Office equipment

Reception room chairs	$ 1,200
Secretarial chair	250
Adding machine	50
Answering machine	175
Computer	3,000
Office desk	500
Executive chair	250

Chiropractic equipment

Anatomical charts and models	$ 1,000
Chiropractic tables, benches and stools	6,000
Diagnostic tools (measuring devices, scales, vital signs, etc.)	1,250
Treatment supplies (disinfectants, gloves, table paper, paper gowns, etc.)	750
X-ray wall stand/grid cabinet, laptop table, etc.	12,000

Remodeling

Room divider, carpeting, paint, etc.	$ 5,000
Electrical wiring	1,500
Miscellaneous	1,000
Total pre-operating expenses	**$48,415**

MONTHLY OPERATING EXPENSES

Monthly operating expenses

Office

Lease (building)	$ 2,000
Lease (X-ray)	1,785
Acct.	225
Telephone	70
Advertising	175
Utilities	175
Office manager	1,530
Equipment loan payment ($100,000/10 years)	1,000
Office supplies	125
Insurances (malpractice, fire, theft)	200
Total monthly office expenses	**$ 7,285**

Personal

Rent	650
Student loan	750
Utilities	175
Telephone	65
Transportation (insurance, gas, maint.)	250
Food	500
Clothing	200
Retirement	400
Miscellaneous	500
Total personal expenses	**$ 3,490**

Office

Monthly	$ 7,285
6 months	43,710
12 months	87,420

Personal

Monthly	3,490
6 months	20,940
12 months	41,880

Combined (office + personal)

Monthly	$ 10,775
6 months	64,650
12 months	129,300

AWARDS AND HONORS

Awards and honors received by Robert Cole include:

- Selected to be in *Who's Who Among Students in American Colleges* as a Student at Sherman College.

- Selected to the National Deans List.

- President of Student Government.

- Administrative Council Representative.

- Strategic Planning Committee Member.

Custom Jewelry/Gift Box Business

Boxes By Benny Inc.

52 Main St.
Adamsville, WI 53000

Paul Greenland

Boxes By Benny creates custom jewelry and gift boxes, with a focus on sales at farmer's markets, art and craft shows, and flea markets.

EXECUTIVE SUMMARY

Business Overview

Located in Adamsville, Wisconsin, Boxes By Benny creates custom jewelry and gift boxes, with a focus on sales at farmer's markets, art and craft shows, and flea markets. The business is the brainchild of Jeffrey and Lindsay Benny, who have decided to channel their artistic and creative abilities into a business venture with tremendous potential.

Prior to establishing the business, Jeffrey worked as a carpenter, focusing mainly on residential construction. When the Great Recession stifled new-home construction, Jeffrey began utilizing his craftsmanship in new ways, producing custom cabinetry for local residents, as well as gift boxes for sale at regional art and craft shows. Jeffrey's wife, Lindsay, a high school art teacher, eventually became involved, producing gift boxes made from unusual materials, including recycled circuit boards.

Jeffrey will devote himself to Boxes By Benny on a full-time basis, while Lindsay will be involved part-time, so that she can continue to pursue her teaching career.

MARKET ANALYSIS

Boxes By Benny's target market is mainly comprised of middle- and upper-income individuals who attend farmer's markets, bazaars, and craft shows. For planning purposes, Boxes By Benny will consider its primary market area to be Adamsville and a surrounding 50-mile region that includes the communities of Sterling, Greenberg, Davis, and Chesterfield. These communities all have events (festivals, craft shows, farmers markets, etc.) throughout the year that will provide the business with multiple exhibition opportunities.

After conducting research into events with the greatest potential, the following were identified as offering the best opportunity during the first year of operations:

- Davis Mall Craft Show (held quarterly)
- Valentine's Day Arts & Crafts Spree (Chesterfield)

- Sterling Farmer's Market
- Annual Greenberg Art Show
- Sterling Craft & Merchandise Show
- Annual Mother's Day Craft Show (Adamsville)
- Adamsville Summer Festival
- Adamsville Farmer's Market
- Adamsville Fall Art & Craft Expo
- Jewelry & Accessory Craft Fair (Sterling)
- Adamsville Home Decor Expo (held twice annually)
- Holiday Craft Bazaar (Davis)

Future Markets

Based on the business' success during its first year, Boxes By Benny will likely exhibit at large public events in Milwaukee, Wisconsin, which is 150 miles away. Although competition will be more intense, this larger metropolitan area will offer strong sales potential.

As Boxes By Benny grows, the owners will consider additional sales channels, including:

- Gift Shop Sales (commission arrangement)
- Retail Stores (commission arrangement)
- Internet Sales

When the business is ready to expand in these areas, detailed market research will be conducted regarding specific gift shops and retail stores that hold the greatest potential in the primary market area. In 2013, the primary market was home to 67 specialty retailers, as well as 25 gift shops.

PRODUCTS & SERVICES

Most of the boxes that Boxes By Benny produces will fall into one of the following categories:

- Cigar Boxes
- Gift Boxes
- Golf Boxes
- Humidors
- Jewelry Boxes
- Puzzle & Game Boxes
- Tea Boxes
- Tea Chests
- Tool Boxes
- Tool Chests
- Watch Boxes
- Wine Boxes

Materials

The majority of Boxes By Benny's creations will be wooden boxes, made from a variety of different woods, including:

- American Black Walnut
- American Elm
- American White Oak
- Aromatic Red Cedar
- Aspen
- Bald Cypress
- Balsa
- Basswood
- Black Cherry
- Butternut
- Chestnut
- Douglas Fir
- Eastern White Pine
- Ebony
- Hickory
- Lauan Plywood
- Mahogany
- Pecan
- Poplar
- Red Oak
- Redwood
- Rosewood
- Southern Yellow Pine
- Spruce SPF
- Sugar Maple
- Sugar Pine
- Teak
- Western Hemlock
- Western Red Cedar
- White Ash
- White Oak
- Yellow Birch

Some of the company's boxes will be produced from recycled boards (e.g., shipping pallets, barn wood, etc.), while others will be produced using exotic or premium hardwoods.

Other unique box designs will be produced using other recycled materials, including circuit boards from computers and other electronic devices, as well as Plexiglas, glass, plastics, and ceramic tiles.

Joinery

In the case of wooden boxes, a wide range of different corner joints will be used, providing strength and durability, as well as a decorative appearance. These include:

- Biscuited Miter
- Keyed Miter
- Splined Miters
- Pinned Rabbet
- Rabbet
- Double Rabbet
- Dado Rabbet
- Finger
- Dovetail
- Half-Blind Dovetail

Special Features

Boxes By Benny will incorporate a number of different special features to give its boxes a unique appearance. These include:

- Unique Pulls (from traditional knobs to bent wire and other items)
- Hinges (traditional and specialty metal hinges, shop-made wooden hinges, leather hinges, and more)
- Lids (rabbeted, sliding, hinged, sawn, raised)
- Padded linings (cloth, felt, cork)

OPERATIONS

Location and Facilities

Boxes By Benny is located in the rural community of Adamsville, Wisconsin. Operations will be based in a 450-square-foot outbuilding on the Benny's property. This location is ideal because it already is home to Jeffrey's woodshop and Lindsay's art studio space. In addition, it offers space for the storage of lumber and other materials needed for the business.

Major Suppliers

Lumber

Boxes By Benny relies upon a number of different suppliers in Wisconsin, including:

- Chering Co.
- Wisconsin Lumber Supply Co.
- Farrington Lumber Inc.
- National Lumber Inc.
- Apple River Lumber Co.

Hardware

Boxes By Benny will utilize a number of local and national hardware suppliers, including:

- Amerock

- Bloomfield & Smith

- RockWare

- Precision Forge Co.

- Menard's

PERSONNEL

Jeffrey Benny

Jeffrey is a member of the United Brotherhood of Carpenters. For most of his career he has worked as a framing and residential carpenter, helping to build new subdivisions and renovate existing homes. However, Jeffrey has always enjoyed millwork and cabinetry, beginning at an early age when he worked on projects with his grandfather. When the Great Recession stifled new-home construction, Jeffrey began utilizing his craftsmanship in new ways, producing custom cabinetry for local residents, as well as gift boxes for sale at regional art and craft shows. Establishing Boxes By Benny will provide him with the opportunity to do this on a full-time basis. In addition to his trade, Jeffrey has pursued small business management courses at Adamsville Community College, and recently received a related certificate.

Lindsay Benny

Lindsay has been an art teacher at Adamsville High School for 12 years. In that role she inspires creativity in students as they work with a variety of materials, including watercolor and acrylic paint, charcoal, clay, and wax. She is especially adept at encouraging students to repurpose/recycle everyday items, and transform them into unique works of art. Lindsay earned a Bachelor of Science degree in Art Education from the University of Wisconsin. In her spare time she enjoys creating her own works of art, including items for sale at craft shows. Lindsay will be involved in Boxes By Benny on a part-time basis, so that she can continue to pursue her teaching career.

GROWTH STRATEGY

Boxes By Benny anticipates that about 60 percent of sales will be attributed to large events. Medium-sized events will account for 30 percent of sales, with smaller events accounting for the remaining 10 percent.

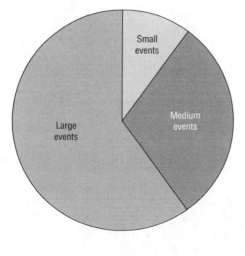

The following table provides a breakdown of unit sales, by type of event, for the first three years of operations. The owners are anticipating annual growth of approximately 10 percent during years two and three. Growth will be attributed to increases in efficiency and economies of scale. Production capabilities will be maximized at this point, with further volume gains requiring additional staff.

	2014	2015	2016
Small events	87	96	105
Medium events	259	285	313
Large events	518	570	627
Total boxes	**864**	**951**	**1,045**

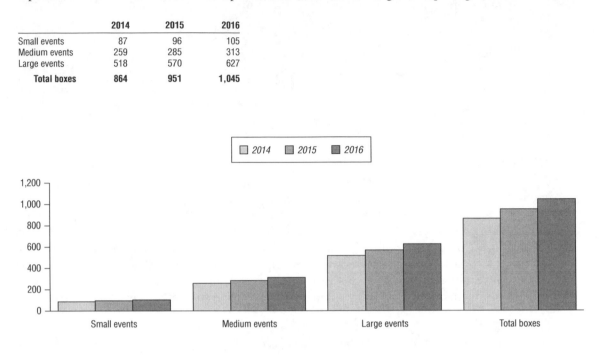

MARKETING & SALES

Boxes By Benny seeks to develop a strong business through positive word-of-mouth. The owners believe that their boxes, which will be adorned with a tag displaying the company name and Web site/ phone number on the bottom, will serve as the ultimate marketing tool. When customers show their new box to friends and family, the ultimate goal is to ensure they ask: "Where did you get that?"

The owners will support their direct sales efforts with a Web site, which will include an extensive photo gallery of boxes that they have created. Although the site initially will not have e-commerce capabilities, prospective customers can contact Boxes By Benny to discuss custom gift boxes. The site will allow individuals to sign up for a quarterly e-mail newsletter. Additionally, it will link to a YouTube channel with videos showing the artists at work. The site also will link to Boxes By Benny's Facebook page, which will include listings of upcoming appearances at art shows and farmer's markets.

Finally, Boxes By Benny will create beautiful, glossy, four-color information cards that will be distributed directly at art shows and farmer's markets. Customers and those with a casual interest can take a card, which will display the owners' unique creations on the front side, along with contact information on the back.

FINANCIAL ANALYSIS

The following table provides sales and profit projections for Boxes By Benny's first three years of operations. Cost of goods sold includes materials, labor, marketing, and production-related energy costs. Additional financial statements have been developed, and are available upon request.

	2014	2015	2016
Small events	$ 6,960	$ 7,680	$ 8,400
Medium events	$20,270	$22,800	$25,040
Large events	$41,440	$45,600	$50,160
Gross sales	**$68,670**	**$76,080**	**$83,600**
Cost of goods sold	$21,600	$23,775	$26,125
Net profit	**$47,070**	**$52,305**	**$57,475**

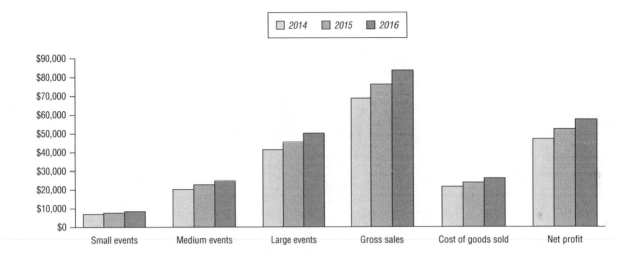

SWOT ANALYSIS

- **Strengths:** Boxes By Benny's offerings will be unique in the marketplace. Exhibiting the finest quality and craftsmanship, the company's boxes will set it apart from the competition.

- **Weaknesses:** The products sold by Boxes By Benny are discretionary in nature, making the business vulnerable to economic downturns that impact consumer discretionary spending.

- **Opportunities:** There is plenty of opportunity in the primary market area, which is characterized by vibrant community interest in handcrafted items and artwork. Boxes By Benny's owners will take advantage of this by offering unique, unusual, and distinctive items of the highest quality.

- **Threats:** Production is limited to Jeffrey and Lindsay Benny. An illness or injury could jeopardize the availability of products, and thus the business itself.

Educational Consulting Firm

CollegeChoice Advisers LLC

17 Berry Glenn Ave.
Litchfield, FL 32400

Paul Greenland

CollegeChoice Advisers LLC is an educational consulting firm focused on academic coaching and college test prep, as well as subject-specific tutoring.

EXECUTIVE SUMMARY

CollegeChoice Advisers LLC is an educational consulting firm focused on academic coaching and college test prep, as well as subject-specific tutoring. Established by high school guidance counselor Burt McCreary and high school math teacher Randy Townsend, CollegeChoice's target market will consist of families with college-bound students, especially those with prospects of being accepted at an exclusive college or university. Burt and Randy will provide the families of exceptional students with the guidance they need to achieve their college admissions goals.

MARKET ANALYSIS

CollegeChoice Advisers is based in Litchfield, Florida in the northeastern corner of Broward County. From a marketing perspective, the owners will focus on prospective clients (e.g., families with middle school- and high school-aged children) residing in adjacent Palm Beach and Martin Counties, which rank among Florida's top five counties by per capita income.

In 2012 Palm Beach County had a combined population of 1.35 million people, or 556,000 households. Those aged 15 to 19 accounted for 5.9% of the population. That year, average household income totaled $81,584. Students in the county are served by the School District of Palm Beach County, which ranks as one of the largest in both the state and the nation. Some students also attend private schools.

In addition, Martin County had a population of 148,508 people, or 64,912 households. Those aged 15 to 19 accounted for 5.2% of the population. Average household income totaled $82,089. The majority of students in the county are served by the Martin County School District, with many also attending private schools.

Future Markets

As defined in the Growth Strategy section of this plan, CollegeChoice Advisors eventually will consider expanding the business to the Florida counties Collier and Monroe, which also rank among the state's highest, in terms of per capita income. In 2012 Collier County had a population of 333,598, or 138,276 households. Those aged 15 to 19 accounted for 5.3% of the population. Average household income totaled $90,174. In addition, Monroe County is home to 74,546 people, or 33,355 households. Those aged 15 to 19 accounted for 4.2% of the population, and average household income was $90,191.

INDUSTRY ANALYSIS

Private tutors and test preparation consultants are part of the larger education industry. According to the Education Industry Association (EIA), spending on all levels of education, from pre-K through post-secondary, was achieving strong growth by 2013. Eclipsed only by healthcare, education industry expenditures were $750 billion and rising, representing about 10 percent of the nation's gross national product.

According to **The New York Times,** data from the research firm EduVentures indicated that tutoring industry revenues were as high as $7 billion as of 2007. By the beginning of the 2010-2011 school year, the EIA indicated that spending on tutors, specifically, was increasing at more than 5 percent annually. Strong demand for academic consulting and tutoring services continued in 2013, as top students faced an increasingly competitive environment for college admissions.

In markets like Manhattan, wealthy individuals pay as much as $250-$400 per hour for elite private tutors, with more individuals paying between $85 per hour and $150 per hour. Nationwide, tutors typically charged rates of $50-$65 per hour.

Like other industries, tutoring and academic consulting professionals are represented by different professional associations, including The National Tutoring Association, the American Tutoring Association, and the Education Industry Association.

PERSONNEL

Randy Townsend

A mathematics teacher at Central High School for 16 years, Randy Townsend is highly regarded as an educator by students, peers, and other faculty members. He is recognized for his skill at presenting complicated mathematical concepts in a way that students can easily understand. In particular, he has an exceptional ability to work with advanced students. In addition to regular classroom instruction, Townsend leads Central High's mathletes program, a program for students who participate in mathematics competitions. In addition, he was part of a committee that developed the Litchfield Consolidated School District's college planning curriculum. In his role with CollegeChoice, Townsend will oversee the firm's tutoring/academic advising offerings.

Burt McCreary

For the past 12 years, Burt McCreary has served as a college admissions counselor at Central High School, where he has gained considerable experience helping a broad range of students plan for their future. In particular, he has enjoyed working with academically advanced students and helping them to secure scholarships. During the 2011-2012 school year alone, Central High's graduating class, which included 200 students, secured more than $5 million in scholarships. McCreary played a role in helping several students gain acceptance to Ivy League schools such as Brown University and Yale University. McCreary earned his undergraduate and graduate education degrees from the University of Michigan. In his role with CollegeChoice, he will be responsible for the firm's college test prep/planning offerings.

The owners of CollegeChoice Advisers possess a wide range of knowledge, skills, and abilities necessary for success as educational consultants and tutors, including:

- Communication

- Listening

- Speaking

- Critical Thinking

- Evaluation

- Relationship Building

- Conflict Resolution

Independent Contractors

In addition to Townsend and McCreary, CollegeChoice will provide services utilizing a staff of independent contractors, who are capable of providing advanced subject specific tutoring in the following subject areas:

- English

- Foreign Language (German, Chinese, Spanish, French)

- Science (Anatomy & Physiology, Biology, Chemistry, Zoology)

- Mathematics (Algebra, Calculus, Geometry, Trigonometry)

- Government

- History

Professional & Advisory Support

CollegeChoice will rely upon Accurate Accounting Services for tax assistance. Legal advice, when needed, will be received from Jonathan M. Myers, an independent attorney. Finally, CollegeChoice has established both checking and merchant accounts with Litchfield Community Bank.

GROWTH STRATEGY

During year one (2013-2014 school year), the owners will launch a marketing initiative during the summer months (June-August), in an effort to secure an initial customer base. The majority of tutoring services will begin in August and conclude in May, with the exception of students needing assistance over the summer. Academic plan development services will be offered at any time, but will be marketed heavily in the winter, with a goal of engaging families during the spring and early summer months, before the beginning of the next school year. Finally, test preparation services will be offered on an ongoing basis, because the ACT and SAT exams are offered at different times throughout the year.

The following table summarizes projected customer volume for the first three years of operations. The test preparation and academic plan development services categories show number of customers, while the tutoring services category shows the number of tutoring sessions.

Test preparation services

	January	February	March	April	May	June	July	August	September	October	November	December	Total
Year 1	6	6	6	7	7	7	8	10	10	11	10	8	**96**
Year 2	9	10	11	11	11	12	12	13	13	14	11	9	**136**
Year 3	10	11	12	12	12	13	13	14	15	14	12	10	**148**

Academic plan development services

	January	February	March	April	May	June	July	August	September	October	November	December	Total
Year 1	2	3	5	6	6	6	5	4	4	4	3	3	**51**
Year 2	4	4	6	8	8	9	7	5	5	5	4	4	**69**
Year 3	6	6	7	9	9	10	8	6	6	6	5	5	**83**

Tutoring services

	January	February	March	April	May	June	July	August	September	October	November	December	Total
Year 1	25	38	43	43	45	10	10	18	43	43	43	43	**726**
Year 2	45	45	50	50	58	15	15	20	50	50	50	50	**903**
Year 3	58	60	63	63	71	20	20	20	63	63	63	63	**1,129**

The owners anticipate revenue growth to be especially strong within the academic plan development category, followed by test preparation, and finally, tutoring (which is offered by independent tutors who pay a 15% commission to us for referrals).

	Year 1	Year 2	Year 3
Test preparation	$ 71,520	$101,320	$110,260
Academic plan development	$102,000	$138,000	$166,000
Tutoring	$ 8,168	$ 10,159	$ 12,701
Total revenue	**$181,688**	**$249,479**	**$288,961**
Net income	**$ 11,788**	**$ 39,329**	**$ 58,361**

By year three, the business will have generated more than $100,000 in net income, which the owners plan to use for the expansion of CollegeChoice Advisors to the high-income Florida counties of Collier and Monroe in year four. Capital will be needed for leasing additional office space and also hiring two additional employees to serve the new geographic market.

SERVICES

Generally speaking, CollegeChoice Advisors will offer the following services:

- Test Preparation
- Academic Plan Development
- Subject-Specific Tutoring

These services may involve advising students in a number of different areas, including:

- Time Management/Organization
- Course Selection
- Citizenship/Volunteering
- Scholarship Identification/Application

- College Application Advisement

- Reading Strategies

- Writing Strategies

- Study Skills Coaching

- Test Anxiety Reduction Strategies

Process

Subject-specific tutoring will be offered on a revenue-sharing/referral basis with a network of highly regarded independent tutors at a rate of $75 per hour. After meeting with families to discuss the needs of their students, we will then make the appropriate referrals.

Test preparation courses, taught by the owners, will be offered on a monthly basis, with a maximum of 15 students per class. The registration fee is $745 per student.

Academic plan development services will be provided directly by the owners. Prospective clients will be provided with a complimentary 30-minute telephone conversation to discuss a student's specific situation and general goals and objectives. If the initial consultation goes well, and the prospective client wishes to proceed with services, then CollegeChoice Advisors will develop a customized plan for the student for a flat fee of $2,000, which includes 10 hours of consultation time. A pre-determined evaluation and adjustment schedule will be developed, so that progress can be reviewed on an ongoing basis.

MARKETING & SALES

CollegeChoice Advisors has developed a marketing plan that involves the following tactics:

1. A Web site with complete details about our business and the services we offer, including an online "intake form" that parents can complete and submit to us at any time.

2. A blog, where the owners will share their insights and experiences regarding education.

3. A presence on both Facebook and Twitter.

4. A public relations strategy that involves sending press releases to local media regarding educational topics, and the advantages of academic planning, test preparation, and tutoring. The owners also will make themselves available for expert interviews on local radio programs and television morning shows.

5. Word-of-mouth marketing, leveraging our strong reputation within the educational community to maintain a steady stream of student referrals.

6. Printed brochures describing our services for parents of prospective students, as well as referral sources (e.g., other teachers).

7. A Yellow Page advertisement.

8. Monthly information sessions with free refreshments, offered at no cost to attendees, describing the effectiveness of academic planning, test preparation, and subject-specific tutoring. Real students will share their stories, providing powerful testimonials.

9. Presentations to area non-profit organizations (e.g., PTAs, church groups, etc.) on education-related issues.

10. A customer referral program that provides a 10 percent discount for each new client that is referred.

11. Exterior signage identifying/promoting CollegeChoice Advisors.

OPERATIONS

Facility & Location

CollegeChoice Advisors has leased space in the Hartsfield Complex, an office building located at 17 Berry Glenn Ave. in Litchfield. This location provides a large meeting space suitable for test preparation classes, office space for each owner, a small reception area, and a restroom. No modifications are needed to the facility, which is easily accessible via main roadways and provides ample parking space for customers.

Hours of Operation

Regular business hours for CollegeChoice Advisors will be Monday through Friday, from 9 AM to 5 PM. However, the owners will work a flexible schedule, allowing them to accommodate evening appointments with families. In addition, some test preparation courses will be offered on Saturdays.

FINANCIAL ANALYSIS

In addition to the following pro forma profit and loss statement, CollegeChoice Advisors has prepared detailed financial projections with the help of their accountant. These projections, which include a summary of minimal startup costs, are available on request.

	Year 1	Year 2	Year 3
Sales			
Tutoring services	$ 8,168	$ 10,159	$ 12,701
Academic plan development	$102,000	$138,000	$166,000
Test preparation services	$ 71,520	$101,320	$110,260
Total	**$181,688**	**$249,479**	**$288,961**
Operating expenses			
Maintenance	$ 350	$ 350	$ 350
Owners' salaries	$135,000	$175,000	$195,000
Office supplies	$ 350	$ 400	$ 450
Advertising	$ 2,000	$ 2,000	$ 2,000
Equipment	$ 1,000	$ 1,000	$ 1,000
Accounting & legal	$ 1,250	$ 950	$ 950
Rent	$ 24,000	$ 24,000	$ 24,000
Telephone	$ 1,000	$ 1,000	$ 1,000
Utilities	$ 1,750	$ 1,800	$ 1,850
Insurance	$ 2,250	$ 2,500	$ 2,750
Internet service	$ 950	$ 1,150	$ 1,250
Total	**$169,900**	**$210,150**	**$230,600**
Net income	**$ 11,788**	**$ 39,329**	**$ 58,361**

Event Planner

Events by Crystal

7834 Hampton Dr.
San Diego, CA 92138

Brenda Kubiac

Events by Crystal is a full-service professional event planning business specializing in corporate meeting planning.

1.0 EXECUTIVE SUMMARY

1.1 Business Overview

Events by Crystal is a California-based sole proprietorship that provides full-service professional event planning services in San Diego. The founder, Crystal Cummings has been involved with event planning for more than five years where she worked exclusively as a corporate meeting planner for Bates Corporation in San Diego accommodating as many as 10,000 guests at one time.

According to *US News & World Report*, event planning is one of the"Top 26 Jobs of 2012" (www.black enterprise.com, 2013). On average, the industry is experiencing salaries up to $76,000 annually. Recent statistics indicate the meeting and event planning profession is growing even through a recovering economy.

Crystal Cummings is a member of the International Special Events Society (ISES), the National Association of Catering Executives (NACE), the Meeting Professionals International (MPI), the Professional Convention Management Association (PCMA), and the San Diego Chapter.

1.2 Mission Statement

Events by Crystal is a full-service event planning company who promises to live up to every clients expectations of their event.

2.0 INDUSTRY/MARKET

2.1 Industry Analysis

The U.S. trade show and event planning industry includes about 4,500 companies with combined annual revenue of about $10 billion. Modest growth is projected for the industry over the next two years. The recovering economy and a rise in corporate spending on travel could drive additional demand for trade show services. The Bureau of Labor Statistics (BLS)"projects meeting, convention, and event planning employment growth of 43.7 percent between 2010 and 2020, adding 31,300 more jobs," adding that"The highest paid in the meeting, convention & event planner profession work in the metropolitan areas of Poughkeepsie, NY...,"earning about $70,790 annually.

Founded in 1987, the primary professional organization within the event planning industry is the International Special Events Society (ISES). Comprised of more than 7,200 professionals in over 38 countries, the mission of ISES"is to educate, advance and promote the special events industry and its network of professionals along with related industries."

2.2 Market Analysis

The city of San Diego ranks as the nation's eighth largest city with 1.3 million residents, while San Diego County has a total population of more than 3 million people. San Diego County encompasses 18 incorporated cities. San Diego is the perfect gathering place for any special event. The city is home to theaters & event facilities, World Resources Simulation Center, San Diego Convention Center, Del Mar Thoroughbred Club, Wave House San Diego, The Abbey on Fifth Avenue—Hornblower Cruises & Events, Real Office Centers, NTC at Liberty Station, the Maritime Museum of San Diego and countless others. By 2020, the city's population is forecast to be 1.54 million people, with 3.54 people in the entire county. San Diego's population base is ideal for an event planning company.

The median age of San Diego's population is 35.6 with over one-quarter under the age of 20 and a mere 11% over 65. About 41.3% of San Diego's workforce over the age of 25 has at least a bachelor's degree. Median household income is $70,149.

2.3 Competition

Crystal searched the yellow pages and online for event planners located in her target market. She also skimmed through specialty magazines, newsletters, and business journals and found few event advertisers. Compared to Crystals Events, other event planners seemed to have less to offer in the way of originality and keeping up with trends. While there are several competing event companies within the primary target area, Crystal already has a successful track record in her targeted market, as well as a personal rapport with former clients, colleagues, and clients.

That's where Events by Crystal sets themselves apart from their competition. As in real estate, location is a huge factor in the success of any event. Events are no longer limited to hotels, convention centers, or restaurants. Events by Crystal plans to think outside the box when it comes to planning events by matching the location to the event. Events can be held at arenas, mansions, museums, wineries, boat charters, cruise ships, dude ranches, boat charters, art galleries, resorts, campgrounds, sporting facilities, and even parking lots depending on the size of the guest list. This is only one method Crystal plans to stand out from her competition.

The"green" trend has become more of a"lifestyle" and event hosts are requesting more in the way of"green" events. Crystal is once again staying ahead of her competition and is fully prepared for this challenge. When a client asks what they offer in the way of an eco-friendly"green event" Crystal won't be caught off guard and will be able to address their needs in a professional manner while carving out her niche at the same time.

3.0 PERSONNEL

3.1 Management Summary

Crystal Cummings is up to the challenge of running her own event planning business out of a home-based office. Prior experience has taught her that running a successful event planning business takes strong administrative skills, computer skills, marketing skills, sales skills, creative skills, execution skills, and project management skills all rolled up together. Crystal has earned the Certified Meeting Professional (CMP) and Certified Special Events Professional (CSEP) through ISES.

3.2 Staffing

On occasion it will be necessary to hire outside help, including staffing agencies, college students for weekend or evening events and colleagues who share the same excitement. When the time comes, event assistants will also be hired. Another option is through networking with professional organizations where professional event planners are more than happy to offer their services.

3.3 Professional and Advisory Support

The company hired an outside accounting company to assist with the initial setup of accounting software to accommodate an event planning company. Legal counsel is providing assistant with client, vendor, and site agreements, as well as any additional formal legal matters prior to that first event. Insurance guidance and coverage was provided by Sandler Insurance. A business account along with a line of credit was set up at San Diego Commercial Bank, including a merchant account for accepting credit card payments.

4.0 STRATEGIES

4.1 Business strategy

In an effort to keep more profits in the company's pocket, Crystal formed strategic partnerships with key vendors who ultimately offered substantial discounts in return for repeat business. The owner plans to take the time to get to know her clients creating long-term relationships, translating into repeat business and referrals. Clients can expect a "hands-on" approach throughout the duration of the event planning process from start to finish. Creating a timeline and sticking to it will ultimately guarantee every event a success, translating into repeat business and referrals.

4.2 Growth strategy

The owner plans to use post-event follow up surveys or questioners, which are among the most common method of market research conducted by event planners. By reaching those in attendance shortly after the event, planners get a better reply and see if their event was successful or there is an area that needs improvement.

When the company out grows its home office space Crystal plans to relocate to a leased office within her primary market and hire two certified event planners to share in the duties of running an event planning company.

5.0 SERVICES

As a full-service event planning company, Events by Crystal plans to offer her services to a host of events which are listed below, but not limited to.

5.1 Corporate/Education

- Board meetings
- Clinics
- Conferences
- Conventions
- Forums
- Board meetings

- Lectures
- Meetings
- Retreats
- Sales meetings
- Seminars
- Shareholder meetings
- Symposiums
- Trainings
- Workshops

5.2 Social Events

- Auctions
- Award banquets
- Book signings
- Concerts
- Expositions
- Fairs
- Fashion shows
- Fundraisers
- Golf tournaments
- Political rallies
- School functions
- Sporting events
- Trade shows
- Weddings
- Community programs

5.3 Vendors

Events by Crystal conducted extensive research of area vendors either through referrals from other planners and venues, or professional trade shows and trade magazines and we're confident that the support system put in place is comprised of the most respected area vendors. The service that the individual vendor will provide is listed below.

- Caterer/bartender
- Florist to provide arrangements (centerpieces, garlands, bouquets)
- Photographer/videographer
- Entertainment agency
- Lighting company (spotlight, strobes, small white lights)
- Prop company (fountain, trellis, palm tree etc.)
- Decor provider

- Staffing company

- Venues

- Tent company

- Transportation/parking personnel

- Rental company

- DJ

- Fabric supply companies (swags, etc.)

- Invitation designer

- Awards and gift companies

- Speakers

- Destination management companies

- Airlines

- Copying services

- Production companies

- Meeting supply companies

- Ground transportation companies

- Exhibition services companies

- Insurance brokers

6.0 MARKETING & SALES

6.1 Advertising and promotion

- Purchase advertisements in relevant publications, including corporate and travel magazines and bridal magazines.

- Build and maintain a Web site showcasing services.

- When it comes to event planners, networking is more effective and less expensive than print advertising. Networking allows meeting people in your own industry.

- Obtain free advertising/publicity compliments of the San Diego Business Journal, San Diego City Beat, San Diego Globe, and San Diego Metropolitan, among others.

- Create business cards with name of business, contact information (phone, fax, e-mail, and Web site address), owners name, specialization, and logo to pass out and ask vendors if I can leave some in their place of business.

- Create tri-fold brochure with all the information listed on the business card. Leave brochures with all the vendors that I work with. Following a successful event Crystal will add photos to the brochures.

- Newsletters will be sent via e-mail prospective, current, and previous clients basically informing clients of anything new or added services.

- Plans to offer a discount package on social event.

7.0 MARKETING PLAN

Events by Crystal plans to maintain an extensive marketing campaign that reaches its targeted market. An overview of both marketing objectives and strategies are listed below.

7.1 Marketing Objectives

- Establish credibility in the social events segment

- Create a professional image

- Get referrals

7.2 Marketing Strategies

- Develop a Web site

- Create a blog

- Create a brochure

- Target the social event segment to gain experience and credibility

- Join San Diego's Chamber of Commerce

8.0 OPERATIONS

For the proposal there will be a small consultation fee of $45.00 that will be applied to client's event if he or she contracts with Events by Crystal. Below is a list of operational duties Events by Crystal after the contract is signed.

- Client consultation

- Setting budgets

- Choosing dates

- Selecting and inspecting a location

- Negotiating with and choosing suppliers

- Arranging transportation

- Booking blocks of hotel rooms

- Arranging catering

- Booking entertainment or speakers

- Writing copy for publicity

- Licensing and permits

8.1 Fees

Fees will vary depending on market segment served. There will be a 50 percent deposit and balance paid the time of the actual event. If the event has a shorter lead time the deposit will be closer to 75 percent. Fees are as follows:

1. For social events the fee will be between 15 and 20 percent of the total cost of the event or $75.00 per hour.

2. For large corporate events a flat fee or "project fee" will average $150.00 per hour plus vendor Commissions or there may be a "not to exceed" figure. For smaller corporate events the company

will charge a fee for services, plus a handling charge for each item contracted; i.e. planner buys flowers and marks up an estimated 15% and charges client.

3. Consultation fee of $45 before presenting proposal for all event segments after initial consultation.

9.0 FINANCIAL ANALYSIS

9. 1 Start-up Expenses

Equipment	$2,000
Advertising/promotion	$ 500
Phone/additional line	$ 80
Copy machine	$ 100
Color laser printer	$ 250
Scanner	$ 100
Digital camera	$ 350
Walkie-talkies	$ 100
Laptop	$ 800
Total	**$4,280**

9.2 Cash Flow Projections 2013

Income

Weddings	$20,000
Holiday parties	$10,000
Fundraisers	$10,000
Corporate meetings	$15,000
Total income all projects	**$55,000**

Expenses

Professional memberships and publications	$ 800
Office supplies	$ 250
Vehicle	$ 7,200
Tax payments	$ 5,600
Insurance	$ 800
Phone	$ 1,440
Equipment	$ 600
Travel	$ 2,000
Marketing	$ 200
Printing	$ 400
Postage	$ 200
Entertainment	$ 600
Total expenses	**$25,970**
Net income	**$29,030**

Food, Diet, & Nutrition Company

THINK THIN WEIGHT LOSS CORPORATION

541 Howe Street, Third Floor
Vancouver, British Columbia V6C 2C2 Canada

*Think Thin Weight Loss Corporation is a leading provider of products and programs in the diet and nutrition industry. This plan, created by Concord Business Development, Inc., of Vancouver, raised over US$4 million for the company. This plan appeared in **Business Plans Handbook, Volume 10.** It has been updated for this edition.*

FINANCIAL HIGHLIGHTS

Industry
Food, diet, and nutrition products.

Mission Statement
Think Thin Weight Loss Corporation is a leading provider of products and programs in the diet and nutrition industry. By offering a superior product line, employing innovative marketing techniques, and developing strategic partnerships with manufacturers and distributors, the company will maintain an uncompromising commitment to quality while ensuring a fair return to shareholders.

Strategic Partnership
Think Thin has entered into a strategic partnership with Garden State Nutritionals, one of the top five largest dietary and nutrition product producers, marketers, and distributors in the world. Think Thin is in negotiations with a number of profitable diet and nutrition-related companies to acquire further products that will add significant revenues to the parent corporation.

Target Market
The U.S. population concerned with health and weight issues.

Capital Requirements
Initial seed round of $1 million; Phase 2 is $3 million; Phase 3, which includes product launch, is $5 million.

Use of Proceeds
Product Development and Sales and Marketing.

Management Projections

By the end of Year 1, the company expects revenues to be $32,976,673; by the end of Year 2, revenues are expected to be $55,280,112; and by the end of Year 3, $70,719,527.

Projected revenues	Year 1	Year 2	Year 3
Net income (loss)	$ 120,480	$ 4,156,067	$ 6,373,541
Sales revenue	$32,976,673	$55,280,112	$70,719,527

CORPORATE SUMMARY

The Opportunity

Think Thin presents the investor with the opportunity to participate in the significant profits of the recession-proof diet and nutrition market. The diet and nutrition products industry is experiencing a powerful trend toward consolidation and financial growth.

Vision

The mandate of the Think Thin Weight Loss Corporation is to identify, develop, or acquire innovative products and programs in the diet and nutrition industry. Dr. Louie Scar, the co-creator of the best-selling diet of all time, the Atkins Diet, developed the initial concept for Think Thin. The business direction of the corporation has evolved from the concept of a single diet product to include a broad-based spectrum of products in the diet and nutrition industry that have solid profit potential. Think Thin Weight Loss Corporation is committed to providing safe, effective, and clinically proven health and weight loss products.

Strategic Partnership

Garden State Nutritionals, a division of Vitaquest International of New Jersey, will supply valuable manufacturing, distribution, and marketing services. Garden State is a world leader in private label and custom manufacturing of dietary supplement products. Garden State's 300,000 square foot manufacturing facility is able to produce up to 4 million bottles of finished packaged goods per week and will fulfill the expected demand for Think Thin's products.

Founded in 1977, Garden State Nutritionals and its affiliate divisions serve hundreds of leading marketers and distributors in more than 75 countries worldwide, including Australia, Western Europe, Japan, and much of the Pacific Rim, with a distribution of 55,000 pharmacies, health food stores, supermarkets, mass merchants, electronic retailers, and an active mail-order database of two million. Producing more than 2,000 new products every year, Garden State has helped pioneer many state-of-the-art technologies in dietary supplement formulations.

Products and Services

Americans spend nearly $50 billion a year on weight loss and nutritional products that for the most part do not work. People are ready for products that will produce results that are healthy, convenient, satisfying, and fit well into today's busy lifestyle. Think Thin is currently in negotiations with a number of weight loss and nutritional product companies that fit this profile. The first of these targeted acquisitions is the Ultimate Lean Routine and Fat Fighter line of products from One World Networks Integrated Technologies Inc. These products were successfully launched in 2010 with revenues of over $8 million in the first year, and over $25 million in the second year. Revenues for the third and current year are projected to be over $40 million. The revenue from these products is predominantly derived from direct response marketing, which has established a base of over 463,000 customers in two years.

Think Thin will expand the considerable success of the Ultimate Lean Routine and Fat Fighter line by introducing these products to the retail market, using the powerful distribution network of Garden State, its strategic partner.

Ultimate Lean Routine and Fat Fighter Products

Greg Isaacs, the inventor of "The Ultimate Lean Routine," is one of Hollywood's most recognized fitness and health gurus. Celebrities that he has trained include Russell Crowe, Melanie Griffith, and Pierce Brosnan. As a high profile fitness figure, Greg Isaacs garners numerous valuable press and promotional opportunities for the Ultimate Lean Routine brands.

The Ultimate Lean Routine and Fat Fighter brands encompass close to twenty nutritional and dietary-related products including: energy bars, dietary bars, powder form weight loss shakes, powder form energy shakes, multi-vitamin/multi-mineral capsules.

The Think Thin Diet

The Think Thin Program is a meal replacement system of prepared drinks that goes beyond simply reducing calories: it reduces hunger and provides a satisfying sense of fullness. Building on 20 years of experience with the remarkable properties of the Mediterranean diet, the company's new weight loss program is fully developed and has been embraced by the medical community. The company's Think Thin canned or bottled meal replacement drinks will be available to the public through retail outlets, online sales, and in conjunction with medical and clinical programs. The cost of each beverage will be comparable to that of Slim-Fast products and other competitors.

The Think Thin Program has been reviewed by the dean of American Nutrition Professor Tony Vanderhelm, M.D., founder of the American Society for Clinical Nutrition, founding Director of the National Institutes of Health and Obesity Research Center, and Emeritus Medical Director of the Vanderhelm Clinic at St. Luke's-Roosevelt Hospital in New York City. Dr. Vanderhelm was also a consultant to the Surgeon General of the United States on human nutrition. Dr. Vanderhelm is on the company's Advisory Board.

MANUFACTURING & DISTRIBUTION

Garden State Nutritionals

As a leading producer of more than $3 billion in finished retail product per year, processing more than 6 billion doses annually and producing up to 4 million bottles of finished package goods per week, Garden State is uniquely qualified to provide support to Think Thin. Garden State's comprehensive suite of support services includes product concept, formulation, laboratory services, package and label design, regulatory affairs, and merchandising services.

Garden State Nutritionals has an established distribution network of 55,000 retail chain accounts. These established client bases, well-developed distribution channels, and state-of-the-art technology infrastructure provide a valuable complement to Think Thin's sales efforts. Think Thin plans to leverage Garden State's distribution strength to accelerate its market penetration across all of its target markets.

Target Market

Think Thin is entering a recession-proof boom market. Currently, 15 percent to 30 percent of adults are on diets, and Americans spend $40 billion to $50 billion a year trying to lose weight. Since 2008 dietary supplement sales are estimated to be growing at a rate of 10-12 percent annually.

- 30 percent of women and 20 percent of men are seeking to lose weight.

- 40 percent each are actively seeking to maintain current weight.

- Most people have attempted to diet using more than one method; on average dieters try one method or another for about six months at the rate of more than one per year for two years.

Studies show that low-carb/high-protein diets such as the Think Thin Program are more popular with consumers—and the Think Thin Program has significant advantages over other such diets. Over half (54%) of popular low-carb/high-protein diet users say that their weight loss to date has either met their goal or exceeded their expectations, compared to only 22 percent of those on a low-fat diet plan.

Marketing Strategy

Think Thin will market its nationally advertised, medically validated line of diet products (the Think Thin Drink, Ultimate Lean Routine, and Fat Fighter) that combine the most popular form of weight loss diet in America today—low carbohydrate, high protein. The company's strategy is to build on the revenue and branding momentum created with the Ultimate Lean Routine and Fat Fighter product lines by taking them to the national retail markets using the distribution network of its strategic partner, Garden State Nutritionals.

For the rollout of the Think Thin products, the company will deploy marketing initiatives aimed at both the general public and the medical community. To ensure the development of a highly effective strategy, Think Thin has entered into an agreement with Greg Louis, the acknowledged marketing genius behind the branding of Tommy Hilfiger, USA Today, ESPN, MTV, and Lean Cuisine, among others. To further complement its marketing and distribution efforts, Think Thin will also be utilizing the well-established relationships Garden State has developed to effectively deliver the company's products to its target markets.

The company's marketing strategy will include high-impact advertising, long-term branding and community building, and expanding its expected solid base of medical support.

- Establish brand awareness with the public and with the medical community

- Differentiate the company's products from the competition, i.e. safe, appetite reducing, high compliance weight loss diet with an effective weight maintenance component

- Develop medical partnerships and support clinical research into weight loss using the company's products

Competition

Atkins Nutritionals

Atkins Nutritionals' low carbohydrate diet bears the closest comparison to the company's Think Thin Program and over the past ten years the company has added a product line of drinks, bars, and supplements to what was originally just a diet book. Atkins' primary weakness is the high level of saturated fats that the diet allows and 30 years of criticism by the medical community for both the content of the diet and lack of research into its long-term effects. Atkins' strength is that the diet tends to work better than most and is generally well liked by its users (at least in comparison with other diets).

Slim-Fast Foods

The company's products offer a low-calorie meal replacement that generally follows accepted guidelines for nutrition, albeit with a too-low fat content if the product was the only food source. Their main weakness is that the diet doesn't work any better than any other low-calorie diet, which means that over the long term and for most people, it doesn't work at all AND is difficult to stay on for any length of time. Slim-Fast Foods sold in 2000 for $2.4 billion dollars (acquired by Unilever).

Medifast

Medifast is a $300 million dollar company that offers meal replacement shakes as part of a low-calorie weight loss program that also includes a wide variety of meals and snacks that are intended to be eaten 5 times per day. Its biggest drawbacks include cost (nearly $400 per month per person, not including other groceries); lack of taste; and difficulty following long-term when faced with small portions and limited choices. Its products can only be ordered online or through a distributor. Forbes listed Medifast as one of the Top 10 Best Small Companies for 2012.

Think Thin Advantage

The strong product line, experienced marketing team, and celebrity and medical endorsements enjoyed by Think Thin will position the company as a leader in the diet and nutrition industry.

COMPANY OVERVIEW

Management Team

Think Thin has assembled a team of experienced medical, management, and marketing professionals with extensive knowledge and experience in public markets and the medical and weight loss field.

Chad H. Steinfeld, Chief Executive Officer and Director

Mr. Steinfeld was the Chairman and CEO of CCA Companies Incorporated and Chairman and CEO of Harwick Companies, Inc., which employed several thousand people worldwide. Chad Steinfeld has built, developed, or operated more than 50 restaurants including Tavern on the Green, which has rapidly evolved into the world's highest grossing restaurant, Maxwell's Plum, and many others. He has also developed health spas and theme parks in North America, Europe, and Asia, including Great Adventure in New Jersey, which is the world's largest independent theme park.

Chad Steinfeld has served as President and Chief Executive Officer of Kitchens of Sara Lee, the world's largest bakery. Mr. Steinfeld was also a Director, Member of the Executive Committee, and Vice President of Consolidated Foods, the parent company of Sara Lee that is ranked within the top 30 companies of the Fortune 500 companies in the United States of America.

Dr. Louie Scar, Chairman of the Board of Directors

The creator of the Think Thin Weight Loss System, Dr. Louie Scar, has researched diet products and appetite control through diet modification for over 30 years. Dr. Scar was the co-creator of the best-selling diet of all time, the Atkins Diet.

Working with his associate, Dr. Dudley Whit, Chief Cardiologist at Harvard University, Dr. Scar achieved world recognition for the prominent role he played in the first-ever international telecommunication transmission of EKG, from Africa to the U.S., opening up a new era of medical communications and consultation.

Sally Lida, President, Director

Sally Lida holds a Cum Laude Baccalaureate Psychology degree from Stony Brook University. She worked for a number of years in research for the Psycho-Physiology Laboratory at Stony Brook, where she received awards for her independent research.

While an executive at DynaTech Nutritionals, she worked on the creation of a formula for the Ultra Herbal Power Slim weight loss product. At DynaTech, Ms. Lida set up an extensive multi-level marketing program, bringing on board a major celebrity endorser.

Greg Louis, Vice-Chairman, Marketing Director, and Director

The youngest inductee into the Art Directors Hall of Fame, Greg Louis is a communications guru—the acknowledged marketing genius behind the branding of Tommy Hilfiger, USA Today, ESPN, MTV, and Lean Cuisine.

Mr. Louis was the founder of Louis USA, a $425 million full-service agency with offices in New York, Chicago, Houston, and Los Angeles.

Kate Whitney, Secretary, Treasurer, and Director

Ms. Whitney brings considerable corporate administration experience in both private and public companies to the Think Thin team. Ms. Whitney has worked for the following firms: Pattinson &

Brewer in England; Cowan, Lipson & Rumney in England; Tupper & Adams in Canada; Legal Freelance Centre in Canada; Ferguson Gifford in Canada; Jones McCloy Peterson in Canada; and Coglon Wizinsky Dadson & Co. in Canada.

Clark Peterson, Director

A graduate of the University of Miami School of Law, Mr. Peterson practiced law for nine years before co-founding Lums Inc., a restaurant chain that grew into 450 units. In 1969, Mr. Peterson purchased Caesars Palace, a 500-room hotel on the Las Vegas strip. Under his guidance, Caesars Palace in Las Vegas grew to 1,750 rooms; he subsequently built Caesars Palace at Tahoe, Nevada, and Atlantic City. In 1990, Mr. Peterson became the Chairman and CEO of the MGM Grand Hotels in Las Vegas.

Clark Peterson has acquired and developed two honeymoon hotels in the Pennsylvania Poconos: Paradise Steam and Cove Haven. In 1984, he started Regent Airlines, a transcontinental luxury airline, which was sold in 1987 to Kirk Kerkorian, principal shareholder of the MGM Motion Picture Studio.

Donald Milne, Director

Mr. Milne is the current Chairman of the IndieProd company. Mr. Milne has been the producer of numerous box office hits such as "Air America," "Footloose," and "L.A. Story" to name but a few. Prior to forming IndieProd, Mr. Milne was Head of Production and President of Columbia Pictures. During his tenure at Columbia, Mr. Milne supervised such projects as "Midnight Express," "The China Syndrome," "Close Encounters of the Third Kind," and "Kramer vs. Kramer."

During Mr. Milne's career, he has garnered 84 Academy Award nominations, of which he received 26. Mr. Milne is a Founding Trustee and Board Member of the Sundance Film Institute in Sundance, Utah, and a Trustee and Board Member of the Museum of Contemporary Art in Los Angeles, California.

Advisory Board

Dr. Tony Vanderhelm, M.D.

Dr. Tony Vanderhelm is Professor Emeritus of Medicine at Columbia University's College of Physicians and Surgeons. Considered the dean of American nutrition, Professor Vanderhelm is the founder of the American Society for Clinical Nutrition, the founding director of the National Institute of Health and Obesity Research Center, and the Founding Medical Director of the Vanderhelm Clinic at St. Luke's-Roosevelt Hospital in New York City.

Professor Vanderhelm was also a consultant to the Surgeon General of the United States on human nutrition and served on the Food and Nutrition Board for the National Academy of Science. The author of over 250 papers in the field of weight and nutrition, Professor Vanderhelm is the recipient of the Distinguished Physician Award from the American College of Physicians.

Dr. James L. Gilford, M.D.

After completing his M.D. at George Washington University, Dr. Gilford enjoyed a long and illustrious career in the Public Service ranks. Early in his career, he headed the national Accident Prevention Program, leading the push for mandatory auto safety belts. After other high-ranking appointments, Dr. Gilford was tapped to become Surgeon General before being appointed Commissioner of the FDA.

Dr. Gilford received numerous honors for his career in public service, including honorary doctorates from the University of Michigan and Emory University, and the coveted Bronfman Prize of the American Public Health Association, the highest public health award in the U.S.

Robert H. Cotter, Ph.D., M.Sc.

Over the course of his impressive career, Mr. Cotter has held senior and consulting positions at leading laboratories responsible for the development and manufacturing processes of numerous pharmaceutical products. He is currently President of Cotter & Fay, Inc., specializing in pharmaceutical plant design, engineering, construction and start-up, and is the President/Principal of a technical consulting service to the chemical process industries, with an emphasis on pertinent regulatory agency requirements.

Maria A. Tolban, Ph.D., R.D.

Dr. Tolban is a registered dietitian and a member of the American Dietetic Association since 1980. She has worked as a clinical and research dietitian and taught graduate college courses in nutrition, counseling, and training. Much of her research has been focused on diets from other cultures and countries and their role in disease prevention and weight control, and she has concentrated her research on diets from the Mediterranean region. An associate of Dr. Scar, they have worked together on appetite control, weight reduction, and nutrition product development since 1985.

Strategic Partnership: Garden State Nutritionals

With the dietary and supplements market set to reach revenues in excess of $60 billion by the end of 2016, Garden State Nutritionals has remained at the forefront of bringing innovative products to meet market changes. For 36 years, this privately-owned corporation has strategically developed, manufactured, marketed, and distributed over 1,000 nutritional supplements. Garden State Nutritionals is a division of Vitaquest International Inc., one of the largest custom vitamin manufacturers in the USA, and Celmark International Inc., a marketing company that specializes in selling nutritional supplements through electronic media and direct response. Vitaquest manufactures over 2,000 new, custom products per year and distributes these products to 75 countries around the globe.

Garden State is located in a modern, 300,000 square-foot building in West Caldwell, New Jersey. This state-of-the-art facility manufactures and packages a wide range of tablets, caplets, two-piece capsules, chewable wafers, effervescents, powdered formulations, liquids and topicals. A total commitment to quality and Good Manufacturing Practices (GMP) is evident by the fact that Garden State received an "A" rating by the National Nutritional Foods Association, the TGA-Certificate of Manufacturing from the Therapeutic Goods Association of Australia and the ACERIS-Quality Assurance Certificate from the Academy of Clinical Environmental Research and Information Services.

Garden State's dietary products are sold nationwide to over 55,000 retail chain accounts. As a marketing driven company, Garden State offers its customers cutting-edge products with value-added services. Such services include: technical advice, expertise from their scientific advisory board, promotions, national advertising and public relation campaigns via television, radio, and print. Garden State offers a full line of multi- and single vitamins and minerals, function-specific products, specialty products for weight loss, energy, herbal teas and supplements, sports nutrition, lotions and oils, and homeopathic products.

Garden State Nutritionals Management

Keith I. Frank, CEO

In his principal duties as CEO of Garden State, Mr. Frank is responsible for overseeing sales and marketing. In his role with Think Thin, Keith Frank is instrumental in identifying key acquisition targets that will considerably enhance the profitability of the company. Mr. Frank graduated from American University with a degree in Marketing Management.

Garden State Nutritionals Research and Development Team

Garden State's research and development team will collaborate with Think Thin to conduct clinical investigations of Think Thin's proposed products. Garden State has assembled a reputable and capable research and development team who are uniquely suited to qualify the products presented by Think Thin. The members of Garden State's research and development team include:

Jan Benedict, Vice President of Marketing and Sales

Mr. Benedict is responsible for formulating, developing, and marketing nutritional and botanical products for all segments of the nutritional market, including: multi-level marketing (MLM), direct sales, electronic media, health care professional, and Internet companies. Jan Benedict is a respected lecturer in North America, has a degree in Chemistry from the University of Notre Dame, and has completed graduate studies in business administration and marketing from the universities of Minnesota and Pennsylvania.

Rick Hendell, Senior Vice President

Prior to joining Garden State, Rick Hendell gained nearly 25 years of experience in all phases of the natural products industry, including product development, manufacturing, research, sales, and marketing. He is a multiple patent holder in enzyme delivery technologies. Mr. Hendell is a well-regarded speaker for seminars and lectures worldwide. Rick majored in biology and chemistry at Fairleigh Dickinson University and William Patterson College.

Seymour "Sy" D. Lavelle, Senior Vice President of Scientific Affairs

Dr. Lavelle serves as Senior Vice President of Scientific Affairs and is responsible for Quality Control, Analytical Development, and Quality Assurance as well as Regulatory/ Information Services for Garden State. Previously employed with Squibb and Johnson & Johnson (Ortho Pharmaceutical Corporation and the R.W. Johnson Pharmaceutical Research Institute), Dr. Lavelle has authored or co-authored over 36 publications and over 80 U.S. patents. Dr. Lavelle has served as an adjunct Professor at the University of Kentucky, holds a Ph.D. in Pharmaceutical Chemistry from the University of Wisconsin, and a B.S. in Pharmacy from Brooklyn College of Pharmacy.

THINK THIN PRODUCTS/PROGRAM

The company's program consists of dietary and nutritional products, including a revolutionary meal replacement formula that reduces appetite. The multiple products Think Thin Weight Loss Corporation initially proposes to acquire and develop in the retail market include:

Nutritional Products

The company's program consists of dietary and nutritional products, including a revolutionary meal replacement formula that reduces appetite. The multiple products Think Thin Weight Loss Corporation initially proposes to acquire and develop in the retail market include:

Lean Routine Products

- Pure Energy plus Shake

- Fat Neutralizer

- Carb Blocker

- Weight Away

- Pure Nutrition

- Enerplex for Women

- Enerplex for Men

- Age Change

- Mind Grow

- Soy Bars Peanut Butter Crunch Bars

- Soy Bars Honey Nut Bars

- Lean Body Guide

- 20 Body Shaping Secrets Guide

Fat Fighter Products
- Fat Fighter

- Desire Fighter

- Fat Fighter System Weight Away

- Fat Fighter System Fat Neutralizer

- Joy of Carbs Guide

The Think Thin meal replacement prepared drink consists of a precise balance between various constituents of foods, mainly carbohydrates, proteins, and fats. Developed by Dr. Louie Scar (the co-creator of the Atkins Diet), the formula for Think Thin is a major departure from competing products currently in the marketplace. In addition to supplying a full range of other nutrients, the products contain the highest level of "healthy" fat possible derived from olive oil. Based on the Harvard University Mediterranean Diet concept, 20 years of field experience, and supported by current mainstream dietary research, it has been concluded that the level and type of fat in the Think Thin product is not harmful. The meal replacement formula's combination of fatty acids and the ratio of various nutrients aid in appetite reduction in a safe and natural way. Because the Think Thin Drink contains only natural food constituents, it does not need to undergo a lengthy FDA approval process.

Differentiating Factors

The company's Think Thin Program can be clearly differentiated from the competition:

- Especially endorsed by leaders in the medical community (unlike the Atkins Diet, which has faced 30 years of criticism).

- Safe weight loss using a natural, monounsaturated fat source (the olive), (unlike the high saturated fats of the Atkins Diet plan).

- An all-in-one product for ease of use and conceptual simplicity (unlike the Atkins Diet line of products with separate vitamin supplements and other products).

- Appetite reduction—due to healthy fat content—so people follow the diet better and stay on it longer (unlike Slim-Fast's low-fat diet which has no appetite reduction).

- Key component of the product is all-natural olive oil, appealing to the growing number of consumers interested in, and even insisting on, natural ingredients and preferring "herbal" treatments.

- Effective, safe, high-compliance weight maintenance plan that follows the Harvard University Mediterranean diet pyramid. A high proportion of the weight stays off.

- It is something new: a new product without the stigma—and failures—associated in the public's mind with other diets.

- It is something old: the romance of the Mediterranean diet and a simpler, healthier way of life.

Components of the Think Thin Drink

- Carbohydrates—low carbohydrate (similar to the Atkins Diet), approximately 30 grams per day rather than the usual 150 grams.

- Protein—high levels of protein from skim milk or soy. Levels will be in accordance with what is currently considered safe by the medical profession.

- Fat—highest level of monounsaturated fats allowable; derived from olive oil.

- Vitamins and minerals added—three cans of the company's Think Thin drink (equivalent to total dietary replacement) will contain 100 percent of the RDA for vitamins and minerals.

- Calorie content per can—approximately 400 calories. Three cans of the company's Think Thin drink (equivalent to total dietary replacement) meet the National Institutes of Health recommendation for a low-calorie diet that promotes a safe rate of weight loss.

- Think Thin breakfast followed by normal lunch, dinner, and snacks. Total calorie reduction conforms to the lesser amount (500 kcal/day) recommended by the National Institutes of Health for the treatment of overweight by low-calorie diet. Weight loss will be approximately 1 to 2 lbs. per week depending on activity level and degree of overweight.

- Think Thin breakfast and lunch followed by normal dinner and snacks. Total calorie reduction conforms to the higher amount (1000 kcal/day) recommended by the National Institutes of Health for the treatment of overweight by low-calorie diet. Weight loss will be approximately 2 to 3 lbs. per week depending on activity level and degree of overweight.

Gardening Consulting Business

Gardening with Gibson LLC

2936 Tanglewood St.
Peterville, WI 53555

Paul Greenland

Gardening with Gibson LLC teaches people the basics about gardening, so they can grow their own vegetables, and also provides advanced guidance for experienced gardeners.

EXECUTIVE SUMMARY

For many years, Roland Gibson earned his living in the field of manufacturing, where he worked as an engineer. However, among friends and neighbors he was known for his vegetable gardens (two of them, which claimed a sizable share of his back yard). On weekday evenings, and on weekends, Roland was a regular fixture in the gardens, which produced an abundance of carrots, corn, green beans, peas, rhubarb, onions, broccoli, turnips, beets, and more. In addition to growing his own vegetables, he was an ambassador for gardening. Long before the "organic" movement, Roland would tell others about the benefits of growing, freely sharing his knowledge and advice when needed.

Forced into early retirement because of a workforce reduction at his employer, Roland has decided to establish his own gardening consulting business. Located in Peterville, Wisconsin, Gardening with Gibson LLC teaches people the basics about gardening, so they can grow their own vegetables, and also provides advanced guidance for experienced gardeners.

MARKET ANALYSIS

By 2013 national interest in gardening had been on the rise for several years. Driven by the economics of the Great Recession, consumers were more interested in the prospect of growing their own food, either for immediate consumption, freezing/canning, or sale. In addition, concerns about genetically modified foods and potentially harmful food additives or ingredients had increased the popularity of organic foodstuffs.

According to the results of a 2012 study from the research firm Scarborough, approximately half of the United States' 164 million homeowners indicated that they had engaged in gardening within the past year. The baby boomer segment, aged 45 to 64, was 10 percent more likely to engage in gardening. Scarborough's study also revealed some other interesting facts about gardeners:

- Full-time Employment: 47%
- Household Income > $100,000: 26%
- College Degree: 33%
- Retired: 22%

In addition, gardeners spend more time on the Internet than non-gardeners. Among those with Internet access, the research indicated that 37% spend at least 10 hours per week online, and 57% report experience with social networking.

Gardening with Gibson is located in Peterville, Wisconsin. According to research sponsored by the Peterville County Extension Service and conducted by Peterville Community College, 58% of county residents have participated in gardening within the last 12 months.

PERSONNEL

Roland Gibson

For many years, Roland Gibson earned his living in the field of manufacturing, where he worked as an engineer for Becker Lampack Manufacturing Co. in Milwaukee, Wisconsin. Over the course of a 20-year career with the organization, Roland assumed positions of greater responsibility, culminating in his role as manager of the engineering services department. In that capacity, he was responsible for overseeing a team of 12 engineers, as well as four support personnel. Additionally, Roland was tasked with managing a six-figure departmental budget, leading training initiatives for department staff, and giving regular presentations to company leadership.

Despite a successful engineering career, among friends and neighbors Roland was known for his vegetable gardens (two of them, which claimed a sizable share of his back yard). On weekday evenings, and on weekends, Roland was a regular fixture in the gardens, which produced an abundance of carrots, corn, green beans, peas, rhubarb, onions, broccoli, turnips, beets, and more. In addition to growing his own vegetables, he was ambassador for gardening. Long before the "organic" movement, Roland would tell others about the benefits of growing, freely sharing his knowledge and advice when needed.

Forced into early retirement because of a workforce reduction at Becker Lampack in 2012, Roland began to perform gardening consulting work by request, on an informal basis. After achieving initial success and identifying market demand, Roland decided to formally establish Gardening with Gibson LLC. This new opportunity will enable him to utilize his business experience in combination with his true passion for gardening and working with others.

GROWTH STRATEGY

Year One:
Establish the Gardening with Gibson brand name in the community. Build on the momentum gained from doing one year of gardening consulting on an informal basis, and the subsequent positive word-of-mouth promotion that has followed. Achieve publication-related sales of approximately $10,000. Become a member of the Peterville Better Business Bureau and Chamber of Commerce. Sell 130 general gardening consulting packages and at least 200 intensive packages. Achieve gross revenues of $61,185.

Year Two:
Continue to build Gardening with Gibson's reputation in the local community. Increase publication sales revenue to $20,000. Sell 140 general gardening consulting packages and 215 intensive packages. Achieve gross revenues of $84,325.

Year Three:

Focus on maintaining Gardening with Gibson's reputation in the community. Increase publication sales revenue to $36,000. Sell 150 general gardening consulting packages and 220 intensive packages. Achieve gross revenues of $119,700.

SERVICES

Gardening with Gibson will offer individual and group consulting services focusing mainly on outdoor vegetable gardens. Roland has some knowledge pertaining to other types of gardens (e.g., flower gardens, greenhouse gardening, herb gardens), and will offer limited consulting services in those areas.

General Consulting Packages

Roland has developed general consulting packages that cover a broad range of topics based on a customer's level of experience. These include:

- Gardening for Beginners
- Intermediate Gardening
- Advanced Gardening

Each package includes five hours of Roland's time, for a total cost of $150. Customers receive an information packet with general tips and information, which can be used as a reference guide throughout the gardening season. Roland meets with customers for two hours (prior to the beginning of the season) in their homes, walking them through the guide, answering questions, helping them to develop plans, etc. Then, the remaining three hours can be used throughout the season, as customers are going through the gardening process.

Intensive Consulting Packages

In addition, Gibson also has developed consulting packages that offer intensive assistance in specific areas, including:

- Planning/Site Selection
- Gardening Tool Selection
- Soil Preparation/Composting
- Crop Selection
- Garden Maintenance
- Pest and Disease Control
- Plant Propagation (creating new plants from bulbs, seeds, etc.)

These packages provide three hours of consulting time for $75. Roland also has developed specific information packets that explore each topic in detail. These are presented to customers prior to the beginning of the gardening season, along with one hour of discussion time. Then, the remaining two hours of consulting services can be used during the gardening season, when needed.

Hourly Assistance

Customers may purchase consulting time individually or in addition to the above packages at a rate of $35.

Roland also offers consulting services to provide tips and assistance regarding specific types of plants, based on his many years of experience. In addition to his time, Roland has produced tip sheets for specific types of vegetables. Going beyond general information, these include considerations specific to the local climate and soil. Consulting/tip sheets are available for many different types of vegetables, including (but not limited to):

- Beans
- Beets
- Cabbages
- Carrots
- Cherry tomatoes
- Corn
- Cucumbers
- Eggplants
- Green tomatoes
- Horseradish
- Hot peppers
- Leeks
- Lettuce
- Potatoes
- Radishes
- Rhubarb
- Scallions
- Soybeans
- Spinach
- Sunflowers
- Squash
- Tomatillos
- Turnips

Publications

Finally, Roland markets his information guides individually (e.g., without any consulting time).

Beginner/Intermediate/Advanced Gardening Guides ($50)

Intensive Guides ($35)

Vegetable Tip Sheets ($15)

Publications are available in electronic (PDF) format, via download from the Gardening with Gibson Web site. Purchase can be made via credit card, PayPal, etc. Roland will mail printed guides to customers for an additional $5 fee.

MARKETING & SALES

Gardening with Gibson has developed a marketing strategy that includes the following tactics for growing the business:

1. A four-color, tri-fold brochure describing the business and services provided.

2. Business card magnets that can be distributed at gardening shows, garden centers, local businesses, and special events.

3. Vehicle graphic magnets to generate mobile exposure for the business.

4. Relationship building with the county extension service, farmer's market organizers, garden centers, and greenhouses to generate referrals.

5. Regular gardening-related presentations to local service organizations (e.g., Rotary, etc.), churches, retiree groups, and special interest clubs, with a goal of generating referrals and positive word-of-mouth exposure.

6. "Refer-a-Friend" Program. Recognizing that word-of-mouth referrals will be crucial for growing the business, Gardening with Gibson will give existing customers a free vegetable tip sheet for referrals to others. Additionally, a 10% discount will be provided to the new customer.

7. A media relations strategy that involves guest appearances/columns focused on gardening. In particular, Roland has made arrangements with **The Peterville Times,** a free local newspaper, to write a regular gardening column, offering tips to both prospective and experienced gardeners, based on the time of year and local climate conditions. A local AM radio station also has provided him with an opportunity to do a weekly gardening radio program during the summer months, providing listeners with an opportunity to call in with gardening-related questions.

8. A Web site with complete details about the business and services offered. A local Web developer has been hired to create a site with e-commerce capabilities, so that Gardening with Gibson can sell consulting packages and PDF publications online via credit card, PayPal, and other electronic payment methods.

9. A listing in the Peterville Yellow Pages.

OPERATIONS

Location

Gardening with Gibson will operate from a home office in Roland Gibson's residence at 2936 Tanglewood St. in Peterville, Wisconsin.

Telecommunications

Because most of his time will be spent "in the field," Roland Gibson will utilize a mobile phone to communicate with and receive messages from clients.

Insurance

Gardening with Gibson has secured a liability insurance policy to cover the scope of services provided on customers' property. A copy of the policy is available for review upon request.

Availability

Gardening with Gibson will offer consulting services between January and October. During the months of November and December, the business will focus on marketing and sales, with a strong emphasis on selling consulting packages as gifts for the upcoming gardening year. No consulting services will be provided during those two months. Based on Roland's experience providing services on an informal basis in 2012-13, he anticipates working the following hours (broken down by category) in 2014:

	January	February	March	April	May	June	July	August	September	October
General packages	20	66	86	88	65	65	65	65	65	65
Intensive packages	16	48	74	68	68	68	68	68	68	68
Hourly consulting	5	7	10	12	15	15	15	15	10	7
Monthly hours	41	121	170	168	148	148	148	148	143	140

FINANCIAL ANALYSIS

Roland Gibson will provide the initial start-up funding (from savings) needed to establish Gardening with Gibson. This will involve $3,000 to develop his publication library, with the assistance of a freelance writer; $4,000 for Web site development; as well as $6,000 to cover remaining marketing expenses.

Sales Unit Forecast

Roland Gibson has prepared the following unit sales forecast for Gardening with Gibson's first three years of operation:

Category	2014	2015	2016
General packages	130	140	150
Intensive packages	206	215	220
Hourly consulting	111	120	140
Publications	325	665	1,160
General guides	110	215	375
Intensive guides	60	125	275
Vegetable tip sheets	155	325	510
Gardening seminars	10	12	15

Pro-Forma Balance Sheet

In addition, the following pro-forma balance sheet has been prepared for the same time period:

Category	2014	2015	2016
General packages	$19,500	$21,000	$ 22,500
Intensive packages	$15,450	$16,125	$ 16,500
Hourly consulting	$ 3,885	$ 4,200	$ 4,900
Publications	$ 9,925	$20,000	$ 36,025
General guides	$ 5,500	$10,750	$ 18,750
Intensive guides	$ 2,100	$ 4,375	$ 9,625
Vegetable tip sheets	$ 2,325	$ 4,875	$ 7,650
Gardening seminars	$ 2,500	$ 3,000	$ 3,750
	$61,185	**$84,325**	**$119,700**

Additional financial statements have been prepared by Johnson & Lighthouse Accountancy, and are available upon request.

Health and Wellness Coaching Business

Keating Health Consultants LLC

45 Green St.
Pinewood Ridge, KY 40600

Paul Greenland

Keating Health Consultants LLC is a health and wellness consulting business focused on three areas: personal health coaching; children's health programs; and workplace wellness programs.

EXECUTIVE SUMMARY

Kathy Keating is a registered nurse who has decided to establish Keating Health Consultants LLC, a health and wellness consulting business focused on three areas: personal health coaching; children's health programs; and workplace wellness programs. Keating currently is employed by Pinewood Ridge General Hospital, where she works with patients of different ages and health status. In addition to her nursing background, Keating is a long-time fitness and wellness enthusiast. Overweight as a teenager, she became motivated to improve her health and lose weight during college. Once Keating attained her goals, her passion for better health remained, with an expanded focus on helping others.

After working for 10 years as a staff nurse on the cardiac unit at Pinewood Ridge General Hospital, Keating has spent the past five years working with the organization's Employee Health department. She also served as the chairwoman of a committee to help the hospital establish its own employee wellness program. In addition, Keating volunteered to help the local school district establish a children's health program for Mattingly Elementary. These experiences, coupled with strong community need at the individual and group levels, have strongly influenced Keating, leading to her decision to establish her own health and wellness consultancy.

INDUSTRY ANALYSIS

According to RAND Health's 2012 report, "A Review of the U.S. Workplace Wellness Market," sponsored by the U.S. Department of Labor and the U.S. Department of Health and Human Services, by 2009 the vast majority (92%) of companies with more than 200 employees had wellness programs in place. These programs typically targeted several primary behaviors:

- Exercise (63%)

- Smoking (60%)

- Weight Loss (53%)

The report indicated that although wellness programs were pervasive, participation levels were quite low, with some estimates at less than 20 percent.

At the same time, the report referred to the existence of a national "lifestyle disease epidemic," indicating that factors such as poor nutrition, frequent alcohol consumption, tobacco use, and inactivity were the driving factors behind chronic diseases such as heart disease, pulmonary conditions, and diabetes, according to the Centers for Disease Control and Prevention.

The report's authors, Soeren Mattke, Christopher Schnyer, and Kristin Van Busum, wrote: "Chronic diseases have become a major burden in the United States, as they lead to decreased quality of life, account for severe disability in 25 million Americans, and are the leading cause of death, claiming 1.7 million lives per year. Aside from the health impact, the costs attributed to treating chronic disease are estimated to account for over 75 percent of national health expenditures. Furthermore, while chronic disease was once thought to be a problem of older age groups, the number of working-age adults with a chronic condition has grown by 25 percent in ten years, nearly equaling 58 million people."

While these conditions impact the larger adult population, they also are affecting children. According to a 2013 Statistical Fact Sheet from the American Heart Association/American Stroke Association, compared to 1973-1974, the number of obese children between the ages of 5 and 17 had increased fivefold by 2008-2009, based on data from the Bogalusa Heart Study. The organization indicated that nearly 24 million children between the ages of 2 and 19 are either obese or overweight.

MARKET ANALYSIS

Keating Health Consultants is located in Pinewood Ridge, Kentucky, in Pinewood County. In 2010 more than 31 percent of Kentucky residents were considered obese, according to data from the Division of Nutrition, Physical Activity, and Obesity, National Center for Chronic Disease Prevention and Health Promotion. This placed the state among the highest in the nation for obesity.

This trend is evident locally, according to data from the Pinewood County Health Department. Furthermore, the health department estimates that the number of children in the county with elevated cholesterol levels (51 percent of females and 34 percent of males) is much higher than the national average of approximately 25 percent.

Workplace Wellness Market

According to data from the Pinewood County Economic Development Council, there were approximately 1,500 business establishments in the county in 2012, employing about 26,000 people. The largest employer categories were services (e.g., hotels, automotive repair, health, legal, etc.) (707 establishments, 45.7%); retail (247 establishments, 16%); and finance/insurance/real estate (159 establishments, 10.2%).

Keating Health Consultants will concentrate its efforts on small-to-mid-sized businesses. Locally, a large percentage of establishments fall within the small business category. In 2012 there were about 1,000 businesses with 1 to 4 employees, accounting for nearly 65 percent of all establishments. Businesses with 5 to 9 employees numbered 255 (17% of all establishments). Finally, mid-sized businesses (e.g., those with 50-100 employees) numbered 105 (7% of all establishments).

Personal Health Coaching Market

Keating Health Consultants will provide personal health coaching services for individuals of every age. However, from a marketing standpoint the business will target individuals under the age of 45, with a goal of preventing or reversing chronic health conditions before they lead to serious problems. In 2012 16.2% of Pinewood County residents were between the ages of 25 and 34, while 16.4% were between the ages of 35 and 44. Population growth within these two categories was projected to remain flat for the next five years.

In terms of household income, those aged 25 to 34 can be summarized as follows:

$19,999 or less (53.5%)

$20,000-$39,999 (31.4%)

$40,000-$59,999 (9.6%)

$60,000-$74,999 (2.2%)

$75,000-$99,999 (3%)

Household income for individuals in the 35-to-44 age group can be summarized as follows:

$19,999 or less (21.3%)

$20,000-$39,999 (34.9%)

$40,000-$59,999 (25.6%)

$60,000-$74,999 (8.9%)

$75,000 $99,999 (6.3%)

$100,000-$124,999 (1.2%)

$125,000-$149,999 (0.9%)

$150,000 + (0.5%)

Children's Health Program Market

Initially, children's health programs will be marketed to schools within the Pinewood County School District, beginning with elementary schools (specifically, students in the fourth, fifth, and sixth grades). After the first three years of operation, the focus will expand to middle and high school students. In 2013 the Pinewood County School District included the following schools:

- Buford Elementary
- Early Learning Center
- Elkhorn Middle School
- Mattingly Elementary
- Newman Elementary
- O'Leary Elementary
- Olson Park Middle School
- Parkview High School
- Pinewood County Career and Technical Center
- Pinewood County Community Education Center
- Pinewood County High School
- Racine Elementary School
- Scholl Elementary School
- Starwood Academy

In the long-term, Keating Health Consultants will consider expanding its marketing for children's health programs to other regions throughout Kentucky, and eventually in surrounding states. A detailed breakdown of school districts in these geographies is available upon request.

SERVICES

Keating Health Consultants will concentrate its health and wellness consulting efforts in three main areas:

- Personal Health Coaching

- Children's Health Programs

- Workplace Wellness Programs

Personal Health Coaching

Personal Health Coaching services are tailored to the unique needs of the individual. Keating offers potential clients a free telephone consultation to discuss their situation, challenges, and goals. If the potential customer decides to move forward, they are provided with an agreement specifying the terms of services that will be provided. Typically, these include the following services offered over the course of 12 months for a flat fee (payable in advance) of $500:

- Initial Screening

- Nutritional Analysis

- Results Report

- Health & Fitness Goal Plan

- Consultation Time (up to four hours, as needed)

- One-Year Screening/Goal Adjustments

Children's Health Programs

Keating Health Consultants has developed a children's health program modeled after a successful pilot initiative developed for Mattingly Elementary School. The program seeks to prevent the development of coronary artery disease in children. According to findings from the National Cholesterol Education Program, high cholesterol levels in children increase their likelihood of having high cholesterol during adulthood. By lowering cholesterol levels, many health experts agree that it is possible to decrease the incidence of coronary heart disease in adulthood.

The program includes several elements, including a walking club that begins in August, at the start of the school year, and runs through May. Participating students in the fourth, fifth, and sixth grades receive an initial screening at the beginning of the school year that includes blood pressure, glucose, body mass index, and cholesterol levels. Parents receive detailed reports regarding their children, explaining scores and how they compare to accepted ranges (desired, satisfactory, borderline high, and high). In addition, a coaching session is provided, where parents receive information regarding meal planning, low-fat grocery shopping, family/lifestyle modification strategies, and more. Parents also learn about free apps available for popular mobile phones, which allow them to compare the caloric/fat/sugar content of common food items, in order to identify the best choices.

Participating children are provided with a notebook to track their daily walking progress. Prizes are awarded on a monthly basis for students with the most mileage. Finally, at the end of the year, participants are provided with a congratulatory voucher for free access to a local water park. One grand prize is provided to the student with the greatest number of miles. The program also concludes with a post-test, where the same variables are screened to track progress.

Workplace Wellness Programs

The same elements of the Children's Health Program serve as the nucleus of the Workplace Wellness Program, with some differences. In addition to walking, participants receive guidance regarding other exercise options and programs. Consultations and screenings also are available for tobacco and alcohol use. Incentives are offered to employees by participating employers. These may include lower healthcare premiums, special cash bonuses, extra vacation time, gift items, and more. At the discretion of the participating company, spouses and children may or may not be eligible to participate in the program.

Keating Health Consultants will focus its marketing efforts on small and mid-sized companies (e.g., those with fewer than 100 employees), in an attempt to provide an impactful, cost-effective solution to an underserved market.

OPERATIONS

Keating Health Consultants will operate from a home office, with minimal overhead. Operations will rest heavily upon the equipment needed to perform health screenings, including:

- Blood Pressure Monitor ($893)

- Professional Lipid Panel Analysis Machine with Printer ($799)

Several different suppliers have been identified, in order for the business to procure the materials needed for ongoing operations (costs for these items are factored directly into service packages):

- Powder-free Nitrile Gloves

- Thermal Paper Labels

- Test Strips

- Paper (for Reports)

- Notebooks

- Parent Information Packets

PERSONNEL

Kathy Keating is a registered nurse who currently is employed by Pinewood Ridge General Hospital, where she works with patients of different ages and health status. In addition to her nursing background, Keating is a long-time fitness and wellness enthusiast. Overweight as a teenager, she became motivated to improve her health and lose weight during college. Once Keating attained her goals, her passion for better health remained, with an expanded focus on helping others.

After working for 10 years as a staff nurse on the cardiac unit at Pinewood Ridge General Hospital, Keating has spent the past five years working with the organization's Employee Health department. She also served as the chairwoman of a committee to help the hospital establish its own employee wellness program. In addition, Keating volunteered to help the local school district establish a children's health program for Mattingly Elementary. These experiences, coupled with strong community need at the individual and group levels, have strongly influenced Keating, leading to her decision to establish her own health and wellness consultancy.

Professional & Advisory Support

Keating Health Consultants will utilize Bowen Accounting for tax assistance. Legal advice, when needed, will be received from West & Farrel, a local law firm. Finally, both checking and merchant accounts have been established with Pinewood Community Bank.

GROWTH STRATEGY

The following table outlines the anticipated growth for Keating Health Consultants during the first three years of operations. Growth in the Children's Health Program category is based on units of 60 students (e.g., two grade classrooms per school), with the expectation that programming will be introduced to all 4th grade classes in the Pinewood Schools during the first year, followed by the addition of grade 5 in year two, and grade 6 in year three.

Health coaching program volume projections

	2014	2015	2016
Personal health coaching	60	90	120
Children's health programs	6	12	18
Workplace wellness programs			
10 employees	10	20	30
30 employees	4	6	8
60 employees	1	2	3
100 employees	0	1	2

MARKETING & SALES

A detailed marketing strategy has been developed for Keating Health Consultants, and is available upon request. Following is a summary of our key marketing strategies for each service category:

Workplace Wellness Programs

The business primarily will rely upon direct marketing (especially direct mail) to reach small businesses throughout the Pinewood market. Mailing list data has been secured from a local list broker, as well as the Chamber of Commerce, and arrangements have been made with a local mail house for a sustained mailing campaign. Mailings will consist of a letter summarizing Kathy Keating's credentials and experience, along with the benefits of developing a workplace wellness program. Kathy will make follow-up phone calls to business owners approximately two weeks after each mail drop, with a goal of scheduling a sales consultation.

Children's Health Programs

Kathy Keating will utilize her existing relationship with the school district, stemming from the successful pilot program she conducted at Mattingly Elementary, to implement programs at all of the district's elementary schools during the first three years.

Personal Health Coaching

Personal health coaching services initially will be marketed by distributing literature to dietitians, family physicians, and health clubs throughout Pinewood County. Keating will make personal visits to distribute literature, with hopes of having conversations with potential referral sources. Keating anticipates that the business will then begin growing via word-of-mouth, as existing clients make referrals to their friends and family.

FINANCIAL ANALYSIS

The following projections show anticipated costs and net profits from the three different categories of services that Keating Health Consultants will provide during the first three years of operations:

Health programming revenue projections

	2014	2015	2016
Personal health coaching	30	60	90
Revenue	$15,000	$30,000	$ 45,000
Cost	$ 5,500	$11,100	$ 16,650
Net profit	$ 9,500	$18,900	$ 28,350
Children's health programs			
Revenue	$27,180	$54,361	$ 81,541
Cost	$23,635	$47,270	$ 70,906
Net profit	$ 3,545	$ 7,091	$ 10,635
Workplace wellness programs			
Revenue	$50,160	$91,008	$131,856
Cost	$37,156	$67,414	$ 97,671
Net profit	$13,004	$23,594	$ 34,185
Total net profit	**$26,049**	**$49,585**	**$ 73,170**

Projections indicate that the business will sustain a net loss of $12,293 during the first year, achieve a modest profit of $1,885 during year two, and a profit of $14,920 in year three. Expansion of programs to the middle and high school levels during years four and five, and beyond Pinewood in the long-term, should result in continued net revenue growth. However, the use of additional labor (perhaps on a contract basis) will be required to accommodate the additional screening volumes.

Three-year pro forma profit & loss

	2014	2015	2016
Net revenue	**$26,049**	**$49,585**	**$73,170**
Operating expenses			
Miscellaneous	$ 350	$ 350	$ 350
Salary	$30,000	$40,000	$50,000
Office supplies	$ 350	$ 400	$ 450
Marketing	$ 2,000	$ 2,000	$ 2,000
Equipment	$ 2,642	$ 2,000	$ 1,000
Accounting & legal	$ 1,250	$ 950	$ 950
Insurance	$ 1,750	$ 2,000	$ 2,250
Internet service	$ 950	$ 1,150	$ 1,250
Total	**$38,342**	**$47,700**	**$58,250**
Net income	**($12,293)**	**$ 1,885**	**$14,920**

The owner is providing $15,000 from personal savings to cover initial operating costs, and is seeking bank financing in the amount of $20,000, in the form of a five-year term loan, to provide additional operating capital.

In-Home Senior Adult Services

HANNAH'S HELPING HAND, LLC

65420 Marlin Ave.
Clearwater, FL 33762

Fran Fletcher

Hannah's Helping Hand is an in home senior adult services business owned and operated by Hannah Edmonds. The Clearwater, Florida business is a sole proprietorship LLC that specializes in providing a variety of in-home services to clients with mild to moderate cognitive impairment.

EXECUTIVE SUMMARY

Hannah's Helping Hand is an in home senior adult services business owned and operated by Hannah Edmonds. The Clearwater, Florida business is a sole proprietorship LLC that specializes in providing a variety of in-home services to clients with mild to moderate cognitive impairment.

The future is bright for workers in the home health/personal care industry. According to the Bureau of Labor statistics, this industry will increase 70% from 2010 to 2020. These projections may even be higher in Florida, where residents over the age of 65 comprise an estimated 17% of the state's population.

Ms. Edmonds has 2 years of experience, serving as the primary caregiver for her grandmother who suffered from dementia. While caring for her grandmother, Ms. Edmonds realized she had a passion for helping the elderly. She was appalled by the lack of affordable in-home care available to people with dementia related illnesses that wish to live independently for as long as possible. Thus, the idea for Hannah's Helping Hand was born.

There are several other in-home senior care service businesses in the area, but none that cater solely to senior adults with mild to moderate cognitive impairment. Ms. Edmonds is confident that Hannah's Helping Hand will succeed in this niche of senior care. A variety of appointment types will be available. Assistance offered during these in-home visits includes:

- Companion Services—daily/weekly check-ins
- Business Services—assist with mail, paying bills, making/keeping track of appointments
- Transportation Services—drive clients to medical appointments, supermarket, post office
- Shopping Services—perform household shopping
- Cooking Services—prepare nutritious meals
- Cleaning Services—provide light housekeeping
- Laundry Services—assist with laundry

- Hygiene Services—ensure that the client maintains personal hygiene

- Miscellaneous Services—changing light bulbs, etc.

Hannah's Helping Hand will obtain clients predominantly through referrals. Ms. Edmonds will list her services through the Clearwater Retirement Association, Alzheimer's Services of America Clearwater Chapter, the Clearwater Council on Aging, and various medical offices in the community.

Ms. Edmonds is seeking a business line of credit in the amount of $10,000 to finance her venture. Financing will cover start-up fees and personal expenses for three months. Start-up fees are minimal, so the line of credit will provide a cushion while the business is building its client base. Ms. Edmonds expects her appointment schedule to reach maximum capacity within six months. She expects a pre-tax profit of $2,800 the first year and pre-tax profits of $15,000 in subsequent years. Ms. Edmonds plans to repay the line of credit within three years.

COMPANY DESCRIPTION

Location

Hannah's Helping Hand, LLC is located in Clearwater, Florida. Ms. Edmonds plans to work out of her home since services will be provided on-site at the client's residence.

Hours of Operations

In-home services will be available by appointment Monday through Friday 8 a.m. until 5:30 p.m. Night and weekend appointments are available upon request.

PERSONNEL

Hannah Edmonds (Owner)

Ms. Edmonds will provide all in-home services. She has 2 years experience providing care to senior adults with mild to moderate cognitive impairment. She received specialized training in providing care to clients with dementia through Alzheimer's Services of America. She also maintains CPR and first aid certification through courses offered at the local community college.

PRODUCTS AND SERVICES

Services

In-home care services will be provided for clients experiencing mild to moderate cognitive impairment, as defined by Alzheimer's Services of America, and will enable these clients to maintain independence, live at home, and sustain a normal lifestyle as long as possible. Ms. Edmonds will work together with clients' families to monitor cognitive and functional abilities. She will help families determine when additional help or services are needed as the impairment progresses. Hannah's Helping Hand will offer:

- Companion Services—daily/weekly check-ins

- Business Services—assist with mail, paying bills, making/keeping track of appointments

- Transportation Services—drive clients to medical appointments, supermarket, post office

- Shopping Services—perform household shopping

- Cooking Services—prepare nutritious meals

- Cleaning Services—provide light housekeeping
- Laundry Services—assist with laundry
- Hygiene Services—ensure that the client maintains personal hygiene
- Miscellaneous Services—changing light bulbs, etc.

MARKET ANALYSIS

Industry Overview

According to the Bureau of Labor Statistics, jobs in the home health/personal care industry are expected to increase 70% from 2010 to 2020. These projections may even be higher in Florida, where residents over the age of 65 comprise an estimated 17% of the state's population.

According to census data, 23% of Clearwater, Florida residents are age 65 and older. Clearwater ranks as one of the top 10 U.S. cities with the largest retirement population, with 24,000 senior adults calling the city home.

Most senior adults will require some form of personal care services during their lifetime. According to data obtained from Alzheimer's Services of America, the number of senior adults with dementia related illnesses is rising at an astronomical rate. Caring for senior adults with cognitive impairments such as dementia or Alzheimer's can be quite difficult for family members. According to Alzheimer's Services of America, approximately 15% of caregivers are long distance caregivers, living an hour or more from their loved one. Hannah's Helping Hand is available to fill this gap in care.

Target Market

Hannah's Helping Hand will market its services to senior adults in the Clearwater area with mild to moderate cognitive impairment that wish to maintain their independence and live alone with minimal help. To qualify for Hannah's Helping Hand in-home care services, clients must be able to dress, bathe, and toilet independently.

Competition

There are currently three senior adult in-home care providers within a five-mile radius. However, none of these cater exclusively to clients with dementia related illnesses.

1. Senior Sitter Services, 1024 Lagoon Ln.; offers around the clock care
2. Seniors First, 3835 Back Beach Rd.; offers transportation and light cleaning
3. Baybrook Senior Services, 6400 Baybrook Ave.; offers transportation, therapy, and medical services

GROWTH STRATEGY

Hannah's Helping Hand believes it has found a healthcare niche in Clearwater. The growth strategy of the company is to make a name for itself as the best, most caring and competent in-home senior adult caregiver for clients with mild to moderate cognitive impairment in the area. Ms. Edmonds will achieve this growth one client at a time with her deep understanding about the needs of older adults with memory issues. When offering services to someone with dementia and related problems, Ms. Edmonds knows that it is imperative to work in a manner that gains the trust of the client and their families. Ms. Edmonds' schedule will only allow her to work with ten clients at the time. Being the sole proprietor will enable her to build and nurture personal relationships with her clients, which will set her apart from other in-home care providers in the area.

SALES AND MARKETING

Referrals will be the backbone of the company's marketing strategy. Hannah's Helping Hand will seek endorsements from key area organizations, including the Clearwater Retirement Association, Alzheimer's Services of America Clearwater Chapter, and the Clearwater Council on Aging. However, while she is building clientele and a great reputation, Ms. Edmonds has identified avenues for bringing clients to her business.

Hannah's Helping Hand will market the following:

- Personalized care for senior adults with mild to moderate cognitive impairment

- Reasonable hourly rates

- Endorsements from local physicians, the Clearwater Retirement Association, Alzheimer's Services of America Clearwater Chapter, and the Clearwater Council on Aging

ADVERTISING

Initial advertising will include:

- Social media

- Local newspaper

- Caregivers.com

In addition to conventional advertising, the company will rely on quality in-home care to generate clients through referrals.

APPOINTMENTS

Appointment Availability

	Monday	Tuesday	Wednesday	Thursday	Friday	Saturday	Sunday
8:00 to 11:00	A.M. Client 3 days a week	A.M. Client 2 days a week	A.M. Client 3 days a week	A.M. Client 2 days a week	A.M. Client 3 days a week	Visits scheduled by the hour	Visits scheduled by the hour
11:00	Commuting time	Commuting time	Commuting time	Commuting time	Commuting time		
11:30 to 2:30	P.M. Client 3 days a week	P.M. Client 2 days a week	P.M. Client 3 days a week	P.M. Client 2 days a week	P.M. Client 3 days a week		
2:30	Commuting time	Commuting time	Commuting time	Commuting time	Commuting time		
3:00	1 hour visit	2 hour visit	1 hour visit	1 hour visit	2 hour visit		
4:00	Commute		Commute	Commute			
4:30	1 hour visit		1 hour visit	1 hour visit			
5:00							
5:30							

Types of Appointments

Using the Available Appointments chart, Ms. Edmonds estimates that she will only be able to accept up to 10 clients. Appointments include:

- 3 hours weekly (1- hour visits); help with medication, mail, bills, cleaning, or short errands

- 3 hours daily (Monday, Wednesday, Friday); help with medication, mail, bills, shopping, errands, doctor visits, cooking, cleaning

- 3 hours daily (Tuesday and Thursday); help with medication, mail, bills, shopping, errands, doctor visits, cooking, cleaning

- 2 hours weekly (2- hour visit); help with medication, mail, bills, shopping, errands, doctor visits, cooking, cleaning

- 1 hour weekly; help with medication, mail, bills, or short errands

- Night/Weekend clients (by the hour)

FINANCIAL ANALYSIS

Start-up costs

Estimated Start-up Costs

Uniforms	$ 200
License, bond, insurance	$ 500
Advertisement	$ 100
Legal fees (LLC)	$1,000
Total	**$1,800**

Estimated Monthly Income

Monthly income will be determined by number of clients and hours worked. Appointments will be scheduled according to the following chart:

Prices for Services

Service	Price
Companion	$35/hour
Transportation	$35/hour
Shopping	$35/hour
Cooking	$35/hour
Cleaning	$35/hour
Business	$35/hour
Laundry	$35/hour
Hygiene	$35/hour
Miscellaneous	$35/hour
Night (after 6 p.m.)	$50/hour
Weekend (Friday 6 p.m.–Sunday 8 a.m.)	$50/hour

Ms. Edmonds believes that her time will be split into the following service segments:

Service segments

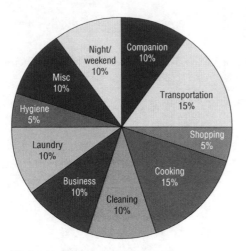

Estimated Monthly Expenses

Expenses will be kept to a minimum. Ms. Edmonds would like to earn $3,200 monthly. However, the number of clients and scheduled services will determine her salary.

Monthly Expenses

Loan payment	$ 300
Phone/Internet	$ 100
Gas	$ 400
Insurance	$ 200
Wages for Ms. Edmonds (est.)	$3,200
Total	**$4,200**

Profit/Loss

Ms. Edmonds conservatively estimates that in the first month of operation, she may only work ten hours a week, which will result in $1,400 of income. When the schedule is at full capacity, gross income will be $5,600 per month. Ms. Edmonds hopes her schedule will be fully booked by Month 6. These figures do not include night and weekend work, which will be on an as-needed basis.

Ms. Edmonds conservatively estimates that her expenses will increase about 2% a year. She does not expect to raise service prices during the first three years, so income is expected to plateau after Month 6. Hannah's Helping Hand should realize a pre-tax profit of approximately $2,800 the first year and $15,000 in Years 2 and 3. These profits will be used to purchase a company van.

Estimated profits months 1–6

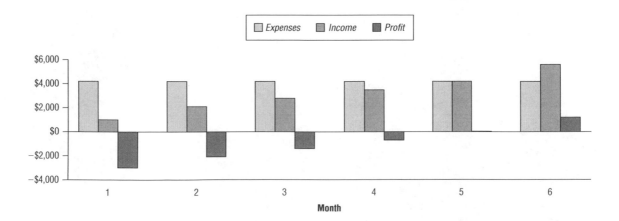

Estimated profits months 7–12

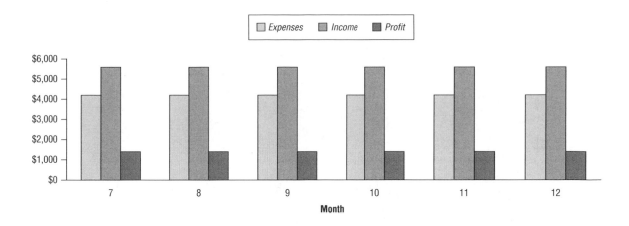

Estimated profits years 1–3

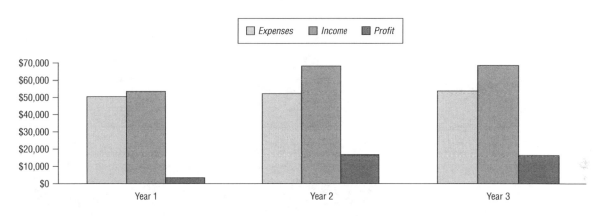

Financing

Ms. Edmonds will obtain a business line of credit for $10,000, the amount needed to cover the start-up costs and three months' expenses. Ms. Edmonds will use her home as collateral for the line of credit and plans to repay the line of credit in the third year of operation. She has budgeted $300 per month for loan repayment, but will pay additional principal if possible.

Repayment Plan

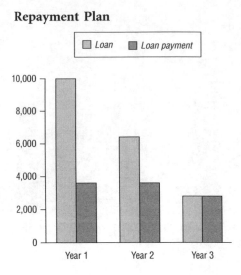

Ms. Edmonds will pay approximately $3,600 per year until the loan is paid in full during the third year of business.

Internet Cafe

Surf Brew Cafe, LLC

5328 Sunnydale Dr.
Orlando, FL 32087

Brenda Kubiac

Surf Brew Cafe, LLC is an Internet cafe that will provide computers with internet access to a wide audience for personal or business use for a set fee or monthly membership.

1.0 EXECUTIVE SUMMARY

Surf Brew Cafe, LLC is a Florida-based limited liability Internet cafe located in Orlando. The cafe will provide Internet access to computers for a set fee or a monthly membership. Other services include the sale of computer hardware, onsite computer repair, printing, scanning, faxing, CD/DVD burning, and free computer lessons for seniors. Additional services include an espresso bar, hot and cold beverages, Panini's, sandwiches, and sweets. The firms' founder, Mr. Michael Benson owned and operated a computer repair shop where he also built computers for 10 years before deciding to open an Internet cafe.

Internet cafes have become very popular and since the fees are related to time, the profitability of the square foot is enormous. Emphasis was placed on creating an inviting environment that visitors will feel the second they walk through the door, from just the right lighting to a water fountain directly within view and plenty of room to move around and mingle. The focus is to make the cafe a community hub where everyone can come and feel at home.

Besides standard computer stations, there are tables and chairs for visitors that walk in off the street to get a bite to eat while they catch up on their daily emails. Moreover, Wi-Fi makes it easy for visitors to check their email, etc. from their laptops or netbooks. The gaming computers are located far enough away from where the tables and chairs are placed to keep the atmosphere pleasant for all patrons.

The owner has gone to great lengths to advertise Surf Brew Cafe, LLC's grand opening and has left no one out. From flyers posted on public bulletin boards to advertising in the local newspaper, including an announcement on the local radio station, the grand opening will be the beginning of a revolving door. The cafe will stay on top of new game releases, promote client opinion with the help of a suggestion box, and weekly gaming or menu specials will further entice returning clients.

1.1 Mission Statement

Surf Brew Cafe, LLC will create an Internet cafe business that will accommodate and cater to the needs of college students, gamers, local business professionals, business travelers, vacationers, as well as lots of foot traffic with particular focus on both new and returning customers.

1.2 Finance

The company has retained law firm, Anderson & Slater P.C. to assist with the legal aspects of operating an Internet cafe, including and not limited to obtaining business licenses, health department permit, the company name, review of the lease and so on. The owner will handle the ongoing daily and weekly bookkeeping to monitor the cafes progress throughout the first year in case changes are needed, while accountant, Amy DeNeve was retained to carry out the quarterly and year-end financial reports.

1.3 Sales Forecasts

Mr. Benson expects nothing less than exponential growth for the first three years Surf Brew Cafe, LLC is open. In the event that the economy slows, Mr. Benson believes he would not be affected by the downturn since the cafes prices are reasonable enough to sustain an economic slump. It's a proven fact that when the economy slows consumers look for more economical ways of entertainment. Since the cafe is located within a high traffic area with such a diverse product mix the business wouldn't be affected if a few services were suspended or the cafes menu trimmed for a short time.

1.4 Expansion Plan

The company plans to add additional computer stations and services if needed. However, if extra cash flow is needed the company will diversify its' product mix further to include the sale of computers. While there is currently lots of controversy surrounding "digital gambling" like blackjack in Internet cafes, especially in the state of Florida where lawmakers are busy closing them down, however, depending on the outcome the owner of Surf Brew Cafe, LLC may consider it. The owner is contemplating "digital gambling" like blackjack and bingo in the cafe, but waiting to hear the outcome from lawmakers who are busy closing them down.

2.0 COMPANY AND FINANCING SUMMARY

Surf Brew Cafe, LLC is a registered corporation in the state of Florida and is fully financed by founder, Mr. Michael Benson. The estimated cost to get an Internet cafe up and running is anywhere from $8,000-$100,000 depending on the number of computers. The owner's previous experience in building computers is a huge asset entering into the Internet cafe business, especially since the cost of computers is the largest challenge for entrepreneurs entering the market. While he has 15 computers from his former business, he will be able to build the 10 remaining computers at a fraction of the cost it would be to purchase new computers.

3.0 PRODUCTS AND SERVICES

Surf Brew Cafe, LLC will offer basic computer usage and multi-gaming computer stations on a pre-pay and monthly basis. Clients will also be able to print, scan, fax, and burn CDs/DVDs. To attract seniors, Mr. Benson plans to offer and conduct free basic computer lessons Monday and Wednesday mornings from 9:00 a.m. to 11:00 a.m. According to the U.S. Census Bureau, computer usage for those over the age of 65 has more than doubled between 2000 and 2011. During that same time, internet usage among those over 65 years jumped higher from 15 percent to 42 percent. Still, there are a number of seniors who shy away from adapting to technology. *The Senior Citizen Journal* "attributes the lag largely due to anxiety over the unknown."(www.asaging.org, 2012)

3.1 Computer Time

Computer rate: $5.00 per half hour minimum

Pre-pay 1 hour	$ 9.00 (10% off)
Pre-pay 2 hours	$16.00 (20% off)
Pre-pay 3 hours	$21.00 (30% off)
Pre-pay 4 hours	$24.00 (40% off)
Pre-pay 6 hours	$30.00 (50% off)
Membership 10 hours	$40.00 (60% off)

Printing and scanning

B&W prints	$ 0.50 per page
Color prints	$ 0.75 per page
Scanned items	$ 1.75 per scan

Fax

Local fax	$ 0.75 per page
Faxes received	$ 0.75 per page
U.S. & Canada	$ 1.50 first page
	$ 0.75 each additional page
International	$ 4.00 first page
	$ 0.50 each additional page

3.2 Other Services

Espresso bar	Small	Large
Coffee	$1.18	$1.50
Café au lait	$1.45	$2.10
Espresso	$1.25	$2.25
Americano	$1.75	$2.50
Macchiato	$1.25	$2.25
Cappuccino	$2.75	$3.30
Latte	$2.50	$3.00
Mocha	$2.75	$3.25
Iced coffee	$1.25	$1.75
Iced tea	$1.25	$1.75
Iced cappuccino	$2.75	$3.25
Iced latte	$2.75	$3.50
Iced mocha	$2.75	$3.50
Iced chai	$2.75	$3.50
Fruit smoothies		$3.25
Hot beverages		
Tea varieties	$1.10	$1.60
Hot chocolate	$1.75	$2.25
Chai	$1.50	$2.10
Cold drinks	**One size**	
Pop	$1.25	
Water	$0.75	
Fruit drinks	$1.50	
Orange juice	$1.75	

3.3 Menu

Panini's	**$4.25**
Caponata, mozzarella and basil panini	
Roasted vegetable, tofu and pesto panini	
Pulled barbecued chicken panini with swiss and red onion	
Brie and smoked turkey panini	
Sandwiches/chips	**$4.25**
Turkey & swiss	
Tuna salad served with lettuce, tomato and mayo	
Meat balls and cheese served with sauce	
Italian sub	
Sweets	**$2.75**
Strawberry cheese cake	
Chocolate cake	
Apple/lemon/blueberry tart	
Rice/chocolate/vanilla pudding	
Assorted pastries	**$1.75**
Assorted cookies	**$1.18**

4.0 STRATEGIC & MARKET ANALYSIS

4.1 Industry Analysis

According to the National Coffee Drinking Study released by the National Coffee Association (www.ncausa.org, 2012), 40% of 18-24 year olds were drinking coffee daily, up 31% compared to 2010. The same study reported 54% of adult's age 25-39 consumed coffee daily, up compared to 44% in 2010. In addition, strong increases in demand for specialty coffee drinks surged by 50% since 2007, according to David Sprinkle, publisher of Packaged Facts (www.packagedfacts.com, 2012). That trend continued during the first quarter of 2013, with a reported 83% of Americans acknowledged they drank coffee. Gourmet coffee consumption continued to rise with 31% of the population drinking gourmet coffee on a daily basis.

4.2 Market Analysis

The residential and business districts in downtown Orlando are thriving. The total population in the greater Orlando area is approximately 2.1 million, while an estimated 51 million tourists visit Orlando annually. Thus, many of the 51 million tourists would likely benefit from an Internet cafe that is conveniently located in Orlando. According to data compiled by Pew Research Center (pewinternet.org, 2012), 65 percent of the U.S. adult population have a high-speed broadband connection at home. That leaves another 35 percent that have a need at one time or another to access the Internet either for personal or business use. The cafe is strategically located across from the University of Central Florida, home to 49,900 students whom fall into the category of prime Internet cafe visitors.

4.3 Target Market

- Business travelers

- College students

- Local seniors

- Gamers

- Tourists

- Foot traffic

- Local business people

- Office workers

4.4 Competition

Following a preliminary market study, Mr. Michael Benson found two other Internet cafes located in the Orlando area; however the formats and services were completely different than the Surf Brew Cafe, LLC. The first, Gaming Center Cafe focuses on gaming only with a couple of vending machines for coffee, hot chocolate, pop and snacks and the second, Pass Time Cafe has 10 computers and offers coffee, tea, pop, cookies, and chips. In addition, both are over 30 miles from the Surf Brew Cafe, LLC so they pose no real threat.

Strengths:
- Location/layout

- 25 computers

- Convenient hours of operation

- Variety of menu items and specialty coffee at competitive prices

- Business experience

- IT experience

- Extra services

- Variety of PC games

Weaknesses:
- New business

- Another Internet cafe or coffee house with similar services could open within close proximity

5.0 MARKETING PLAN

Surf Brew Cafe, LLC plans to run a hard marketing campaign that will reach each and every possible individual in its target market prior to the grand opening, including previous business associates and customers. An overview of both marketing objectives and strategies are listed below.

5.1 Marketing Objectives
- Build and foster loyalty

- Cater to all age groups

- Strive for repeat cafe visitors

- Increase traffic

- Get the word out about the grand opening of the Internet cafe

5.2 Marketing Strategies
1. Build a Web site announcing weekly specials, new games, top gamers, etc.

2. Promote grand opening.

3. Personally visit local businesses in the target market to find out what their needs are and pass out coupons for free cups of coffee the day of the grand opening.

4. Visit the University of Central Florida to meet with the editor of the university newspaper to announce the opening of Surf Brew Cafe, LLC in their next publication, as well as post on student bulletin boards.

5. Pass out flyers personally and post on public bulletin boards.

6. Advertise in the *Orlando Business Journal, Orlando Post,* and the *East Orlando Sun* local newspapers.

7. Pay for local radio time on station WDBO announcing the grand opening one week before.

8. Social networking via Facebook, Twitter, and LinkedIn.

9. Online advertising using Facebook.

10. Contact former business associates and customers to announce new business venture and personally invite them to grand opening.

6.0 OPERATIONS

6.1 Organization

Surf Brew Cafe, LLC is owned and will be operated by Mr. Michael Benson, who holds a Bachelor's Degree in Information Technology with 10 years' experience as an IT specialist. The owner will be responsible for all services except the espresso bar and food items. A total of three part-time college students will be hired who will alternate shifts to work the espresso bar and food counter during the cafes peak hours so that owner can concentrate on delivering excellent customer service. The owner's wife, Emily will be responsible for keeping the kitchen running smoothly.

6.2 Suppliers

Surf Brew Cafe, LLC has supplier agreements set in place to fulfill the cafes menu with Sharps Meat Market who will supply deli meats and cheeses, The Sweet Shop and the local Farmer's Market who will supply the sweets and fresh produce daily. The bakery Shoppe will deliver fresh breads on a daily basis and coffee will be supplied by Coffee & Tea Express. Other local suppliers include Pastries & More and Andy's Meats & Veggies who will act as backup suppliers in the event problems arise with original suppliers.

6.3 Hours

Surf Brew Cafe, LLC will be open for business Monday through Saturday from 8:00 a.m. to midnight and Sunday from 11:00 a.m. to 10:00 p.m.

6.4 Facility and location

Surf Brew Cafe, LLC is conveniently located five minutes east from downtown Orlando within the business district located at 5328 Sunnydale Dr. directly across from the University of Central Florida, home to 49,900 students. The leased 1,700 square foot building is well equipped to handle the daily operations of an Internet cafe, including ample lighting, parking, and is also wheelchair accessible. There is extra space to add another 10 computer stations if needed. There will be additional electrical outlets installed by the owner's brother, Richard who is a licensed electrician whom will also assist with setting up the computer stations.

Surf Brew Cafe, LLC will be equipped with both a wired (LAN) and a wireless (Wi-Fi) network to accommodate 25 computers and visitors personal laptops or netbooks, including one server computer that will control the clients and networking hardware. The server computer will be equipped with Internet Cafe management software to monitor user's accounts, charge Point of Service (POS) items including cash drawer and receipt printer, as well as get the latest statistics, logs and detailed reports. The software is also equipped with monitoring print jobs and billing directly to customer's account, manual timers to track usage of laptops and computers, and 300 plus games and more.

The building was formerly a diner making it easy to convert to an Internet cafe equipped with a kitchen including a walk-in cooler, gas grill for making sandwiches, display case, snack bar, coffee machines, etc. However, the company will have to invest in a commercial espresso machine. There is also a small office to house the central computer and storage room that is ideal for computer repairs.

Startup costs

Lease deposit	$ 1,500
Startup utilities	$ 300
Legal fees	$ 500
Business licenses	$ 200
Web site	$ 100
Advertising	$ 1,000
Management software	$ 700
Phone line	$ 100
Internet connection	$ 100 per month
Printer/photocopier/scanner	$ 1,000
Computers/software	$ 5,000
Commercial espresso machine	$ 1,500
Suppliers	$ 1,750
Total startup costs	**$13,750**

6.5 Projected Startup costs

7.0 FINANCIAL ANALYSIS

Surf Brew Cafe, LLC's three-year income statement below shows an estimated net profit of $44,440 for the first year followed by an estimated net profit of $78,620 for the second year and $135,198 for the third year.

7.1 Three-Year Income Statement

	Year 1	Year 2	Year 3
Customer volume	10,337	14,998	18,010
Total revenues	$82,152	$135,397	$198,190
Total cost of goods	$21,104	$ 38,320	$ 42,743
Total expenses	$16,608	$ 18,457	$ 20,249
Net profit	**$44,440**	**$ 78,620**	**$135,198**

Landscape Contractor

Cantalupo Landscape Services, Inc.

PO Box 9980
Lake MoheganNew York 10547

Cantalupo Landscape Services, Inc. is a New York based corporation that will provide landscape contracting, landscape architecture, and lawn moving/lawn care services in its targeted market. The Company was founded by Vincent Cantalupo.

1.0 EXECUTIVE SUMMARY

The purpose of this business plan is to raise $100,000 for the development of a landscape contractor while showcasing the expected financials and operations over the next three years. Cantalupo Landscape Services, Inc. is a New York based corporation that will provide landscape contracting, landscape architecture, and lawn moving/lawn care services in its targeted market. The Company was founded by Vincent Cantalupo.

1.1 The Services

As mentioned above, Cantalupo Landscape Services intends to operate in a multifaceted capacity by offering general landscape contracting, specialized landscape architecture, and general lawn care and lawn moving services to the general public. Despite recent economic turmoil, busy professionals/ executives and property management firms have continued to need these services on a weekly, bi-weekly, and monthly basis.

At the onset of operations, the Company intends to partner with several local property management firms and real estate based companies that have regular lawn care and landscape contracting needs. These relationships will ensure that the business generates a continuous stream of revenue on a month to month basis.

The third section of the business plan will further describe the services offered by Cantalupo Landscape Services.

1.2 Financing

Mr. Cantalupo is seeking to raise $100,000 from as a bank loan. The interest rate and loan agreement are to be further discussed during negotiation. This business plan assumes that the business will receive a 10 year loan with a 9% fixed interest rate. The financing will be used for the following:

- Acquisition for lawn care and landscaping equipment.

- Financing for the first six months of operation.

- Capital to purchase a company vehicle.

Mr. Cantalupo will contribute $10,000 to the venture.

1.3 Mission Statement

The mission of Cantalupo Landscape Services' is to become the recognized leader in its targeted market for landscape contracting, landscape architecture, and general lawn care services.

1.4 Management Team

The Company was founded by Vincent Cantalupo. Mr. Cantalupo has more than 10 years of experience in the landscape architecture and landscape contracting industry. Through his expertise, he will be able to bring the operations of the business to profitability within its first year of operations.

1.5 Sales Forecasts

Mr. Cantalupo expects a strong rate of growth at the start of operations. Below are the expected financials over the next three years.

Proforma profit and loss (yearly)

Year	1	2	3
Sales	$443,100	$531,720	$622,112
Operating costs	$301,410	$312,521	$324,015
EBITDA	$ 91,050	$158,431	$226,999
Taxes, interest, and depreciation	$ 47,265	$ 69,174	$ 94,818
Net profit	$ 43,785	$ 89,257	$132,180

Sales, operating costs, and profit forecast

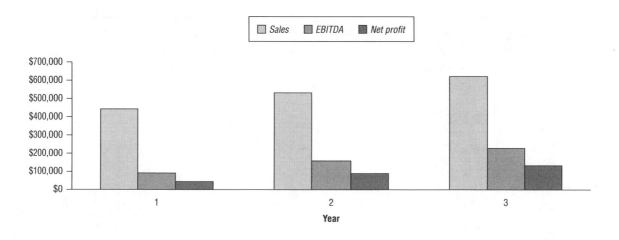

1.6 Expansion Plan

The Founder expects that the business will aggressively expand during the first three years of operation. Mr. Cantalupo intends to implement marketing campaigns that will effectively target individuals and property managers within the target market.

2.0 COMPANY AND FINANCING SUMMARY

2.1 Registered Name and Corporate Structure

The Company is registered as a corporation in the State of New York.

2.2 Required Funds

At this time, Cantalupo Landscape Services requires $100,000 of debt funds. Below is a breakdown of how these funds will be used:

Projected startup costs

Initial lease payments and deposits	$ 10,000
Working capital	$ 35,000
FF&E	$ 10,000
Leasehold improvements	$ 5,000
Security deposits	$ 5,000
Insurance	$ 2,500
Vehicle and landscaping equipment	$ 30,000
Marketing budget	$ 7,500
Miscellaneous and unforeseen costs	$ 5,000
Total startup costs	**$110,000**

Use of funds

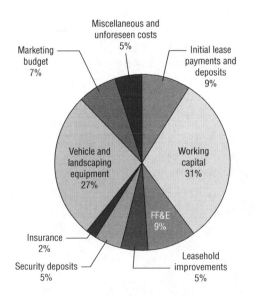

2.3 Investor Equity

Mr. Cantalupo is not seeking an investment from a third party at this time.

2.4 Management Equity

Vincent Cantalupo owns 100% of Cantalupo Landscape Services, Inc.

2.5 Exit Strategy

If the business is very successful, Mr. Cantalupo may seek to sell the business to a third party for a significant earnings multiple. Most likely, the Company will hire a qualified business broker to sell the business on behalf of Cantalupo Landscape Services. Based on historical numbers, the business could fetch a sales premium of up to 4 times earnings.

3.0 PRODUCTS AND SERVICES

Below is a description of the landscaping/mowing services offered by Cantalupo Landscape Services.

3.1 Landscape Contracting

The primary segment of the business is providing landscape contracting and landscape architecture services to the general public. These services will include designing landscapes and redesigning/renewing existing landscape structures on behalf of the Company's clients. The Company will recognize revenues from both the aggregate sale of specialized landscape contracting services as well as per hour fees from landscape architecture planning and drafting.

At the onset of operations, Mr. Cantalupo intends to partner with a number of local and regional real estate developers, real estate investment firms, and property management companies that have a regular need for landscape contracting work. The fifth section of the business plan will further document the marketing plans of Cantalupo Landscape Services.

3.2 Lawn Mowing Services and Sales of Trees/Plants

The secondary segment of the business, lawn moving services and sales of trees/plants, will actually generate the bulk of the Company's revenues. The business intends on having a lawn care crew of approximately five people that will mow lawns for homeowners and property management firm clients on a weekly or bi-weekly basis. Lawn mowing services will generate the most revenue for the business, although it will generate only 30% of the Company's pre-tax profits.

In conjunction with the Company's landscape architecture and contracting services, the business will generate tertiary streams of revenue from the sale of trees and plants that will be used in conjunction with landscape architecture plans. The Company will earn significant high margins on the sales of these plants and trees, which will be sourced from local nurseries and farms.

4.0 STRATEGIC AND MARKET ANALYSIS

4.1 Economic Outlook

This section of the analysis will detail the economic climate, the landscape contracting industry, the customer profile, and the competition that the business will face as it progresses through its business operations.

Currently, the economic market condition in the United States is moderate. The meltdown of the sub prime mortgage market coupled with increasing gas prices has led many people to believe that the US is on the cusp of a double dip economic recession. This slowdown in the economy has also greatly impacted real estate sales, which has halted to historical lows. However, and as will be discussed later in the business plan, landscaping companies typically operate with a certain level of economic immunity as the people that use these services typically are upper middle and upper income people that are too busy to tend to their own lawn care and landscaping matters.

4.2 Industry Analysis

In the United States, there are more than 80,000 businesses that operate in a capacity that is substantially similar or identical to those of the Company. Each year, the landscape contractors and lawn mowing services generate more than $29 billion dollars per year. Additionally, the businesses aggregately employ more than 200,000 people nationwide, and provide gross annual payrolls in excess of $13 billion dollars.

The industry has experienced solid growth as the number of real estate developers building property in the United States has swelled with the rise in general housing and building prices. However, in the event of a severe economic recession, Management expects that the Company may see a decline in revenues. Lawn care and landscape contracting services are expensive, and as such, decreases in general economic output will result in decreases of revenue to the Company. However, Management will combat these deleterious economic changes by developing ongoing relationships with wealthy homeowners and property management firms that require regular landscape contracting and lawn care services.

4.3 Customer Profile

The average client will be a middle to upper middle class man or woman living in the Company's target market. Common traits among clients will include:

- Annual household income exceeding $50,000

- Lives or works no more than 15 miles from the Company's location.

- Will spend $100 to $250 per month on the Company's services.

4.4 Competition

Landscape contracting is an extremely competitive market. Within any area, there are a number of businesses that operate in a similar capacity to the Company. However, Management (in order to maintain a regularity of revenue and cash flow) intends to heavily partner with real estate firms that require landscape maintenance on an ongoing basis. Additionally, the business will differentiate itself from other companies in the market by sourcing the highest quality flowers and trees that will be planted within residential and commercial real estate.

5.0 MARKETING PLAN

Cantalupo Landscape Services intends to maintain an extensive marketing campaign that will ensure maximum visibility for the business in its targeted market. Below is an overview of the marketing strategies and objectives of Cantalupo Landscape Services.

5.1 Marketing Objectives

- Develop an online presence by developing a website and placing the Company's name and contact information with online directories.

- Implement a local campaign with the Company's targeted market via the use of flyers, local newspaper advertisements, and word of mouth.

- Establish relationships with property management firms within the targeted market.

5.2 Marketing Strategies

Mr. Cantalupo intends on using a number of marketing strategies that will allow Cantalupo Landscape Services to easily target homeowners and property management firms within the target market. These strategies include traditional print advertisements and ads placed on search engines on the Internet. Below is a description of how the business intends to market its services to the general public.

Cantalupo Landscape Services will also use an internet based strategy. The Company will have an expansive website that showcases the plants and trees that can be installed into a client's property. Additionally, the preliminary fees associated with landscape contracting will be shown on the website. Many people feel much more comfortable doing business with companies when they know the price that they will be paying for contracted plants/trees and related services. Prior to the onset of operations, the business will hire a website development firm to integrate this type of functionality into the website.

Finally, Cantalupo Landscape Services will develop ongoing relationships with property management firms that require continued upkeep of their client's properties. This will ensure that the business generates substantial and predictable revenues on a monthly basis.

5.3 Pricing

For ongoing maintenance, the business expects to generate $100 to $250 per month depending on the size of the property. Initial fees for planting flowers and trees will be $1,500 to $5,000.

6.0 ORGANIZATIONAL PLAN AND PERSONNEL SUMMARY

6.1 Corporate Organization

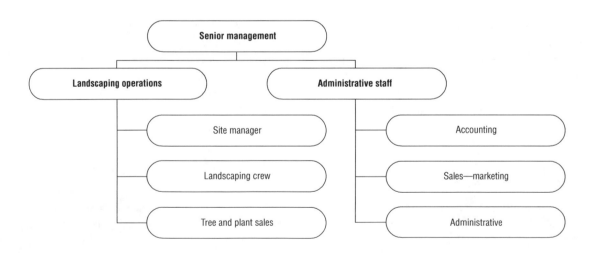

6.2 Organizational Budget

Personnel plan—yearly

Year	1	2	3
Owner	$ 35,000	$ 36,050	$ 37,132
Site manager	$ 44,000	$ 45,320	$ 46,680
Landscaping crew	$ 98,000	$100,940	$103,968
Bookkeeper (P/T)	$ 12,500	$ 12,875	$ 13,261
Administrative	$ 38,000	$ 39,140	$ 40,314
Total	**$227,500**	**$234,325**	**$241,355**

Numbers of personnel

Owner	1	1	1
Site manager	2	2	2
Landscaping crew	7	7	7
Bookkeeper (P/T)	1	1	1
Administrative	2	2	2
Totals	**13**	**13**	**13**

Personnel expense breakdown

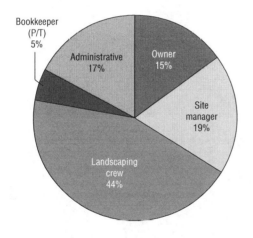

7.0 FINANCIAL PLAN

7.1 Underlying Assumptions

The Company has based its proforma financial statements on the following:

- Cantalupo Landscape Services will have an annual revenue growth rate of 16% per year.

- The Owner will acquire $100,000 of debt funds to develop the business.

- The loan will have a 10 year term with a 9% interest rate.

7.2 Sensitivity Analysis

In the event of an economic downturn, the business may have a decline in its revenues. However, landscape and lawn mowing services are typically in demand during seasonal months as the people that enroll in these services are often busy professionals that will continue to be able to afford the Company's services despite deleterious changes in the economy. Additionally, the business intends to develop ongoing relationships with property management firms, which will ensure a continued stream of referral revenue for the business.

7.3 Source of Funds

Financing

Equity contributions

Management investment	$ 10,000.00
Total equity financing	**$ 10,000.00**
Banks and lenders	
Banks and lenders	$100,000.00
Total debt financing	**$100,000.00**
Total financing	**$110,000.00**

7.4 General Assumptions

General assumptions

Year	1	2	3
Short term interest rate	9.5%	9.5%	9.5%
Long term interest rate	10.0%	10.0%	10.0%
Federal tax rate	33.0%	33.0%	33.0%
State tax rate	5.0%	5.0%	5.0%
Personnel taxes	15.0%	15.0%	15.0%

7.5 Profit and Loss Statements

Proforma profit and loss (yearly)

Year	1	2	3
Sales	**$443,100**	**$531,720**	**$622,112**
Cost of goods sold	$ 50,640	$ 60,768	$ 71,099
Gross margin	88.57%	88.57%	88.57%
Operating income	**$392,460**	**$470,952**	**$551,014**
Expenses			
Payroll	$227,500	$234,325	$241,355
General and administrative	$ 13,200	$ 13,728	$ 14,277
Marketing expenses	$ 2,216	$ 2,659	$ 3,111
Professional fees and licensure	$ 5,219	$ 5,376	$ 5,537
Insurance costs	$ 1,987	$ 2,086	$ 2,191
Travel and vehicle costs	$ 7,596	$ 8,356	$ 9,191
Rent and utilities	$ 4,250	$ 4,463	$ 4,686
Miscellaneous costs	$ 5,317	$ 6,381	$ 7,465
Payroll taxes	$ 34,125	$ 35,149	$ 36,203
Total operating costs	**$301,410**	**$312,521**	**$324,015**
EBITDA	**$ 91,050**	**$158,431**	**$226,999**
Federal income tax	$ 30,047	$ 49,599	$ 72,445
State income tax	$ 4,553	$ 7,515	$ 10,977
Interest expense	$ 8,738	$ 8,131	$ 7,468
Depreciation expenses	$ 3,929	$ 3,929	$ 3,929
Net profit	**$ 43,785**	**$ 89,257**	**$132,180**
Profit margin	**9.88%**	**16.79%**	**21.25%**

Sales, operating costs, and profit forecast

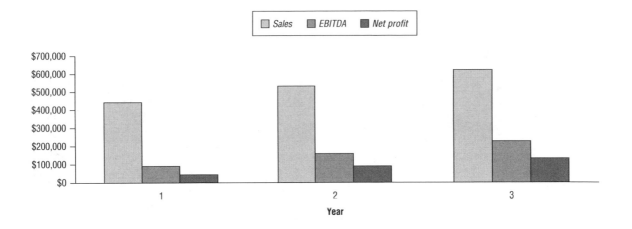

7.6 Cash Flow Analysis

Proforma cash flow analysis—yearly

Year	1	2	3
Cash from operations	$ 47,713	$ 93,186	$136,109
Cash from receivables	$ 0	$ 0	$ 0
Operating cash inflow	**$ 47,713**	**$ 93,186**	**$136,109**
Other cash inflows			
Equity investment	$ 10,000	$ 0	$ 0
Increased borrowings	$100,000	$ 0	$ 0
Sales of business assets	$ 0	$ 0	$ 0
A/P increases	$ 37,902	$ 43,587	$ 50,125
Total other cash inflows	**$147,902**	**$ 43,587**	**$ 50,125**
Total cash inflow	**$195,615**	**$136,773**	**$186,234**
Cash outflows			
Repayment of principal	$ 6,463	$ 7,070	$ 7,733
A/P decreases	$ 24,897	$ 29,876	$ 35,852
A/R increases	$ 0	$ 0	$ 0
Asset purchases	$ 55,000	$ 23,296	$ 34,027
Dividends	$ 33,399	$ 65,230	$ 95,276
Total cash outflows	**$119,760**	**$125,473**	**$172,888**
Net cash flow	**$ 75,856**	**$ 11,300**	**$ 13,346**
Cash balance	**$ 75,856**	**$ 87,156**	**$100,502**

Proforma cash flow (yearly)

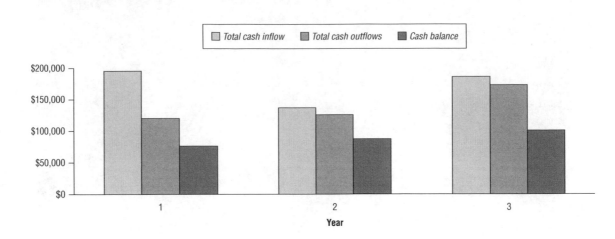

7.7 Balance Sheet

Proforma balance sheet—yearly

Year	1	2	3
Assets			
Cash	$ 75,856	$ 87,156	$100,502
Amortized expansion costs	$ 15,000	$ 17,330	$ 20,732
Landscaping and vehicle assets	$ 30,000	$ 47,472	$ 72,993
FF&E	$ 10,000	$ 13,494	$ 18,599
Accumulated depreciation	($ 3,929)	($ 7,857)	($ 11,786)
Total assets	**$126,927**	**$157,595**	**$201,040**
Liabilities and equity			
Accounts payable	$ 13,005	$ 26,716	$ 40,990
Long term liabilities	$ 93,537	$ 86,467	$ 79,397
Other liabilities	$ 0	$ 0	$ 0
Total liabilities	**$106,542**	**$113,183**	**$120,387**
Net worth	**$ 20,385**	**$ 44,413**	**$ 80,654**
Total liabilities and equity	**$126,927**	**$157,595**	**$201,040**

Proforma balance sheet

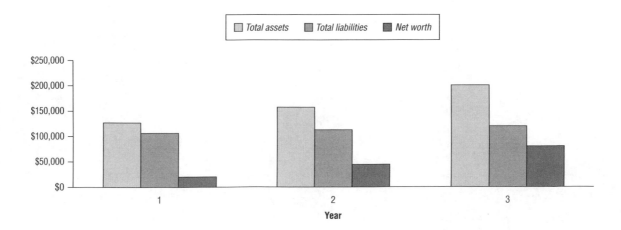

7.8 Breakeven Analysis

Monthly break even analysis

Year	1	2	3
Monthly revenue	$ 28,358	$ 29,404	$ 30,485
Yearly revenue	$340,301	$352,846	$365,824

Break even analysis

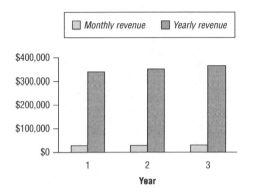

7.9 Business Ratios

Business ratios—yearly

Year	1	2	3
Sales			
Sales growth	0.00%	20.00%	17.00%
Gross margin	88.60%	88.60%	88.60%
Financials			
Profit margin	9.88%	16.79%	21.25%
Assets to liabilities	1.19	1.39	1.67
Equity to liabilities	0.19	0.39	0.67
Assets to equity	6.23	3.55	2.49
Liquidity			
Acid test	0.71	0.77	0.83
Cash to assets	0.60	0.55	0.50

7.10 Three Year Profit and Loss Statement

Profit and loss statement (first year)

Months	1	2	3	4	5	6	7
Sales	$35,000	$35,350	$35,700	$36,050	$36,400	$36,750	$37,100
Cost of goods sold	$ 4,000	$ 4,040	$ 4,080	$ 4,120	$ 4,160	$ 4,200	$ 4,240
Gross margin	88.60%	88.60%	88.60%	88.60%	88.60%	88.60%	88.60%
Operating income	**$31,000**	**$31,310**	**$31,620**	**$31,930**	**$32,240**	**$32,550**	**$32,860**
Expenses							
Payroll	$18,958	$18,958	$18,958	$18,958	$18,958	$18,958	$18,958
General and administrative	$ 1,100	$ 1,100	$ 1,100	$ 1,100	$ 1,100	$ 1,100	$ 1,100
Marketing expenses	$ 185	$ 185	$ 185	$ 185	$ 185	$ 185	$ 185
Professional fees and licensure	$ 435	$ 435	$ 435	$ 435	$ 435	$ 435	$ 435
Insurance costs	$ 166	$ 166	$ 166	$ 166	$ 166	$ 166	$ 166
Travel and vehicle costs	$ 633	$ 633	$ 633	$ 633	$ 633	$ 633	$ 633
Rent and utilities	$ 354	$ 354	$ 354	$ 354	$ 354	$ 354	$ 354
Miscellaneous costs	$ 443	$ 443	$ 443	$ 443	$ 443	$ 443	$ 443
Payroll taxes	$ 2,844	$ 2,844	$ 2,844	$ 2,844	$ 2,844	$ 2,844	$ 2,844
Total operating costs	**$25,117**	**$25,117**	**$25,117**	**$25,117**	**$25,117**	**$25,117**	**$25,117**
EBITDA	**$ 5,883**	**$ 6,193**	**$ 6,503**	**$ 6,813**	**$ 7,123**	**$ 7,433**	**$ 7,743**
Federal income tax	$ 2,373	$ 2,397	$ 2,421	$ 2,445	$ 2,468	$ 2,492	$ 2,516
State income tax	$ 360	$ 363	$ 367	$ 370	$ 374	$ 378	$ 381
Interest expense	$ 750	$ 746	$ 742	$ 738	$ 734	$ 730	$ 726
Depreciation expense	$ 327	$ 327	$ 327	$ 327	$ 327	$ 327	$ 327
Net profit	**$ 2,072**	**$ 2,359**	**$ 2,645**	**$ 2,932**	**$ 3,219**	**$ 3,505**	**$ 3,792**

Profit and loss statement (first year cont.)

Month	8	9	10	11	12	1
Sales	$37,450	$37,800	$38,150	$38,500	$38,850	$443,100
Cost of goods sold	$ 4,280	$ 4,320	$ 4,360	$ 4,400	$ 4,440	$ 50,640
Gross margin	88.60%	88.60%	88.60%	88.60%	88.60%	88.60%
Operating income	**$33,170**	**$33,480**	**$33,790**	**$34,100**	**$34,410**	**$392,460**
Expenses						
Payroll	$18,958	$18,958	$18,958	$18,958	$18,958	$227,500
General and administrative	$ 1,100	$ 1,100	$ 1,100	$ 1,100	$ 1,100	$ 13,200
Marketing expenses	$ 185	$ 185	$ 185	$ 185	$ 185	$ 2,216
Professional fees and licensure	$ 435	$ 435	$ 435	$ 435	$ 435	$ 5,219
Insurance costs	$ 166	$ 166	$ 166	$ 166	$ 166	$ 1,987
Travel and vehicle costs	$ 633	$ 633	$ 633	$ 633	$ 633	$ 7,596
Rent and utilities	$ 354	$ 354	$ 354	$ 354	$ 354	$ 4,250
Miscellaneous costs	$ 443	$ 443	$ 443	$ 443	$ 443	$ 5,317
Payroll taxes	$ 2,844	$ 2,844	$ 2,844	$ 2,844	$ 2,844	$ 34,125
Total operating costs	**$25,117**	**$25,117**	**$25,117**	**$25,117**	**$25,117**	**$301,410**
EBITDA	**$ 8,053**	**$ 8,363**	**$ 8,673**	**$ 8,983**	**$ 9,293**	**$ 91,050**
Federal income tax	$ 2,539	$ 2,563	$ 2,587	$ 2,611	$ 2,634	$ 30,047
State income tax	$ 385	$ 388	$ 392	$ 396	$ 399	$ 4,553
Interest expense	$ 722	$ 718	$ 714	$ 710	$ 706	$ 8,738
Depreciation expense	$ 327	$ 327	$ 327	$ 327	$ 327	$ 3,929
Net profit	**$ 4,079**	**$ 4,365**	**$ 4,652**	**$ 4,939**	**$ 5,226**	**$ 43,785**

Profit and loss statement (second year)

Quarter	Q1	2 Q2	Q3	Q4	2
Sales	**$106,344**	**$132,930**	**$143,564**	**$148,882**	**$531,720**
Cost of goods sold	$ 12,154	$ 15,192	$ 16,407	$ 17,015	$ 60,768
Gross margin	88.60%	88.60%	88.60%	88.60%	88.60%
Operating income	**$ 94,190**	**$117,738**	**$127,157**	**$131,867**	**$470,952**
Expenses					
Payroll	$ 46,865	$ 58,581	$ 63,268	$ 65,611	$234,325
General and administrative	$ 2,746	$ 3,432	$ 3,707	$ 3,844	$ 13,728
Marketing expenses	$ 532	$ 665	$ 718	$ 744	$ 2,659
Professional fees and licensure	$ 1,075	$ 1,344	$ 1,451	$ 1,505	$ 5,376
Insurance costs	$ 417	$ 522	$ 563	$ 584	$ 2,086
Travel and vehicle costs	$ 1,671	$ 2,089	$ 2,256	$ 2,340	$ 8,356
Rent and utilities	$ 893	$ 1,116	$ 1,205	$ 1,250	$ 4,463
Miscellaneous costs	$ 1,276	$ 1,595	$ 1,723	$ 1,787	$ 6,381
Payroll taxes	$ 7,030	$ 8,787	$ 9,490	$ 9,842	$ 35,149
Total operating costs	**$ 62,504**	**$ 78,130**	**$ 84,381**	**$ 87,506**	**$312,521**
EBITDA	**$ 31,686**	**$ 39,608**	**$ 42,776**	**$ 44,361**	**$158,431**
Federal income tax	$ 9,920	$ 12,400	$ 13,392	$ 13,888	$ 49,599
State income tax	$ 1,503	$ 1,879	$ 2,029	$ 2,104	$ 7,515
Interest expense	$ 2,092	$ 2,053	$ 2,013	$ 1,973	$ 8,131
Depreciation expense	$ 982	$ 982	$ 902	$ 982	$ 3,920
Net profit	**$ 17,189**	**$ 22,294**	**$ 24,360**	**$ 25,414**	**$ 89,257**

Profit and loss statement (third year)

Quarter	Q1	3 Q2	Q3	Q4	3
Sales	**$124,422**	**$155,528**	**$167,970**	**$174,191**	**$622,112**
Cost of goods sold	$ 14,220	$ 17,775	$ 19,197	$ 19,908	$ 71,099
Gross margin	88.60%	88.60%	88.60%	88.60%	88.60%
Operating income	**$110,203**	**$137,753**	**$148,774**	**$154,284**	**$551,014**
Expenses					
Payroll	$ 48,271	$ 60,339	$ 65,166	$ 67,579	$241,355
General and administrative	$ 2,855	$ 3,569	$ 3,855	$ 3,998	$ 14,277
Marketing expenses	$ 622	$ 778	$ 840	$ 871	$ 3,111
Professional fees and licensure	$ 1,107	$ 1,384	$ 1,495	$ 1,550	$ 5,537
Insurance costs	$ 438	$ 548	$ 591	$ 613	$ 2,191
Travel and vehicle costs	$ 1,838	$ 2,298	$ 2,482	$ 2,574	$ 9,191
Rent and utilities	$ 937	$ 1,171	$ 1,265	$ 1,312	$ 4,686
Miscellaneous costs	$ 1,493	$ 1,866	$ 2,016	$ 2,090	$ 7,465
Payroll taxes	$ 7,241	$ 9,051	$ 9,775	$ 10,137	$ 36,203
Total operating costs	**$ 64,803**	**$ 81,004**	**$ 87,484**	**$ 90,724**	**$324,015**
EBITDA	**$ 45,400**	**$ 56,750**	**$ 61,290**	**$ 63,560**	**$226,999**
Federal income tax	$ 14,489	$ 18,111	$ 19,560	$ 20,285	$ 72,445
State income tax	$ 2,195	$ 2,744	$ 2,964	$ 3,073	$ 10,977
Interest expense	$ 1,932	$ 1,889	$ 1,846	$ 1,802	$ 7,468
Depreciation expense	$ 982	$ 982	$ 982	$ 982	$ 3,929
Net profit	**$ 25,802**	**$ 33,023**	**$ 35,938**	**$ 37,418**	**$132,180**

7.11 Three Year Cash Flow Analysis

Cash flow analysis (first year)

Month	1	2	3	4	5	6	7
Cash from operations	$ 2,400	$ 2,686	$ 2,973	$ 3,259	$ 3,546	$ 3,833	$ 4,119
Cash from receivables	$ 0	$ 0	$ 0	$ 0	$ 0	$ 0	$ 0
Operating cash inflow	**$ 2,400**	**$ 2,686**	**$ 2,973**	**$ 3,259**	**$ 3,546**	**$ 3,833**	**$ 4,119**
Other cash inflows							
Equity investment	$ 10,000	$ 0	$ 0	$ 0	$ 0	$ 0	$ 0
Increased borrowings	$100,000	$ 0	$ 0	$ 0	$ 0	$ 0	$ 0
Sales of business assets	$ 0	$ 0	$ 0	$ 0	$ 0	$ 0	$ 0
A/P increases	$ 3,159	$ 3,159	$ 3,159	$ 3,159	$ 3,159	$ 3,159	$ 3,159
Total other cash inflows	**$113,159**	**$ 3,159**	**$ 3,159**	**$ 3,159**	**$ 3,159**	**$ 3,159**	**$ 3,159**
Total cash inflow	**$115,558**	**$ 5,845**	**$ 6,131**	**$ 6,418**	**$ 6,704**	**$ 6,991**	**$ 7,278**
Cash outflows							
Repayment of principal	$ 517	$ 521	$ 525	$ 528	$ 532	$ 536	$ 540
A/P decreases	$ 2,075	$ 2,075	$ 2,075	$ 2,075	$ 2,075	$ 2,075	$ 2,075
A/R increases	$ 0	$ 0	$ 0	$ 0	$ 0	$ 0	$ 0
Asset purchases	$ 55,000	$ 0	$ 0	$ 0	$ 0	$ 0	$ 0
Dividends	$ 0	$ 0	$ 0	$ 0	$ 0	$ 0	$ 0
Total cash outflows	**$ 57,592**	**$ 2,595**	**$ 2,599**	**$ 2,603**	**$ 2,607**	**$ 2,611**	**$ 2,615**
Net cash flow	**$ 57,967**	**$ 3,249**	**$ 3,532**	**$ 3,815**	**$ 4,097**	**$ 4,380**	**$ 4,663**
Cash balance	**$ 57,967**	**$61,216**	**$64,748**	**$68,562**	**$72,660**	**$77,039**	**$81,702**

Cash flow analysis (first year cont.)

Month	8	9	10	11	12	1
Cash from operations	$ 4,406	$ 4,693	$ 4,980	$ 5,266	$ 5,553	$ 47,713
Cash from receivables	$ 0	$ 0	$ 0	$ 0	$ 0	$ 0
Operating cash inflow	**$ 4,406**	**$ 4,693**	**$ 4,980**	**$ 5,266**	**$ 5,553**	**$ 47,713**
Other cash inflows						
Equity investment	$ 0	$ 0	$ 0	$ 0	$ 0	$ 10,000
Increased borrowings	$ 0	$ 0	$ 0	$ 0	$ 0	$100,000
Sales of business assets	$ 0	$ 0	$ 0	$ 0	$ 0	$ 0
A/P increases	$ 3,159	$ 3,159	$ 3,159	$ 3,159	$ 3,159	$ 37,902
Total other cash inflows	**$ 3,159**	**$ 3,159**	**$ 3,159**	**$ 3,159**	**$ 3,159**	**$147,902**
Total cash inflow	**$ 7,565**	**$ 7,851**	**$ 8,138**	**$ 8,425**	**$ 8,712**	**$195,615**
Cash outflows						
Repayment of principal	$ 545	$ 549	$ 553	$ 557	$ 561	$ 6,463
A/P decreases	$ 2,075	$ 2,075	$ 2,075	$ 2,075	$ 2,075	$ 24,897
A/R increases	$ 0	$ 0	$ 0	$ 0	$ 0	$ 0
Asset purchases	$ 0	$ 0	$ 0	$ 0	$ 0	$ 55,000
Dividends	$ 0	$ 0	$ 0	$ 0	$33,399	$ 33,399
Total cash outflows	**$ 2,619**	**$ 2,623**	**$ 2,627**	**$ 2,632**	**$36,035**	**$119,760**
Net cash flow	**$ 4,945**	**$ 5,228**	**$ 5,511**	**$ 5,793**	**−$27,323**	**$ 75,856**
Cash balance	**$86,647**	**$91,875**	**$97,386**	**$103,179**	**$75,856**	**$ 75,856**

Cash flow analysis (second year)

Quarter	Q1	2 Q2	Q3	Q4	2
Cash from operations	$18,637	$23,296	$25,160	$26,092	$ 93,186
Cash from receivables	$ 0	$ 0	$ 0	$ 0	$ 0
Operating cash inflow	**$18,637**	**$23,296**	**$25,160**	**$26,092**	**$ 93,186**
Other cash inflows					
Equity investment	$ 0	$ 0	$ 0	$ 0	$ 0
Increased borrowings	$ 0	$ 0	$ 0	$ 0	$ 0
Sales of business assets	$ 0	$ 0	$ 0	$ 0	$ 0
A/P increases	$ 8,717	$10,897	$11,769	$12,204	$ 43,587
Total other cash inflows	**$ 8,717**	**$10,897**	**$11,769**	**$12,204**	**$ 43,587**
Total cash inflow	**$27,355**	**$34,193**	**$36,929**	**$38,296**	**$136,773**
Cash outflows					
Repayment of principal	$ 1,708	$ 1,747	$ 1,787	$ 1,827	$ 7,070
A/P decreases	$ 5,975	$ 7,469	$ 8,067	$ 8,365	$ 29,876
A/R increases	$ 0	$ 0	$ 0	$ 0	$ 0
Asset purchases	$ 4,659	$ 5,824	$ 6,290	$ 6,523	$ 23,296
Dividends	$13,046	$16,308	$17,612	$18,264	$ 65,230
Total cash outflows	**$26,389**	**$31,348**	**$33,756**	**$34,980**	**$125,473**
Net cash flow	**$ 1,966**	**$ 2,845**	**$ 3,173**	**$ 3,316**	**$ 11,300**
Cash balance	**$77,821**	**$80,667**	**$83,840**	**$87,156**	**$ 87,156**

Cash flow analysis (third year)

Quarter	Q1	3 Q2	Q3	Q4	3
Cash from operations	$27,222	$34,027	$36,749	$ 38,110	$136,109
Cash from receivables	$ 0	$ 0	$ 0	$ 0	$ 0
Operating cash inflow	**$27,222**	**$34,027**	**$36,749**	**$ 38,110**	**$136,109**
Other cash inflows					
Equity investment	$ 0	$ 0	$ 0	$ 0	$ 0
Increased borrowings	$ 0	$ 0	$ 0	$ 0	$ 0
Sales of business assets	$ 0	$ 0	$ 0	$ 0	$ 0
A/P increases	$10,025	$12,531	$13,534	$ 14,035	$ 50,125
Total other cash inflows	**$10,025**	**$12,531**	**$13,534**	**$ 14,035**	**$ 50,125**
Total cash inflow	**$37,247**	**$46,559**	**$50,283**	**$ 52,146**	**$186,234**
Cash outflows					
Repayment of principal	$ 1,869	$ 1,911	$ 1,954	$ 1,999	$ 7,733
A/P decreases	$ 7,170	$ 8,963	$ 9,680	$ 10,038	$ 35,852
A/R increases	$ 0	$ 0	$ 0	$ 0	$ 0
Asset purchases	$ 6,805	$ 8,507	$ 9,187	$ 9,528	$ 34,027
Dividends	$19,055	$23,819	$25,725	$ 26,677	$ 95,276
Total cash outflows	**$34,900**	**$43,200**	**$46,546**	**$ 48,242**	**$172,888**
Net cash flow	**$ 2,347**	**$ 3,359**	**$ 3,737**	**$ 3,903**	**$ 13,346**
Cash balance	**$89,503**	**$92,862**	**$96,599**	**$100,502**	**$100,502**

Marketing Consultant

Shapiro Consulting, LLC

182 Haggerty St.
Chicago, IL 60654

Brenda Kubiac

Shapiro Consulting, LLC is an independent marketing consultant specializing in integrated marketing services related to Web marketing.

1.0 EXECUTIVE SUMMARY

1.1 Business Overview

Following a 13-year marketing career, Mr. Brandon Shapiro decided to become an independent marketing consultant. Through both experience and extensive market research, Mr. Shapiro learned there was a profound need in the area of Web marketing within startup, small and medium-sized companies. While a large number of the targeted companies were spending more on Web marketing, compared to traditional advertising they had no idea how to measure how they were doing.

Local Commerce Monitor (LCM) (www.biakelsey.com, 2012) reported that "While total annual spending on advertising and promotion remained flat, ... SMBs are allocating more of their marketing dollars to digital presence assets," according to Steve Marshall, director of research at BIA/Kelsey adding that "From Web presence and mobile websites to social media, small businesses are building deeper and broader engagement with customers across a range of digital presence platforms."

It's a proven fact, consultants in general are more valuable and in demand when they are an expert in a specific field rather than a generalist in a wide range of fields. That's where Shapiro Consulting, LLC comes in with both experience and expertise in the field of Web marketing. The firm expects nothing less than long-term relationships with clients by being totally committed and consistently providing the highest levels of customer service. As an avid public speaker, and numerous articles written on the subject of marketing, in particular Web marketing there is no reason to believe the firm will not succeed.

Mr. Shapiro is a member of the American Marketing Association of which he has been a long time contributor to both the *Journal of Marketing* and *Journal of Marketing Research*. He is also a member of the Association of Professional Consultants.

1.2 Mission Statement

The mission of the company is to provide startup, small and medium-sized companies the knowledge and skill needed to master and benefit from Web marketing with the ultimate goal of increasing client sales and profits within the marketplace, while maintaining the highest standard of honesty and ethics in all business practices.

2.0 STRATEGIC & MARKET ANALYSIS

2.1 Market Analysis

With more than 260,000 businesses, Chicago is a prime market when your sights are focused on startup, small to mid-sized businesses, or any size for that matter. With over 400 corporate headquarters, 30 S&P 500 companies, 29 Fortune 500 headquarters, and 10 Fortune Global 500 headquarters it's obvious Chicago is a prime market for marketing consultants who should expect high returns for their services. In 2012 alone, 129 new and expanding companies came online in which translated into 34.8 million square feet of expansions.

According to the Small Business Advocacy Council (SBAC), of the 1.1 million businesses in Illinois, an estimated 870,000 are self-employed. The SBAC also reported that approximately half the state's employees work at small to medium-sized companies. Through outside research of marketing consultants, Mr. Shapiro learned the majority of firms focus on management marketing. He also learned his prices are reasonably priced compared to his peers.

2.2 Industry Analysis

According to the Small Business Administration (SBA), "The small business sector in America occupies 30-50% of all commercial space, an estimated 2—34 billion square feet," adding that "the small business sector is growing rapidly. While corporate America has been 'downsizing,' the rate of small business 'start-ups' has grown, and the rate for small business failures has declined."

In "Small Business by the Numbers," released by the National Small Business Association revealed over 70 million Americans either work or are owners of small businesses. In fact, 99.7 percent of all employer firms are small businesses. According to the Census Bureau's Survey of Business Owners, an estimated half or 51.6 percent of all businesses were home-based businesses.

2.3 Target Market

The firm has identified a great local market populated with fast-growing small businesses within the Chicago Metropolitan area. The firm plans to target home-based businesses on a consulting basis to help them grow their Web marketing efforts, including the new companies that have recently opened.

2.4 Competition

Companies in Chicago and the surrounding metropolitan area command the expertise of marketing professionals to grow their businesses, however there are many marketing consultants vying for the same companies. It is up to the marketing consultant to sell its services and Shapiro Consulting, LLC has carved out a particular niche that separates the firm from its competition.

Strengths:
- Level of experience
- The scope of small businesses in Chicago with a real need for Shapiro's services

Weaknesses:
- Need to establish credibility of new firm
- Need to build client base

3.0 MANAGEMENT SUMMARY

Shapiro Consulting, LLC is owned and operated by Mr. Brandon Shapiro, a seasoned marketing consultant spanning 13 years and counting. With an MBA under his belt from the University of Illinois at Chicago he joined Armstrong Marketing, Inc. where he worked as a management analyst prior to opening Shapiro Consulting, LLC.

4.0 PROFESSIONAL AND ADVISORY SUPPORT

The firm has retained Miller & Schuller P.C. to assist with the legal aspects of operating a home-based marketing consultant business. Draper Accounting Services set the firm up using QuickBooks that can conveniently print checks, pay bills, and track expenses; invoice customers and track payments and sales taxes; generate reports, including profit and loss, statement of cash flows, balance sheet, sales reports, and more; tracks information for taxes to share with accountant. A line of credit was established at Chicago Commercial Bank, a business checking account was opened, including a merchant account for accepting credit card payments.

5.0 GROWTH STRATEGY

The firm plans to focus on word-of-mouth referrals and if necessary, the owner is prepared to expand beyond local markets in the event they become saturated.

1. Pay close attention when compiling proposal or letter of intent. Be clear of the agreed upon project, intended results with pricing clearly stated.

2. Keep in touch with clients.

3. Stay within clients' budget

4. Always be prompt.

5. Keep clients informed.

6. Know and recognize competition.

7. Continue delivering speeches.

8. Promote potential clients by offering workshops and seminars.

9. Network through community events.

10. Always be accessible to clients and potential clients.

11. Stay up-to-date on up-and-coming technology and marketing trends to inform prior and new clients.

12. Reward clients with a discount on next project for referrals along with a thank you note.

13. Build a contact database with contact's name and title, address and phone, fax, e-mail, and marketing needs.

6.0 PRODUCTS AND SERVICES

Shapiro Consulting, LLC provides a clear understanding of what Web marketing is and how startup, small and medium-sized businesses can benefit.

- How to build content and compete effectively

- How to build a keyword list to optimize company website

- How to create and manage mailing lists

- How to incorporate social media that gets results

- Improved search engine ranking and increased site traffic

- Online press release

- Web analytics to boost profits

- Importance of the tagline

- How to benefit from blogs

- Online articles and newsletters

- Viral marketing

- Mobile marketing

- Tracking system

- YouTube video marketing

- Custom blog themes

Fees

Shapiro Consulting, LLC plans to price marketing services either hourly at $145 per hour, on a per-item or per project basis. As a means to keep a money flow, Shapiro Consulting, LLC offers a 1% discount for invoices paid in less than 30 days. The firm will continue to monitor competitor's fees and adjust accordingly. The firm has learned that e-mail invoicing works best, especially when there is a question or concern by the client since it will be addressed sooner rather than later holding up payment. Project-related expenses such as business travel, copying; phone calls, courier or overnight mailing service, postage, etc. will be considered reimbursable expenses and will be specified in the contract.

6.1 Other services

The firm also provides startup, small and medium-sized companies 1 or 2 day onsite social media workshop with the company's social media team. Fees will be based on number of days and on level of Web marketing discussed. Topics covered include how to collect testimonials, interpreting sales statistics, measuring social media, search engines and how they work, integrating e-mail in social media, putting together a webcast, webinar, or web conference and more. The firm also offers consulting services by the hour at $100.

Fees

Half-day (up to 4 hours)—$2,000-$3,500

Full-day (6-8 hours)—$4,000-$6,000

7.0 MARKETING PLAN

Shapiro Consulting, LLC plans to maintain an extensive marketing campaign that reaches its targeted market. An overview of both marketing objectives and strategies are listed below.

7.1 Marketing Objectives

- Establish credibility

- Create a professional image

- Referrals

7.2 Marketing Strategies

The firm plans to revisit their marketing efforts to see what's working and eliminate what isn't.

1. Continue building portfolio

2. Build partnership with clients

3. Deliver proposals or letters of intent to clients personally

4. Always monitor competitors

5. Start a free electronic newsletter

6. Networking with potential clients

7. Become a member of the Chamber of Commerce

8. Provide free initial consultation

9. Offer new client discount of $15

10. Have a minimum of three references

11. Use of mailing lists

12. Walk-ins

13. Cold calls

14. Build Web site

8.0 OPERATIONS

A support system has been put in place to focus on the principle business, marketing. The company has hired Ms. Amy Sloan who is going to work a couple mornings a week as an assistant. As the workload increases Ms. Sloan will become a full-time employee of Shapiro Consulting, LLC. In addition, Shapiro Consulting, LLC signed up with Armstrong Temp Service in the event the firm is overwhelmed with clients than time to accommodate. The firm also plans to sub-contract work to other trustworthy independent marketing consultants when the marketing project is out of their scope of work or unable to handle the extra workload. The firm will consider moving into leased office space and hire additional employees, including consultants if the number of clients exceeds expectations.

9.0 FINANCIAL ANALYSIS

9.1 2013 balance sheet

Revenue

Consulting/billable hours—$141,000

Onsite consulting—$12,000

Public speaking—$1,500

Article contribution—$1,000

Total revenue—$155,500

9.2 Expenses

Business License—$250

Business liability Insurance—$400

Small safe for back-up disks—$200

Two worktables—$100

Two file cabinets—$100

Bookshelves—$75

Desk/chair—$200

Home security system (optional)—$500

2 line phone—$100

Computer equipment—$2,000

Fax/copier/scanner—$100

Office supplies (paper, folders, pens, etc.)—$500

Internet access—$100

Professional services (lawyer, accountant, etc.)—$500

Professional memberships—$350

Advertising—$1,000

Web site—$100

Travel (airfare, hotel, rental cars)—$1,000

Postage (overnight fees)—$500

Salary—$20,000

Total—$28,075

Net income—$127,425

Martial Arts School

Zen Martial Arts

PO Box 6721
Elmhurst, NY 11373

BizPlanDB.com

Zen Martial Arts is a New York based corporation that will provide many levels of martial arts training (specifically focused on Karate) as well sales of apparel/martial arts goods to customers in its targeted market. The Company was founded by Chelsea Wolfbauer.

1.0 EXECUTIVE SUMMARY

The purpose of this business plan is to raise $100,000 for the development of a martial arts school/studio while showcasing the expected financials and operations over the next three years. Zen Martial Arts is a New York based corporation that will provide many levels of martial arts training (specifically focused on Karate) as well sales of apparel/martial arts goods to customers in its targeted market. The Company was founded by Chelsea Wolfbauer.

1.1 The Services

Zen Martial Arts will provide its customers with white belt through black belt instruction for learning karate. The Company anticipates having 200 students enrolled in the Company's class services on a monthly basis. The facility will provide instruction for people aged 3 and older. Classes will be held on a daily basis.

For younger and middle school aged children, Zen Martial Arts will offer after school and summer camp programs that provide intensive training.

Finally, the business will generate secondary revenue streams from the sale of apparel and related martial arts merchandise sold at the Company's location.

The third section of the business plan will further describe the services offered by Zen Martial Arts.

1.2 Financing

Ms. Wolfbauer is seeking to raise $100,000 from as a bank loan. The interest rate and loan agreement are to be further discussed during negotiation. This business plan assumes that the business will receive a 10 year loan with a 9% fixed interest rate. The financing will be used for the following:

- Development of the Company's location.
- Financing for the first six months of operation.
- Capital to purchase inventory.

Ms. Wolfbauer will contribute $10,000 to the venture.

135

1.3 Mission Statement

Zen Martial Arts' mission is to become the recognized local leader for providing martial arts instruction while concurrently boosting customers (both children and adults) self-esteem and self-defense abilities.

1.4 Management Team

The Company was founded by Chelsea Wolfbauer. Ms. Wolfbauer has more than 10 years of experience in the martial arts industry. Through his expertise, she will be able to bring the operations of the business to profitability within its first year of operations.

1.5 Sales Forecasts

Ms. Wolfbauer expects a strong rate of growth at the start of operations. Below are the expected financials over the next three years.

Proforma profit and loss (yearly)

Year	1	2	3
Sales	$487,578	$585,094	$684,560
Operating costs	$286,453	$297,697	$309,360
EBITDA	$116,074	$185,335	$255,787
Taxes, interest, and depreciation	$ 56,953	$ 79,576	$105,937
Net profit	$ 59,121	$105,759	$149,851

Sales, operating costs, and profit forecast

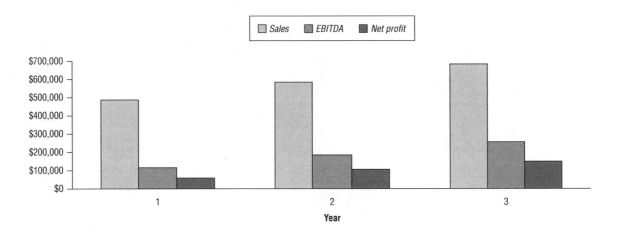

1.6 Expansion Plan

The Founder expects that the business will aggressively expand during the first three years of operation. Ms. Wolfbauer intends to implement marketing campaigns that will effectively target individuals (and families with children) within the target market.

2.0 COMPANY AND FINANCING SUMMARY

2.1 Registered Name and Corporate Structure

The Company is registered as a corporation in the State of New York.

2.2 Required Funds

At this time, Zen Martial Arts requires $100,000 of debt funds. Below is a breakdown of how these funds will be used:

Projected startup costs

Initial lease payments and deposits	$ 10,000
Working capital	$ 35,000
FF&E	$ 23,000
Leasehold improvements	$ 5,000
Security deposits	$ 5,000
Insurance	$ 2,500
Inventory	$ 17,000
Marketing budget	$ 7,500
Miscellaneous and unforeseen costs	$ 5,000
Total startup costs	**$110,000**

Use of funds

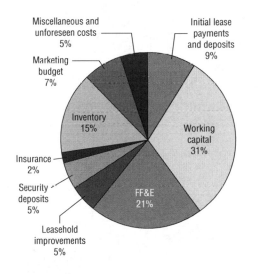

2.3 Investor Equity

Ms. Wolfbauer is not seeking an investment from a third party at this time.

2.4 Management Equity

Chelsea Wolfbauer owns 100% of Zen Martial Arts, Inc.

2.5 Exit Strategy

If the business is very successful, Ms. Wolfbauer may seek to sell the business to a third party for a significant earnings multiple. Most likely, the Company will hire a qualified business broker to sell the business on behalf of Zen Martial Arts, Inc. Based on historical numbers, the business could fetch a sales premium of up to 4 times earnings.

3.0 PRODUCTS AND SERVICES

Below is a description of the services offered by Zen Martial Arts.

3.1 Martial Arts Instruction

As stated in the executive summary, Zen Martial Arts will teach a full range of classes for people of all ages and experience levels. The Company's instructors will be black belt ranked that are capable of training individuals ages 3 and up in the Chinese martial art. Ms. Wolfbauer anticipates that the business will have 200 students enrolled at any given time.

Each class to be offered by the business will be specific to the level and age of the participants.

The Company will also develop after school programs that are specifically geared towards elementary and middle school aged children. Ms. Wolfbauer intends to generate referrals from local schools to drive interest in these programs. During the summer, Zen Martial Arts, Inc. intends to operate a summer camp which will provide intensive training to students in the same age range as the after school programs.

It should be noted that the Company will always comply with all regulations regarding the employment of people that work with children. Each employee retained by the Company will undergo an extensive background check coupled with a drug test. The business only hires people that are qualified to handle the needs of children and those that do not have any past criminal record.

3.2 Sales of Martial Arts Apparel and Related Products

The Company's secondary revenue streams will come from the sale of martial arts apparel (such as karate uniforms) as well as gloves, belts, and other merchandise associated with the Company's martial arts instruction programs. Ms. Wolfbauer anticipates that this aspect of the business will generate 25% of the Company's aggregate revenues.

4.0 STRATEGIC AND MARKET ANALYSIS

4.1 Economic Outlook

This section of the analysis will detail the economic climate, the martial arts teaching industry, the customer profile, and the competition that the business will face as it progresses through its business operations.

Currently, the economic market condition in the United States is moderate. The meltdown of the sub prime mortgage market coupled with increasing gas prices has led many people to believe that the US is on the cusp of a double dip economic recession. This slowdown in the economy has also greatly impacted real estate sales, which has halted to historical lows.

4.2 Industry Analysis

There are over 2,000 martial arts training establishments in the United States. These businesses produce over $4 billon dollars a year in gross receipts. Additionally, the business employs over 50,000 people, and generates payroll figures of $1.45 billion dollars a year. The industry has experienced a tremendous rate of growth over the last ten years.

Studies have shown that parents are now spending 500% more on children per year (adjusted for inflation). Additionally, there is an extremely fast growing problem with obesity in the United States among children and adults alike. According to the Department of Health and Human Services, 1 and 3 children will contract diabetes in their lifetime as a result of obesity. As such, martial arts instruction provides these potential customers with a method of managing and improving their health while concurrently increasing their self confidence.

4.3 Customer Profile

Zen Martial Arts' average client will be a middle to upper middle class man or woman (including parents that are simply enrolling their children) living in the Company's target market. Common traits among clients will include:

- Annual household income exceeding $50,000

- Lives or works no more than 15 miles from the Company's location.

- Will spend $125 to $200 per month on martial arts instruction for themselves or their children.

4.4 Competition

Martial arts instruction is a highly specialized field. Ms. Wolfbauer has extensive experience in a number of disciplines as it relates to self defense and martial arts. As such, the business (due to Ms. Wolfbauer's expansive knowledge and tutelage abilities) will be able to retain a strong competitive advantage as she is well versed in a number of different types of martial arts training. Additionally, the Company will maintain a strong competitive advantage over other competitors by keeping fees reasonably priced so that individuals from all socioeconomic classes can participate in his programs outlined in the third section of the business plan.

5.0 MARKETING PLAN

Zen Martial Arts intends to maintain an extensive marketing campaign that will ensure maximum visibility for the business in its targeted market. Below is an overview of the marketing strategies and objectives of the Company.

5.1 Marketing Objectives

- Develop an online presence by developing a website and placing the Company's name and contact information with online directories.

- Implement a local campaign with the Company's targeted market via the use of flyers, local newspaper advertisements, and word of mouth advertising.

- Establish relationships with local teachers/gym coaches within the targeted market.

5.2 Marketing Strategies

Ms. Wolfbauer intends on using a number of marketing strategies that will allow Zen Martial Arts to easily target men, women, and families within the target market. These strategies include traditional print advertisements and ads placed on search engines on the Internet. Below is a description of how the business intends to market its services to the general public.

Zen Martial Arts will also maintain a website that showcases the many disciplines of martial arts offered by the Company. The business will also integrate e-commerce functionality into the website so that individuals can register themselves (or their children) directly into classes. On the website, the fees and class schedules will be posted on a weekly basis. Competitors within this area do not offer the same level of ease as it relates to this matter, and Zen Martial Arts will retain a strong degree of advantage by offering this functionality to its customers.

The Company will maintain a sizable amount of print and traditional advertising methods within local markets to promote the martial art instruction services that the Company is selling. Finally, Ms. Wolfbauer will develop referral relationships with local teachers and schools to further increase enrollment in the Company's after school and summer camp programs.

5.3 Pricing

Zen Martial Arts, Inc. will charge $125 per month for weekly instruction regarding martial arts. The business, for each new customer, will also charge a one time $75 registration fee.

6.0 ORGANIZATIONAL PLAN AND PERSONNEL SUMMARY

6.1 Corporate Organization

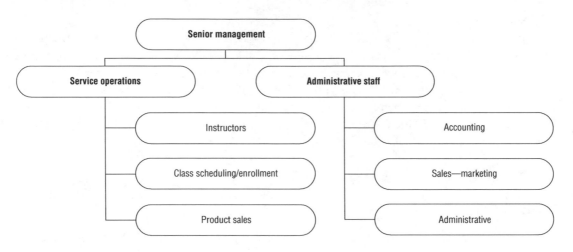

6.2 Organizational Budget

Personnel plan—yearly

Year	1	2	3
Owner	$ 40,000	$ 41,200	$ 42,436
Assistant manager	$ 35,000	$ 36,050	$ 37,132
Martial arts instructors	$ 81,000	$ 83,430	$ 85,933
Bookkeeper (P/T)	$ 12,500	$ 12,875	$ 13,261
Administrative	$ 22,000	$ 22,660	$ 23,340
Total	**$190,500**	**$196,215**	**$202,101**

Numbers of personnel			
Owner	1	1	1
Assistant manager	1	1	1
Martial arts instructors	3	3	3
Bookkeeper (P/T)	1	1	1
Administrative	1	1	1
Totals	**7**	**7**	**7**

Personnel expense breakdown

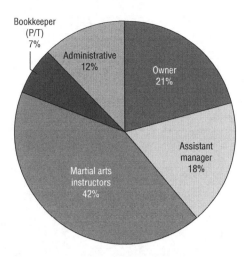

7.0 FINANCIAL PLAN

7.1 Underlying Assumptions

The Company has based its proforma financial statements on the following:

- Zen Martial Arts, Inc. will have an annual revenue growth rate of 16% per year.

- The Owner will acquire $100,000 of debt funds to develop the business.

- The loan will have a 10 year term with a 9% interest rate.

7.2 Sensitivity Analysis

The Company's revenues are moderately sensitive to changes in the general economy. However, the demand among children and teens for healthy lifestyles is growing as parents realize the importance of children having a physical outlet (like martial arts). Management expects that many parents will classify their children's martial art instruction as a necessity and will continue to pay for monthly fees regardless of the general economic climate.

7.3 Source of Funds

Financing

Equity contributions	
Management investment	$ 10,000.00
Total equity financing	**$ 10,000.00**
Banks and lenders	
Banks and lenders	$ 100,000.00
Total debt financing	**$100,000.00**
Total financing	**$110,000.00**

7.4 General Assumptions

General assumptions

Year	1	2	3
Short term interest rate	9.5%	9.5%	9.5%
Long term interest rate	10.0%	10.0%	10.0%
Federal tax rate	33.0%	33.0%	33.0%
State tax rate	5.0%	5.0%	5.0%
Personnel taxes	15.0%	15.0%	15.0%

7.5 Profit and Loss Statements

Proforma profit and loss (yearly)

Year	1	2	3
Sales	**$487,578**	**$585,094**	**$684,560**
Cost of goods sold	$ 85,051	$102,061	$119,412
Gross margin	82.56%	82.56%	82.56%
Operating income	**$402,527**	**$483,032**	**$565,148**
Expenses			
Payroll	$190,500	$196,215	$202,101
General and administrative	$ 14,400	$ 14,976	$ 15,575
Marketing expenses	$ 5,851	$ 7,021	$ 8,215
Professional fees and licensure	$ 5,219	$ 5,376	$ 5,537
Insurance costs	$ 7,500	$ 7,875	$ 8,269
Travel and vehicle costs	$ 8,500	$ 9,350	$ 10,285
Rent and utilities	$ 24,250	$ 25,463	$ 26,736
Miscellaneous costs	$ 1,658	$ 1,989	$ 2,328
Payroll taxes	$ 28,575	$ 29,432	$ 30,315
Total operating costs	**$286,453**	**$297,697**	**$309,360**
EBITDA	**$116,074**	**$185,335**	**$255,787**
Federal income tax	$ 38,304	$ 58,477	$ 81,945
State income tax	$ 5,804	$ 8,860	$ 12,416
Interest expense	$ 8,738	$ 8,131	$ 7,468
Depreciation expenses	$ 4,107	$ 4,107	$ 4,107
Net profit	**$ 59,121**	**$105,759**	**$149,851**
Profit margin	**12.13%**	**18.08%**	**21.89%**

Sales, operating costs, and profit forecast

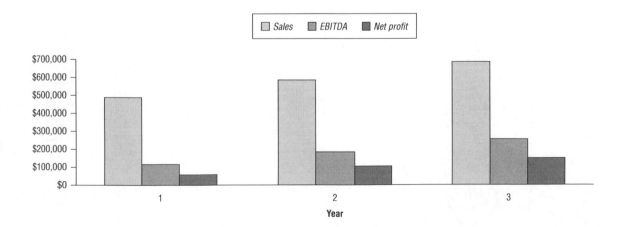

7.6 Cash Flow Analysis

Proforma cash flow analysis—yearly

Year	1	2	3
Cash from operations	$ 63,228	$109,866	$153,958
Cash from receivables	$ 0	$ 0	$ 0
Operating cash inflow	**$ 63,228**	**$109,866**	**$153,958**
Other cash inflows			
Equity investment	$ 10,000	$ 0	$ 0
Increased borrowings	$100,000	$ 0	$ 0
Sales of business assets	$ 0	$ 0	$ 0
A/P increases	$ 37,902	$ 43,587	$ 50,125
Total other cash inflows	**$147,902**	**$ 43,587**	**$ 50,125**
Total cash inflow	**$211,130**	**$153,454**	**$204,083**
Cash outflows			
Repayment of principal	$ 6,463	$ 7,070	$ 7,733
A/P decreases	$ 24,897	$ 29,876	$ 35,852
A/R increases	$ 0	$ 0	$ 0
Asset purchases	$ 57,500	$ 27,467	$ 38,489
Dividends	$ 44,260	$ 76,907	$107,771
Total cash outflows	**$133,120**	**$141,319**	**$189,845**
Net cash flow	**$ 78,010**	**$ 12,135**	**$ 14,239**
Cash balance	**$ 78,010**	**$ 90,145**	**$104,383**

Proforma cash flow (yearly)

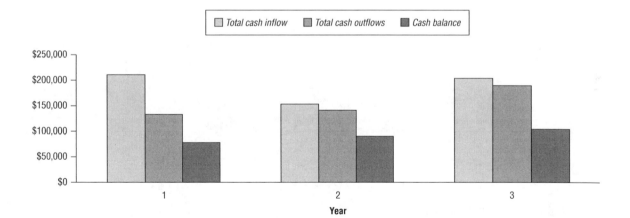

7.7 Balance Sheet

Proforma balance sheet—yearly

Year	1	2	3
Assets			
Cash	$ 78,010	$ 90,145	$104,383
Amortized development/expansion costs	$ 17,500	$ 20,247	$ 24,096
Inventory	$ 17,000	$ 30,733	$ 49,978
FF&E	$ 23,000	$ 33,987	$ 49,382
Accumulated depreciation	($ 4,107)	($ 8,214)	($ 12,321)
Total assets	**$131,403**	**$166,897**	**$215,518**
Liabilities and equity			
Accounts payable	$ 13,005	$ 26,716	$ 40,990
Long term liabilities	$ 93,537	$ 86,467	$ 79,397
Other liabilities	$ 0	$ 0	$ 0
Total liabilities	**$106,542**	**$113,183**	**$120,387**
Net worth	**$ 24,861**	**$ 53,714**	**$ 95,131**
Total liabilities and equity	**$131,403**	**$166,897**	**$215,518**

Proforma balance sheet

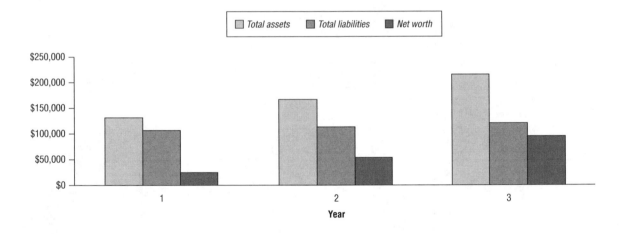

7.8 Breakeven Analysis

Monthly break even analysis

Year	1	2	3
Monthly revenue	$ 28,915	$ 30,050	$ 31,227
Yearly revenue	$346,978	$360,598	$374,726

Break even analysis

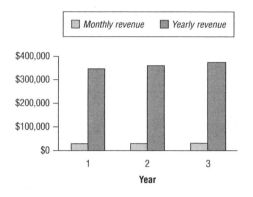

7.9 Business Ratios

Business ratios—yearly

Year	1	2	3
Sales			
Sales growth	0.00%	20.00%	17.00%
Gross margin	82.60%	82.60%	82.60%
Financials			
Profit margin	12.13%	18.08%	21.89%
Assets to liabilities	1.23	1.47	1.79
Equity to liabilities	0.23	0.47	0.79
Assets to equity	5.29	3.11	2.27
Liquidity			
Acid test	0.73	0.80	0.87
Cash to assets	0.59	0.54	0.48

7.10 Three Year Profit and Loss Statement

Profit and loss statement (first year)

Months	1	2	3	4	5	6	7
Sales	$39,900	$40,033	$40,166	$40,299	$40,432	$40,565	$40,698
Cost of goods sold	$ 6,960	$ 6,983	$ 7,006	$ 7,030	$ 7,053	$ 7,076	$ 7,099
Gross margin	82.60%	82.60%	82.60%	82.60%	82.60%	82.60%	82.60%
Operating income	$32,940	$33,050	$33,160	$33,269	$33,379	$33,489	$33,599
Expenses							
Payroll	$15,875	$15,875	$15,875	$15,875	$15,875	$15,875	$15,875
General and administrative	$ 1,200	$ 1,200	$ 1,200	$ 1,200	$ 1,200	$ 1,200	$ 1,200
Marketing expenses	$ 488	$ 488	$ 488	$ 488	$ 488	$ 488	$ 488
Professional fees and licensure	$ 435	$ 435	$ 435	$ 435	$ 435	$ 435	$ 435
Insurance costs	$ 625	$ 625	$ 625	$ 625	$ 625	$ 625	$ 625
Travel and vehicle costs	$ 708	$ 708	$ 708	$ 708	$ 708	$ 708	$ 708
Rent and utilities	$ 2,021	$ 2,021	$ 2,021	$ 2,021	$ 2,021	$ 2,021	$ 2,021
Miscellaneous costs	$ 138	$ 138	$ 138	$ 138	$ 138	$ 138	$ 138
Payroll taxes	$ 2,381	$ 2,381	$ 2,381	$ 2,381	$ 2,381	$ 2,381	$ 2,381
Total operating costs	$23,871	$23,871	$23,871	$23,871	$23,871	$23,871	$23,871
EBITDA	$ 9,069	$ 9,179	$ 9,289	$ 9,398	$ 9,508	$ 9,618	$ 9,728
Federal income tax	$ 3,135	$ 3,145	$ 3,155	$ 3,166	$ 3,176	$ 3,187	$ 3,197
State income tax	$ 475	$ 477	$ 478	$ 480	$ 481	$ 483	$ 484
Interest expense	$ 750	$ 746	$ 742	$ 738	$ 734	$ 730	$ 726
Depreciation expense	$ 342	$ 342	$ 342	$ 342	$ 342	$ 342	$ 342
Net profit	$ 4,367	$ 4,469	$ 4,570	$ 4,672	$ 4,774	$ 4,876	$ 4,977

Profit and loss statement (first year cont.)

Month	8	9	10	11	12	1
Sales	**$40,831**	**$40,964**	**$41,097**	**$41,230**	**$41,363**	**$487,578**
Cost of goods sold	$ 7,122	$ 7,146	$ 7,169	$ 7,192	$ 7,215	$ 85,051
Gross margin	82.60%	82.60%	82.60%	82.60%	82.60%	82.60%
Operating income	**$33,709**	**$33,818**	**$33,928**	**$34,038**	**$34,148**	**$402,527**
Expenses						
Payroll	$ 15,875	$ 15,875	$ 15,875	$ 15,875	$ 15,875	$190,500
General and administrative	$ 1,200	$ 1,200	$ 1,200	$ 1,200	$ 1,200	$ 14,400
Marketing expenses	$ 488	$ 488	$ 488	$ 488	$ 488	$ 5,851
Professional fees and licensure	$ 435	$ 435	$ 435	$ 435	$ 435	$ 5,219
Insurance costs	$ 625	$ 625	$ 625	$ 625	$ 625	$ 7,500
Travel and vehicle costs	$ 708	$ 708	$ 708	$ 708	$ 708	$ 8,500
Rent and utilities	$ 2,021	$ 2,021	$ 2,021	$ 2,021	$ 2,021	$ 24,250
Miscellaneous costs	$ 138	$ 138	$ 138	$ 138	$ 138	$ 1,658
Payroll taxes	$ 2,381	$ 2,381	$ 2,381	$ 2,381	$ 2,381	$ 28,575
Total operating costs	**$23,871**	**$23,871**	**$23,871**	**$23,871**	**$23,871**	**$286,453**
EBITDA	**$ 9,838**	**$ 9,947**	**$10,057**	**$10,167**	**$10,277**	**$116,074**
Federal income tax	$ 3,208	$ 3,218	$ 3,229	$ 3,239	$ 3,250	$ 38,304
State income tax	$ 486	$ 488	$ 489	$ 491	$ 492	$ 5,804
Interest expense	$ 722	$ 718	$ 714	$ 710	$ 706	$ 8,738
Depreciation expense	$ 342	$ 342	$ 342	$ 342	$ 342	$ 4,107
Net profit	**$ 5,079**	**$ 5,181**	**$ 5,283**	**$ 5,385**	**$ 5,487**	**$ 59,121**

Profit and loss statement (second year)

Quarter	Q1	2 Q2	Q3	Q4	2
Sales	**$117,019**	**$146,273**	**$157,975**	**$163,826**	**$585,094**
Cost of goods sold	$ 20,412	$ 25,515	$ 27,557	$ 28,577	$102,061
Gross margin	82.60%	82.60%	82.60%	82.60%	82.60%
Operating income	**$ 96,606**	**$120,758**	**$130,419**	**$135,249**	**$483,032**
Expenses					
Payroll	$ 39,243	$ 49,054	$ 52,978	$ 54,940	$196,215
General and administrative	$ 2,995	$ 3,744	$ 4,044	$ 4,193	$ 14,976
Marketing expenses	$ 1,404	$ 1,755	$ 1,896	$ 1,966	$ 7,021
Professional fees and licensure	$ 1,075	$ 1,344	$ 1,451	$ 1,505	$ 5,376
Insurance costs	$ 1,575	$ 1,969	$ 2,126	$ 2,205	$ 7,875
Travel and vehicle costs	$ 1,870	$ 2,338	$ 2,525	$ 2,618	$ 9,350
Rent and utilities	$ 5,093	$ 6,366	$ 6,875	$ 7,130	$ 25,463
Miscellaneous costs	$ 398	$ 497	$ 537	$ 557	$ 1,989
Payroll taxes	$ 5,886	$ 7,358	$ 7,947	$ 8,241	$ 29,432
Total operating costs	**$ 59,539**	**$ 74,424**	**$ 80,378**	**$ 83,355**	**$297,697**
EBITDA	**$ 37,067**	**$ 46,334**	**$ 50,041**	**$ 51,894**	**$185,335**
Federal income tax	$ 11,695	$ 14,619	$ 15,789	$ 16,374	$ 58,477
State income tax	$ 1,772	$ 2,215	$ 2,392	$ 2,481	$ 8,860
Interest expense	$ 2,092	$ 2,053	$ 2,013	$ 1,973	$ 8,131
Depreciation expense	$ 1,027	$ 1,027	$ 1,027	$ 1,027	$ 4,107
Net profit	**$ 20,481**	**$ 26,420**	**$ 28,819**	**$ 30,040**	**$105,759**

Profit and loss statement (third year)

Quarter	Q1	3 Q2	Q3	Q4	3
Sales	**$136,912**	**$171,140**	**$184,831**	**$191,677**	**$684,560**
Cost of goods sold	$ 23,882	$ 29,853	$ 32,241	$ 33,435	$119,412
Gross margin	82.60%	82.60%	82.60%	82.60%	82.60%
Operating income	**$113,030**	**$141,287**	**$152,590**	**$158,241**	**$565,148**
Expenses					
Payroll	$ 40,420	$ 50,525	$ 54,567	$ 56,588	$202,101
General and administrative	$ 3,115	$ 3,894	$ 4,205	$ 4,361	$ 15,575
Marketing expenses	$ 1,643	$ 2,054	$ 2,218	$ 2,300	$ 8,215
Professional fees and licensure	$ 1,107	$ 1,384	$ 1,495	$ 1,550	$ 5,537
Insurance costs	$ 1,654	$ 2,067	$ 2,233	$ 2,315	$ 8,269
Travel and vehicle costs	$ 2,057	$ 2,571	$ 2,777	$ 2,880	$ 10,285
Rent and utilities	$ 5,347	$ 6,684	$ 7,219	$ 7,486	$ 26,736
Miscellaneous costs	$ 466	$ 582	$ 628	$ 652	$ 2,328
Payroll taxes	$ 6,063	$ 7,579	$ 8,185	$ 8,488	$ 30,315
Total operating costs	**$ 61,872**	**$ 77,340**	**$ 83,527**	**$ 86,621**	**$309,360**
EBITDA	**$ 51,157**	**$ 63,947**	**$ 69,063**	**$ 71,620**	**$255,787**
Federal income tax	$ 16,389	$ 20,406	$ 22,125	$ 22,945	$ 81,945
State income tax	$ 2,483	$ 3,104	$ 3,352	$ 3,476	$ 12,416
Interest expense	$ 1,932	$ 1,889	$ 1,846	$ 1,802	$ 7,468
Depreciation expense	$ 1,027	$ 1,027	$ 1,027	$ 1,027	$ 4,107
Net profit	**$ 29,327**	**$ 37,441**	**$ 40,712**	**$ 42,371**	**$149,851**

7.11 Three Year Cash Flow Analysis

Cash flow analysis (first year)

Month	1	2	3	4	5	6	7
Cash from operations	$ 4,709	$ 4,811	$ 4,913	$ 5,014	$ 5,116	$ 5,218	$ 5,320
Cash from receivables	$ 0	$ 0	$ 0	$ 0	$ 0	$ 0	$ 0
Operating cash inflow	**$ 4,709**	**$ 4,811**	**$ 4,913**	**$ 5,014**	**$ 5,116**	**$ 5,218**	**$ 5,320**
Other cash inflows							
Equity investment	$ 10,000	$ 0	$ 0	$ 0	$ 0	$ 0	$ 0
Increased borrowings	$100,000	$ 0	$ 0	$ 0	$ 0	$ 0	$ 0
Sales of business assets	$ 0	$ 0	$ 0	$ 0	$ 0	$ 0	$ 0
A/P increases	$ 3,159	$ 3,159	$ 3,159	$ 3,159	$ 3,159	$ 3,159	$ 3,159
Total other cash inflows	**$113,159**	**$ 3,159**	**$ 3,159**	**$ 3,159**	**$ 3,159**	**$ 3,159**	**$ 3,159**
Total cash inflow	**$117,868**	**$ 7,970**	**$ 8,071**	**$ 8,173**	**$ 8,275**	**$ 8,376**	**$ 8,478**
Cash outflows							
Repayment of principal	$ 517	$ 521	$ 525	$ 528	$ 532	$ 536	$ 540
A/P decreases	$ 2,075	$ 2,075	$ 2,075	$ 2,075	$ 2,075	$ 2,075	$ 2,075
A/R increases	$ 0	$ 0	$ 0	$ 0	$ 0	$ 0	$ 0
Asset purchases	$ 57,500	$ 0	$ 0	$ 0	$ 0	$ 0	$ 0
Dividends	$ 0	$ 0	$ 0	$ 0	$ 0	$ 0	$ 0
Total cash outflows	**$ 60,092**	**$ 2,595**	**$ 2,599**	**$ 2,603**	**$ 2,607**	**$ 2,611**	**$ 2,615**
Net cash flow	**$ 57,776**	**$ 5,374**	**$ 5,472**	**$ 5,570**	**$ 5,668**	**$ 5,765**	**$ 5,863**
Cash balance	**$ 57,776**	**$63,151**	**$68,623**	**$74,192**	**$79,860**	**$85,625**	**$91,488**

Cash flow analysis (first year cont.)

Month	8	9	10	11	12	1
Cash from operations	$ 5,422	$ 5,523	$ 5,625	$ 5,727	$ 5,829	$ 63,228
Cash from receivables	$ 0	$ 0	$ 0	$ 0	$ 0	$ 0
Operating cash inflow	**$ 5,422**	**$ 5,523**	**$ 5,625**	**$ 5,727**	**$ 5,829**	**$ 63,228**
Other cash inflows						
Equity investment	$ 0	$ 0	$ 0	$ 0	$ 0	$ 10,000
Increased borrowings	$ 0	$ 0	$ 0	$ 0	$ 0	$100,000
Sales of business assets	$ 0	$ 0	$ 0	$ 0	$ 0	$ 0
A/P increases	$ 3,159	$ 3,159	$ 3,159	$ 3,159	$ 3,159	$ 37,902
Total other cash inflows	**$ 3,159**	**$ 3,159**	**$ 3,159**	**$ 3,159**	**$ 3,159**	**$147,902**
Total cash inflow	**$ 8,580**	**$ 8,682**	**$ 8,784**	**$ 8,886**	**$ 8,988**	**$211,130**
Cash outflows						
Repayment of principal	$ 545	$ 549	$ 553	$ 557	$ 561	$ 6,463
A/P decreases	$ 2,075	$ 2,075	$ 2,075	$ 2,075	$ 2,075	$ 24,897
A/R increases	$ 0	$ 0	$ 0	$ 0	$ 0	$ 0
Asset purchases	$ 0	$ 0	$ 0	$ 0	$ 0	$ 57,500
Dividends	$ 0	$ 0	$ 0	$ 0	$44,260	$ 44,260
Total cash outflows	**$ 2,619**	**$ 2,623**	**$ 2,627**	**$ 2,632**	**$46,896**	**$133,120**
Net cash flow	**$ 5,961**	**$ 6,059**	**$ 6,156**	**$ 6,254**	**−$37,908**	**$ 78,010**
Cash balance	**$97,449**	**$103,508**	**$109,664**	**$115,918**	**$78,010**	**$ 78,010**

Cash flow analysis (second year)

Quarter	Q1	2 Q2	Q3	Q4	2
Cash from operations	$21,973	$27,467	$29,664	$30,763	$109,866
Cash from receivables	$ 0	$ 0	$ 0	$ 0	$ 0
Operating cash inflow	**$21,973**	**$27,467**	**$29,664**	**$30,763**	**$109,866**
Other cash inflows					
Equity investment	$ 0	$ 0	$ 0	$ 0	$ 0
Increased borrowings	$ 0	$ 0	$ 0	$ 0	$ 0
Sales of business assets	$ 0	$ 0	$ 0	$ 0	$ 0
A/P increases	$ 8,717	$10,897	$11,769	$12,204	$ 43,587
Total other cash inflows	**$ 8,717**	**$10,897**	**$11,769**	**$12,204**	**$ 43,587**
Total cash inflow	**$30,691**	**$38,363**	**$41,433**	**$42,967**	**$153,454**
Cash outflows					
Repayment of principal	$ 1,708	$ 1,747	$ 1,787	$ 1,827	$ 7,070
A/P decreases	$ 5,975	$ 7,469	$ 8,067	$ 8,365	$ 29,876
A/R increases	$ 0	$ 0	$ 0	$ 0	$ 0
Asset purchases	$ 5,493	$ 6,867	$ 7,416	$ 7,691	$ 27,467
Dividends	$15,381	$19,227	$20,765	$21,534	$ 76,907
Total cash outflows	**$28,558**	**$35,310**	**$38,034**	**$39,417**	**$141,319**
Net cash flow	**$ 2,132**	**$ 3,054**	**$ 3,398**	**$ 3,550**	**$ 12,135**
Cash balance	**$80,142**	**$83,196**	**$86,595**	**$90,145**	**$ 90,145**

Cash flow analysis (third year)

Quarter	Q1	Q2	Q3	Q4	3
Cash from operations	$30,792	$38,489	$ 41,569	$ 43,108	$153,958
Cash from receivables	$ 0	$ 0	$ 0	$ 0	$ 0
Operating cash inflow	**$30,792**	**$38,489**	**$ 41,569**	**$ 43,108**	**$153,958**
Other cash inflows					
Equity investment	$ 0	$ 0	$ 0	$ 0	$ 0
Increased borrowings	$ 0	$ 0	$ 0	$ 0	$ 0
Sales of business assets	$ 0	$ 0	$ 0	$ 0	$ 0
A/P increases	$10,025	$12,531	$ 13,534	$ 14,035	$ 50,125
Total other cash inflows	**$10,025**	**$12,531**	**$ 13,534**	**$ 14,035**	**$ 50,125**
Total cash inflow	**$40,817**	**$51,021**	**$ 55,103**	**$ 57,143**	**$204,083**
Cash outflows					
Repayment of principal	$ 1,869	$ 1,911	$ 1,954	$ 1,999	$ 7,733
A/P decreases	$ 7,170	$ 8,963	$ 9,680	$ 10,038	$ 35,852
A/R increases	$ 0	$ 0	$ 0	$ 0	$ 0
Asset purchases	$ 7,698	$ 9,622	$ 10,392	$ 10,777	$ 38,489
Dividends	$21,554	$26,943	$ 29,098	$ 30,176	$107,771
Total cash outflows	**$38,291**	**$47,439**	**$ 51,125**	**$ 52,990**	**$189,845**
Net cash flow	**$ 2,526**	**$ 3,582**	**$ 3,978**	**$ 4,153**	**$ 14,239**
Cash balance	**$92,670**	**$96,252**	**$100,230**	**$104,383**	**$104,383**

Medical Billing Service

Medical Billing Solutions, LLC

248 Linwood Ave.
Worchester, Massachusetts 01605

Brenda Kubiac

Medical Billing Solutions, LLC is an independent medical billing and electronic claims processing business.

1.0 EXECUTIVE SUMMARY

1.1 Business Overview

An article published by Healthcare Business & Technology (www.healthcarebusinesstech.com, 2013) states "It is estimated that doctors in the U.S. leave approximately $125 billion on the table each year due to poor billing practices," adding that, "It is estimated that up to 80% of medical bills contain errors." That's where professional Medical Billers come in—to handle the task of collecting and allowing the doctors to care for their patients.

Medical Billing Solutions, LLC is a Massachusetts-based limited liability medical billing company located in Worchester. The firms' founder, Victoria Caldwell has obtained the necessary certification, business license, and business and liability insurance for conducting a medical billing business in the state of Massachusetts.

Ms. Caldwell is entering the market with both experience as a medical biller and two clients signed up. Through extensive marketing efforts and referrals the firm expects to sign up no less than six additional clients during the first year of operation with a total of 25 or more by the end of the third year. At that time, the firm will relocate from a 400 square foot home-based office to leased office space large enough to bring two full-time medical billing and coders inside the firm. While not a large part of the business, Medical Billing Solutions, LLC also provides consulting services on an as needed basis at $45 per hour.

Ms. Caldwell is an active member of the American Medical Billing Association (AMBA). She plans to continue soliciting for additional clients, including group medical practices, home health agencies, physical therapy practices, psychiatrists, physician offices, psychologists and other allied health professionals in order to meet her goal of 25 clients or more by the close of her third year of operation. Ms. Caldwell is working on obtaining her medical coding certification to compliment her medical billing certification, which in turn will ultimately add to Medical Billing Solutions, LLC bottom line.

1.2 Goals and Objectives

Ms. Caldwell is committed to becoming a strategic player among her peers working in the healthcare industry as a full-practice management medical billing and coding professional. While Ms. Caldwell's title is a medical billing specialist, she is working towards obtaining her medical coding certification through the American Health Information Management Association (AHIMA). Upon completion, her new role as a Certified Professional Coder (CPC) will compliment her Certified Medical Reimbursement Specialist (CMRS) certification and boost her credibility. She is striving to be a stand out in the medical billing and coding profession throughout Worchester and the surrounding area. By attaining her medical coding certification she is well on her way to reaching her goal.

1.3 The Services

Medical Billing Solutions, LLC will perform medical billing for clients, including submitting electronic claims and paper claims in accordance with government regulations and private payer policies to billing patients and tracking accounts payable and receivable. Other services include follow-up on claim status, settling claim denials, and submitting appeals. The firm will also offer consulting services upon request. Both medical billing and consulting services will be performed between the hours of 9:00 a.m. to 5 p.m. Monday through Friday.

1.4 Finance

The company has retained Schellar & Schellar P.C. to assist with the legal aspects of operating a home-based medical billing service business. In addition, Ms. Caldwell brought in Draper Accounting Services, to walk her through every step prior to opening, from installing invoicing and bookkeeping software and setting up books to advising of the best tax structure for her purpose. A line of credit was established at Huron Commercial Bank, a business checking account was opened, and a bank credit card was issued.

1.5 Mission Statement

Medical Billing Solutions, LLC will drastically reduce the amount of time it takes to collect from insurance companies and lower the rejection rate for claims from 30 percent to fewer than 2 percent. Clients will see an immediate cost savings by outsourcing their billing. The firm will also offer clients the highest quality of customer service and privacy.

1.6 Sales Forecasts

Medical Billing Solutions, LLC expects to be profitable during the first year of operation. According to some industry analysts, home-based medical billers can generate an estimated $40,000 annually compared to a medical billing and coding firm that can generate well over $100,000 per year.

1.7 Expansion Plan

Following the first year of operation the firm will provide full-practice management to family practitioners by providing quality billing and patient accounting, as well as sign up an additional 10 clients by the end of the second year with a total of 25 or more by the close of the third year. At that time, the company will move from home office space to leased office space within close proximity of current clients and hire two experienced medical billing and coding professionals.

2.0 COMPANY AND FINANCING SUMMARY

Medical Billing Solutions, LLC is a registered corporation in the state of Massachusetts and is fully financed by founder Victoria Caldwell.

2.1 Management Summary

The company was founded by Victoria Caldwell who received her Certified Medical Reimbursement Specialist (CMRS) certification from the American Medical Billing Association (AMBA). Prior to certification, Victoria spent eight years working as a medical receptionist for Focus Medical Group located in Worcester, Massachusetts. During her tenure, part of her duties included submitting medical claims for payment.

3.0 PRODUCTS AND SERVICES

- Prepare electronic/paper claims (CMS 1500 forms) to insurance companies
- Simple data entry, such as patient information
- Sending out patients' information
- Follow-up on all unpaid insurance claims via email/fax/phone etc.
- Compile reports that are of interest to the doctor
- Office space adheres with HIPAA privacy standards (locked filing cabinet and computer access restricted)
- Consulting services

3.1 Fees
- Set-up fee for clearinghouse account—$300 monthly
- Doctor enrollment form—$50 monthly
- Electronic claims transmissions—$2 to $3
- Paper claims transmissions—$5 to $20
- Reports—$4 each
- Consulting—$45 per hour

4.0 STRATEGIC & MARKET ANALYSIS

4.1 Industry Analysis
According to the Agency for Healthcare Research and Quality (AHRQ), "the United States spends a larger share of its gross domestic product (GDP) on health care than any other major industrialized country. Expenditures for health Care represent nearly one-seventh of the Nation's GDP, and they continue to be one of the fastest growing components of the Federal budget. There are over 35 million hospital stays in the United States every year and during most of these stays, multiple procedures are performed. Three of 5 patients in U.S. hospitals receive at least one procedure during their hospital stay. One in 5 receives three or more."

The Department of Labor Statistics reported the medical billing industry is expected to excel faster than any other occupation from 2010 to 2014. According to the U.S. Department of Health and Human Services Centers for Medicare and Medicaid, health spending will continue to grow by 6.9 percent through 2016. By then, health-care spending will total $4.1 trillion and account for about 19.6 percent of the gross domestic product (GDP). At that time, the United States Bureau of Labor Statistics (BLS) suggested there will be 200,000 medical coders working in the United States.

Additionally, as the population ages, namely the baby boomers there will be an increasing need for both medical and dental services. One of the most important industry developments is the push by the U.S. Presidential Administration to have medical resources available for about 32 million uninsured Americans by 2014 that will ultimately lead to more hospital and doctor's visits, as well as the need for Medical Insurance Billers.

4.2 Market Analysis
During the initial market survey, Ms. Caldwell also learned there are still many within the healthcare industry taking care of their medical billing needs in-house. She doesn't view this as an obstacle, but a need for her services.

A preliminary study of the target market found three other medical billing companies in the Worcester metropolitan area; however, they only offer claims submission with no follow-up services so they pose no threat. Further market research revealed additional medical billers offering full-service, but are not located within a 50-mile radius of Medical Billing Solutions, LLC.

4.3 Target Market

Target prosperous neighborhoods where residents actually have money to go to the doctors. Then, the focus turns to the doctor's offices, medical buildings, clinics, etc. within and around the targeted area. The medical doctors then become the target, especially those who during the initial market analysis were taking care of their medical billing needs in-house and have not been able to consistently submit claims in a timely manner.

4.4 Competition

Strengths:
- Medical billing certification
- Detail oriented
- Good math and data entry skills
- Understanding of insurance claims procedures
- Understanding of medical terms
- Understanding of basic medical diagnosis codes
- Understanding of Medical law (HIPAA) and ethics
- Excellent keyboarding skills
- Two clients under contract

Weaknesses:
- Lack of certification and experience in medical coding
- Competition
- Quoting prices (by percentage, per claim fee, flat monthly fee or hourly rate fee)
- Lack of clients

5.0 MARKETING PLAN

Medical Billing Solutions, LLC plans to examine its target market by interviewing in-house medical billers, as well as potential clients by both a direct survey and face-to-face. This will be accomplished by contacting prospective clients directly by phone or by mail to explain services and set up an initial meeting. An overview of both marketing objectives and strategies are listed below.

5.1 Marketing Objectives
- Establish relationships with other medical billing professionals
- Know what my clients' needs are so they are met
- Learn what potential clients lack in their medical billing needs
- Network daily
- Continue to establish credibility
- Sign up a minimum of six additional clients during the first year of operation
- Always be accessible

5.2 Marketing Strategies

1. Attend local networking events, medical conferences, medical trade shows or other events where hospital administrators and other medical professionals in my target market are among the attendees.

2. Reach targeted market via face-to-face, local newspaper advertisements, and word-of-mouth.

3. Maintain a presence in various business journals along with ads appearing on the Internet.

4. Contact clients and prospects directly to find out what their needs are.

5. Network with medical professionals and other medical billers and coders through LinkedIn, Facebook, and Twitter.

6. Compare services and fees with those of competitors within the same market to compete effectively.

7. Investigate how competitors within my target market are charging to determine if I will charge an hourly rate or flat rate for services.

8. Establish relationships and promote business by joining medical associations.

9. Market services to physicians' offices, hospitals, clinics and other medical professionals.

10. Conduct a direct survey to learn how doctor's medical billing needs are being addressed.

11. Provide high level of customer service.

12. List Medical Billing Solutions, LLC in medical directories, online and in print.

13. Volunteer for fundraisers.

5.3 Marketing and Advertising

Medical Billing Solutions, LLC plans to run an extensive marketing and advertising campaign within its target market.

- Direct mailing

- Face-to-face

- Cold calling

- Referrals from satisfied clients

- Flyers

- Advertise in area hospital and clinic newsletters.

- Create a Web site listing services, mission statement, hours of operation, business location, contact information for potential clients, why I started my business, why a potential client should choose Medical Billing Solutions, LLC, and itemized pricing range, links to web presences, and testimonials from satisfied clients.

- Create flyers and brochures with services offered, hours of operation, location, why and when I opened the business, experience in medical billing, and rates.

6.0 OPERATIONS

The company plans to operate out of home-based office located at 248 Linwood Ave. Upon a close observation of competitors pricing within the target market, the company plans to set medical billing services in the range of $2 to $3 per claim. Upon completion of medical coding certification during the first six months of operation, the firm will become a full-practice management medical billing and coding business. To reflect the added services, fees will be adjusted to $3.50 to $4.50 per claim. The initial startup costs will range anywhere from $2,000 to $10,000.

The company plans to check in on clients periodically with the use of a client assessment survey to monitor results and see if the client's needs are being met and if anything needs to be changed or added. The firm has obtained the necessary forms listed below from the United Clearinghouse and is prepared to begin operations.

- Medical claims and billing agreement between the United Clearinghouse and Medical Billing Solutions, LLC

- Authorization for credit card charge on a monthly basis for services and fees rendered

- Provider enrollment form for each client for services

- Signed payment agreement

- Completed provider information form for each client to enroll them in the clearinghouse

- A signed contract for between Medical Billing Solutions, LLC and United Clearinghouse outlining the services Medical Billing Solutions, LLC will be utilizing

7.0 FINANCIAL ANALYSIS

Medical Billing Solutions, LLCs pro-forma balance sheet for 2013, 2014, and 2015 is below followed with the projected revenue and net revenue for the same time period.

7.1 Three-Year Income Statement

	2013	2014	2015
Revenue			
Medical billing	$27,200	$47,500	$ 78,000
Consulting	$ 4,500	$12,000	$ 17,000
Other services	$ 1,100	$ 2,140	$ 5,590
Total revenue	**$32,800**	**$61,640**	**$100,590**
Expenses			
Computer & peripherals	$ 2,000	$ 0	$ 500
Flash drive backup	$ 40	$ 0	$ 0
Uninterruptible power supply	$ 100	$ 0	$ 0
Surge protector	$ 50	$ 0	$ 0
Accounting	$ 350	$ 550	$ 725
Legal	$ 200	$ 225	$ 260
Coding Professional Certification (CPC)	$ 1,397	$ 0	$ 0
Business/liability insurance	$ 500	$ 750	$ 1,100
Professional memberships	$ 224	$ 224	$ 224
Advertising & marketing	$ 600	$ 500	$ 400
Clearing house support fees	$ 300	$ 300	$ 300
CMS 1,500 forms (case of 2,500)	$ 35	$ 70	$ 105
Business license	$ 100	$ 0	$ 0
Multi-function fax/printer/copier	$ 300	$ 0	$ 0
Digital recording software	$ 495	$ 0	$ 0
Medical transcription software	$ 250	$ 0	$ 0
Medical billing/coding software	$ 549	$ 549	$ 549
Medical billing coding reference books	$ 169	$ 0	$ 0
Invoicing/book keeping software	$ 150	$ 0	$ 0
Phone system	$ 100	$ 0	$ 0
Answering machine	$ 40	$ 0	$ 0
File cabinet with lock	$ 100	$ 0	$ 100
Postage meter	$ 40	$ 0	$ 0
Miscellaneous office supplies	$ 500	$ 700	$ 1,000
Travel	$ 900	$ 900	$ 900
Total expenses	**$ 9,489**	**$ 4,768**	**$ 6,163**
Net income	**$23,311**	**$56,872**	**$ 94,427**

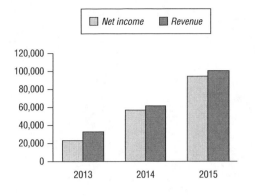

Motel

Staten Island Inn

56669 Main St.
Staten Island, NY 10312

BizPlanDB.com

Staten Island Inn is a New York based corporation that will provide lodging and related services for its targeted market. The Company was founded in 2009 by John Peck

1.0 EXECUTIVE SUMMARY

The purpose of this business plan is to raise $1,000,000 for the development of a motel while showcasing the expected financials and operations over the next three years. Staten Island Inn is a New York based corporation that will provide lodging and related services for its targeted market. The Company was founded in 2009 by John Peck.

1.1 The Services

The Company intends to develop a 20 room motel facility that will feature a number of amenities including high speed internet access, phone usage, and a fully stocked vending machine. At this time, Mr. Peck is sourcing a number of potential general contractors and real estate agents to determine whether the facility should be purchased or built from scratch.

Staten Island Inn will employ a full time maid service to ensure that each room provides customers with comfortable lodgings for their nightly stays.

The third section of the business plan will further describe the services offered by Staten Island Inn.

1.2 Financing

Mr. Peck is seeking to raise $1,000,000 from as a bank loan. The interest rate and loan agreement are to be further discussed during negotiation. This business plan assumes that the business will receive a 30 year loan with a 9% fixed interest rate. The financing will be used for the following:

- Development of the Company's location.
- Financing for the first six months of operation.
- Capital to purchase beds, furniture, and other motel equipment.

Mr. Peck will contribute $100,000 to the venture.

1.3 Mission Statement

Staten Island Inn's mission is to provide customers with comfortable lodgings and many other amenities including high speed internet access, cable TV, and phone usage.

1.4 Management Team

The Company was founded by John Peck. Mr. Peck has more than 10 years of experience in the hotel industry. Through his expertise, he will be able to bring the operations of the business to profitability within its first year of operations.

1.5 Sales Forecasts

Mr. Peck expects a strong rate of growth at the start of operations. Below are the expected financials over the next three years.

Proforma profit and loss (yearly)

Year	1	2	3
Sales	$691,524	$829,829	$970,900
Operating costs	$319,358	$346,652	$375,255
EBITDA	$286,635	$380,540	$475,560
Taxes, interest, and depreciation	$203,501	$204,693	$240,366
Net profit	$ 83,134	$180,704	$240,051

Sales, operating costs, and profit forecast

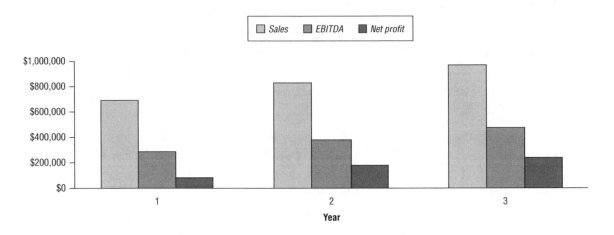

1.6 Expansion Plan

The Founder expects that the business will aggressively expand during the first three years of operation. Mr. Peck intends to implement marketing campaigns that will effectively target individuals and business travelers within the target market.

2.0 COMPANY AND FINANCING SUMMARY

2.1 Registered Name and Corporate Structure

The Company is registered as a corporation in the State of New York.

2.2 Required Funds

At this time, Staten Island Inn requires $1,000,000 of debt funds. Below is a breakdown of how these funds will be used:

Projected startup costs

Initial lease payments (3 months)	$	10,000
Working capital	$	120,000
FF&E	$	45,000
Leasehold improvements	$	5,000
Security deposits	$	5,000
Insurance	$	2,500
Facility acquisition	$	900,000
Marketing budget	$	7,500
Miscellaneous and unforeseen costs	$	5,000
Total startup costs		**$1,100,000**

2.3 Investor Equity

Mr. Peck is not seeking an investment from a third party at this time.

2.4 Management Equity

John Peck owns 100% of Staten Island Inn

2.5 Exit Strategy

If the business is very successful, Mr. Peck may seek to sell the business to a third party for a significant earnings multiple. Most likely, the Company will hire a qualified business broker to sell the business on behalf of Staten Island Inn. Based on historical numbers, the business could fetch a sales premium of up to 9 times earnings.

3.0 PRODUCTS AND SERVICES

Below is a description of the lodging services offered by Staten Island Inn.

3.1 Lodging Services

The Company intends to offer a motel room on a nightly basis for travelers. The room will have many amenities, including, but not limited to:

- A large sized room with a queen sized bed
- Full cable television
- Room Service
- In room mini-bar
- Daily housekeeping

As the Company expands, Management intends to offer more amenities and services so that we can consistently add value for the customers' experience.

4.0 STRATEGIC AND MARKET ANALYSIS

4.1 Economic Outlook

This section of the analysis will detail the economic climate, the motel industry, the customer profile, and the competition that the business will face as it progresses through its business operations.

Currently, the economic market condition in the United States is moderate. The meltdown of the sub prime mortgage market coupled with increasing gas prices has led many people to believe that the US is on the cusp of a double dip economic recession. This slowdown in the economy has also greatly impacted real estate sales, which has halted to historical lows. However, motels in highly populated metropolitan areas operate with great economic stability as people will continue to require lodging despite deleterious changes in the general economy.

4.2 Industry Analysis

The motel industry in the United States is an extremely fragmented industry that has a number of different operators working in many markets. There are a few large corporations that offer motel rooms on a national scale. Although these are large businesses, their portion of the overall motel market is very limited.

According to a US Economic Census report, there are over 43,000 individual motel facilities in the United States. It is a $74 billion dollar per year industry that employees approximately 1.7 million people.

The hotel/motel industry is mature. The future growth rate of the industry is expected to remain in line with the growth of the general economy.

4.3 Customer Profile

Staten Island Inn's average client will be a middle to upper middle class man or woman. Common traits among clients will include:

- Annual household income exceeding $50,000

- Will spend $100 per night at Staten Island Inn

- 75% of guests will be business travelers

- 25% of guests will be local residents of people visiting on vacation

4.4 Competition

Staten Island Inn will retain a competitive advantage among other places of lodging within the area by being able to remain flexible on price. As will be discussed in the next section of the business plan, the Company will have all of its rooms available for immediate booking on popular travel focused websites. This will ensure that the Company has an extremely high occupancy rate while concurrently ensuring that Staten Island Inn is generating revenue and is cash flow positive at all times. The business will also offer discounts during popular tourist seasons, which will set the Company apart from its competition even further. The demand for quality motel rooms within the greater New York metropolitan area is very strong, and while there are many competitors within the area, the business will be able to thrive within this market.

5.0 MARKETING PLAN

Staten Island Inn intends to maintain an extensive marketing campaign that will ensure maximum visibility for the business in its targeted market. Below is an overview of the marketing strategies and objectives of Staten Island Inn.

5.1 Marketing Objectives

- Develop an online presence by developing a website and placing the Company's name and contact information with online directories.

- Place Staten Island Inn's name within online travel sites such as Expedia, Travelocity, and Orbitz.

- Implement a local campaign with the Company's targeted market via the use of flyers, local newspaper advertisements, and word of mouth.

- Establish relationships with travel agents within the targeted market.

5.2 Marketing Strategies

Mr. Peck intends on using a number of marketing strategies that will allow Staten Island Inn to easily target business and vacationing travelers within the target market. These strategies include traditional print advertisements and ads placed on search engines on the Internet. Below is a description of how the business intends to market its services to the general public.

The Company will maintain a sizable amount of print and traditional advertising methods within local markets to promote the lodging that the Company is selling. The Company will also place advertisements within airports located within 50 miles of Staten Island Inn.

Staten Island Inn, as discussed above, will also aggressively engage sites such as Expedia, Travelocity, and Orbitz in order to have individuals place reservations with the Company. As many people now use these websites in order to find places of lodging, Mr. Peck will aggressively list the availability and competitive pricing associated with the rooms available at Staten Island Inn. The business will also have its own website from which individuals can directly make reservations for rooms.

5.3 Pricing
Staten Island Inn will charge approximately $100 per night for occupancy of a room.

6.0 ORGANIZATIONAL PLAN AND PERSONNEL SUMMARY

6.1 Corporate Organization

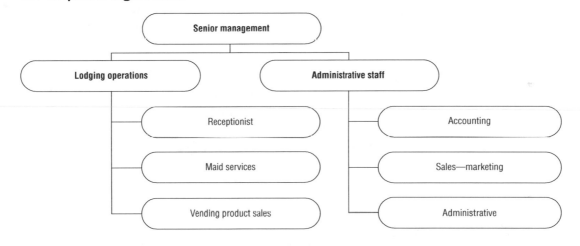

6.2 Organizational Budget

Personnel plan—yearly

Year	1	2	3
Owners	$ 80,000	$ 82,400	$ 84,872
Manager	$ 35,000	$ 36,050	$ 37,132
Assistant	$ 32,500	$ 33,475	$ 34,479
Maids	$ 37,500	$ 51,500	$ 66,306
Receptionist	$ 44,000	$ 45,320	$ 46,680
Total	**$229,000**	**$248,745**	**$269,469**

Numbers of personnel

Owners	2	2	2
Manager	1	1	1
Assistant	1	1	1
Maids	3	4	5
Receptionist	2	2	2
Totals	**9**	**10**	**11**

Personnel expense breakdown

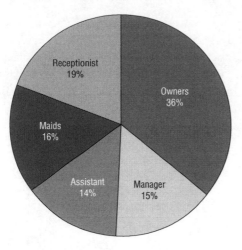

7.0 FINANCIAL PLAN

7.1 Underlying Assumptions

The Company has based its proforma financial statements on the following:

- Staten Island Inn will have an annual revenue growth rate of 16% per year.

- The Owner will acquire $1,000,000 of debt funds to develop the business.

- The loan will have a 30 year term with a 9% interest rate.

7.2 Sensitivity Analysis

In the event of an economic downturn, the business may have a decline in its revenues. However, lodging services are continually demanded by business travelers, and only a severe economic recession would result in a decline in Staten Island Inn's revenues.

7.3 Source of Funds

Financing

Equity contributions

Investor(s)	$ 100,000.00
Total equity financing	**$ 100,000.00**
Banks and lenders	
Banks and lenders	$ 1,000,000.00
Total debt financing	**$1,000,000.00**
Total financing	**$1,100,000.00**

7.4 General Assumptions

General assumptions

Year	1	2	3
Short term interest rate	9.5%	9.5%	9.5%
Long term interest rate	10.0%	10.0%	10.0%
Federal tax rate	33.0%	33.0%	33.0%
State tax rate	5.0%	5.0%	5.0%
Personnel taxes	15.0%	15.0%	15.0%

7.5 Profit and Loss Statements

Proforma profit and loss (yearly)

Year	1	2	3
Sales	**$691,524**	**$829,829**	**$970,900**
Cost of goods sold	$ 85,531	$102,637	$120,085
Gross margin	87.63%	87.63%	87.63%
Operating income	**$605,993**	**$727,192**	**$850,815**
Expenses			
Payroll	$229,000	$248,745	$269,469
General and administrative	$ 25,200	$ 26,208	$ 27,256
Marketing expenses	$ 3,458	$ 4,149	$ 4,854
Professional fees and licensure	$ 5,219	$ 5,376	$ 5,537
Insurance costs	$ 1,987	$ 2,086	$ 2,191
Travel and vehicle costs	$ 7,596	$ 8,356	$ 9,191
Rent and utilities	$ 4,250	$ 4,463	$ 4,686
Miscellaneous costs	$ 8,298	$ 9,958	$ 11,651
Payroll taxes	$ 34,350	$ 37,312	$ 40,420
Total operating costs	**$319,358**	**$346,652**	**$375,255**
EBITDA	**$286,635**	**$380,540**	**$475,560**
Federal income tax	$ 94,590	$ 96,181	$127,769
State income tax	$ 14,332	$ 14,573	$ 19,359
Interest expense	$ 89,723	$ 89,082	$ 88,381
Depreciation expenses	$ 4,857	$ 4,857	$ 4,857
Net profit	**$ 83,134**	**$180,704**	**$240,051**
Profit margin	**12.02%**	**21.78%**	**24.72%**

Sales, operating costs, and profit forecast

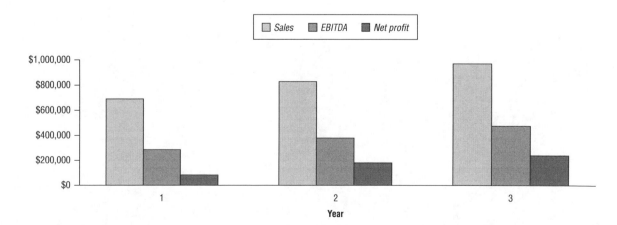

7.6 Cash Flow Analysis

Proforma cash flow analysis—yearly

Year	1	2	3
Cash from operations	$ 87,991	$187,704	$247,051
Cash from receivables	$ 0	$ 0	$ 0
Operating cash inflow	**$ 87,991**	**$187,704**	**$247,051**
Other cash inflows			
Equity investment	$ 100,000	$ 0	$ 0
Increased borrowings	$ 1,000,000	$ 0	$ 0
Sales of business assets	$ 0	$ 0	$ 0
A/P increases	$ 37,902	$ 43,587	$ 50,125
Total other cash inflows	**$1,137,902**	**$ 43,587**	**$ 50,125**
Total cash inflow	**$1,225,893**	**$231,291**	**$297,176**
Cash outflows			
Repayment of principal	$ 6,832	$ 7,473	$ 8,174
A/P decreases	$ 24,897	$ 29,876	$ 35,852
A/R increases	$ 0	$ 0	$ 0
Asset purchases	$ 975,000	$ 46,926	$ 61,763
Dividends	$ 61,594	$131,393	$172,936
Total cash outflows	**$1,068,323**	**$215,668**	**$278,724**
Net cash flow	**$ 157,570**	**$ 15,623**	**$ 18,452**
Cash balance	**$ 157,570**	**$173,194**	**$191,646**

Proforma cash flow (yearly)

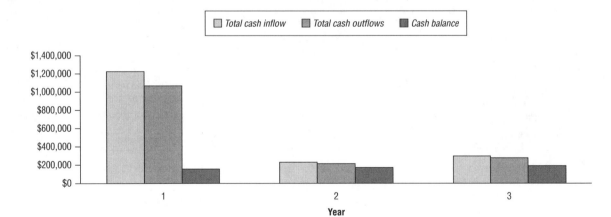

7.7 Balance Sheet

Proforma balance sheet—yearly

Year	1	2	3
Assets			
Cash	$ 157,570	$ 173,194	$ 191,646
Amortized expansion costs	$ 15,000	$ 19,693	$ 25,869
Inventory	$ 25,000	$ 60,195	$ 106,517
FF&E	$ 45,000	$ 52,039	$ 61,303
Miscellaneous assets	$ 13,000	$ 14,950	$ 17,193
Real estate	$ 954,000	$1,011,240	$1,071,914
Accumulated depreciation	($ 7,000)	($ 14,000)	($ 21,000)
Total assets	**$1,202,570**	**$1,317,310**	**$1,453,442**
Liabilities and equity			
Accounts payable	$ 13,005	$ 26,716	$ 40,990
Long term liabilities	$ 993,168	$ 985,695	$ 978,222
Other liabilities	$ 8,200	$ 8,528	$ 8,869
Total liabilities	**$1,014,373**	**$1,020,939**	**$1,028,081**
Net worth	**$ 188,197**	**$ 296,371**	**$ 425,361**
Total liabilities and equity	**$1,202,570**	**$1,317,310**	**$1,453,442**

Proforma balance sheet

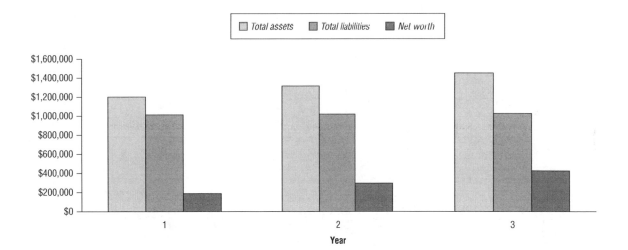

7.8 Breakeven Analysis

Monthly break even analysis

Year	1	2	3
Monthly revenue	$ 30,369	$ 32,965	$ 35,685
Yearly revenue	$364,432	$395,579	$428,219

Break even analysis

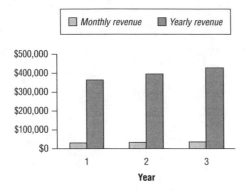

7.9 Business Ratios

Business ratios—yearly

Year	1	2	3
Sales			
Sales growth	0.00%	20.00%	17.00%
Gross margin	87.60%	87.60%	87.60%
Financials			
Profit margin	11.71%	21.78%	24.72%
Assets to liabilities	1.19	1.29	1.41
Equity to liabilities	0.19	0.29	0.41
Assets to equity	6.39	4.44	3.42
Liquidity			
Acid test	0.16	0.17	0.19
Cash to assets	0.13	0.13	0.13

7.10 Three Year Profit and Loss Statement

Profit and loss statement (first year)

Months	1	2	3	4	5	6	7
Sales	**$57,000**	**$57,114**	**$57,228**	**$57,342**	**$57,456**	**$57,570**	**$57,684**
Cost of goods sold	$ 7,050	$ 7,064	$ 7,078	$ 7,092	$ 7,106	$ 7,121	$ 7,135
Gross margin	87.60%	87.60%	87.60%	87.60%	87.60%	87.60%	87.60%
Operating income	**$49,950**	**$50,050**	**$50,150**	**$50,250**	**$50,350**	**$50,450**	**$50,549**
Expenses							
Payroll	$19,083	$19,083	$19,083	$19,083	$19,083	$19,083	$19,083
General and administrative	$ 2,100	$ 2,100	$ 2,100	$ 2,100	$ 2,100	$ 2,100	$ 2,100
Marketing expenses	$ 288	$ 288	$ 288	$ 288	$ 288	$ 288	$ 288
Professional fees and licensure	$ 435	$ 435	$ 435	$ 435	$ 435	$ 435	$ 435
Insurance costs	$ 166	$ 166	$ 166	$ 166	$ 166	$ 166	$ 166
Travel and vehicle costs	$ 633	$ 633	$ 633	$ 633	$ 633	$ 633	$ 633
Rent and utilities	$ 354	$ 354	$ 354	$ 354	$ 354	$ 354	$ 354
Miscellaneous costs	$ 692	$ 692	$ 692	$ 692	$ 692	$ 692	$ 692
Payroll taxes	$ 2,863	$ 2,863	$ 2,863	$ 2,863	$ 2,863	$ 2,863	$ 2,863
Total operating costs	**$26,613**	**$26,613**	**$26,613**	**$26,613**	**$26,613**	**$26,613**	**$26,613**
EBITDA	**$23,337**	**$23,437**	**$23,537**	**$23,637**	**$23,736**	**$23,836**	**$23,936**
Federal income tax	$ 7,797	$ 7,812	$ 7,828	$ 7,843	$ 7,859	$ 7,875	$ 7,890
State income tax	$ 1,181	$ 1,184	$ 1,186	$ 1,188	$ 1,191	$ 1,193	$ 1,195
Interest expense	$ 7,500	$ 7,496	$ 7,492	$ 7,488	$ 7,483	$ 7,479	$ 7,475
Depreciation expense	$ 583	$ 583	$ 583	$ 583	$ 583	$ 583	$ 583
Net profit	**$ 6,275**	**$ 6,362**	**$ 6,448**	**$ 6,534**	**$ 6,620**	**$ 6,706**	**$ 6,792**

Profit and loss statement (first year cont.)

Month	8	9	10	11	12	1
Sales	**$57,798**	**$57,912**	**$58,026**	**$58,140**	**$58,254**	**$691,524**
Cost of goods sold	$ 7,149	$ 7,163	$ 7,177	$ 7,191	$ 7,205	$ 85,531
Gross margin	87.60%	87.60%	87.60%	87.60%	87.60%	87.60%
Operating income	**$50,649**	**$50,749**	**$50,849**	**$50,949**	**$51,049**	**$605,993**
Expenses						
Payroll	$19,083	$19,083	$19,083	$19,083	$19,083	$229,000
General and administrative	$ 2,100	$ 2,100	$ 2,100	$ 2,100	$ 2,100	$ 25,200
Marketing expenses	$ 288	$ 288	$ 288	$ 288	$ 288	$ 3,458
Professional fees and licensure	$ 435	$ 435	$ 435	$ 435	$ 435	$ 5,219
Insurance costs	$ 166	$ 166	$ 166	$ 166	$ 166	$ 1,987
Travel and vehicle costs	$ 633	$ 633	$ 633	$ 633	$ 633	$ 7,596
Rent and utilities	$ 354	$ 354	$ 354	$ 354	$ 354	$ 4,250
Miscellaneous costs	$ 692	$ 692	$ 692	$ 692	$ 692	$ 8,298
Payroll taxes	$ 2,863	$ 2,863	$ 2,863	$ 2,863	$ 2,863	$ 34,350
Total operating costs	**$26,613**	**$26,613**	**$26,613**	**$26,613**	**$26,613**	**$319,358**
EBITDA	**$24,036**	**$24,136**	**$24,236**	**$24,336**	**$24,436**	**$286,635**
Federal income tax	$ 7,906	$ 7,921	$ 7,937	$ 7,953	$ 7,968	$ 94,590
State income tax	$ 1,198	$ 1,200	$ 1,203	$ 1,205	$ 1,207	$ 14,332
Interest expense	$ 7,471	$ 7,466	$ 7,462	$ 7,458	$ 7,453	$ 89,723
Depreciation expense	$ 583	$ 583	$ 583	$ 583	$ 583	$ 7,000
Net profit	**$ 6,878**	**$ 6,965**	**$ 7,051**	**$ 7,137**	**$ 7,224**	**$ 80,991**

Profit and loss statement (second year)

Quarter	Q1	2 Q2	Q3	Q4	2
Sales	$165,966	$207,457	$224,054	$232,352	$829,829
Cost of goods sold	$ 20,527	$ 25,659	$ 27,712	$ 28,738	$102,637
Gross margin	87.60%	87.60%	87.60%	87.60%	87.60%
Operating income	$145,438	$181,798	$196,342	$203,614	$727,192
Expenses					
Payroll	$ 49,749	$ 62,186	$ 67,161	$ 69,649	$248,745
General and administrative	$ 5,242	$ 6,552	$ 7,076	$ 7,338	$ 26,208
Marketing expenses	$ 830	$ 1,037	$ 1,120	$ 1,162	$ 4,149
Professional fees and licensure	$ 1,075	$ 1,344	$ 1,451	$ 1,505	$ 5,376
Insurance costs	$ 417	$ 522	$ 563	$ 584	$ 2,086
Travel and vehicle costs	$ 1,671	$ 2,089	$ 2,256	$ 2,340	$ 8,356
Rent and utilities	$ 893	$ 1,116	$ 1,205	$ 1,250	$ 4,463
Miscellaneous costs	$ 1,992	$ 2,489	$ 2,689	$ 2,788	$ 9,958
Payroll taxes	$ 7,462	$ 9,328	$ 10,074	$ 10,447	$ 37,312
Total operating costs	$ 69,330	$ 86,663	$ 93,596	$ 97,063	$346,652
EBITDA	$ 76,108	$ 95,135	$102,746	$106,551	$380,540
Federal income tax	$ 19,236	$ 24,045	$ 25,969	$ 26,931	$ 96,181
State income tax	$ 2,915	$ 3,643	$ 3,935	$ 4,080	$ 14,573
Interest expense	$ 22,333	$ 22,292	$ 22,250	$ 22,207	$ 89,082
Depreciation expense	$ 1,750	$ 1,750	$ 1,750	$ 1,750	$ 7,000
Net profit	$ 29,874	$ 43,405	$ 48,842	$ 51,583	$173,704

Profit and loss statement (third year)

Quarter	Q1	3 Q2	Q3	Q4	3
Sales	$194,180	$242,725	$262,143	$271,852	$970,900
Cost of goods sold	$ 24,017	$ 30,021	$ 32,423	$ 33,624	$120,085
Gross margin	0.0%	0.0%	0.0%	0.0%	0.0%
Operating income	$170,163	$212,704	$229,720	$238,228	$850,815
Expenses					
Payroll	$ 53,894	$ 67,367	$ 72,757	$ 75,451	$269,469
General and administrative	$ 5,451	$ 6,814	$ 7,359	$ 7,632	$ 27,256
Marketing expenses	$ 971	$ 1,214	$ 1,311	$ 1,359	$ 4,854
Professional fees and licensure	$ 1,107	$ 1,384	$ 1,495	$ 1,550	$ 5,537
Insurance costs	$ 438	$ 548	$ 591	$ 613	$ 2,191
Travel and vehicle costs	$ 1,838	$ 2,298	$ 2,482	$ 2,574	$ 9,191
Rent and utilities	$ 937	$ 1,171	$ 1,265	$ 1,312	$ 4,686
Miscellaneous costs	$ 2,330	$ 2,913	$ 3,146	$ 3,262	$ 11,651
Payroll taxes	$ 8,084	$ 10,105	$ 10,913	$ 11,318	$ 40,420
Total operating costs	$ 75,051	$ 93,814	$101,319	$105,071	$375,255
EBITDA	$ 95,112	$118,890	$128,401	$133,157	$475,560
Federal income tax	$ 25,554	$ 31,942	$ 34,498	$ 35,775	$127,769
State income tax	$ 3,872	$ 4,840	$ 5,227	$ 5,421	$ 19,359
Interest expense	$ 22,163	$ 22,119	$ 22,073	$ 22,026	$ 88,381
Depreciation expense	$ 1,750	$ 1,750	$ 1,750	$ 1,750	$ 7,000
Net profit	$ 41,773	$ 58,239	$ 64,854	$ 68,185	$233,051

7.11 Three Year Cash Flow Analysis

Cash flow analysis (first year)

Month	1	2	3	4	5	6	7
Cash from operations	$ 6,275	$ 6,362	$ 6,448	$ 6,534	$ 6,620	$ 6,706	$ 6,792
Cash from receivables	$ 0	$ 0	$ 0	$ 0	$ 0	$ 0	$ 0
Operating cash inflow	**$ 6,275**	**$ 6,362**	**$ 6,448**	**$ 6,534**	**$ 6,620**	**$ 6,706**	**$ 6,792**
Other cash inflows							
Equity investment	$ 100,000	$ 0	$ 0	$ 0	$ 0	$ 0	$ 0
Increased borrowings	$1,000,000	$ 0	$ 0	$ 0	$ 0	$ 0	$ 0
Sales of business assets	$ 0	$ 0	$ 0	$ 0	$ 0	$ 0	$ 0
A/P increases	$ 3,159	$ 3,159	$ 3,159	$ 3,159	$ 3,159	$ 3,159	$ 3,159
Total other cash inflows	**$1,103,159**	**$ 3,159**	**$ 3,159**	**$ 3,159**	**$ 3,159**	**$ 3,159**	**$ 3,159**
Total cash inflow	**$1,109,434**	**$ 9,520**	**$ 9,606**	**$ 9,692**	**$ 9,778**	**$ 9,864**	**$ 9,951**
Cash outflows							
Repayment of principal	$ 546	$ 550	$ 554	$ 559	$ 563	$ 567	$ 571
A/P decreases	$ 2,075	$ 2,075	$ 2,075	$ 2,075	$ 2,075	$ 2,075	$ 2,075
A/R increases	$ 0	$ 0	$ 0	$ 0	$ 0	$ 0	$ 0
Asset purchases	$ 975,000	$ 0	$ 0	$ 0	$ 0	$ 0	$ 0
Dividends	$ 0	$ 0	$ 0	$ 0	$ 0	$ 0	$ 0
Total cash outflows	**$ 977,621**	**$ 2,625**	**$ 2,629**	**$ 2,633**	**$ 2,638**	**$ 2,642**	**$ 2,646**
Net cash flow	**$ 131,813**	**$ 6,895**	**$ 6,977**	**$ 7,059**	**$ 7,141**	**$ 7,223**	**$ 7,305**
Cash balance	**$ 131,813**	**$138,708**	**$145,685**	**$152,744**	**$159,884**	**$167,107**	**$174,412**

Cash flow analysis (first year cont.)

Month	8	9	10	11	12	1
Cash from operations	$ 6,878	$ 6,965	$ 7,051	$ 7,137	$ 7,224	$ 80,991
Cash from receivables	$ 0	$ 0	$ 0	$ 0	$ 0	$ 0
Operating cash inflow	**$ 6,878**	**$ 6,965**	**$ 7,051**	**$ 7,137**	**$ 7,224**	**$ 80,991**
Other cash inflows						
Equity investment	$ 0	$ 0	$ 0	$ 0	$ 0	$ 100,000
Increased borrowings	$ 0	$ 0	$ 0	$ 0	$ 0	$1,000,000
Sales of business assets	$ 0	$ 0	$ 0	$ 0	$ 0	$ 0
A/P increases	$ 3,159	$ 3,159	$ 3,159	$ 3,159	$ 3,159	$ 37,902
Total other cash inflows	**$ 3,159**	**$ 3,159**	**$ 3,159**	**$ 3,159**	**$ 3,159**	**$1,137,902**
Total cash inflow	**$ 10,037**	**$ 10,123**	**$ 10,209**	**$ 10,296**	**$ 10,382**	**$1,218,893**
Cash outflows						
Repayment of principal	$ 576	$ 580	$ 584	$ 589	$ 593	$ 6,832
A/P decreases	$ 2,075	$ 2,075	$ 2,075	$ 2,075	$ 2,075	$ 24,897
A/R increases	$ 0	$ 0	$ 0	$ 0	$ 0	$ 0
Asset purchases	$ 0	$ 0	$ 0	$ 0	$ 0	$ 975,000
Dividends	$ 0	$ 0	$ 0	$ 0	$ 61,594	$ 61,594
Total cash outflows	**$ 2,650**	**$ 2,655**	**$ 2,659**	**$ 2,663**	**$ 64,262**	**$1,068,323**
Net cash flow	**$ 7,387**	**$ 7,469**	**$ 7,550**	**$ 7,632**	**−$ 53,880**	**$ 150,570**
Cash balance	**$181,798**	**$189,267**	**$196,817**	**$204,450**	**$150,570**	**$ 150,570**

Cash flow analysis (second year)

Quarter	Q1	2 Q2	Q3	Q4	2
Cash from operations	$ 37,541	$ 46,926	$ 50,680	$ 52,557	$187,704
Cash from receivables	$ 0	$ 0	$ 0	$ 0	$ 0
Operating cash inflow	**$ 37,541**	**$ 46,926**	**$ 50,680**	**$ 52,557**	**$187,704**
Other cash inflows					
Equity investment	$ 0	$ 0	$ 0	$ 0	$ 0
Increased borrowings	$ 0	$ 0	$ 0	$ 0	$ 0
Sales of business assets	$ 0	$ 0	$ 0	$ 0	$ 0
A/P increases	$ 8,717	$ 10,897	$ 11,769	$ 12,204	$ 43,587
Total other cash inflows	**$ 8,717**	**$ 10,897**	**$ 11,769**	**$ 12,204**	**$ 43,587**
Total cash inflow	**$ 46,258**	**$ 57,823**	**$ 62,449**	**$ 64,762**	**$231,291**
Cash outflows					
Repayment of principal	$ 1,806	$ 1,847	$ 1,889	$ 1,931	$ 7,473
A/P decreases	$ 5,975	$ 7,469	$ 8,067	$ 8,365	$ 29,876
A/R increases	$ 0	$ 0	$ 0	$ 0	$ 0
Asset purchases	$ 9,385	$ 11,732	$ 12,670	$ 13,139	$ 46,926
Dividends	$ 26,279	$ 32,848	$ 35,476	$ 36,790	$131,393
Total cash outflows	**$ 43,445**	**$ 53,896**	**$ 58,101**	**$ 60,226**	**$215,668**
Net cash flow	**$ 2,813**	**$ 3,927**	**$ 4,347**	**$ 4,535**	**$ 15,623**
Cash balance	**$153,384**	**$157,311**	**$161,658**	**$166,194**	**$166,194**

Cash flow analysis (third year)

Quarter	Q1	3 Q2	Q3	Q4	3
Cash from operations	$ 49,410	$ 61,763	$ 66,704	$ 69,174	$247,051
Cash from receivables	$ 0	$ 0	$ 0	$ 0	$ 0
Operating cash inflow	**$ 49,410**	**$ 61,763**	**$ 66,704**	**$ 69,174**	**$247,051**
Other cash inflows					
Equity investment	$ 0	$ 0	$ 0	$ 0	$ 0
Increased borrowings	$ 0	$ 0	$ 0	$ 0	$ 0
Sales of business assets	$ 0	$ 0	$ 0	$ 0	$ 0
A/P increases	$ 10,025	$ 12,531	$ 13,534	$ 14,035	$ 50,125
Total other cash inflows	**$ 10,025**	**$ 12,531**	**$ 13,534**	**$ 14,035**	**$ 50,125**
Total cash inflow	**$ 59,435**	**$ 74,294**	**$ 80,238**	**$ 83,209**	**$297,176**
Cash outflows					
Repayment of principal	$ 1,975	$ 2,020	$ 2,066	$ 2,113	$ 8,174
A/P decreases	$ 7,170	$ 8,963	$ 9,680	$ 10,038	$ 35,852
A/R increases	$ 0	$ 0	$ 0	$ 0	$ 0
Asset purchases	$ 12,353	$ 15,441	$ 16,676	$ 17,294	$ 61,763
Dividends	$ 34,587	$ 43,234	$ 46,693	$ 48,422	$172,936
Total cash outflows	**$ 56,085**	**$ 69,658**	**$ 75,114**	**$ 77,867**	**$278,724**
Net cash flow	**$ 3,350**	**$ 4,637**	**$ 5,123**	**$ 5,343**	**$ 18,452**
Cash balance	**$169,544**	**$174,180**	**$179,303**	**$184,646**	**$184,646**

Plumbing Service

Sierra Plumbing Services, Inc.

500 Vernon Street
Roseville, CA 95678

Claire Moore MBA

Sierra Plumbing Services, Inc. is based in Roseville, California and will provide plumbing services for cities in the Sierra foothills area including: Roseville, Lincoln, Penryn, Loomis, Newcastle, Rocklin, Auburn, and Colfax.

EXECUTIVE SUMMARY

Sierra Plumbing Services, Inc. is based in Roseville, California and will provide plumbing services for cities in the Sierra foothills area including: Roseville, Lincoln, Penryn, Loomis, Newcastle, Rocklin, Auburn, and Colfax. We have chosen to serve both residential and commercial customers with a comprehensive roster of specialized services ranging from drain cleaning to sewer line inspection and repair.

The purpose of this business plan is to serve as a blueprint for future growth. It is our intention to grow Sierra Plumbing Services, Inc. into an enterprise that employs two additional plumbers within the next five years and eventually grows to a staff of 12 full-time plumbers plus support staff. Growth strategies past year three are not covered in this business plan.

Company founder, James Bluth has over 15 years experience in residential and commercial service and repair. Bluth was one of the first plumbing professionals in Placer County to use the trenchless sewer and water line replacement system also known as Pipe Bursting or Trenchless Technology.

Sierra Plumbing Services, Inc. will employ only licensed and certified professionals rather than plumbing technicians. Our dedication to quality as well as our commitment to prompt customer service will create our competitive advantage and enable us to develop our share of the market.

According to the 2011 Placer County Economic and Demographic Profile, Placer County is, "one of California's fastest growing counties and a key component of the Sacramento Region's economy" The county's growth rate has earned it a ranking of 56th on the U.S. Census Bureau's list of the "100 Fastest Growing U.S. Counties with 10,000 or more Population in 2009: April 1, 2000 to July 1, 2009." Placer County ranks third in growth rate among all California counties in its rate of population growth from January 2009 to January 2010.

While Placer County real estate activity was negatively affected during the housing downturn and recession, it remains competitive and is now experiencing a resurgence as the country emerges from the recession. The local government's favorable attitude toward economic development has led to an increase in both residential and commercial real estate activity.

The demand for both residential and commercial real estate space continues to rise. Sierra Plumbing Services, Inc. is well-positioned to grow along with the rest of Placer County.

Objectives

Company objective for years one through three include the following:

- Establish Sierra Plumbing Services, Inc. as a recognized brand.

- Develop a reputation for providing quality service and prompt attention to customer needs.

- Achieve a level of revenues that will allow for future growth.

Mission

Sierra Plumbing Services, Inc. provides residential and commercial customers prompt and effective plumbing solutions. We stand behind our work and strive to meet and exceed the needs and expectations of our customers.

While it is the mission of Sierra Plumbing to provide quality service, it is not our goal to be the lowest priced player in the marketplace. Part of our branding and promotional strategy includes the fact that we may cost a little more than much of our competition but you get what you pay for. Uniforms and background checks cost money as does training and development. Our services will be priced at a point that not only covers our costs but ensures productivity.

Company Summary

Sierra Plumbing Services, Inc. was formed in 2013 by James Bluth who began his career in 1990 after completing a program of study and apprenticeship in a plumbing training program sponsored by the Plumbing-Heating-Cooling Contractors Association (PHCC). In 1990, Bluth was granted a California state plumbing contractor's license issued by the Contractors State License Board (CSLB).

Between 1990 and 2013 Bluth utilized his skills and training in a number of venues including: sales and service for a nationally known retail company, a local plumbing services franchise company, and a locally-owned plumbing service company. In 2012 Bluth began to develop his plan for opening his own service company and has financed the company start-up through the use of his personal savings.

Currently Bluth is the only employee but his plans are to expand the company over the next five years and add two licensed plumbers and a heating and cooling expert. Bluth's wife, Marianne, assists in maintaining the accounting records for the business. The company operates out of Bluth's home.

Start-up Requirements

The following items have already been secured to start the business:

Legal fees for incorporation and filing fees	$ 2,000
QuickBooks software	$ 300
PC computer/printer	$ 700
Office software	$ 200
Business license	$ 250
Trade name registration	$ 200
Liability insurance	$ 100
Misc. tools (pipe wrenches, clamp set, thread chaser, flaring tool set, thread seal tape, pipe snakes manual and electric)	$ 1,000
Advertising: signage for truck, business cards, yellow pages, newspaper	$ 850
Pickup truck: 2007 Toyota	$12,000
Office furniture (used)	$ 900
Storage rack and tool box, liner for truck	$ 480
Total	**$18,980**

Based on experience and research, James Bluth has determined that the following items are required in order to begin operations:

Office supplies: stationery, forms, business checks	$ 150
Supplies: gas, solder etc.	$ 400
Web site creation	$ 900
Advertising: design, writing, printing of flyers, brochures	$ 400
Materials: pipes, cords, pipe cutters, propane torch, saws, fittings	$ 500
Total	**$2,350**

Ongoing expenses will include:

Bank fees including credit card processing estimated	$ 50/month
Liability insurance	$100/month
Truck insurance	$ 95/month
Advertising	$100/month
Web site hosting	$ 15/month
Truck: gas	$350/month
Rental unit: equipment and supplies storage	$ 75/month
Cell phone	$ 85/month

Company Ownership

Sierra Plumbing Services, Inc. is a C corporation with its headquarters at Bluth's home located at 500 Vernon Street in Roseville, California. Corporate officers include: James Bluth, president, Carl Bluth, vice president, Marianne Bluth, secretary-treasurer.

PRODUCTS AND SERVICES

Sierra Plumbing Services, Inc. will offer plumbing services to both residential and commercial customers located in Placer County, CA. We will provide service for new home construction as well as for existing structures. Through the use of mobile accounting apps, we will be able to create on-site estimates that accurately outline the job to be done and associated costs. In this way we will build a reputation for accurate job pricing and ensure customer satisfaction.

Services offered include:

- drain cleaning and repair

- sewer cleaning and repair

- sewer video pipe inspection

- trenchless sewer replacement

- water line repair and replacement

- tankless water heater installation and service

- toilet replacement

Because James Bluth is the only plumber on staff, he plans on being available for customers Tuesdays through Thursdays from 8 a.m. to 6 p.m. and Fridays from 8 a.m. to 4 p.m. As revenues grow priority will be given to adding staff and increasing service hours.

MARKET ANALYSIS

Sierra Plumbing Services, Inc. will serve residential and commercial customers in Placer County, California which has been identified as one of the fastest growing counties in the country. As the economy emerges from the effects of the housing crisis and the recession, Placer County is already experiencing a drop in the number of foreclosure sales. This drop points to a growth in the real estate market and is good news for an area that was hit especially hard by the recession.

According to the 2011 Placer County Economic and Demographic Profile, Placer County has experienced extensive growth in both commercial and residential construction and real estate activity over the past decade. Despite the negative downturns due to the recession, Placer County still remains competitive relative to other markets in the Sacramento and Bay Area regions.

Growth is expected to continue because Placer County is a popular spot for Bay Area retirees and businesses that desire a better quality of life combined with affordable living costs. In fact growth in Placer County during the past year is unique in that it is comprised primarily of "in-migration" from other areas rather than from births. This appeal for residents relocating to Placer County is expected to continue through at least 2020.

Another sign of growth is the January 8, 2013 endorsement by the Board of Supervisors of the Next Economy Regional Prosperity Plan, a broad-based campaign to stimulate job growth, investment and innovation in several counties, including Placer County.

It is expected that customers will primarily consist of residential rather than commercial jobs because Sierra Plumbing is limited to one plumber. The added advantage of residential customers is the receipt of payment at the time of service rather than the cost of carrying accounts receivable that is expected when dealing with commercial customers.

Our ideal customer is a homeowner who wants plumbing work done quickly and efficiently and is will to pay for quality service. This customer prefers not to be a do-it-yourselfer and recognizes that a valuable service will be priced accordingly.

MARKET STRATEGY

Because plumbing services are often needed at a moment's notice, it's important to market the business in a way that will enable customers to find and remember Sierra Plumbing. Service businesses in general gain business primarily through referrals. Therefore Sierra Plumbing is committed to maintaining extraordinary customer satisfaction.

- **The web:** A web presence will be developed with the assistance of a professional web site creator. James and Marianne will add a blog to the site where they will post regular articles with information of interest to the public about how to care for their plumbing, how to hire a plumbing professional, and more.

- **Social media:** Social media tools such as Facebook and FourSquare will be used to ensure that Sierra Plumbing has an identifiable presence. Contact information including Bluth's cell phone number will be listed on all sites. Future plans include the addition of a YouTube channel with video demonstrations of plumbing topics and fun facts and tips.

- **Networking:** Bluth has joined a local networking group that operates on the principle of sharing leads. Other group members include a realtor, insurance agent, and accountant. Networking with other business owners will be key to Sierra Plumbing's success. Not only will affiliations with other professionals such as realtors and insurance agents be stressed, Bluth will maintain and develop his relationships with complementary professionals in plumbing and HVAC specialties. In this way job leads can be shared, for example, when Bluth is unavailable, he can refer the job to a fellow plumber and hopefully reap a referral in return in the future.

- **Direct mail:** A program of direct mail will be used to regularly send flyers to realtors and insurance agents in the county. Mailings will rotate with one city being targeted each month. Cooperation with other plumbers also opens the possibility of sharing large jobs in new construction or in commercial venues that Bluth might otherwise not be able to cover.

- **Newsletter:** A monthly newsletter will be mailed to existing customers in order to keep Sierra Plumbing top of mind. The newsletter will contain articles, tips, and fun facts of interest to homeowners.

- **Referrals:** The ability to build trust with a customer through an accurate quote that creates no surprises, will build a loyal following and in turn, numerous happy referrals. Both paper and magnet business cards will be handed out liberally to help customers keep Sierra Plumbing top of mind. A membership on Angie's List will be purchased so that customers can post comments. Posts will be monitored so that any customers who post unfavorable comments can be contacted and resolved.

- **Trucks:** All trucks used by Sierra Plumbing will have a custom paint job that will include the company name, logo, phone number, web address, list of primary services, geographic areas served.

- **Yellow pages:** All but replaced by the web, yellow pages are still used by a segment of the population. A listing here on a year after year basis will help to establish the brand and build recognition.

The QuickBooks apps will make accounting easier too by taking estimates and converting them into sales receipts that record the sale and payment into the accounting system, eliminating the need for duplication of data entry. The web-based app also makes customer management easier through the storage of customer contact information and maintenance of a complete history of estimates and jobs.

Maintaining customer contact information will provide the ability to conduct direct mail campaigns with customers. Regular contact through direct mail will include such campaigns as:

- annual calendar imprinted with Sierra Plumbing contact information
- periodic "Refer a friend - Get a discount"
- periodic "Specials" such as discounts on sewer pipe inspections
- mailing a monthly newsletter with useful information for homeowners

Other practices that will distinguish Sierra Plumbing from other plumbing services include:

- all calls will be returned within one hour during normal business hours Tuesday through Friday
- estimates given prior to work being done and guaranteed to be accurate
- cleanup after job completion
- employees are identifiable by their company uniforms
- employees undergo background check prior to hire
- hand-written "thank you" notes sent to customers after service

Plumbing Service Analysis

In the state of California a plumbing contractor's license is required for projects that cost more than $500. Earning the contractor's license (C-36) requires the following:

- be at least 18 years of age

- four years of experience as a journeyman, foreman, supervisor, or contractor

- approval from the state licensing board for permission to sit for required exams

- passing a business law exam and a trade exam

- working capital of at least $2,500

- filing a bond of $10,000 with the Registrar

- fingerprinting, proof of workers' compensation coverage or exemption

The Contractors State License Board (CSLB) administers licensing exams. Licenses must be renewed every two years. There is no continuing education requirement.

COMPETITION

There are several plumbing services that serve Placer County so Sierra Plumbing Services, Inc. will have to find a way to rise above the noise and establish its own brand. The competition falls within identifiable types:

Locally owned companies: similar to Sierra Plumbing Services, Inc. these companies are willing to travel throughout the county to serve customers. Some have a staff of employees allowing them to answer calls seven days a week. Like Sierra Plumbing, these companies offer a variety of services.

Franchise companies: affiliation with a national franchise gives these companies instant recognition.

COMPETITIVE EDGE

One of the complaints most often heard about contractors is that they do not follow up or even show up when they say they will. Contained within Sierra Plumbing's mission statement and embedded in its business approach is the commitment to maintaining clear and consistent contact with customers and following through on calls, appointments, and services to the customer's satisfaction.

Key among these commitments is a program of continued contact through the use of:

- the company web site and blog

- monthly newsletter

- coupon and specials throughout the year

- social media presence on Facebook, Twitter and FourSquare

- hand-written "thank you" notes after service

James Bluth has gained a detailed knowledge of plumbing skills but also has a deep knowledge of customer needs and concerns through his years in retail sales and service for a major home improvement retail company. Through thousands of interactions with homeowners, Bluth has developed and honed his skills in working with customers to diagnose and solve their plumbing needs.

Through his retail experience, Bluth has also gained many industry and individual contacts. He knows what companies make the best parts and provide the best service. Sierra Plumbing customers will benefit by being able to get the best parts from companies that stand behind their products. They can save time and money by relying on Bluth's knowledge and contacts when it comes to buying parts and furnishings for their plumbing needs.

MANAGEMENT

Company founder, James Bluth has over 15 years experience in residential and commercial service and repair. Bluth was one of the first plumbing professionals in Placer County to use the trenchless sewer and water line replacement system also known as Pipe Bursting or Trenchless Technology.

Sierra Plumbing Services, Inc. was formed in 2013 by James Bluth who began his career in 1990 after completing a program of study and apprenticeship in a plumbing training program sponsored by the Plumbing-Heating-Cooling Contractors Association (PHCC). In 1990, Bluth was granted a California state plumbing contractor's license issued by the Contractors State License Board (CSLB).

Between 1990 and 2013 Bluth utilized his skills and training in a number of venues including: sales and service for a nationally known retail company, a local plumbing services franchise company, and a locally-owned plumbing service company. In 2012 Bluth began to develop his plan for opening his own service company and has financed the company start-up through the use of his personal savings. Sierra Plumbing Services, Inc. began officially in March of 2013 after Bluth quit his job.

PERSONNEL PLAN

James Bluth will be the only employee for the first year of operations as Sierra Plumbing develops its brand identity. During this time, James Bluth, Jr. will continue to work toward his certification as a plumber and heating/cooling specialist in the state of California. In year two James Bluth, Jr. will join the company. At that time funding for an additional truck will be obtained through an equity credit line on the Bluth family home. The truck will be leased to the corporation which will pay for insurance, license and maintenance as well as gas and repairs for the truck.

The addition of James Bluth, Jr. will enable Sierra Plumbing to offer services Mondays through Saturdays and to diversify its service offerings to include heating/cooling as well as plumbing services. In year five, the company will hire an additional plumber and acquire an additional truck.

Personnel plan	Year 1	Year 2	Year 3
James Bluth	$24,000	$36,000	$39,000
James Bluth, Jr.		$36,000	$36,000
Total people	1	2	2
Total payroll	**$24,000**	**$72,000**	**$75,000**

FINANCIAL PLAN

Projected Profit and Loss

	Year 1	Year 2	Year 3
Sales	**$75,000**	**$150,000**	**$200,000**
Direct cost of materials	$ 7,200	$ 15,000	$ 23,000
Other costs of labor	$ 0	$ 0	$ 0
Total cost of sales	**$ 7,200**	**$ 15,000**	**$ 23,000**
Gross margin	$67,800	$135,000	$177,000
Gross margin %	90.40%	90.00%	88.50%
Expenses			
Payroll	$24,000	$ 72,000	$ 75,000
Depreciation	$ 2,800	$ 4,800	$ 4,800
Rent	$ 900	$ 1,200	$ 1,200
Utilities	$ 0	$ 0	$ 0
Insurance	$ 3,000	$ 6,000	$ 6,000
Payroll taxes/workers comp	$ 2,400	$ 7,200	$ 7,500
Telephone	$ 850	$ 1,600	$ 1,800
Advertising/web site	$ 1,400	$ 2,400	$ 3,600
Truck gas/repairs	$ 4,500	$ 11,000	$ 12,000
Legal fees	$ 2,450	$ 0	$ 0
Employee benefits	$ 3,600	$ 10,800	$ 11,250
Dues subscriptions	$ 450	$ 800	$ 850
Truck lease		$ 3,600	$ 3,600
Other expenses	$ 500	$ 700	$ 900
Total operating expenses	**$46,850**	**$122,100**	**$128,500**
Profit before interest and taxes	$20,950	$ 12,900	$ 48,500
EBITDA	$23,750	$ 17,700	$ 53,300
Interest expense	$ 0	$ 0	$ 0
Taxes incurred	$ 5,238	$ 3,225	$ 12,125
Net profit after taxes	**$15,713**	**$ 9,675**	**$ 36,375**
Net profit/sales	**20.95%**	**6.45%**	**18.19%**

Projected Balance Sheet

Proforma balance sheet

	Year 1	Year 2	Year 3
Assets			
Current assets			
Cash	$ 4,000	$19,901	$51,384
Other current assets	$ 550	$ 450	$ 450
Total current assets	**$ 4,550**	**$20,351**	**$51,834**
Long-term assets			
Long-term assets	$15,580	$15,580	$15,580
Accumulated depreciation	($ 5,453)	($ 4,051)	($ 2,430)
Total long-term assets	**$10,127**	**$11,529**	**$13,150**
Total assets	**$14,677**	**$31,880**	**$64,984**
Liabilities and capital			
Current liabilities			
Accounts payable	$ 0	$ 0	$ 0
Other current liabilities	$ 0	$ 1,400	$ 1,600
Subtotal current liabilities	$ 0	$ 1,400	$ 1,600
Long-term liabilities	$ 0	$ 0	$ 0
Total liabilities	**$ 0**	**$ 1,400**	**$ 1,600**
Earnings	$15,713	$ 9,675	$36,375
Total capital	**$14,677**	**$30,480**	**$63,384**
Total liabilities and capital	**$14,677**	**$31,880**	**$64,984**

Profit by year

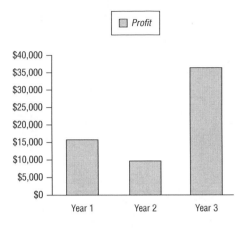

SOURCES

http://www.youngentrepreneur.com/startingup/how-to-guides/how-to-start-a-plumbing-business/

http://smallbusiness.chron.com/open-plumbing-business-2467.html

http://www.thefinanceresource.com/free_business_plans/free_plumbing_contractor_business_plan.aspx

http://www.bplans.com/plumbing_business_plan/executive_summary_fc.php#.UI7FM65Vot0/
?affiliate=smallbusi7

http://plumbingmarketingprofits.com/plumbing-marketing-interview-with-the-clean-plumber-
s?utm_source=dlvr.it&utm_medium=feed

http://www.time.com/time/nation/article/0,8599,1851673,00.html

http://www.plumbingzone.com/f4/gross-sales-per-truck-187-000-00-a-25531/

http://www.cslb.ca.gov/Resources/FormsAndApplications/ApplicationForOriginalContractorsLicense.pdf

http://www.labormarketinfo.edd.ca.gov/OccGuides/LicenseDetail.aspx?Li-
cId=69940%20%20%20%20%20

Vending Machine Business

Brenner's Vending Services

48350 DelRay Blvd.
Troy, MI 48085

Brenda Kubiac

Brenner's Vending Services, LLC is a vending machine service business.

1.0 EXECUTIVE SUMMARY

1.1 Business Overview

Brenner's Vending Services, LLC is a Michigan-based limited liability vending machine business located in Troy. Formerly, the owner, David Brenner spent several years servicing vending machines as a technician before he decided to start his own vending machine business and become part of the nearly $20 billion snack and vending industry. David joins the small segment of vending operators that comprised 77 percent of operators in 2011. Throughout those seven years he learned that if you want to succeed as a vendor operator it's all in how you value your customers. Not only do you listen to their requests, but more importantly their complaints. Not only has David Brenner witnessed first-hand how not to run a vending service business, he has established ties and relationships within the industry along the way.

The owner has targeted four high traffic manufacturing areas and has negotiated a percentage of profits with clients and is ready to start his vending business. The company also signed a contract with a large industrial office complex slated to open during the second year of operation for coffee vending equipment. David Brenner is an active member of the National Automatic Merchandising Association (NAMA) of which keeps vendors on top of industry trends and technological advances directly related to the vending industry.

1.2 Mission Statement

Brenner's Vending Services promises to fulfill customer's expectations by delivering exceptional products and customer service at all times.

2.0 INDUSTRY/MARKET

2.1 Industry Analysis

According to the Bureau of Labor Statistics, the average vending machine operator makes about $70.58 per hour. There were a reported 29,375 vendor operators working in the industry in 2012. According to IBISWorld industry analyst Dale Schmidt, "rising food costs and less-populated public places have translated into lost earnings for vending machines" adding that "operators will work to better meet demand by offering a wider selection of food, including a further push into healthy snacks. However, the operator's will still rely heavily on soda and candy even with the increasing focus on healthy eating, hindering industry growth" (www.ibisworld.com, 2012).

The medium sized vending operators (revenues between $5 million and $10 million) continue to lose market share to larger vending operators who have the means to compete within the highly competitive industry. However, the smaller operators (revenues under $1 million) profit because of less operating costs and they are able to foster relationships with their clients and keep contracts in place longer.

Established in 1936, the National Automatic Merchandising Association's (NAMA) mission is to "collectively advance and promote the automatic merchandising and coffee service industries." (www.nama.org, 2013) NAMA plans to launch a major campaign directed especially at those aged 18-27 in conversation surrounding the latest vending machines, products, and high-tech upgrades with the help of social networking.

2.2 MARKET ANALYSIS

According to the *Automatic Merchandiser* magazine's State of the Vending Industry Report, vending sales totaled nearly $20 billion in 2012. Also, market research company NPD Group released its 2012 report titled "Snacking in America" that revealed 53 percent of consumer's snack two or three times per day.

During Brenner's Vending Services, LLC market assessment, the company discovered a need for coffee vending in the workplace. According to the National Automatic Merchandising Association's (NAMA) 2012 Coffee Research Project, *Office Beverage Strengths and Opportunities*, 49 percent of employees would drink more coffee on the job if "espressos, lattes or other ways of serving coffee were available."

With statistics like these there is no reason to fail as a vending operator unless you're not watching the market, your competitor's prices, relocating under-performing machines, keeping your machines stocked, changing product selection as a result of customer feedback, or nurturing relationships with both your customers and clients.

2.3 Competition

Even though vendor operators in general face intense competition, with a population of 57,251 people residing in Troy, vending machine operators should be able to share in the prosperity of vending.

3.0 PERSONNEL

3.1 Management Summary

The company was started by David Brenner who has been around the vending industry for seven years employed as a vending machine repair technician for Baller Vending Services, Inc. located in Royal Oak MI. David received his certification from industry trade group, the National Automatic Merchandising Association (NAMA). David feels he has a competitive edge as he embarks on his new business venture.

3.2 Professional and Advisory Support

Brenner's Vending Services, LLC has hired Sloan Accounting Agency to set up an accounting system that will be appropriate for a home-based vending business. Legal counsel was provided by Simon & Company to address all the legal matters including writing up the contract between Brenner's Vending Services, LLC and clients. To maneuver through insurance guidelines and fully protect Brenner's Vending Services, LLC, in particular, $1 million in liability insurance was obtained through Damon Insurance Co.

4.0 STRATEGIES

4.1 Business Strategy

Monitor vending products, especially the so-called healthy line to see what is producing large returns compared to products if any that may need to be substituted with other products.

4.2 Growth Strategy

Brenner's Vending Services, LLC will strive for a 150 to 200 percent return on products and continue to extend its route by purchasing additional vending machines and locating them in high prone traffic areas within a 60-mile radius of each other along with other perks to increase revenue during the first three year of operation. Continue to monitor target market for changes that could off-set original assessment from the first year.

- **Year One:** Purchase a total of 4 vending machines and place along the route in high-traffic areas that compliment and not compete with competitor's machines.

- **Year Two:** Purchase and locate four Cup of Jo Coffee Bar Hot beverage vending machines that grind coffee beans for freshly brewed coffee, café mocha and cappuccino, French vanilla and decaf coffee at industrial office complex. Pass out flyers around the office about the new vending machine that accepts credit/debit cards. Coffee items will be purchased from Java Wholesalers, Inc. located in Ferndale, MI. The company will invest in remote monitoring software that alerts vending operator when a vending machine needs to be filled at a given location and which products.

- **Year Three:** Have a total of 15 vending machines located in profitable locations along targeted route equipped with dollar bill acceptors and permit cashless payment.

5.0 PRODUCTS AND SERVICES

Products include Four Combination Treasures snack vending machines stocked with brand recognized candy, chips, cookies, healthy snacks and more. These machines will be re-stocked when they are half-full at all times.

6.0 MARKETING & SALES

6.1 Advertising and Promotion

- Listed company contact information in the online Vending Yellow Pages Directory

- Attend industry trade shows

- Build Web site showcasing vending machines and location, vendor items etc.

- Follow-up with clients to see if they are satisfied or have any concern

- To retain client base the company plans to hire a marketing firm to conduct a survey to determine if Brenner's Vending Services, LLC is delivering what customers want and expect after six months in operation

- Handle complaints and special requests

- Build customer loyalty

- Continue developing and fostering relationships

- Join open forums to get questions answered as they come up from other vendors

- Pass out free samples

- Network with industry professionals and other owners

- Monitor machines and re-locate if the location is not meeting sales expectations

- Continue to keep a watchful eye on competitor's vending machines for price increases

7.0 OPERATIONS

Following extensive research through various channels the company decided to invest in used vending machines versus purchasing new. David Brenner located the ideal equipment from one vendor getting out of the business and purchased four vending machines for $2,000. Since vending machines normally last 40 years and these are eight years old repairs should be kept to a minimum. Snacks and candy will be purchased at area big-box store or other online wholesalers.

Business owners view the vending machine in their establishment as a convenience to both their employees and customers. A commission of 0 to 20 percent of the net profit is discussed and followed by a contract signing guaranteeing the location, normally for one year. The machine can then be put in place and filled. To continue for the next year another contract will be signed by both parties involved.

8.0 FINANCIAL ANALYSIS

8.1 Start-up Inventory Expenses

Inventory	Estimated unit cost	Unit count per vendor	Estimated cost per vendor	Total for 4 vendors
Row 1/Salty snacks				
Doritos	0.32	10	$3.20	$12.80
Cheetos	0.30	10	3.00	12.00
Kettle Brand Baked Potato Chips, Sea Salt	0.29	10	2.90	11.60
Fritos	0.32	10	3.20	12.80
Sun Chips	0.29	10	2.90	11.60
Snyder's Pretzels	0.31	10	3.10	12.40
Laurel Hill Multigrain Tortilla Chips	0.33	10	3.30	13.20
Lays Bar-b-que Chips	0.32	10	3.20	12.80
Pringles	0.34	10	3.40	13.60
Ruffles Sour Cream & Onion	0.32	10	3.20	12.80
Row 2/Cookies/Crackers				
Ritz Bits	0.30	10	3.00	12.00
Oreo Cookies	0.30	10	3.30	13.20
Lays Chips	0.30	10	3.00	12.00
Nabisco Chocolate	0.30	10	3.00	12.00
Chip Cookies Animal Crackers	0.30	10	3.00	12.00
Row 3/Candy				
Reese's Peanut Butter Cups	0.38	10	3.80	15.20
m&m's	0.38	10	3.80	15.20
Twix	0.38	10	3.80	15.20
Milky Way	0.38	10	3.80	15.20
Snickers	0.38	10	3.80	15.20
Butterfinger	0.38	10	3.80	15.20
Kit Kat	0.38	10	3.80	15.20
Skittles	0.36	10	3.80	15.20
3 Musketeers	0.38	10	3.80	15.20
PayDay	0.38	10	3.80	15.20
Row 4/Snack bars				
Nestle Crunch	0.38	10	3.80	15.20
Twizzlers	0.36	10	3.60	14.40
Almond Joy	0.38	8	3.04	12.16
Mounds	0.38	8	3.04	12.16
Hershey Chocolate	0.38	10	3.80	15.20
Hershey Almond	0.38	10	3.80	15.20
York Peppermint Pieces	0.38	8	3.80	15.20
Hershey Milk Duds	0.36	8	2.88	11.52
Dove	0.41	8	3.28	13.12
Row 5/Gum & Mints				
Eclipse	0.24	15	3.60	14.40
Orbit	0.25	15	3.75	15.00
Ice Breakers	0.33	15	4.95	19.80
Stride Sweet Cinnamon	0.30	15	4.50	18.00
Dentyne	0.26	15	3.90	15.60
Trident Passionberry Twist	0.26	15	3.90	15.60
Row 6/Pastries				
Kellogg's Pop Tarts	0.42	10	4.20	16.80
Yellow Zinger	0.40	10	4.00	16.00
Pound Cake	0.39	10	3.90	15.60
Carrot Cake	0.39	10	3.90	15.60
Blueberry Muffins	0.42	10	4.20	16.80
Cheese Danish	0.43	10	4.30	17.20
Honey Bun	0.45	10	4.50	18.00
Cinnamon Roll	0.39	10	3.90	15.60
Donuts	0.39	10	3.90	15.60
Cup Cakes	0.38	10	3.80	15.20

8.1 Start-up Inventory Expenses cont.

Inventory	Estimated unit cost	Unit count per vendor	Estimated cost per vendor	Total for 4 vendors
Row 7/Healthy snacks				
Cereal & Granola Bar	0.52	8	4.16	16.64
CLIF Bar	0.78	5	3.90	15.60
Eden Foods Nuts, Seeds & Berries	0.62	5	3.10	12.40
Geru Natural Energy Drink	0.84	8	6.72	26.88
Stonefield Farms Non-dairy Smoothie	0.89	10	8.90	35.60
Apple Crisps	0.42	5	2.10	8.40
Veggie Chips	0.41	5	2.05	8.20
Fruit & Nut Bar	0.52	8	4.16	16.64
Kopali Organics Trail Mix	0.91	5	4.55	18.20
Tofurky Original Jurky	0.89	5	4.45	17.80
Penta Purified Water	0.32	50	16.00	64.00
Beginning inventory				**$964.12**
First refill				**$482.06**
Total start-up				**$1,446.18**

8.2 2013 balance sheet

Revenue

Vending machine #1	$ 27,270
Vending machine #2	$ 52,318
Vending machine #3	$ 19,345
Vending machine #4	$ 31,689
Total revenue	**$130,622**

8.3 Expenses

Office equipment	$ 2,000.00
Marketing/advertising	$ 500.00
Truck lease	$ 650.00
Insurance	$ 1,000.00
Licenses and fees	$ 300.00
Professional fees	$ 250.00
Misc. office supply	$ 250.00
Delivery/moving/freight	$ 800.00
Vending equipment	$ 4,000.00
Inventory	$ 1,446.18
Currency Counter	$ 500.00
Total	**$ 11,696.18**
Net income	**$118,925.82**

BUSINESS PLAN TEMPLATE

USING THIS TEMPLATE

A business plan carefully spells out a company's projected course of action over a period of time, usually the first two to three years after the start-up. In addition, banks, lenders, and other investors examine the information and financial documentation before deciding whether or not to finance a new business venture. Therefore, a business plan is an essential tool in obtaining financing and should describe the business itself in detail as well as all important factors influencing the company, including the market, industry, competition, operations and management policies, problem solving strategies, financial resources and needs, and other vital information. The plan enables the business owner to anticipate costs, plan for difficulties, and take advantage of opportunities, as well as design and implement strategies that keep the company running as smoothly as possible.

This template has been provided as a model to help you construct your own business plan. Please keep in mind that there is no single acceptable format for a business plan, and that this template is in no way comprehensive, but serves as an example.

The business plans provided in this section are fictional and have been used by small business agencies as models for clients to use in compiling their own business plans.

GENERIC BUSINESS PLAN

Main headings included below are topics that should be covered in a comprehensive business plan. They include:

Business Summary

Purpose

Provides a brief overview of your business, succinctly highlighting the main ideas of your plan.

Includes

- Name and Type of Business
- Description of Product/Service
- Business History and Development
- Location
- Market
- Competition
- Management
- Financial Information
- Business Strengths and Weaknesses
- Business Growth

Table of Contents

Purpose

Organized in an Outline Format, the Table of Contents illustrates the selection and arrangement of information contained in your plan.

Includes

- Topic Headings and Subheadings
- Page Number References

Business History and Industry Outlook

Purpose

Examines the conception and subsequent development of your business within an industry specific context.

Includes

- Start-up Information
- Owner/Key Personnel Experience
- Location
- Development Problems and Solutions
- Investment/Funding Information
- Future Plans and Goals
- Market Trends and Statistics
- Major Competitors
- Product/Service Advantages
- National, Regional, and Local Economic Impact

Product/Service

Purpose

Introduces, defines, and details the product and/or service that inspired the information of your business.

Includes

- Unique Features
- Niche Served
- Market Comparison
- Stage of Product/Service Development
- Production
- Facilities, Equipment, and Labor
- Financial Requirements
- Product/Service Life Cycle
- Future Growth

Market Examination

Purpose

Assessment of product/service applications in relation to consumer buying cycles.

Includes

- Target Market
- Consumer Buying Habits
- Product/Service Applications
- Consumer Reactions
- Market Factors and Trends
- Penetration of the Market
- Market Share
- Research and Studies
- Cost
- Sales Volume and Goals

Competition

Purpose

Analysis of Competitors in the Marketplace.

Includes

- Competitor Information
- Product/Service Comparison
- Market Niche
- Product/Service Strengths and Weaknesses
- Future Product/Service Development

Marketing

Purpose

Identifies promotion and sales strategies for your product/service.

Includes

- Product/Service Sales Appeal
- Special and Unique Features
- Identification of Customers
- Sales and Marketing Staff
- Sales Cycles
- Type of Advertising/ Promotion
- Pricing
- Competition
- Customer Services

Operations

Purpose

Traces product/service development from production/inception to the market environment.

Includes

- Cost Effective Production Methods
- Facility
- Location
- Equipment
- Labor
- Future Expansion

Administration and Management

Purpose

Offers a statement of your management philosophy with an in-depth focus on processes and procedures.

Includes

- Management Philosophy
- Structure of Organization
- Reporting System
- Methods of Communication
- Employee Skills and Training
- Employee Needs and Compensation
- Work Environment
- Management Policies and Procedures
- Roles and Responsibilities

Key Personnel

Purpose

Describes the unique backgrounds of principle employees involved in business.

Includes

- Owner(s)/Employee Education and Experience
- Positions and Roles
- Benefits and Salary
- Duties and Responsibilities
- Objectives and Goals

Potential Problems and Solutions

Purpose

Discussion of problem solving strategies that change issues into opportunities.

Includes

- Risks
- Litigation
- Future Competition
- Economic Impact
- Problem Solving Skills

Financial Information

Purpose

Secures needed funding and assistance through worksheets and projections detailing financial plans, methods of repayment, and future growth opportunities.

Includes

- Financial Statements
- Bank Loans
- Methods of Repayment
- Tax Returns

- Start-up Costs
- Projected Income (3 years)
- Projected Cash Flow (3 Years)
- Projected Balance Statements (3 years)

Appendices

Purpose

Supporting documents used to enhance your business proposal.

Includes

- Photographs of product, equipment, facilities, etc.
- Copyright/Trademark Documents
- Legal Agreements
- Marketing Materials
- Research and or Studies

- Operation Schedules
- Organizational Charts
- Job Descriptions
- Resumes
- Additional Financial Documentation

Fictional Food Distributor

Commercial Foods, Inc.

3003 Avondale Ave.
Knoxville, TN 37920

This plan demonstrates how a partnership can have a positive impact on a new business. It demonstrates how two individuals can carve a niche in the specialty foods market by offering gourmet foods to upscale restaurants and fine hotels. This plan is fictional and has not been used to gain funding from a bank or other lending institution.

STATEMENT OF PURPOSE

Commercial Foods, Inc. seeks a loan of $75,000 to establish a new business. This sum, together with $5,000 equity investment by the principals, will be used as follows:

- Merchandise inventory $25,000
- Office fixture/equipment $12,000
- Warehouse equipment $14,000
- One delivery truck $10,000
- Working capital $39,000
- Total $100,000

DESCRIPTION OF THE BUSINESS

Commercial Foods, Inc. will be a distributor of specialty food service products to hotels and upscale restaurants in the geographical area of a 50 mile radius of Knoxville. Richard Roberts will direct the sales effort and John Williams will manage the warehouse operation and the office. One delivery truck will be used initially with a second truck added in the third year. We expect to begin operation of the business within 30 days after securing the requested financing.

MANAGEMENT

A. Richard Roberts is a native of Memphis, Tennessee. He is a graduate of Memphis State University with a Bachelor's degree from the School of Business. After graduation, he worked for a major manufacturer of specialty food service products as a detail sales person for five years, and, for the past three years, he has served as a product sales manager for this firm.

B. John Williams is a native of Nashville, Tennessee. He holds a B.S. Degree in Food Technology from the University of Tennessee. His career includes five years as a product development chemist in gourmet food products and five years as operations manager for a food service distributor.

Both men are healthy and energetic. Their backgrounds complement each other, which will ensure the success of Commercial Foods, Inc. They will set policies together and personnel decisions will be made jointly. Initial salaries for the owners will be $1,000 per month for the first few years. The spouses of both principals are successful in the business world and earn enough to support the families.

They have engaged the services of Foster Jones, CPA, and William Hale, Attorney, to assist them in an advisory capacity.

PERSONNEL

The firm will employ one delivery truck driver at a wage of $8.00 per hour. One office worker will be employed at $7.50 per hour. One part-time employee will be used in the office at $5.00 per hour. The driver will load and unload his own trucks. Mr. Williams will assist in the warehouse operation as needed to assist one stock person at $7.00 per hour. An additional delivery truck and driver will be added the third year.

LOCATION

The firm will lease a 20,000 square foot building at 3003 Avondale Ave., in Knoxville, which contains warehouse and office areas equipped with two-door truck docks. The annual rental is $9,000. The building was previously used as a food service warehouse and very little modification to the building will be required.

PRODUCTS AND SERVICES

The firm will offer specialty food service products such as soup bases, dessert mixes, sauce bases, pastry mixes, spices, and flavors, normally used by upscale restaurants and nice hotels. We are going after a niche in the market with high quality gourmet products. There is much less competition in this market than in standard run of the mill food service products. Through their work experiences, the principals have contacts with supply sources and with local chefs.

THE MARKET

We know from our market survey that there are over 200 hotels and upscale restaurants in the area we plan to serve. Customers will be attracted by a direct sales approach. We will offer samples of our products and product application data on use of our products in the finished prepared foods. We will cultivate the chefs in these establishments. The technical background of John Williams will be especially useful here.

COMPETITION

We find that we will be only distributor in the area offering a full line of gourmet food service products. Other foodservice distributors offer only a few such items in conjunction with their standard product line. Our survey shows that many of the chefs are ordering products from Atlanta and Memphis because of a lack of adequate local supply.

SUMMARY

Commercial Foods, Inc. will be established as a foodservice distributor of specialty food in Knoxville. The principals, with excellent experience in the industry, are seeking a $75,000 loan to establish the business. The principals are investing $25,000 as equity capital.

The business will be set up as an S Corporation with each principal owning 50% of the common stock in the corporation.

FICTIONAL HARDWARE STORE

OSHKOSH HARDWARE, INC.

123 Main St.
Oshkosh, WI 54901

The following plan outlines how a small hardware store can survive competition from large discount chains by offering products and providing expert advice in the use of any product it sells. This plan is fictional and has not been used to gain funding from a bank or other lending institution.

EXECUTIVE SUMMARY

Oshkosh Hardware, Inc. is a new corporation that is going to establish a retail hardware store in a strip mall in Oshkosh, Wisconsin. The store will sell hardware of all kinds, quality tools, paint, and housewares. The business will make revenue and a profit by servicing its customers not only with needed hardware but also with expert advice in the use of any product it sells.

Oshkosh Hardware, Inc. will be operated by its sole shareholder, James Smith. The company will have a total of four employees. It will sell its products in the local market. Customers will buy our products because we will provide free advice on the use of all of our products and will also furnish a full refund warranty.

Oshkosh Hardware, Inc. will sell its products in the Oshkosh store staffed by three sales representatives. No additional employees will be needed to achieve its short and long range goals. The primary short range goal is to open the store by October 1, 1994. In order to achieve this goal a lease must be signed by July 1, 1994 and the complete inventory ordered by August 1, 1994.

Mr. James Smith will invest $30,000 in the business. In addition, the company will have to borrow $150,000 during the first year to cover the investment in inventory, accounts receivable, and furniture and equipment. The company will be profitable after six months of operation and should be able to start repayment of the loan in the second year.

THE BUSINESS

The business will sell hardware of all kinds, quality tools, paint, and housewares. We will purchase our products from three large wholesale buying groups.

In general our customers are homeowners who do their own repair and maintenance, hobbyists, and housewives. Our business is unique in that we will have a complete line of all hardware items and will be able to get special orders by overnight delivery. The business makes revenue and profits by servicing our customers not only with needed hardware but also with expert advice in the use of any product we sell. Our major costs for bringing our products to market are cost of merchandise of 36%, salaries of $45,000, and occupancy costs of $60,000.

Oshkosh Hardware, Inc.'s retail outlet will be located at 1524 Frontage Road, which is in a newly developed retail center of Oshkosh. Our location helps facilitate accessibility from all parts of town and reduces our delivery costs. The store will occupy 7500 square feet of space. The major equipment involved in our business is counters and shelving, a computer, a paint mixing machine, and a truck.

THE MARKET

Oshkosh Hardware, Inc. will operate in the local market. There are 15,000 potential customers in this market area. We have three competitors who control approximately 98% of the market at present. We feel we can capture 25% of the market within the next four years. Our major reason for believing this is that our staff is technically competent to advise our customers in the correct use of all products we sell.

After a careful market analysis, we have determined that approximately 60% of our customers are men and 40% are women. The percentage of customers that fall into the following age categories are:

Under 16: 0%

17-21: 5%

22-30: 30%

31-40: 30%

41-50: 20%

51-60: 10%

61-70: 5%

Over 70: 0%

The reasons our customers prefer our products is our complete knowledge of their use and our full refund warranty.

We get our information about what products our customers want by talking to existing customers. There seems to be an increasing demand for our product. The demand for our product is increasing in size based on the change in population characteristics.

SALES

At Oshkosh Hardware, Inc. we will employ three sales people and will not need any additional personnel to achieve our sales goals. These salespeople will need several years experience in home repair and power tool usage. We expect to attract 30% of our customers from newspaper ads, 5% of our customers from local directories, 5% of our customers from the yellow pages, 10% of our customers from family and friends, and 50% of our customers from current customers. The most cost effect source will be current customers. In general our industry is growing.

MANAGEMENT

We would evaluate the quality of our management staff as being excellent. Our manager is experienced and very motivated to achieve the various sales and quality assurance objectives we have set. We will use a management information system that produces key inventory, quality assurance, and sales data on a weekly basis. All data is compared to previously established goals for that week, and deviations are the primary focus of the management staff.

GOALS IMPLEMENTATION

The short term goals of our business are:

1. Open the store by October 1, 1994
2. Reach our breakeven point in two months
3. Have sales of $100,000 in the first six months

In order to achieve our first short term goal we must:

1. Sign the lease by July 1, 1994
2. Order a complete inventory by August 1, 1994

In order to achieve our second short term goal we must:

1. Advertise extensively in Sept. and Oct.
2. Keep expenses to a minimum

In order to achieve our third short term goal we must:

1. Promote power tool sales for the Christmas season
2. Keep good customer traffic in Jan. and Feb.

The long term goals for our business are:

1. Obtain sales volume of $600,000 in three years
2. Become the largest hardware dealer in the city
3. Open a second store in Fond du Lac

The most important thing we must do in order to achieve the long term goals for our business is to develop a highly profitable business with excellent cash flow.

FINANCE

Oshkosh Hardware, Inc. Faces some potential threats or risks to our business. They are discount house competition. We believe we can avoid or compensate for this by providing quality products complimented by quality advice on the use of every product we sell. The financial projections we have prepared are located at the end of this document.

JOB DESCRIPTION-GENERAL MANAGER

The General Manager of the business of the corporation will be the president of the corporation. He will be responsible for the complete operation of the retail hardware store which is owned by the corporation. A detailed description of his duties and responsibilities is as follows.

Sales

Train and supervise the three sales people. Develop programs to motivate and compensate these employees. Coordinate advertising and sales promotion effects to achieve sales totals as outlined in budget. Oversee purchasing function and inventory control procedures to insure adequate merchandise at all times at a reasonable cost.

Finance

Prepare monthly and annual budgets. Secure adequate line of credit from local banks. Supervise office personnel to insure timely preparation of records, statements, all government reports, control of receivables and payables, and monthly financial statements.

Administration

Perform duties as required in the areas of personnel, building leasing and maintenance, licenses and permits, and public relations.

Organizations, Agencies, & Consultants

A listing of Associations and Consultants of interest to entrepreneurs, followed by the ten Small Business Administration Regional Offices, Small Business Development Centers, Service Corps of Retired Executives offices, and Venture Capital and Finance Companies.

Associations

This section contains a listing of associations and other agencies of interest to the small business owner. Entries are listed alphabetically by organization name.

American Business Women's Association
9100 Ward Pkwy.
PO Box 8728
Kansas City, MO 64114-0728
(800)228-0007
E-mail: abwa@abwa.org
Website: http://www.abwa.org
Jeanne Banks, National President

American Franchisee Association
53 W Jackson Blvd., Ste. 1157
Chicago, IL 60604
(312)431-0545
E-mail: info@franchisee.org
Website: http://www.franchisee.org
Susan P. Kezios, President

American Independent Business Alliance
222 S Black Ave.
Bozeman, MT 59715
(406)582-1255
E-mail: info@amiba.net
Website: http://www.amiba.net
Jennifer Rockne, Director

American Small Businesses Association
206 E College St., Ste. 201
Grapevine, TX 76051
800-942-2722
E-mail: info@asbaonline.org
Website: http://www.asbaonline.org/

American Women's Economic Development Corporation
216 East 45th St., 10th Floor
New York, NY 10017
(917)368-6100

Fax: (212)986-7114
E-mail: info@awed.org
Website: http://www.awed.org
Roseanne Antonucci, Exec. Dir.

Association for Enterprise Opportunity
1601 N Kent St., Ste. 1101
Arlington, VA 22209
(703)841-7760
Fax: (703)841-7748
E-mail: aeo@assoceo.org
Website: http://www.micro
enterpriseworks.org
Bill Edwards, Exec.Dir.

Association of Small Business Development Centers
c/o Don Wilson
8990 Burke Lake Rd.
Burke, VA 22015
(703)764-9850
Fax: (703)764-1234
E-mail: info@asbdc-us.org
Website: http://www.asbdc-us.org
Don Wilson, Pres./CEO

BEST Employers Association
2505 McCabe Way
Irvine, CA 92614
(949)253-4080
800-433-0088
Fax: (714)553-0883
E-mail: info@bestlife.com
Website: http://www.bestlife.com
Donald R. Lawrenz, CEO

Center for Family Business
PO Box 24219
Cleveland, OH 44124
(440)460-5409
E-mail: grummi@aol.com
Dr. Leon A. Danco, Chm.

Coalition for Government Procurement
1990 M St. NW, Ste. 400
Washington, DC 20036
(202)331-0975
E-mail: info@thecgp.org
Website: http://www.coalgovpro.org
Paul Caggiano, Pres.

Employers of America
PO Box 1874
Mason City, IA 50402-1874
(641)424-3187
800-728-3187
Fax: (641)424-1673
E-mail: employer@employerhelp.org
Website: http://www.employerhelp.org
Jim Collison, Pres.

Family Firm Institute
200 Lincoln St., Ste. 201
Boston, MA 02111
(617)482-3045
Fax: (617)482-3049
E-mail: ffi@ffi.org
Website: http://www.ffi.org
Judy L. Green, Ph.D., Exec.Dir.

Independent Visually Impaired Enterprisers
500 S 3rd St., Apt. H
Burbank, CA 91502
(818)238-9321
E-mail: abazyn@bazyn
communications.com
http://www.acb.org/affiliates
Adris Bazyn, Pres.

International Association for Business Organizations
3 Woodthorn Ct., Ste. 12
Owings Mills, MD 21117
(410)581-1373
E-mail: nahbb@msn.com
Rudolph Lewis, Exec. Officer

International Council for Small Business
The George Washington University School of Business and Public Management
2115 G St. NW, Ste. 403
Washington, DC 20052
(202)994-0704
Fax: (202)994-4930
E-mail: icsb@gwu.edu
Website: http://www.icsb.org
Susan G. Duffy. Admin.

International Small Business Consortium
3309 Windjammer St.
Norman, OK 73072
E-mail: sb@isbc.com
Website: http://www.isbc.com

Kauffman Center for Entrepreneurial Leadership
4801 Rockhill Rd.
Kansas City, MO 64110-2046
(816)932-1000
E-mail: info@kauffman.org
Website: http://www.entreworld.org

National Alliance for Fair Competition
3 Bethesda Metro Center, Ste. 1100
Bethesda, MD 20814
(410)235-7116
Fax: (410)235-7116
E-mail: ampesq@aol.com
Tony Ponticelli, Exec.Dir.

National Association for the Self-Employed
PO Box 612067
DFW Airport
Dallas, TX 75261-2067
(800)232-6273
E-mail: mpetron@nase.org
Website: http://www.nase.org
Robert Hughes, Pres.

National Association of Business Leaders
4132 Shoreline Dr., Ste. J & H
Earth City, MO 63045
Fax: (314)298-9110
E-mail: nabl@nabl.com
Website: http://www.nabl.com/
Gene Blumenthal, Contact

National Association of Private Enterprise
PO Box 15550
Long Beach, CA 90815
888-224-0953

Fax: (714)844-4942
Website: http://www.napeonline.net
Laura Squiers, Exec.Dir.

National Association of Small Business Investment Companies
666 11th St. NW, Ste. 750
Washington, DC 20001
(202)628-5055
Fax: (202)628-5080
E-mail: nasbic@nasbic.org
Website: http://www.nasbic.org
Lee W. Mercer, Pres.

National Business Association
PO Box 700728
5151 Beltline Rd., Ste. 1150
Dallas, TX 75370
(972)458-0900
800-456-0440
Fax: (972)960-9149
E-mail: info@nationalbusiness.org
Website: http://www.national business.org
Raj Nisankarao, Pres.

National Business Owners Association
PO Box 111
Stuart, VA 24171
(276)251-7500
(866)251-7505
Fax: (276)251-2217
E-mail: membershipservices@nboa.org
Website: http://www.rvmdb.com.nboa
Paul LaBarr, Pres.

National Center for Fair Competition
PO Box 220
Annandale, VA 22003
(703)280-4622
Fax: (703)280-0942
E-mail: kentonp1@aol.com
Kenton Pattie, Pres.

National Family Business Council
1640 W. Kennedy Rd.
Lake Forest, IL 60045
(847)295-1040
Fax: (847)295-1898
E-mail: lmsnfbc@email.msn.com
Jogn E. Messervey, Pres.

National Federation of Independent Business
53 Century Blvd., Ste. 250
Nashville, TN 37214
(615)872-5800
800-NFIBNOW
Fax: (615)872-5353
Website: http://www.nfib.org
Jack Faris, Pres. and CEO

National Small Business Association
1156 15th St. NW, Ste. 1100
Washington, DC 20005
(202)293-8830
800-345-6728
Fax: (202)872-8543
E-mail: press@nsba.biz
Website: http://www.nsba.biz
Rob Yunich, Dir. of Communications

PUSH Commercial Division
930 E 50th St.
Chicago, IL 60615-2702
(773)373-3366
Fax: (773)373-3571
E-mail: info@rainbowpush.org
Website: http://www.rainbowpush.org
Rev. Willie T. Barrow, Co-Chm.

Research Institute for Small and Emerging Business
722 12th St. NW
Washington, DC 20005
(202)628-8382
Fax: (202)628-8392
E-mail: info@riseb.org
Website: http://www.riseb.org
Allan Neece, Jr., Chm.

Sales Professionals USA
PO Box 149
Arvada, CO 80001
(303)534-4937
888-736-7767
E-mail: salespro@salesprofessionals-usa.com
Website: http://www.salesprofessionals-usa.com
Sharon Herbert, Natl. Pres.

Score Association - Service Corps of Retired Executives
409 3rd St. SW, 6th Fl.
Washington, DC 20024
(202)205-6762
800-634-0245
Fax: (202)205-7636
E-mail: media@score.org
Website: http://www.score.org
W. Kenneth Yancey, Jr., CEO

Small Business and Entrepreneurship Council
1920 L St. NW, Ste. 200
Washington, DC 20036
(202)785-0238
Fax: (202)822-8118
E-mail: membership@sbec.org
Website: http://www.sbecouncil.org
Karen Kerrigan, Pres./CEO

Small Business in Telecommunications
1331 H St. NW, Ste. 500
Washington, DC 20005
(202)347-4511
Fax: (202)347-8607
E-mail: sbt@sbthome.org
Website: http://www.sbthome.org
Lonnie Danchik, Chm.

Small Business Legislative Council
1010 Massachusetts Ave. NW, Ste. 540
Washington, DC 20005
(202)639-8500
Fax: (202)296-5333
E-mail: email@sblc.org
Website: http://www.sblc.org
John Satagaj, Pres.

Small Business Service Bureau
554 Main St.
PO Box 15014
Worcester, MA 01615-0014
(508)756-3513
800-343-0939
Fax: (508)770-0528
E-mail: membership@sbsb.com
Website: http://www.sbsb.com
Francis R. Carroll, Pres.

**Small Publishers Association
of North America**
1618 W Colorado Ave.
Colorado Springs, CO 80904
(719)475-1726
Fax: (719)471-2182
E-mail: span@spannet.org
Website: http://www.spannet.org
Scott Flora, Exec. Dir.

SOHO America
PO Box 941
Hurst, TX 76053-0941
800-495-SOHO
E-mail: soho@1sas.com
Website: http://www.soho.org

**Structured Employment Economic
Development Corporation**
915 Broadway, 17th Fl.
New York, NY 10010
(212)473-0255
Fax: (212)473-0357
E-mail: info@seedco.org
Website: http://www.seedco.org
William Grinker, CEO

Support Services Alliance
107 Prospect St.
Schoharie, NY 12157
800-836-4772

E-mail: info@ssamembers.com
Website: http://www.ssainfo.com
Steve COle, Pres.

**United States Association for Small
Business and Entrepreneurship**
975 University Ave., No. 3260
Madison, WI 53706
(608)262-9982
Fax: (608)263-0818
E-mail: jgillman@wisc.edu
Website: http://www.ususbe.org
Joan Gillman, Exec. Dir.

Consultants

This section contains a listing of consultants specializing in small business development. It is arranged alphabetically by country, then by state or province, then by city, then by firm name.

Canada

Alberta

Common Sense Solutions
3405 16A Ave.
Edmonton, AB, Canada
(403)465-7330
Fax: (403)465-7380
E-mail: gcoulson@comsense
solutions.com
Website: http://www.comsense
solutions.com

Varsity Consulting Group
School of Business
University of Alberta
Edmonton, AB, Canada T6G 2R6
(780)492-2994
Fax: (780)492-5400
Website: http://www.bus.ualberta.ca/vcg

Viro Hospital Consulting
42 Commonwealth Bldg., 9912-106
St. NW
Edmonton, AB, Canada T5K 1C5
(403)425-3871
Fax: (403)425-3871
E-mail: rpb@freenet.edmonton.ab.ca

British Columbia

SRI Strategic Resources Inc.
4330 Kingsway, Ste. 1600
Burnaby, BC, Canada V5H 4G7
(604)435-0627
Fax: (604)435-2782

E-mail: inquiry@sri.bc.ca
Website: http://www.sri.com

Andrew R. De Boda Consulting
1523 Milford Ave.
Coquitlam, BC, Canada V3J 2V9
(604)936-4527
Fax: (604)936-4527
E-mail: deboda@intergate.bc.ca
Website: http://www.ourworld.
compuserve.com/homepages/deboda

The Sage Group Ltd.
980 - 355 Burrard St.
744 W Haistings, Ste. 410
Vancouver, BC, Canada V6C 1A5
(604)669-9269
Fax: (604)669-6622

Tikkanen-Bradley
1345 Nelson St., Ste. 202
Vancouver, BC, Canada V6E 1J8
(604)669-0583
E-mail: webmaster@tikkanen
bradley.com
Website: http://www.tikkanenbradley.com

Ontario

The Cynton Co.
17 Massey St.
Brampton, ON, Canada L6S 2V6
(905)792-7769
Fax: (905)792-8116
E-mail: cynton@home.com
Website: http://www.cynton.com

Begley & Associates
RR 6
Cambridge, ON, Canada N1R 5S7
(519)740-3629
Fax: (519)740-3629
E-mail: begley@in.on.ca
Website: http://www.in.on.ca/~begley/
index.htm

CRO Engineering Ltd.
1895 William Hodgins Ln.
Carp, ON, Canada K0A 1L0
(613)839-1108
Fax: (613)839-1406
E-mail: J.Grefford@ieee.ca
Website: http://www.geocities.com/
WallStreet/District/7401/

Task Enterprises
Box 69, RR 2 Hamilton
Flamborough, ON, Canada L8N 2Z7
(905)659-0153
Fax: (905)659-0861

HST Group Ltd.
430 Gilmour St.
Ottawa, ON, Canada K2P 0R8
(613)236-7303
Fax: (613)236-9893

Harrison Associates
BCE Pl.
181 Bay St., Ste. 3740
PO Box 798
Toronto, ON, Canada M5J 2T3
(416)364-5441
Fax: (416)364-2875

TCI Convergence Ltd. Management Consultants
99 Crown's Ln.
Toronto, ON, Canada M5R 3P4
(416)515-4146
Fax: (416)515-2097
E-mail: tci@inforamp.net
Website: http://tciconverge.com/index.1.html

Ken Wyman & Associates Inc.
64B Shuter St., Ste. 200
Toronto, ON, Canada M5B 1B1
(416)362-2926
Fax: (416)362-3039
E-mail: kenwyman@compuserve.com

JPL Business Consultants
82705 Metter Rd.
Wellandport, ON, Canada L0R 2J0
(905)386-7450
Fax: (905)386-7450
E-mail: plamarch@freenet.npiec.on.ca

Quebec

The Zimmar Consulting Partnership Inc.
Westmount
PO Box 98
Montreal, QC, Canada H3Z 2T1
(514)484-1459
Fax: (514)484-3063

Saskatchewan

Trimension Group
No. 104-110 Research Dr.
Innovation Place, SK, Canada S7N 3R3
(306)668-2560
Fax: (306)975-1156
E-mail: trimension@trimension.ca
Website: http://www.trimension.ca

Corporate Management Consultants
40 Government Road - PO Box 185
Prud Homme, SK, Canada, S0K 3K0
(306)654-4569
Fax: (650)618-2742

E-mail: cmccorporatemanagement@shaw.ca
Website: http://www.Corporatemanagementconsultants.com
Gerald Rekve

United States

Alabama

Business Planning Inc.
300 Office Park Dr.
Birmingham, AL 35223-2474
(205)870-7090
Fax: (205)870-7103

Tradebank of Eastern Alabama
546 Broad St., Ste. 3
Gadsden, AL 35901
(205)547-8700
Fax: (205)547-8718
E-mail: mansion@webex.com
Website: http://www.webex.com/~tea

Alaska

AK Business Development Center
3335 Arctic Blvd., Ste. 203
Anchorage, AK 99503
(907)562-0335
Free: 800-478-3474
Fax: (907)562-6988
E-mail: abdc@gci.net
Website: http://www.abdc.org

Business Matters
PO Box 287
Fairbanks, AK 99707
(907)452-5650

Arizona

Carefree Direct Marketing Corp.
8001 E Serene St.
PO Box 3737
Carefree, AZ 85377-3737
(480)488-4227
Fax: (480)488-2841

Trans Energy Corp.
1739 W 7th Ave.
Mesa, AZ 85202
(480)827-7915
Fax: (480)967-6601
E-mail: aha@clean-air.org
Website: http://www.clean-air.org

CMAS
5125 N 16th St.
Phoenix, AZ 85016

(602)395-1001
Fax: (602)604-8180

Comgate Telemanagement Ltd.
706 E Bell Rd., Ste. 105
Phoenix, AZ 85022
(602)485-5708
Fax: (602)485-5709
E-mail: comgate@netzone.com
Website: http://www.comgate.com

Moneysoft Inc.
1 E Camelback Rd. #550
Phoenix, AZ 85012
Free: 800-966-7797
E-mail: mbray@moneysoft.com

Harvey C. Skoog
PO Box 26439
Prescott Valley, AZ 86312
(520)772-1714
Fax: (520)772-2814

LMC Services
8711 E Pinnacle Peak Rd., No. 340
Scottsdale, AZ 85255-3555
(602)585-7177
Fax: (602)585-5880
E-mail: louws@earthlink.com

Sauerbrun Technology Group Ltd.
7979 E Princess Dr., Ste. 5
Scottsdale, AZ 85255-5878
(602)502-4950
Fax: (602)502-4292
E-mail: info@sauerbrun.com
Website: http://www.sauerbrun.com

Gary L. McLeod
PO Box 230
Sonoita, AZ 85637
Fax: (602)455-5661

Van Cleve Associates
6932 E 2nd St.
Tucson, AZ 85710
(520)296-2587
Fax: (520)296-3358

California

Acumen Group Inc.
(650)949-9349
Fax: (650)949-4845
E-mail: acumen-g@ix.netcom.com
Website: http://pw2.netcom.com/~janed/acumen.html

On-line Career and Management Consulting
420 Central Ave., No. 314
Alameda, CA 94501

(510)864-0336
Fax: (510)864-0336
E-mail: career@dnai.com
Website: http://www.dnai.com/~career

Career Paths-Thomas E. Church & Associates Inc.
PO Box 2439
Aptos, CA 95001
(408)662-7950
Fax: (408)662-7955
E-mail: church@ix.netcom.com
Website: http://www.careerpaths-tom.com

Keck & Co. Business Consultants
410 Walsh Rd.
Atherton, CA 94027
(650)854-9588
Fax: (650)854-7240
E-mail: info@keckco.com
Website: http://www.keckco.com

Ben W. Laverty III, PhD, REA, CEI
4909 Stockdale Hwy., Ste. 132
Bakersfield, CA 93309
(661)283-8300
Free: 800-833-0373
Fax: (661)283-8313
E-mail: cstc@cstcsafety.com
Website: http://www.cstcsafety.com/cstc

Lindquist Consultants-Venture Planning
225 Arlington Ave.
Berkeley, CA 94707
(510)524-6685
Fax: (510)527-6604

Larson Associates
PO Box 9005
Brea, CA 92822
(714)529-4121
Fax: (714)572-3606
E-mail: ray@consultlarson.com
Website: http://www.consultlarson.com

Kremer Management Consulting
PO Box 500
Carmel, CA 93921
(408)626-8311
Fax: (408)624-2663
E-mail: ddkremer@aol.com

W and J PARTNERSHIP
PO Box 2499
18876 Edwin Markham Dr.
Castro Valley, CA 94546
(510)583-7751
Fax: (510)583-7645
E-mail: wamorgan@wjpartnership.com
Website: http://www.wjpartnership.com

JB Associates
21118 Gardena Dr.
Cupertino, CA 95014
(408)257-0214
Fax: (408)257-0216
E-mail: semarang@sirius.com

House Agricultural Consultants
PO Box 1615
Davis, CA 95617-1615
(916)753-3361
Fax: (916)753-0464
E-mail: infoag@houseag.com
Website: http://www.houseag.com/

3C Systems Co.
16161 Ventura Blvd., Ste. 815
Encino, CA 91436
(818)907-1302
Fax: (818)907 1357
E-mail: mark@3CSysCo.com
Website: http://www.3CSysCo.com

Technical Management Consultants
3624 Westfall Dr.
Encino, CA 91436-4154
(818)784-0626
Fax: (818)501-5575
E-mail: tmcrs@aol.com

RAINWATER-GISH & Associates, Business Finance & Development
317 3rd St., Ste. 3
Eureka, CA 95501
(707)443-0030
Fax: (707)443-5683

Global Tradelinks
451 Pebble Beach Pl.
Fullerton, CA 92835
(714)441-2280
Fax: (714)441-2281
E-mail: info@globaltradelinks.com
Website: http://www.globaltradelinks.com

Strategic Business Group
800 Cienaga Dr.
Fullerton, CA 92835-1248
(714)449-1040
Fax: (714)525-1631

Burnes Consulting
20537 Wolf Creek Rd.
Grass Valley, CA 95949
(530)346-8188
Free: 800-949-9021
Fax: (530)346-7704
E-mail: kent@burnesconsulting.com
Website: http://www.burnesconsulting.com

Pioneer Business Consultants
9042 Garfield Ave., Ste. 312
Huntington Beach, CA 92646
(714)964-7600

Beblie, Brandt & Jacobs Inc.
16 Technology, Ste. 164
Irvine, CA 92618
(714)450-8790
Fax: (714)450-8799
E-mail: darcy@bbjinc.com
Website: http://198.147.90.26

Fluor Daniel Inc.
3353 Michelson Dr.
Irvine, CA 92612-0650
(949)975-2000
Fax: (949)975-5271
E-mail: sales.consulting@fluordaniel.com
Website: http://www.fluordaniel consulting.com

MCS Associates
18300 Von Karman, Ste. 710
Irvine, CA 92612
(949)263-8700
Fax: (949)263-0770
E-mail: info@mcsassociates.com
Website: http://www.mcsassociates.com

Inspired Arts Inc.
4225 Executive Sq., Ste. 1160
La Jolla, CA 92037
(619)623-3525
Free: 800-851-4394
Fax: (619)623-3534
E-mail: info@inspiredarts.com
Website: http://www.inspiredarts.com

The Laresis Companies
PO Box 3284
La Jolla, CA 92038
(619)452-2720
Fax: (619)452-8744

RCL & Co.
PO Box 1143
737 Pearl St., Ste. 201
La Jolla, CA 92038
(619)454-8883
Fax: (619)454-8880

Comprehensive Business Services
3201 Lucas Cir.
Lafayette, CA 94549
(925)283-8272
Fax: (925)283-8272

The Ribble Group
27601 Forbes Rd., Ste. 52
Laguna Niguel, CA 92677

Organizations, Agencies, & Consultants

(714)582-1085
Fax: (714)582-6420
E-mail: ribble@deltanet.com

Norris Bernstein, CMC
9309 Marina Pacifica Dr. N
Long Beach, CA 90803
(562)493-5458
Fax: (562)493-5459
E-mail: norris@ctecomputer.com
Website: http://foodconsultants.com/
bernstein/

Horizon Consulting Services
1315 Garthwick Dr.
Los Altos, CA 94024
(415)967-0906
Fax: (415)967-0906

Brincko Associates Inc.
1801 Avenue of the Stars, Ste. 1054
Los Angeles, CA 90067
(310)553-4523
Fax: (310)553-6782

**Rubenstein/Justman Management
Consultants**
2049 Century Park E, 24th Fl.
Los Angeles, CA 90067
(310)282-0800
Fax: (310)282-0400
E-mail: info@rjmc.net
Website: http://www.rjmc.net

F.J. Schroeder & Associates
1926 Westholme Ave.
Los Angeles, CA 90025
(310)470-2655
Fax: (310)470-6378
E-mail: fjsacons@aol.com
Website: http://www.mcninet.com/
GlobalLook/Fjschroe.html

Western Management Associates
5959 W Century Blvd., Ste. 565
Los Angeles, CA 90045-6506
(310)645-1091
Free: (888)788-6534
Fax: (310)645-1092
E-mail: gene@cfoforrent.com
Website: http://www.cfoforrent.com

Darrell Sell and Associates
Los Gatos, CA 95030
(408)354-7794
E-mail: darrell@netcom.com

Leslie J. Zambo
3355 Michael Dr.
Marina, CA 93933
(408)384-7086

Fax: (408)647-4199
E-mail: 104776.1552@compuserve.com

Marketing Services Management
PO Box 1377
Martinez, CA 94553
(510)370-8527
Fax: (510)370-8527
E-mail: markserve@biotechnet.com

William M. Shine Consulting Service
PO Box 127
Moraga, CA 94556-0127
(510)376-6516

Palo Alto Management Group Inc.
2672 Bayshore Pky., Ste. 701
Mountain View, CA 94043
(415)968-4374
Fax: (415)968-4245
E-mail: mburwen@pamg.com

BizplanSource
1048 Irvine Ave., Ste. 621
Newport Beach, CA 92660
Free: 888-253-0974
Fax: 800-859-8254
E-mail: info@bizplansource.com
Website: http://www.bizplansource.com
Adam Greengrass, President

The Market Connection
4020 Birch St., Ste. 203
Newport Beach, CA 92660
(714)731-6273
Fax: (714)833-0253

Muller Associates
PO Box 7264
Newport Beach, CA 92658
(714)646-1169
Fax: (714)646-1169

International Health Resources
PO Box 329
North San Juan, CA 95960-0329
(530)292-1266
Fax: (530)292-1243
Website: http://www.futureof
healthcare.com

NEXUS - Consultants to Management
PO Box 1531
Novato, CA 94948
(415)897-4400
Fax: (415)898-2252
E-mail: jimnexus@aol.com

Aerospcace.Org
PO Box 28831
Oakland, CA 94604-8831

(510)530-9169
Fax: (510)530-3411
Website: http://www.aerospace.org

Intelequest Corp.
722 Gailen Ave.
Palo Alto, CA 94303
(415)968-3443
Fax: (415)493-6954
E-mail: frits@iqix.com

McLaughlin & Associates
66 San Marino Cir.
Rancho Mirage, CA 92270
(760)321-2932
Fax: (760)328-2474
E-mail: jackmcla@msn.com

**Carrera Consulting Group, a division
of Maximus**
2110 21st St., Ste. 400
Sacramento, CA 95818
(916)456-3300
Fax: (916)456-3306
E-mail: central@carreraconsulting.com
Website: http://www.carreraconsulting.com

**Bay Area Tax Consultants and Bayhill
Financial Consultants**
1150 Bayhill Dr., Ste. 1150
San Bruno, CA 94066-3004
(415)952-8786
Fax: (415)588-4524
E-mail: baytax@compuserve.com
Website: http://www.baytax.com/

AdCon Services, LLC
8871 Hillery Dr.
Dan Diego, CA 92126
(858)433-1411
E-mail: adam@adconservices.com
Website: http://www.adconservices.com
Adam Greengrass

California Business Incubation Network
101 W Broadway, No. 480
San Diego, CA 92101
(619)237-0559
Fax: (619)237-0521

G.R. Gordetsky Consultants Inc.
11414 Windy Summit Pl.
San Diego, CA 92127
(619)487-4939
Fax: (619)487-5587
E-mail: gordet@pacbell.net

Freeman, Sullivan & Co.
131 Steuart St., Ste. 500
San Francisco, CA 94105
(415)777-0707

Free: 800-777-0737
Fax: (415)777-2420
Website: http://www.fsc-research.com

Ideas Unlimited
2151 California St., Ste. 7
San Francisco, CA 94115
(415)931-0641
Fax: (415)931-0880

Russell Miller Inc.
300 Montgomery St., Ste. 900
San Francisco, CA 94104
(415)956-7474
Fax: (415)398-0620
E-mail: rmi@pacbell.net
Website: http://www.rmisf.com

PKF Consulting
425 California St., Ste. 1650
San Francisco, CA 94104
(415)421-5378
Fax: (415)956-7708
E-mail: callahan@pkfc.com
Website: http://www.pkfonline.com

Welling & Woodard Inc.
1067 Broadway
San Francisco, CA 94133
(415)776-4500
Fax: (415)776-5067

Highland Associates
16174 Highland Dr.
San Jose, CA 95127
(408)272-7008
Fax: (408)272-4040

ORDIS Inc.
6815 Trinidad Dr.
San Jose, CA 95120-2056
(408)268-3321
Free: 800-446-7347
Fax: (408)268-3582
E-mail: ordis@ordis.com
Website: http://www.ordis.com

Stanford Resources Inc.
20 Great Oaks Blvd., Ste. 200
San Jose, CA 95119
(408)360-8400
Fax: (408)360-8410
E-mail: sales@stanfordsources.com
Website: http://www.stanfordresources.com

Technology Properties Ltd. Inc.
PO Box 20250
San Jose, CA 95160
(408)243-9898
Fax: (408)296-6637
E-mail: sanjose@tplnet.com

Helfert Associates
1777 Borel Pl., Ste. 508
San Mateo, CA 94402-3514
(650)377-0540
Fax: (650)377-0472

Mykytyn Consulting Group Inc.
185 N Redwood Dr., Ste. 200
San Rafael, CA 94903
(415)491-1770
Fax: (415)491-1251
E-mail: info@mcgi.com
Website: http://www.mcgi.com

Omega Management Systems Inc.
3 Mount Darwin Ct.
San Rafael, CA 94903-1109
(415)499-1300
Fax: (415)492-9490
E-mail: omegamgt@ix.nctcom.com

The Information Group Inc.
4675 Stevens Creek Blvd., Ste. 100
Santa Clara, CA 95051
(408)985-7877
Fax: (408)985-2945
E-mail: dvincent@tig-usa.com
Website: http://www.tig-usa.com

Cast Management Consultants
1620 26th St., Ste. 2040N
Santa Monica, CA 90404
(310)828-7511
Fax: (310)453-6831

Cuma Consulting Management
Box 724
Santa Rosa, CA 95402
(707)785-2477
Fax: (707)785-2478

The E-Myth Academy
131B Stony Cir., Ste. 2000
Santa Rosa, CA 95401
(707)569-5600
Free: 800-221-0266
Fax: (707)569-5700
E-mail: info@e-myth.com
Website: http://www.e-myth.com

Reilly, Connors & Ray
1743 Canyon Rd.
Spring Valley, CA 91977
(619)698-4808
Fax: (619)460-3892
E-mail: davidray@adnc.com

Management Consultants
Sunnyvale, CA 94087-4700
(408)773-0321

RJR Associates
1639 Lewiston Dr.
Sunnyvale, CA 94087
(408)737-7720
E-mail: bobroy@rjrassoc.com
Website: http://www.rjrassoc.com

Schwafel Associates
333 Cobalt Way, Ste. 21
Sunnyvale, CA 94085
(408)720-0649
Fax: (408)720-1796
E-mail: schwafel@ricochet.net
Website: http://www.patca.org

Staubs Business Services
23320 S Vermont Ave.
Torrance, CA 90502-2940
(310)830-9128
Fax: (310)830-9128
E-mail: Harry_L_Staubs@Lamg.com

Out of Your Mind...and Into the Marketplace
13381 White Sands Dr.
Tustin, CA 92780-4565
(714)544-0248
Free: 800-419-1513
Fax: (714)730-1414
E-mail: lpinson@aol.com
Website: http://www.business-plan.com

Independent Research Services
PO Box 2426
Van Nuys, CA 91404-2426
(818)993-3622

Ingman Company Inc.
7949 Woodley Ave., Ste. 120
Van Nuys, CA 91406-1232
(818)375-5027
Fax: (818)894-5001

Innovative Technology Associates
3639 E Harbor Blvd., Ste. 203E
Ventura, CA 93001
(805)650-9353

Grid Technology Associates
20404 Tufts Cir.
Walnut, CA 91789
(909)444-0922
Fax: (909)444-0922
E-mail: grid_technology@msn.com

Ridge Consultants Inc.
100 Pringle Ave., Ste. 580
Walnut Creek, CA 94596
(925)274-1990
Fax: (510)274-1956
E-mail: info@ridgecon.com
Website: http://www.ridgecon.com

Bell Springs Publishing
PO Box 1240
Willits, CA 95490
(707)459-6372
E-mail: bellsprings@sabernet
Website: http://www.bellsprings.com

Hutchinson Consulting and Appraisal
23245 Sylvan St., Ste. 103
Woodland Hills, CA 91367
(818)888-8175
Free: 800-977-7548
Fax: (818)888-8220
E-mail: r.f.hutchinson-cpa@worldnet.
att.net

Colorado

Sam Boyer & Associates
4255 S Buckley Rd., No. 136
Aurora, CO 80013
Free: 800-785-0485
Fax: (303)766-8740
E-mail: samboyer@samboyer.com
Website: http://www.samboyer.com/

Ameriwest Business Consultants Inc.
PO Box 26266
Colorado Springs, CO 80936
(719)380-7096
Fax: (719)380-7096
E-mail: email@abchelp.com
Website: http://www.abchelp.com

GVNW Consulting Inc.
2270 La Montana Way
Colorado Springs, CO 80936
(719)594-5800
Fax: (719)594-5803
Website: http://www.gvnw.com

M-Squared Inc.
755 San Gabriel Pl.
Colorado Springs, CO 80906
(719)576-2554
Fax: (719)576-2554

Thornton Financial FNIC
1024 Centre Ave., Bldg. E
Fort Collins, CO 80526-1849
(970)221-2089
Fax: (970)484-5206

TenEyck Associates
1760 Cherryville Rd.
Greenwood Village, CO 80121-1503
(303)758-6129
Fax: (303)761-8286

Associated Enterprises Ltd.
13050 W Ceder Dr., Unit 11
Lakewood, CO 80228

(303)988-6695
Fax: (303)988-6739
E-mail: ael1@classic.msn.com

The Vincent Company Inc.
200 Union Blvd., Ste. 210
Lakewood, CO 80228
(303)989-7271
Free: 800-274-0733
Fax: (303)989-7570
E-mail: vincent@vincentco.com
Website: http://www.vincentco.com

Johnson & West Management Consultants Inc.
7612 S Logan Dr.
Littleton, CO 80122
(303)730-2810
Fax: (303)730-3219

Western Capital Holdings Inc.
10050 E Applwood Dr.
Parker, CO 80138
(303)841-1022
Fax: (303)770-1945

Connecticut

Stratman Group Inc.
40 Tower Ln.
Avon, CT 06001-4222
(860)677-2898
Free: 800-551-0499
Fax: (860)677-8210

Cowherd Consulting Group Inc.
106 Stephen Mather Rd.
Darien, CT 06820
(203)655-2150
Fax: (203)655-6427

Greenwich Associates
8 Greenwich Office Park
Greenwich, CT 06831-5149
(203)629-1200
Fax: (203)629-1229
E-mail: lisa@greenwich.com
Website: http://www.greenwich.com

Follow-up News
185 Pine St., Ste. 818
Manchester, CT 06040
(860)647-7542
Free: 800-708-0696
Fax: (860)646-6544
E-mail: Followupnews@aol.com

Lovins & Associates Consulting
309 Edwards St.
New Haven, CT 06511
(203)787-3367

Fax: (203)624-7599
E-mail: Alovinsphd@aol.com
Website: http://www.lovinsgroup.com

JC Ventures Inc.
4 Arnold St.
Old Greenwich, CT 06870-1203
(203)698-1990
Free: 800-698-1997
Fax: (203)698-2638

Charles L. Hornung Associates
52 Ned's Mountain Rd.
Ridgefield, CT 06877
(203)431-0297

Manus
100 Prospect St., S Tower
Stamford, CT 06901
(203)326-3880
Free: 800-445-0942
Fax: (203)326-3890
E-mail: manus1@aol.com
Website: http://www.RightManus.com

RealBusinessPlans.com
156 Westport Rd.
Wilton, CT 06897
(914)837-2886
E-mail: ct@realbusinessplans.com
Website: http://www.RealBusinessPlans.com
Tony Tecce

Delaware

Focus Marketing
61-7 Habor Dr.
Claymont, DE 19703
(302)793-3064

Daedalus Ventures Ltd.
PO Box 1474
Hockessin, DE 19707
(302)239-6758
Fax: (302)239-9991
E-mail: daedalus@mail.del.net

The Formula Group
PO Box 866
Hockessin, DE 19707
(302)456-0952
Fax: (302)456-1354
E-mail: formula@netaxs.com

Selden Enterprises Inc.
2502 Silverside Rd., Ste. 1
Wilmington, DE 19810-3740
(302)529-7113
Fax: (302)529-7442
E-mail: selden2@bellatlantic.net
Website: http://www.seldenenterprises.com

District of Columbia

Bruce W. McGee and Associates
7826 Eastern Ave. NW, Ste. 30
Washington, DC 20012
(202)726-7272
Fax: (202)726-2946

McManis Associates Inc.
1900 K St. NW, Ste. 700
Washington, DC 20006
(202)466-7680
Fax: (202)872-1898
Website: http://www.mcmanis-mmi.com

Smith, Dawson & Andrews Inc.
1000 Connecticut Ave., Ste. 302
Washington, DC 20036
(202)835-0740
Fax: (202)775-8526
E-mail: webmaster@sda-inc.com
Website: http://www.sda-inc.com

Florida

BackBone, Inc.
20404 Hacienda Court
Boca Raton, FL 33498
(561)470-0965
Fax: 516-908-4038
E-mail: BPlans@backboneinc.com
Website: http://www.backboneinc.com
Charles Epstein, President

Whalen & Associates Inc.
4255 Northwest 26 Ct.
Boca Raton, FL 33434
(561)241-5950
Fax: (561)241-7414
E-mail: drwhalen@ix.netcom.com

E.N. Rysso & Associates
180 Bermuda Petrel Ct.
Daytona Beach, FL 32119
(386)760-3028
E-mail: erysso@aol.com

Virtual Technocrats LLC
560 Lavers Circle, #146
Delray Beach, FL 33444
(561)265-3509
E-mail: josh@virtualtechnocrats.com;
info@virtualtechnocrats.com
Website: http://www.virtualtechno
crats.com
Josh Eikov, Managing Director

Eric Sands Consulting Services
6193 Rock Island Rd., Ste. 412
Fort Lauderdale, FL 33319
(954)721-4767
Fax: (954)720-2815
E-mail: easands@aol.com
Website: http://www.ericsandsconsultig.com

Professional Planning Associates, Inc.
1975 E. Sunrise Blvd. Suite 607
Fort Lauderdale, FL 33304
(954)764-5204
Fax: 954-463-4172
E-mail: Mgoldstein@proplana.com
Website: http://proplana.com
Michael Goldstein, President

Host Media Corp.
3948 S 3rd St., Ste. 191
Jacksonville Beach, FL 32250
(904)285-3239
Fax: (904)285-5618
E-mail: msconsulting@compuserve.com
Website: http://www.media
servicesgroup.com

William V. Hall
1925 Brickell, Ste. D-701
Miami, FL 33129
(305)856-9622
Fax: (305)856-4113
E-mail: williamvhall@compuserve.com

F.A. McGee Inc.
800 Claughton Island Dr., Ste. 401
Miami, FL 33131
(305)377-9123

Taxplan Inc.
Mirasol International Ctr.
2699 Collins Ave.
Miami Beach, FL 33140
(305)538-3303

T.C. Brown & Associates
8415 Excalibur Cir., Apt. B1
Naples, FL 34108
(941)594-1949
Fax: (941)594-0611
E-mail: tcater@naples.net.com

RLA International Consulting
713 Lagoon Dr.
North Palm Beach, FL 33408
(407)626-4258
Fax: (407)626-5772

Comprehensive Franchising Inc.
2465 Ridgecrest Ave.
Orange Park, FL 32065
(904)272-6567
Free: 800-321-6567
Fax: (904)272-6750
E-mail: theimp@cris.com
Website: http://www.franchise411.com

Hunter G. Jackson Jr. - Consulting Environmental Physicist
PO Box 618272
Orlando, FL 32861-8272
(407)295-4188
E-mail: hunterjackson@juno.com

F. Newton Parks
210 El Brillo Way
Palm Beach, FL 33480
(561)833-1727
Fax: (561)833-4541

Avery Business Development Services
2506 St. Michel Ct.
Ponte Vedra Beach, FL 32082
(904)285-6033
Fax: (904)285-6033

Strategic Business Planning Co.
PO Box 821006
South Florida, FL 33082-1006
(954)704-9100
Fax: (954)438-7333
E-mail: info@bizplan.com
Website: http://www.bizplan.com

Dufresne Consulting Group Inc.
10014 N Dale Mabry, Ste. 101
Tampa, FL 33618-4426
(813)264-4775
Fax: (813)264-9300
Website: http://www.dcgconsult.com

Agrippa Enterprises Inc.
PO Box 175
Venice, FL 34284-0175
(941)355-7876
E-mail: webservices@agrippa.com
Website: http://www.agrippa.com

Center for Simplified Strategic Planning Inc.
PO Box 3324
Vero Beach, FL 32964-3324
(561)231-3636
Fax: (561)231-1099
Website: http://www.cssp.com

Georgia

Marketing Spectrum Inc.
115 Perimeter Pl., Ste. 440
Atlanta, GA 30346
(770)395-7244
Fax: (770)393-4071

Business Ventures Corp.
1650 Oakbrook Dr., Ste. 405
Norcross, GA 30093
(770)729-8000
Fax: (770)729-8028

Informed Decisions Inc.
100 Falling Cheek
Sautee Nacoochee, GA 30571
(706)878-1905
Fax: (706)878-1802
E-mail: skylake@compuserve.com

Tom C. Davis & Associates, P.C.
3189 Perimeter Rd.
Valdosta, GA 31602
(912)247-9801
Fax: (912)244-7704
E-mail: mail@tcdcpa.com
Website: http://www.tcdcpa.com/

Illinois

TWD and Associates
431 S Patton
Arlington Heights, IL 60005
(847)398-6410
Fax: (847)255-5095
E-mail: tdoo@aol.com

Management Planning Associates Inc.
2275 Half Day Rd., Ste. 350
Bannockburn, IL 60015-1277
(847)945-2421
Fax: (847)945-2425

Phil Faris Associates
86 Old Mill Ct.
Barrington, IL 60010
(847)382-4888
Fax: (847)382-4890
E-mail: pfaris@meginsnet.net

Seven Continents Technology
787 Stonebridge
Buffalo Grove, IL 60089
(708)577-9653
Fax: (708)870-1220

Grubb & Blue Inc.
2404 Windsor Pl.
Champaign, IL 61820
(217)366-0052
Fax: (217)356-0117

ACE Accounting Service Inc.
3128 N Bernard St.
Chicago, IL 60618
(773)463-7854
Fax: (773)463-7854

AON Consulting Worldwide
200 E Randolph St., 10th Fl.
Chicago, IL 60601
(312)381-4800
Free: 800-438-6487
Fax: (312)381-0240
Website: http://www.aon.com

FMS Consultants
5801 N Sheridan Rd., Ste. 3D
Chicago, IL 60660
(773)561-7362
Fax: (773)561-6274

Grant Thornton
800 1 Prudential Plz.
130 E Randolph St.
Chicago, IL 60601
(312)856-0001
Fax: (312)861-1340
E-mail: gtinfo@gt.com
Website: http://www.grantthornton.com

Kingsbury International Ltd.
5341 N Glenwood Ave.
Chicago, IL 60640
(773)271-3030
Fax: (773)728-7080
E-mail: jetlag@mcs.com
Website: http://www.kingbiz.com

MacDougall & Blake Inc.
1414 N Wells St., Ste. 311
Chicago, IL 60610-1306
(312)587-3330
Fax: (312)587-3699
E-mail: jblake@compuserve.com

James C. Osburn Ltd.
6445 N. Western Ave., Ste. 304
Chicago, IL 60645
(773)262-4428
Fax: (773)262-6755
E-mail: osburnltd@aol.com

Tarifero & Tazewell Inc.
211 S Clark
Chicago, IL 60690
(312)665-9714
Fax: (312)665-9716

Human Energy Design Systems
620 Roosevelt Dr.
Edwardsville, IL 62025
(618)692-0258
Fax: (618)692-0819

China Business Consultants Group
931 Dakota Cir.
Naperville, IL 60563
(630)778-7992
Fax: (630)778-7915
E-mail: cbcq@aol.com

Center for Workforce Effectiveness
500 Skokie Blvd., Ste. 222
Northbrook, IL 60062
(847)559-8777
Fax: (847)559-8778

E-mail: office@cwelink.com
Website: http://www.cwelink.com

Smith Associates
1320 White Mountain Dr.
Northbrook, IL 60062
(847)480-7200
Fax: (847)480-9828

Francorp Inc.
20200 Governors Dr.
Olympia Fields, IL 60461
(708)481-2900
Free: 800-372-6244
Fax: (708)481-5885
E-mail: francorp@aol.com
Website: http://www.francorpinc.com

Camber Business Strategy Consultants
1010 S Plum Tree Ct
Palatine, IL 60078-0986
(847)202-0101
Fax: (847)705-7510
E-mail: camber@ameritech.net

Partec Enterprise Group
5202 Keith Dr.
Richton Park, IL 60471
(708)503-4047
Fax: (708)503-9468

Rockford Consulting Group Ltd.
Century Plz., Ste. 206
7210 E State St.
Rockford, IL 61108
(815)229-2900
Free: 800-667-7495
Fax: (815)229-2612
E-mail: rligus@RockfordConsulting.com
Website: http://www.Rockford
Consulting.com

RSM McGladrey Inc.
1699 E Woodfield Rd., Ste. 300
Schaumburg, IL 60173-4969
(847)413-6900
Fax: (847)517-7067
Website: http://www.rsmmcgladrey.com

A.D. Star Consulting
320 Euclid
Winnetka, IL 60093
(847)446-7827
Fax: (847)446-7827
E-mail: startwo@worldnet.att.net

Indiana

Modular Consultants Inc.
3109 Crabtree Ln.
Elkhart, IN 46514

(219)264-5761
Fax: (219)264-5761
E-mail: sasabo5313@aol.com

Midwest Marketing Research
PO Box 1077
Goshen, IN 46527
(219)533-0548
Fax: (219)533-0540
E-mail: 103365.654@compuserve

Ketchum Consulting Group
8021 Knue Rd., Ste. 112
Indianapolis, IN 46250
(317)845-5411
Fax: (317)842-9941

MDI Management Consulting
1519 Park Dr.
Munster, IN 46321
(219)838-7909
Fax: (219)838-7909

Iowa

McCord Consulting Group Inc.
4533 Pine View Dr. NE
PO Box 11024
Cedar Rapids, IA 52410
(319)378-0077
Fax: (319)378-1577
E-mail: smmccord@hom.com
Website: http://www.mccordgroup.com

Management Solutions L.C.
3815 Lincoln Pl. Dr.
Des Moines, IA 50312
(515)277-6408
Fax: (515)277-3506
E-mail: wasunimers@uswest.net

Grandview Marketing
15 Red Bridge Dr.
Sioux City, IA 51104
(712)239-3122
Fax: (712)258-7578
E-mail: eandrews@pionet.net

Kansas

Assessments in Action
513A N Mur-Len
Olathe, KS 66062
(913)764-6270
Free: (888)548-1504
Fax: (913)764-6495
E-mail: lowdene@qni.com
Website: http://www.assessments-in-action.com

Maine

Edgemont Enterprises
PO Box 8354
Portland, ME 04104
(207)871-8964
Fax: (207)871-8964

Pan Atlantic Consultants
5 Milk St.
Portland, ME 04101
(207)871-8622
Fax: (207)772-4842
E-mail: pmurphy@maine.rr.com
Website: http://www.panatlantic.net

Maryland

Clemons & Associates Inc.
5024-R Campbell Blvd.
Baltimore, MD 21236
(410)931-8100
Fax: (410)931-8111
E-mail: info@clemonsmgmt.com
Website: http://www.clemonsmgmt.com

Imperial Group Ltd.
305 Washington Ave., Ste. 204
Baltimore, MD 21204-6009
(410)337-8500
Fax: (410)337-7641

Leadership Institute
3831 Yolando Rd.
Baltimore, MD 21218
(410)366-9111
Fax: (410)243-8478
E-mail: behconsult@aol.com

Burdeshaw Associates Ltd.
4701 Sangamore Rd.
Bethesda, MD 20816 2508
(301)229-5800
Fax: (301)229-5045
E-mail: jstacy@burdeshaw.com
Website: http://www.burdeshaw.com

Michael E. Cohen
5225 Pooks Hill Rd., Ste. 1119 S
Bethesda, MD 20814
(301)530-5738
Fax: (301)530-2988
E-mail: mecohen@crosslink.net

World Development Group Inc.
5272 River Rd., Ste. 650
Bethesda, MD 20816-1405
(301)652-1818
Fax: (301)652-1250
E-mail: wdg@has.com
Website: http://www.worlddg.com

Swartz Consulting
PO Box 4301
Crofton, MD 21114-4301
(301)262-6728

Software Solutions International Inc.
9633 Duffer Way
Gaithersburg, MD 20886
(301)330-4136
Fax: (301)330-4136

Strategies Inc.
8 Park Center Ct., Ste. 200
Owings Mills, MD 21117
(410)363-6669
Fax: (410)363-1231
E-mail: strategies@strat1.com
Website: http://www.strat1.com

Hammer Marketing Resources
179 Inverness Rd.
Severna Park, MD 21146
(410)544-9191
Fax: (305)675-3277
E-mail: info@gohammer.com
Website: http://www.gohammer.com

Andrew Sussman & Associates
13731 Kretsinger
Smithsburg, MD 21783
(301)824-2943
Fax: (301)824-2943

Massachusetts

Geibel Marketing and Public Relations
PO Box 611
Belmont, MA 02478-0005
(617)484-8285
Fax: (617)489 3567
E-mail: jgeibel@geibelpr.com
Website: http://www.geibelpr.com

Bain & Co.
2 Copley Pl.
Boston, MA 02116
(617)572-2000
Fax: (617)572-2427
E-mail: corporate.inquiries@bain.com
Website: http://www.bain.com

Mehr & Co.
62 Kinnaird St.
Cambridge, MA 02139
(617)876-3311
Fax: (617)876-3023
E-mail: mehrco@aol.com

Monitor Company Inc.
2 Canal Park
Cambridge, MA 02141

(617)252-2000
Fax: (617)252-2100
Website: http://www.monitor.com

Information & Research Associates
PO Box 3121
Framingham, MA 01701
(508)788-0784

Walden Consultants Ltd.
252 Pond St.
Hopkinton, MA 01748
(508)435-4882
Fax: (508)435-3971
Website: http://www.waldencon
sultants.com

Jeffrey D. Marshall
102 Mitchell Rd.
Ipswich, MA 01938-1219
(508)356-1113
Fax: (508)356-2989

Consulting Resources Corp.
6 Northbrook Park
Lexington, MA 02420
(781)863-1222
Fax: (781)863-1441
E-mail: res@consultingresources.net
Website: http://www.consulting
resources.net

Planning Technologies Group L.L.C.
92 Hayden Ave.
Lexington, MA 02421
(781)778-4678
Fax: (781)861-1099
E-mail: ptg@plantech.com
Website: http://www.plantech.com

Kalba International Inc.
23 Sandy Pond Rd.
Lincoln, MA 01773
(781)259-9589
Fax: (781)259-1460
E-mail: info@kalbainternational.com
Website: http://www.kalbainter
national.com

VMB Associates Inc.
115 Ashland St.
Melrose, MA 02176
(781)665-0623
Fax: (425)732-7142
E-mail: vmbinc@aol.com

The Company Doctor
14 Pudding Stone Ln.
Mendon, MA 01756
(508)478-1747
Fax: (508)478-0520

Data and Strategies Group Inc.
190 N Main St.
Natick, MA 01760
(508)653-9990
Fax: (508)653-7799
E-mail: dsginc@dsggroup.com
Website: http://www.dsggroup.com

The Enterprise Group
73 Parker Rd.
Needham, MA 02494
(617)444-6631
Fax: (617)433-9991
E-mail: lsacco@world.std.com
Website: http://www.enterprise-group.com

PSMJ Resources Inc.
10 Midland Ave.
Newton, MA 02458
(617)965-0055
Free: 800-537-7765
Fax: (617)965-5152
E-mail: psmj@tiac.net
Website: http://www.psmj.com

Scheur Management Group Inc.
255 Washington St., Ste. 100
Newton, MA 02458-1611
(617)969-7500
Fax: (617)969-7508
E-mail: smgnow@scheur.com
Website: http://www.scheur.com

I.E.E.E., Boston Section
240 Bear Hill Rd., 202B
Waltham, MA 02451-1017
(781)890-5294
Fax: (781)890-5290

Business Planning and Consulting Services
20 Beechwood Ter.
Wellesley, MA 02482
(617)237-9151
Fax: (617)237-9151

Michigan

Walter Frederick Consulting
1719 South Blvd.
Ann Arbor, MI 48104
(313)662-4336
Fax: (313)769-7505

Fox Enterprises
6220 W Freeland Rd.
Freeland, MI 48623
(517)695-9170
Fax: (517)695-9174
E-mail: foxjw@concentric.net
Website: http://www.cris.com/~foxjw

G.G.W. and Associates
1213 Hampton
Jackson, MI 49203
(517)782-2255
Fax: (517)782-2255

Altamar Group Ltd.
6810 S Cedar, Ste. 2-B
Lansing, MI 48911
(517)694-0910
Free: 800-443-2627
Fax: (517)694-1377

Sheffieck Consultants Inc.
23610 Greening Dr.
Novi, MI 48375-3130
(248)347-3545
Fax: (248)347-3530
E-mail: cfsheff@concentric.net

Rehmann, Robson PC
5800 Gratiot
Saginaw, MI 48605
(517)799-9580
Fax: (517)799-0227
Website: http://www.rrpc.com

Francis & Co.
17200 W 10 Mile Rd., Ste. 207
Southfield, MI 48075
(248)559-7600
Fax: (248)559-5249

Private Ventures Inc.
16000 W 9 Mile Rd., Ste. 504
Southfield, MI 48075
(248)569-1977
Free: 800-448-7614
Fax: (248)569-1838
E-mail: pventuresi@aol.com

JGK Associates
14464 Kerner Dr.
Sterling Heights, MI 48313
(810)247-9055
Fax: (248)822-4977
E-mail: kozlowski@home.com

Minnesota

Health Fitness Corp.
3500 W 80th St., Ste. 130
Bloomington, MN 55431
(612)831-6830
Fax: (612)831-7264

Consatech Inc.
PO Box 1047
Burnsville, MN 55337
(612)953-1088
Fax: (612)435-2966

Robert F. Knotek
14960 Ironwood Ct.
Eden Prairie, MN 55346
(612)949-2875

DRI Consulting
7715 Stonewood Ct.
Edina, MN 55439
(612)941-9656
Fax: (612)941-2693
E-mail: dric@dric.com
Website: http://www.dric.com

Markin Consulting
12072 87th Pl. N
Maple Grove, MN 55369
(612)493-3568
Fax: (612)493-5744
E-mail: markin@markinconsulting.com
Website: http://www.markin
consulting.com

Minnesota Cooperation Office for Small Business & Job Creation Inc.
5001 W 80th St., Ste. 825
Minneapolis, MN 55437
(612)830-1230
Fax: (612)830-1232
E-mail: mncoop@msn.com
Website: http://www.mnco.org

Enterprise Consulting Inc.
PO Box 1111
Minnetonka, MN 55345
(612)949-5909
Fax: (612)906-3965

Amdahl International
724 1st Ave. SW
Rochester, MN 55902
(507)252-0402
Fax: (507)252-0402
E-mail: amdahl@best-service.com
Website: http://www.wp.com/amdahl int

Power Systems Research
1365 Corporate Center Curve, 2nd Fl.
St. Paul, MN 55121
(612)905-8400
Free: (888)625-8612
Fax: (612)454-0760
E-mail: Barb@Powersys.com
Website: http://www.powersys.com

Missouri

Business Planning and Development Corp.
4030 Charlotte St.
Kansas City, MO 64110
(816)753-0495

E-mail: humph@bpdev.demon.co.uk
Website: http://www.bpdev.demon.co.uk

CFO Service
10336 Donoho
St. Louis, MO 63131
(314)750-2940
E-mail: jskae@cfoservice.com
Website: http://www.cfoservice.com

Nebraska

International Management Consulting Group Inc.
1309 Harlan Dr., Ste. 205
Bellevue, NE 68005
(402)291-4545
Free: 800-665-IMCG
Fax: (402)291-4343
E-mail: imcg@neonramp.com
Website: http://www.mgtcon
sulting.com

Heartland Management Consulting Group
1904 Barrington Pky.
Papillion, NE 68046
(402)339-2387
Fax: (402)339-1319

Nevada

The DuBois Group
865 Tahoe Blvd., Ste. 108
Incline Village, NV 89451
(775)832-0550
Free: 800-375-2935
Fax: (775)832-0556
E-mail: DuBoisGrp@aol.com

New Hampshire

Wolff Consultants
10 Buck Rd.
Hanover, NH 03755
(603)643-6015

BPT Consulting Associates Ltd.
12 Parmenter Rd., Ste. B-6
Londonderry, NH 03053
(603)437-8484
Free: (888)278-0030
Fax: (603)434-5388
E-mail: bptcons@tiac.net
Website: http://www.bptconsulting.com

New Jersey

Bedminster Group Inc.
1170 Rte. 22 E
Bridgewater, NJ 08807

(908)500-4155
Fax: (908)766-0780
E-mail: info@bedminstergroup.com
Website: http://www.bedminster
group.com
Fax: (202)806-1777
Terry Strong, Acting Regional Dir.

Delta Planning Inc.
PO Box 425
Denville, NJ 07834
(913)625-1742
Free: 800-672-0762
Fax: (973)625-3531
E-mail: DeltaP@worldnet.att.net
Website: http://deltaplanning.com

Kumar Associates Inc.
1004 Cumbermeade Rd.
Fort Lee, NJ 07024
(201)224-9480
Fax: (201)585-2343
E-mail: mail@kumarassociates.com
Website: http://kumarassociates.com

John Hall & Company Inc.
PO Box 187
Glen Ridge, NJ 07028
(973)680-4449
Fax: (973)680-4581
E-mail: jhcompany@aol.com

Market Focus
PO Box 402
Maplewood, NJ 07040
(973)378-2470
Fax: (973)378-2470
E-mail: mcss66@marketfocus.com

Vanguard Communications Corp.
100 American Rd.
Morris Plains, NJ 07950
(973)605-8000
Fax: (973)605-8329
Website: http://www.vanguard.net/

ConMar International Ltd.
1901 US Hwy. 130
North Brunswick, NJ 08902
(732)940-8347
Fax: (732)274-1199

KLW New Products
156 Cedar Dr.
Old Tappan, NJ 07675
(201)358-1300
Fax: (201)664-2594
E-mail: lrlarsen@usa.net
Website: http://www.klwnew
products.com

PA Consulting Group
315A Enterprise Dr.
Plainsboro, NJ 08536
(609)936-8300
Fax: (609)936-8811
E-mail: info@paconsulting.com
Website: http://www.pa-consulting.com

Aurora Marketing Management Inc.
66 Witherspoon St., Ste. 600
Princeton, NJ 08542
(908)904-1125
Fax: (908)359-1108
E-mail: aurora2@voicenet.com
Website: http://www.auroramarketing.net

Smart Business Supersite
88 Orchard Rd., CN-5219
Princeton, NJ 08543
(908)321-1924
Fax: (908)321-5156
E-mail: irv@smartbiz.com
Website: http://www.smartbiz.com

Tracelin Associates
1171 Main St., Ste. 6K
Rahway, NJ 07065
(732)381-3288

Schkeeper Inc.
130-6 Bodman Pl.
Red Bank, NJ 07701
(732)219-1965
Fax: (732)530-3703

Henry Branch Associates
2502 Harmon Cove Twr.
Secaucus, NJ 07094
(201)866-2008
Fax: (201)601-0101
E-mail: hbranch161@home.com

Robert Gibbons & Company Inc.
46 Knoll Rd.
Tenafly, NJ 07670-1050
(201)871-3933
Fax: (201)871-2173
E-mail: crisisbob@aol.com

PMC Management Consultants Inc.
6 Thistle Ln.
Three Bridges, NJ 08887-0332
(908)788-1014
Free: 800-PMC-0250
Fax: (908)806-7287
E-mail: int@pmc-management.com
Website: http://www.pmc-management.com

R.W. Bankart & Associates
20 Valley Ave., Ste. D-2

Westwood, NJ 07675-3607
(201)664-7672

New Mexico

Vondle & Associates Inc.
4926 Calle de Tierra, NE
Albuquerque, NM 87111
(505)292-8961
Fax: (505)296-2790
E-mail: vondle@aol.com

InfoNewMexico
2207 Black Hills Rd., NE
Rio Rancho, NM 87124
(505)891-2462
Fax: (505)896-8971

New York

Powers Research and Training Institute
PO Box 78
Bayville, NY 11709
(516)628-2250
Fax: (516)628-2252
E-mail: powercocch@compuserve.com
Website: http://www.nancypowers.com

Consortium House
296 Wittenberg Rd.
Bearsville, NY 12409
(845)679-8867
Fax: (845)679-9248
E-mail: eugenegs@aol.com
Website: http://www.chpub.com

Progressive Finance Corp.
3549 Tiemann Ave.
Bronx, NY 10469
(718)405-9029
Free: 800-225-8381
Fax: (718)405-1170

Wave Hill Associates Inc.
2621 Palisade Ave., Ste. 15-C
Bronx, NY 10463
(718)549-7368
Fax: (718)601-9670
E-mail: pepper@compuserve.com

Management Insight
96 Arlington Rd.
Buffalo, NY 14221
(716)631-3319
Fax: (716)631-0203
E-mail: michalski@foodservice insight.com
Website: http://www.foodservice insight.com

Samani International Enterprises, Marions Panyaught Consultancy
2028 Parsons
Flushing, NY 11357-3436
(917)287-8087
Fax: 800-873-8939
E-mail: vjp2@biostrategist.com
Website: http://www.biostrategist.com

Marketing Resources Group
71-58 Austin St.
Forest Hills, NY 11375
(718)261-8882

Mangabay Business Plans & Development Subsidiary of Innis Asset Allocation
125-10 Queens Blvd., Ste. 2202
Kew Gardens, NY 11415
(905)527-1947
Fax: 509-472-1935
E-mail: mangabay@mangabay.com
Website: http://www.mangabay.com
Lee Toh, Managing Partner

ComputerEase Co.
1301 Monmouth Ave.
Lakewood, NY 08701
(212)406-9464
Fax: (914)277-5317
E-mail: crawfordc@juno.com

Boice Dunham Group
30 W 13th St.
New York, NY 10011
(212)924-2200
Fax: (212)924-1108

Elizabeth Capen
27 E 95th St.
New York, NY 10128
(212)427-7654
Fax: (212)876-3190

Haver Analytics
60 E 42nd St., Ste. 2424
New York, NY 10017
(212)986-9300
Fax: (212)986-5857
E-mail: data@haver.com
Website: http://www.haver.com

The Jordan, Edmiston Group Inc.
150 E 52nd Ave., 18th Fl.
New York, NY 10022
(212)754-0710
Fax: (212)754-0337

KPMG International
345 Park Ave.
New York, NY 10154-0102
(212)758-9700

Fax: (212)758-9819
Website: http://www.kpmg.com

Mahoney Cohen Consulting Corp.
111 W 40th St., 12th Fl.
New York, NY 10018
(212)490-8000
Fax: (212)790-5913

Management Practice Inc.
342 Madison Ave.
New York, NY 10173-1230
(212)867-7948
Fax: (212)972-5188
Website: http://www.mpiweb.com

Moseley Associates Inc.
342 Madison Ave., Ste. 1414
New York, NY 10016
(212)213-6673
Fax: (212)687-1520

Practice Development Counsel
60 Sutton Pl. S
New York, NY 10022
(212)593-1549
Fax: (212)980-7940
E-mail: pwhaserot@pdcounsel.com
Website: http://www.pdcounsel.com

Unique Value International Inc.
575 Madison Ave., 10th Fl.
New York, NY 10022-1304
(212)605-0590
Fax: (212)605-0589

The Van Tulleken Co.
126 E 56th St.
New York, NY 10022
(212)355-1390
Fax: (212)755-3061
E-mail: newyork@vantullcken.com

Vencon Management Inc.
301 W 53rd St.
New York, NY 10019
(212)581-8787
Fax: (212)397-4126
Website: http://www.venconinc.com

Werner International Inc.
55 E 52nd, 29th Fl.
New York, NY 10055
(212)909-1260
Fax: (212)909-1273
E-mail: richard.downing@rgh.com
Website: http://www.wernertex.com

Zimmerman Business Consulting Inc.
44 E 92nd St., Ste. 5-B
New York, NY 10128

(212)860-3107
Fax: (212)860-7730
E-mail: ljzzbci@aol.com
Website: http://www.zbcinc.com

Overton Financial
7 Allen Rd.
Peekskill, NY 10566
(914)737-4649
Fax: (914)737-4696

Stromberg Consulting
2500 Westchester Ave.
Purchase, NY 10577
(914)251-1515
Fax: (914)251-1562
E-mail: strategy@stromberg_consul
ting.com
Website: http://www.stromberg_
consulting.com

Innovation Management Consulting Inc.
209 Dewitt Rd.
Syracuse, NY 13214-2006
(315)425-5144
Fax: (315)445-8989
E-mail: missonneb@axess.net

M. Clifford Agress
891 Fulton St.
Valley Stream, NY 11580
(516)825-8955
Fax: (516)825-8955

Destiny Kinal Marketing Consultancy
105 Chemung St.
Waverly, NY 14892
(607)565-8317
Fax: (607)565-4083

Valutis Consulting Inc.
5350 Main St., Ste. 7
Williamsville, NY 14221-5338
(716)634-2553
Fax: (716)634-2554
E-mail: valutis@localnet.com
Website: http://www.valutisconsulting.com

North Carolina

Best Practices L.L.C.
6320 Quadrangle Dr., Ste. 200
Chapel Hill, NC 27514
(919)403-0251
Fax: (919)403-0144
E-mail: best@best:in/class
Website: http://www.best-in-class.com

Norelli & Co.
Bank of America Corporate Ctr.
100 N Tyron St., Ste. 5160

Charlotte, NC 28202-4000
(704)376-5484
Fax: (704)376-5485
E-mail: consult@norelli.com
Website: http://www.norelli.com

North Dakota

Center for Innovation
4300 Dartmouth Dr.
PO Box 8372
Grand Forks, ND 58202
(701)777-3132
Fax: (701)777-2339
E-mail: bruce@innovators.net
Website: http://www.innovators.net

Ohio

Transportation Technology Services
208 Harmon Rd.
Aurora, OH 44202
(330)562-3596

Empro Systems Inc.
4777 Red Bank Expy., Ste. 1
Cincinnati, OH 45227-1542
(513)271-2042
Fax: (513)271-2042

Alliance Management International Ltd.
1440 Windrow Ln.
Cleveland, OH 44147-3200
(440)838-1922
Fax: (440)838-0979
E-mail: bgruss@amiltd.com
Website: http://www.amiltd.com

Bozell Kamstra Public Relations
1301 E 9th St., Ste. 3400
Cleveland, OH 44114
(216)623-1511
Fax: (216)623-1501
E-mail: jfeniger@cleveland.bozellk
amstra.com
Website: http://www.bozellk
amstra.com

Cory Dillon Associates
111 Schreyer Pl. E
Columbus, OH 43214
(614)262-8211
Fax: (614)262-3806

Holcomb Gallagher Adams
300 Marconi, Ste. 303
Columbus, OH 43215
(614)221-3343
Fax: (614)221-3367
E-mail: riadams@acme.freenet.oh.us

Young & Associates
PO Box 711
Kent, OH 44240
(330)678-0524
Free: 800-525-9775
Fax: (330)678-6219
E-mail: online@younginc.com
Website: http://www.younginc.com

Robert A. Westman & Associates
8981 Inversary Dr. SE
Warren, OH 44484-2551
(330)856-4149
Fax: (330)856-2564

Oklahoma

Innovative Partners L.L.C.
4900 Richmond Sq., Ste. 100
Oklahoma City, OK 73118
(405)840-0033
Fax: (405)843-8359
E-mail: ipartners@juno.com

Oregon

INTERCON - The International Converting Institute
5200 Badger Rd.
Crooked River Ranch, OR 97760
(541)548-1447
Fax: (541)548-1618
E-mail: johnbowler@
crookedriverranch.com

Talbott ARM
HC 60, Box 5620
Lakeview, OR 97630
(541)635-8587
Fax: (503)947-3482

Management Technology Associates Ltd.
2768 SW Sherwood Dr, Ste. 105
Portland, OR 97201-2251
(503)224-5220
Fax: (503)224-5334
E-mail: lcuster@mta-ltd.com
Website: http://www.mgmt-tech.com

Pennsylvania

Healthscope Inc.
400 Lancaster Ave.
Devon, PA 19333
(610)687-6199
Fax: (610)687-6376
E-mail: health@voicenet.com
Website: http://www.healthscope.net/

Elayne Howard & Associates Inc.
3501 Masons Mill Rd., Ste. 501

Huntingdon Valley, PA 19006-3509
(215)657-9550

GRA Inc.
115 West Ave., Ste. 201
Jenkintown, PA 19046
(215)884-7500
Fax: (215)884-1385
E-mail: gramail@gra-inc.com
Website: http://www.gra-inc.com

Mifflin County Industrial Development Corp.
Mifflin County Industrial Plz.
6395 SR 103 N
Bldg. 50
Lewistown, PA 17044
(717)242-0393
Fax: (717)242-1842
E-mail: mcide@acsworld.net

Autech Products
1289 Revere Rd.
Morrisville, PA 19067
(215)493-3759
Fax: (215)493-9791
E-mail: autech4@yahoo.com

Advantage Associates
434 Avon Dr.
Pittsburgh, PA 15228
(412)343-1558
Fax: (412)362-1684
E-mail: ecocba1@aol.com

Regis J. Sheehan & Associates
Pittsburgh, PA 15220
(412)279-1207

James W. Davidson Company Inc.
23 Forest View Rd.
Wallingford, PA 19086
(610)566-1462

Puerto Rico

Diego Chevere & Co.
Metro Parque 7, Ste. 204
Metro Office
Caparra Heights, PR 00920
(787)774-9595
Fax: (787)774-9566
E-mail: dcco@coqui.net

Manuel L. Porrata and Associates
898 Munoz Rivera Ave., Ste. 201
San Juan, PR 00927
(787)765-2140
Fax: (787)754-3285
E-mail: m_porrata@manuelporrata.com
Website: http://manualporrata.com

South Carolina

Aquafood Business Associates
PO Box 13267
Charleston, SC 29422
(843)795-9506
Fax: (843)795-9477
E-mail: rraba@aol.com

Profit Associates Inc.
PO Box 38026
Charleston, SC 29414
(803)763-5718
Fax: (803)763-5719
E-mail: bobrog@awod.com
Website: http://www.awod.com/gallery/business/proasc

Strategic Innovations International
12 Executive Ct.
Lake Wylie, SC 29710
(803)831-1225
Fax: (803)831-1177
E-mail: stratinnov@aol.com
Website: http://www.strategicinnovations.com

Minus Stage
Box 4436
Rock Hill, SC 29731
(803)328-0705
Fax: (803)329-9948

Tennessee

Daniel Petchers & Associates
8820 Fernwood CV
Germantown, TN 38138
(901)755-9896

Business Choices
1114 Forest Harbor, Ste. 300
Hendersonville, TN 37075-9646
(615)822-8692
Free: 800-737-8382
Fax: (615)822-8692
E-mail: bz-ch@juno.com

RCFA Healthcare Management Services L.L.C.
9648 Kingston Pke., Ste. 8
Knoxville, TN 37922
(865)531-0176
Free: 800-635-4040
Fax: (865)531-0722
E-mail: info@rcfa.com
Website: http://www.rcfa.com

Growth Consultants of America
3917 Trimble Rd.
Nashville, TN 37215

(615)383-0550
Fax: (615)269-8940
E-mail: 70244.451@compuserve.com

Texas

Integrated Cost Management Systems Inc.
2261 Brookhollow Plz. Dr., Ste. 104
Arlington, TX 76006
(817)633-2873
Fax: (817)633-3781
E-mail: abm@icms.net
Website: http://www.icms.net

Lori Williams
1000 Leslie Ct.
Arlington, TX 76012
(817)459-3934
Fax: (817)459-3934

Business Resource Software Inc.
2013 Wells Branch Pky., Ste. 305
Austin, TX 78728
Free: 800-423-1228
Fax: (512)251-4401
E-mail: info@brs-inc.com
Website: http://www.brs-inc.com

Erisa Adminstrative Services Inc.
12325 Hymeadow Dr., Bldg. 4
Austin, TX 78750-1847
(512)250-9020
Fax: (512)250-9487
Website: http://www.cserisa.com

R. Miller Hicks & Co.
1011 W 11th St.
Austin, TX 78703
(512)477-7000
Fax: (512)477-9697
E-mail: millerhicks@rmhicks.com
Website: http://www.rmhicks.com

Pragmatic Tactics Inc.
3303 Westchester Ave.
College Station, TX 77845
(409)696-5294
Free: 800-570-5294
Fax: (409)696-4994
E-mail: ptactics@aol.com
Website: http://www.ptatics.com

Perot Systems
12404 Park Central Dr.
Dallas, TX 75251
(972)340-5000
Free: 800-688-4333
Fax: (972)455-4100
E-mail: corp.comm@ps.net
Website: http://www.perotsystems.com

ReGENERATION Partners
3838 Oak Lawn Ave.
Dallas, TX 75219
(214)559-3999
Free: 800-406-1112
E-mail: info@regeneration-partner.com
Website: http://www.regeneration-partners.com

High Technology Associates - Division of Global Technologies Inc.
1775 St. James Pl., Ste. 105
Houston, TX 77056
(713)963-9300
Fax: (713)963-8341
E-mail: hta@infohwy.com

MasterCOM
103 Thunder Rd.
Kerrville, TX 78028
(830)895-7990
Fax: (830)443-3428
E-mail: jmstubblefield@master training.com
Website: http://www.mastertraining.com

PROTEC
4607 Linden Pl.
Pearland, TX 77584
(281)997-9872
Fax: (281)997-9895
E-mail: p.oman@ix.netcom.com

Alpha Quadrant Inc.
10618 Auldine
San Antonio, TX 78230
(210)344-3330
Fax: (210)344-8151
E-mail: mbussone@sbcglobal.net
Website:http://www.a-quadrant.com
Michele Bussone

Bastian Public Relations
614 San Dizier
San Antonio, TX 78232
(210)404-1839
E-mail: lisa@bastianpr.com
Website: http://www.bastianpr.com
Lisa Bastian CBC

Business Strategy Development Consultants
PO Box 690365
San Antonio, TX 78269
(210)696-8000
Free: 800-927-BSDC
Fax: (210)696-8000

Tom Welch, CPC
6900 San Pedro Ave., Ste. 147
San Antonio, TX 78216-6207

(210)737-7022
Fax: (210)737-7022
E-mail: bplan@iamerica.net
Website: http://www.moneywords.com

Utah

Business Management Resource
PO Box 521125
Salt Lake City, UT 84152-1125
(801)272-4668
Fax: (801)277-3290
E-mail: pingfong@worldnet.att.net

Virginia

Tindell Associates
209 Oxford Ave.
Alexandria, VA 22301
(703)683-0109
Fax: 703-783-0219
E-mail: scott@tindell.net
Website: http://www.tindell.net
Scott Lockett, President

Elliott B. Jaffa
2530-B S Walter Reed Dr.
Arlington, VA 22206
(703)931-0040
E-mail: thetrainingdoctor@excite.com
Website: http://www.tregistry.com/jaffa.htm

Koach Enterprises - USA
5529 N 18th St.
Arlington, VA 22205
(703)241-8361
Fax: (703)241-8623

Federal Market Development
5650 Chapel Run Ct.
Centreville, VA 20120-3601
(703)502-8930
Free: 800-821-5003
Fax: (703)502-8929

Huff, Stuart & Carlton
2107 Graves Mills Rd., Ste. C
Forest, VA 24551
(804)316-9356
Free: (888)316-9356
Fax: (804)316-9357
Website: http://www.wealthmgt.net

AMX International Inc.
1420 Spring Hill Rd. , Ste. 600
McLean, VA 22102-3006
(703)690-4100
Fax: (703)643-1279
E-mail: amxmail@amxi.com
Website: http://www.amxi.com

Charles Scott Pugh (Investor)
4101 Pittaway Dr.
Richmond, VA 23235-1022
(804)560-0979
Fax: (804)560-4670

John C. Randall and Associates Inc.
PO Box 15127
Richmond, VA 23227
(804)746-4450
Fax: (804)730-8933
E-mail: randalljcx@aol.com
Website: http://www.johncrandall.com

McLeod & Co.
410 1st St.
Roanoke, VA 24011
(540)342-6911
Fax: (540)344-6367
Website: http://www.mcleodco.com/

Salzinger & Company Inc.
8000 Towers Crescent Dr., Ste. 1350
Vienna, VA 22182
(703)442-5200
Fax: (703)442-5205
E-mail: info@salzinger.com
Website: http://www.salzinger.com

The Small Business Counselor
12423 Hedges Run Dr., Ste. 153
Woodbridge, VA 22192
(703)490-6755
Fax: (703)490-1356

Washington

Burlington Consultants
10900 NE 8th St., Ste. 900
Bellevue, WA 98004
(425)688-3060
Fax: (425)454-4383
E-mail: partners@burlington
consultants.com
Website: http://www.burlington
consultants.com

Perry L. Smith Consulting
800 Bellevue Way NE, Ste. 400
Bellevue, WA 98004-4208
(425)462-2072
Fax: (425)462-5638

St. Charles Consulting Group
1420 NW Gilman Blvd.
Issaquah, WA 98027
(425)557-8708
Fax: (425)557-8731
E-mail: info@stcharlesconsulting.com
Website: http://www.stcharlescon
sulting.com

Independent Automotive Training Services
PO Box 334
Kirkland, WA 98083
(425)822-5715
E-mail: ltunney@autosvccon.com
Website: http://www.autosvccon.com

Kahle Associate Inc.
6203 204th Dr. NE
Redmond, WA 98053
(425)836-8763
Fax: (425)868-3770
E-mail: randykahle@kahleassociates.com
Website: http://www.kahleassociates.com

Dan Collin
3419 Wallingord Ave N, No. 2
Seattle, WA 98103
(206)634-9469
E-mail: dc@dancollin.com
Website: http://members.home.net/
dcollin/

ECG Management Consultants Inc.
1111 3rd Ave., Ste. 2700
Seattle, WA 98101-3201
(206)689-2200
Fax: (206)689-2209
E-mail: ecg@ecgmc.com
Website: http://www.ecgmc.com

Northwest Trade Adjustment Assistance Center
900 4th Ave., Ste. 2430
Seattle, WA 98164-1001
(206)622-2730
Free: 800-667-8087
Fax: (206)622-1105
E-mail: matchingfunds@nwtaac.org
Website: http://www.taacenters.org

Business Planning Consultants
S 3510 Ridgeview Dr.
Spokane, WA 99206
(509)928-0332
Fax: (509)921-0842
E-mail: bpci@nextdim.com

West Virginia

**Stanley & Associates Inc./
BusinessandMarketingPlans.com**
1687 Robert C. Byrd Dr.
Beckley, WV 25801
(304)252-0324
Free: 888-752-6720
Fax: (304)252-0470
E-mail: cclay@charterinternet.com

Website: http://www.Businessand
MarketingPlans.com
Christopher Clay

Wisconsin

White & Associates Inc.
5349 Somerset Ln. S
Greenfield, WI 53221
(414)281-7373
Fax: (414)281-7006
E-mail: wnaconsult@aol.com

Small business administration regional offices

This section contains a listing of Small Business Administration offices arranged numerically by region. Service areas are provided. Contact the appropriate office for a referral to the nearest field office, or visit the Small Business Administration online at www.sba.gov.

Region 1

U.S. Small Business Administration
Region I Office
10 Causeway St., Ste. 812
Boston, MA 02222-1093
Phone: (617)565-8415
Fax: (617)565-8420
Serves Connecticut, Maine, Massachusetts, New Hampshire, Rhode Island, and Vermont.

Region 2

U.S. Small Business Administration
Region II Office
26 Federal Plaza, Ste. 3108
New York, NY 10278
Phone: (212)264-1450
Fax: (212)264-0038
Serves New Jersey, New York, Puerto Rico, and the Virgin Islands.

Region 3

U.S. Small Business Administration
Region III Office
Robert N C Nix Sr. Federal Building
900 Market St., 5th Fl.
Philadelphia, PA 19107
(215)580-2807
Serves Delaware, the District of Columbia, Maryland, Pennsylvania, Virginia, and West Virginia.

Region 4

U.S. Small Business Administration
Region IV Office
233 Peachtree St. NE
Harris Tower 1800
Atlanta, GA 30303
Phone: (404)331-4999
Fax: (404)331-2354
Serves Alabama, Florida, Georgia, Kentucky, Mississippi, North Carolina, South Carolina, and Tennessee.

Region 5

U.S. Small Business Administration
Region V Office
500 W. Madison St.
Citicorp Center, Ste. 1240
Chicago, IL 60661-2511
Phone: (312)353-0357
Fax: (312)353-3426
Serves Illinois, Indiana, Michigan, Minnesota, Ohio, and Wisconsin.

Region 6

U.S. Small Business Administration
Region VI Office
4300 Amon Carter Blvd., Ste. 108
Fort Worth, TX 76155
Phone: (817)684-5581
Fax: (817)684-5588
Serves Arkansas, Louisiana, New Mexico, Oklahoma, and Texas.

Region 7

U.S. Small Business Administration
Region VII Office
323 W. 8th St., Ste. 307
Kansas City, MO 64105-1500
Phone: (816)374-6380
Fax: (816)374-6339
Serves Iowa, Kansas, Missouri, and Nebraska.

Region 8

U.S. Small Business Administration
Region VIII Office
721 19th St., Ste. 400
Denver, CO 80202
Phone: (303)844-0500
Fax: (303)844-0506
Serves Colorado, Montana, North Dakota, South Dakota, Utah, and Wyoming.

Region 9

U.S. Small Business Administration
Region IX Office
330 N Brand Blvd., Ste. 1270
Glendale, CA 91203-2304
Phone: (818)552-3434
Fax: (818)552-3440
Serves American Samoa, Arizona, California, Guam, Hawaii, Nevada, and the Trust Territory of the Pacific Islands.

Region 10

U.S. Small Business Administration
Region X Office
2401 Fourth Ave., Ste. 400
Seattle, WA 98121
Phone: (206)553-5676
Fax: (206)553-4155
Serves Alaska, Idaho, Oregon, and Washington.

Small business development centers

This section contains a listing of all Small Business Development Centers, organized alphabetically by state/U.S. territory, then by city, then by agency name.

Alabama

Alabama SBDC
UNIVERSITY OF ALABAMA
2800 Milan Court Suite 124
Birmingham, AL 35211-6908
Phone: 205-943-6750
Fax: 205-943-6752
E-Mail: wcampbell@provost.uab.edu
Website: http://www.asbdc.org
Mr. William Campbell Jr, State Director

Alaska

Alaska SBDC
UNIVERSITY OF ALASKA - ANCHORAGE
430 West Seventh Avenue, Suite 110
Anchorage, AK 99501
Phone: 907-274 -7232
Fax: 907-274-9524
E-Mail: anerw@uaa.alaska.edu
Website: http://www.aksbdc.org
Ms. Jean R. Wall, State Director

American Samoa

American Samoa SBDC
AMERICAN SAMOA COMMUNITY COLLEGE
P.O. Box 2609
Pago Pago, American Samoa 96799
Phone: 011-684-699-4830
Fax: 011-684-699-6132
E-Mail: htalex@att.net
Mr. Herbert Thweatt, Director

Arizona

Arizona SBDC
MARICOPA COUNTY COMMUNITY COLLEGE
2411 West 14th Street, Suite 132
Tempe, AZ 85281
Phone: 480-731-8720
Fax: 480-731-8729
E-Mail: mike.york@domail.maricopa.edu
Website: http://www.dist.maricopa.edu.sbdc
Mr. Michael York, State Director

Arkansas

Arkansas SBDC
UNIVERSITY OF ARKANSAS
2801 South University Avenue
Little Rock, AR 72204
Phone: 501-324-9043
Fax: 501-324-9049
E-Mail: jmroderick@ualr.edu
Website: http://asbdc.ualr.edu
Ms. Janet M. Roderick, State Director

California

California - San Francisco SBDC
Northern California SBDC Lead Center
HUMBOLDT STATE UNIVERSITY
Office of Economic Development
1 Harpst Street 2006A, Siemens Hall
Arcata, CA, 95521
Phone: 707-826-3922
Fax: 707-826-3206
E-Mail: gainer@humboldt.edu
Ms. Margaret A. Gainer, Regional Director

California - Sacramento SBDC
CALIFORNIA STATE UNIVERSITY - CHICO
Chico, CA 95929-0765
Phone: 530-898-4598
Fax: 530-898-4734

E-Mail: dripke@csuchico.edu
Website: http://gsbdc.csuchico.edu
Mr. Dan Ripke, Interim Regional Director

California - San Diego SBDC
SOUTHWESTERN COMMUNITY
COLLEGE DISTRICT
900 Otey Lakes Road
Chula Vista, CA 91910
Phone: 619-482-6388
Fax: 619-482-6402
E-Mail: dtrujillo@swc.cc.ca.us
Website: http://www.sbditc.org
Ms. Debbie P. Trujillo, Regional Director

California - Fresno SBDC
UC Merced Lead Center
UNIVERSITY OF CALIFORNIA -
MERCED
550 East Shaw, Suite 105A
Fresno, CA 93710
Phone: 559-241-6590
Fax: 559-241-7422
E-Mail: crosander@ucmerced.edu
Website: http://sbdc.ucmerced.edu
Mr. Chris Rosander, State Director

California - Santa Ana SBDC
Tri-County Lead SBDC
CALIFORNIA STATE UNIVERSITY -
FULLERTON
800 North State College Boulevard, LH640
Fullerton, CA 92834
Phone: 714-278-2719
Fax: 714-278-7858
E-Mail: vpham@fullerton.edu
Website: http://www.leadsbdc.org
Ms. Vi Pham, Lead Center Director

California - Los Angeles Region SBDC
LONG BEACH COMMUNITY
COLLEGE DISTRICT
3950 Paramount Boulevard, Ste 101
Lakewood, CA 90712
Phone: 562-938-5004
Fax: 562-938-5030
E-Mail: ssloan@lbcc.edu
Ms. Sheneui Sloan, Interim Lead Center
Director

Colorado

Colorado SBDC
OFFICE OF ECONOMIC
DEVELOPMENT
1625 Broadway, Suite 170
Denver, CO 80202
Phone: 303-892-3864
Fax: 303-892-3848
E-Mail: Kelly.Manning@state.co.us

Website: http://www.state.co.us/oed/sbdc
Ms. Kelly Manning, State Director

Connecticut

Connecticut SBDC
UNIVERSITY OF CONNECTICUT
1376 Storrs Road, Unit 4094
Storrs, CT 06269-1094
Phone: 860-870-6370
Fax: 860-870-6374
E-Mail: richard.cheney@uconn.edu
Website: http://www.sbdc.uconn.edu
Mr. Richard Cheney, Interim State Director

Delaware

Delaware SBDC
DELAWARE TECHNOLOGY PARK
1 Innovation Way, Suite 301
Newark, DE 19711
Phone: 302-831-2747
Fax: 302-831-1423
E-Mail: Clinton.tymes@mvs.udel.edu
Website: http://www.delawaresbdc.org
Mr. Clinton Tymes, State Director

District of Columbia

District of Columbia SBDC
HOWARD UNIVERSITY
2600 6th Street, NW Room 128
Washington, DC 20059
Phone: 202-806-1550
Fax: 202-806-1777
E-Mail: hturner@howard.edu
Website: http://www.dcsbdc.com/
Mr. Henry Turner, Executive Director

Florida

Florida SBDC
UNIVERSITY OF WEST FLORIDA
401 East Chase Street, Suite 100
Pensacola, FL 32502
Phone: 850-473-7800
Fax: 850-473-7813
E-Mail: jcartwri@uwf.edu
Website: http://www.floridasbdc.com
Mr. Jerry Cartwright, State Director

Georgia

Georgia SBDC
UNIVERSITY OF GEORGIA
1180 East Broad Street
Athens, GA 30602
Phone: 706-542-6762
Fax: 706-542-6776
E-mail: aadams@sbdc.uga.edu

Website: http://www.sbdc.uga.edu
Mr. Allan Adams, Interim State Director

Guam

Guam Small Business Development
Center
UNIVERSITY OF GUAM
Pacific Islands SBDC
P.O. Box 5014 - U.O.G. Station
Mangilao, GU 96923
Phone: 671-735-2590
Fax: 671-734-2002
E-mail: casey@pacificsbdc.com
Website: http://www.uog.edu/sbdc
Mr. Casey Jeszenka, Director

Hawaii

Hawaii SBDC
UNIVERSITY OF HAWAII - HILO
308 Kamehameha Avenue, Suite 201
Hilo, HI 96720
Phone: 808-974-7515
Fax: 808-974-7683
E-Mail: darrylm@interpac.net
Website: http://www.hawaii-sbdc.org
Mr. Darryl Mleynek, State Director

Idaho

Idaho SBDC
BOISE STATE UNIVERSITY
1910 University Drive
Boise, ID 83725
Phone: 208-426-3799
Fax: 208-426-3877
E-mail: jhogge@boisestate.edu
Website: http://www.idahosbdc.org
Mr. Jim Hogge, State Director

Illinois

Illinois SBDC
DEPARTMENT OF COMMERCE
AND ECONOMIC OPPORTUNITY
620 E. Adams, S-4
Springfield, IL 62701
Phone: 217-524-5700
Fax: 217-524-0171
E-mail: mpatrilli@ildceo.net
Website: http://www.ilsbdc.biz
Mr. Mark Petrilli, State Director

Indiana

Indiana SBDC
INDIANA ECONOMIC
DEVELOPMENT CORPORATION
One North Capitol, Suite 900
Indianapolis, IN 46204

Phone: 317-234-8872
Fax: 317-232-8874
E-mail: dtrocha@isbdc.org
Website: http://www.isbdc.org
Ms. Debbie Bishop Trocha, State
Director

Iowa

Iowa SBDC
IOWA STATE UNIVERSITY
340 Gerdin Business Bldg.
Ames, IA 50011-1350
Phone: 515-294-2037
Fax: 515-294-6522
E-mail: jonryan@iastate.edu
Website: http://www.iabusnet.org
Mr. Jon Ryan, State Director

Kansas

Kansas SBDC
FORT HAYS STATE UNIVERSITY
214 SW Sixth Street, Suite 301
Topeka, KS 66603
Phone: 785 296 6514
Fax: 785-291-3261
E-mail: ksbdc.wkearns@fhsu.edu
Website: http://www.fhsu.edu/ksbdc
Mr. Wally Kearns, State Director

Kentucky

Kentucky SBDC
UNIVERSITY OF KENTUCKY
225 Gatton College of Business
Economics Building
Lexington, KY 40506-0034
Phone: 859-257-7668
Fax: 859-323-1907
E-mail: lrnaug0@pop.uky.edu
Website: http://www.ksbdc.org
Ms. Becky Naugle, State Director

Louisiana

Louisiana SBDC
**UNIVERSITY OF LOUISIANA -
MONROE**
College of Business Administration
700 University Avenue
Monroe, LA 71209
Phone: 318-342-5506
Fax: 318-342-5510
E-mail: wilkerson@ulm.edu
Website: http://www.lsbdc.org
Ms. Mary Lynn Wilkerson, State
Director

Maine

Maine SBDC
**UNIVERSITY OF SOUTHERN
MAINE**
96 Falmouth Street P.O. Box 9300
Portland, ME 04103
Phone: 207-780-4420
Fax: 207-780-4810
E-mail: jrmassaua@maine.edu
Website: http://www.mainesbdc.org
Mr. John Massaua, State Director

Maryland

Maryland SBDC
UNIVERSITY OF MARYLAND
7100 Baltimore Avenue, Suite 401
College Park, MD 20742
Phone: 301-403-8300
Fax: 301-403-8303
E-mail: rsprow@mdsbdc.umd.edu
Website: http://www.mdsbdc.umd.edu
Ms. Renee Sprow, State Director

Massachusetts

Massachusetts SBDC
UNIVERSITY OF MASSACHUSETTS
School of Management, Room 205
Amherst, MA 01003-4935
Phone: 413-545-6301
Fax: 413-545-1273
E-mail: gep@msbdc.umass.edu
Website: http://msbdc.som.umass.edu
Ms. Georgianna Parkin, State Director

Michigan

Michigan SBTDC
**GRAND VALLEY STATE
UNIVERSITY**
510 West Fulton Avenue
Grand Rapids, MI 49504
Phone: 616-331-7485
Fax: 616-331-7389
E-mail: lopuckic@gvsu.edu
Website: http://www.misbtdc.org
Ms. Carol Lopucki, State Director

Minnesota

Minnesota SBDC
**MINNESOTA SMALL BUSINESS
DEVELOPMENT CENTER**
1st National Bank Building
332 Minnesota Street, Suite E200
St. Paul, MN 55101-1351
Phone: 651-297-5773
Fax: 651-296-5287

E-mail: michael.myhre@state.mn.us
Website: http://www.mnsbdc.com
Mr. Michael Myhre, State Director

Mississippi

Mississippi SBDC
UNIVERSITY OF MISSISSIPPI
B-19 Jeanette Phillips Drive
P.O. Box 1848
University, MS 38677
Phone: 662-915-5001
Fax: 662-915-5650
E-mail: wgurley@olemiss.edu
Website: http://www.olemiss.edu/depts/
mssbdc
Mr. Doug Gurley, Jr., State Director

Missouri

Missouri SBDC
UNIVERSITY OF MISSOURI
1205 University Avenue, Suite 300
Columbia, MO 65211
Phone: 573-882-1348
Fax: 573-884-4297
E-mail: summersm@missouri.edu
Website: http://www.mo-sbdc.org/
index.shtml
Mr. Max Summers, State Director

Montana

Montana SBDC
DEPARTMENT OF COMMERCE
301 South Park Avenue, Room 114 /
P.O. Box 200505
Helena, MT 59620
Phone: 406-841-2746
Fax: 406-444-1872
E-mail: adesch@state.mt.us
Website: http://commerce.state.mt.us/
brd/BRD_SBDC.html
Ms. Ann Desch, State Director

Nebraska

Nebraska SBDC
**UNIVERSITY OF NEBRASKA -
OMAHA**
60th & Dodge Street, CBA Room 407
Omaha, NE 68182
Phone: 402-554-2521
Fax: 402-554-3473
E-mail: rbernier@unomaha.edu
Website: http://nbdc.unomaha.edu
Mr. Robert Bernier, State Director

Nevada

Nevada SBDC
UNIVERSITY OF NEVADA - RENO
Reno College of Business
Administration, Room 411
Reno, NV 89557-0100
Phone: 775-784-1717
Fax: 775-784-4337
E-mail: males@unr.edu
Website: http://www.nsbdc.org
Mr. Sam Males, State Director

New Hampshire

New Hampshire SBDC
UNIVERSITY OF NEW HAMPSHIRE
108 McConnell Hall
Durham, NH 03824-3593
Phone: 603-862-4879
Fax: 603-862-4876
E-mail: Mary.Collins@unh.edu
Website: http://www.nhsbdc.org
Ms. Mary Collins, State Director

New Jersey

New Jersey SBDC
RUTGERS UNIVERSITY
49 Bleeker Street
Newark, NJ 07102-1993
Phone: 973-353-5950
Fax: 973-353-1110
E-mail: bhopper@njsbdc.com
Website: http://www.njsbdc.com/home
Ms. Brenda Hopper, State Director

New Mexico

New Mexico SBDC
SANTA FE COMMUNITY COLLEGE
6401 Richards Avenue
Santa Fe, NM 87505
Phone: 505-428-1362
Fax: 505-471-9469
E-mail: rmiller@santa-fe.cc.nm.us
Website: http://www.nmsbdc.org
Mr. Roy Miller, State Director

New York

New York SBDC
STATE UNIVERSITY OF NEW YORK
SUNY Plaza, S-523
Albany, NY 12246
Phone: 518-443-5398
Fax: 518-443-5275
E-mail: j.king@nyssbdc.org
Website: http://www.nyssbdc.org
Mr. Jim King, State Director

North Carolina

North Carolina SBDTC
UNIVERSITY OF NORTH CAROLINA
5 West Hargett Street, Suite 600
Raleigh, NC 27601
Phone: 919-715-7272
Fax: 919-715-7777
E-mail: sdaugherty@sbtdc.org
Website: http://www.sbtdc.org
Mr. Scott Daugherty, State Director

North Dakota

North Dakota SBDC
UNIVERSITY OF NORTH DAKOTA
1600 E. Century Avenue, Suite 2
Bismarck, ND 58503
Phone: 701-328-5375
Fax: 701-328-5320
E-mail: christine.martin@und.nodak.edu
Website: http://www.ndsbdc.org
Ms. Christine Martin-Goldman, State
Director

Ohio

Ohio SBDC
OHIO DEPARTMENT
OF DEVELOPMENT
77 South High Street
Columbus, OH 43216
Phone: 614-466-5102
Fax: 614-466-0829
E-mail: mabraham@odod.state.oh.us
Website: http://www.ohiosbdc.org
Ms. Michele Abraham, State Director

Oklahoma

Oklahoma SBDC
SOUTHEAST OKLAHOMA STATE
UNIVERSITY
517 University, Box 2584, Station A
Durant, OK 74701
Phone: 580-745-7577
Fax: 580-745-7471
E-mail: gpennington@sosu.edu
Website: http://www.osbdc.org
Mr. Grady Pennington, State Director

Oregon

Oregon SBDC
LANE COMMUNITY COLLEGE
99 West Tenth Avenue, Suite 390
Eugene, OR 97401-3021
Phone: 541-463-5250
Fax: 541-345-6006
E-mail: carterb@lanecc.edu

Website: http://www.bizcenter.org
Mr. William Carter, State Director

Pennsylvania

Pennsylvania SBDC
UNIVERSITY OF PENNSYLVANIA
The Wharton School
3733 Spruce Street
Philadelphia, PA 19104-6374
Phone: 215-898-1219
Fax: 215-573-2135
E-mail: ghiggins@wharton.upenn.edu
Website: http://pasbdc.org
Mr. Gregory Higgins, State Director

Puerto Rico

Puerto Rico SBDC
INTER-AMERICAN UNIVERSITY
OF PUERTO RICO
416 Ponce de Leon Avenue, Union Plaza,
Seventh Floor
Hato Rey, PR 00918
Phone: 787-763-6811
Fax: 787-763-4629
E-mail: cmarti@prsbdc.org
Website: http://www.prsbdc.org
Ms. Carmen Marti, Executive Director

Rhode Island

Rhode Island SBDC
BRYANT UNIVERSITY
1150 Douglas Pike
Smithfield, RI 02917
Phone: 401-232-6923
Fax: 401-232-6933
E-mail: adawson@bryant.edu
Website: http://www.risbdc.org
Ms. Diane Fournaris, Interim State Director

South Carolina

South Carolina SBDC
UNIVERSITY OF SOUTH CAROLINA
College of Business Administration
1710 College Street
Columbia, SC 29208
Phone: 803-777-4907
Fax: 803-777-4403
E-mail: lenti@moore.sc.edu
Website: http://scsbdc.moore.sc.edu
Mr. John Lenti, State Director

South Dakota

South Dakota SBDC
UNIVERSITY OF SOUTH DAKOTA
414 East Clark Street, Patterson Hall
Vermillion, SD 57069

Phone: 605-677-6256
Fax: 605-677-5427
E-mail: jshemmin@usd.edu
Website: http://www.sdsbdc.org
Mr. John S. Hemmingstad, State
Director

Tennessee

Tennessee SBDC
TENNESSEE BOARD OF REGENTS
1415 Murfressboro Road, Suite 540
Nashville, TN 37217-2833
Phone: 615-898-2745
Fax: 615-893-7089
E-mail: pgeho@mail.tsbdc.org
Website: http://www.tsbdc.org
Mr. Patrick Geho, State Director

Texas

Texas-North SBDC
**DALLAS COUNTY COMMUNITY
COLLEGE**
1402 Corinth Street
Dallas, TX 75215
Phone: 214-860-5835
Fax: 214-860-5813
E-mail: emk9402@dcccd.edu
Website: http://www.ntsbdc.org
Ms. Liz Klimback, Region Director

Texas-Houston SBDC
UNIVERSITY OF HOUSTON
2302 Fannin, Suite 200
Houston, TX 77002
Phone: 713-752-8425
Fax: 713-756-1500
E-mail: fyoung@uh.edu
Website: http://sbdcnetwork.uh.edu
Mr. Mike Young, Executive Director

Texas-NW SBDC
TEXAS TECH UNIVERSITY
2579 South Loop 289, Suite 114
Lubbock, TX 79423
Phone: 806-745-3973
Fax: 806-745-6207
E-mail: c.bean@nwtsbdc.org
Website: http://www.nwtsbdc.org
Mr. Craig Bean, Executive Director

**Texas-South-West Texas Border
Region SBDC**
**UNIVERSITY OF TEXAS -
SAN ANTONIO**
501 West Durango Boulevard
San Antonio, TX 78207-4415
Phone: 210-458-2742
Fax: 210-458-2464

E-mail: albert.salgado@utsa.edu
Website: http://www.iedtexas.org
Mr. Alberto Salgado, Region Director

Utah

Utah SBDC
SALT LAKE COMMUNITY COLLEGE
9750 South 300 West
Sandy, UT 84070
Phone: 801-957-3493
Fax: 801-957-3488
E-mail: Greg.Panichello@slcc.edu
Website: http://www.slcc.edu/sbdc
Mr. Greg Panichello, State Director

Vermont

Vermont SBDC
VERMONT TECHNICAL COLLEGE
PO Box 188, 1 Main Street
Randolph Center, VT 05061-0188
Phone: 802-728-9101
Fax: 802-728-3026
E-mail: lquillen@vtc.edu
Website: http://www.vtsbdc.org
Ms. Lenae Quillen-Blume, State Director

Virgin Islands

Virgin Islands SBDC
**UNIVERSITY OF THE VIRGIN
ISLANDS**
8000 Nisky Center, Suite 720
St. Thomas, VI 00802-5804
Phone: 340-776-3206
Fax: 340-775-3756
E-mail: wbush@webmail.uvi.edu
Website: http://rps.uvi.edu/SBDC
Mr. Warren Bush, State Director

Virginia

Virginia SBDC
GEORGE MASON UNIVERSITY
4031 University Drive, Suite 200
Fairfax, VA 22030-3409
Phone: 703-277-7727
Fax: 703-352-8515
E-mail: jkeenan@gmu.edu
Website: http://www.virginiasbdc.org
Ms. Jody Keenan, Director

Washington

Washington SBDC
WASHINGTON STATE UNIVERSITY
534 E. Trent Avenue
P.O. Box 1495
Spokane, WA 99210-1495

Phone: 509-358-7765
Fax: 509-358-7764
E-mail: barogers@wsu.edu
Website: http://www.wsbdc.org
Mr. Brett Rogers, State Director

West Virginia

West Virginia SBDC
**WEST VIRGINIA DEVELOPMENT
OFFICE**
Capital Complex, Building 6, Room 652
Charleston, WV 25301
Phone: 304-558-2960
Fax: 304-558-0127
E-mail: csalyer@wvsbdc.org
Website: http://www.wvsbdc.org
Mr. Conley Salyor, State Director

Wisconsin

Wisconsin SBDC
UNIVERSITY OF WISCONSIN
432 North Lake Street, Room 423
Madison, WI 53706
Phone: 608-263-7794
Fax: 608-263-7830
E-mail: erica.kauten@uwex.edu
Website: http://www.wisconsinsbdc.org
Ms. Erica Kauten, State Director

Wyoming

Wyoming SBDC
UNIVERSITY OF WYOMING
P.O. Box 3922
Laramie, WY 82071-3922
Phone: 307-766-3505
Fax: 307-766-3406
E-mail: DDW@uwyo.edu
Website: http://www.uwyo.edu/sbdc
Ms. Debbie Popp, Acting State Director

Service corps of retired executives (score) offices

*This section contains a listing of all
SCORE offices organized alphabetically by
state/U.S. territory, then by city, then by
agency name.*

Alabama

SCORE Office (Northeast Alabama)
1330 Quintard Ave.
Anniston, AL 36202
(256)237-3536

Organizations, Agencies, & Consultants

SCORE Office (North Alabama)
901 South 15th St, Rm. 201
Birmingham, AL 35294-2060
(205)934-6868
Fax: (205)934-0538

SCORE Office (Baldwin County)
29750 Larry Dee Cawyer Dr.
Daphne, AL 36526
(334)928-5838

SCORE Office (Shoals)
612 S. COurt
Florence, AL 35630
(256)764-4661
Fax: (256)766-9017
E-mail: shoals@shoalschamber.com

SCORE Office (Mobile)
600 S Court St.
Mobile, AL 36104
(334)240-6868
Fax: (334)240-6869

SCORE Office (Alabama Capitol City)
600 S. Court St.
Montgomery, AL 36104
(334)240-6868
Fax: (334)240-6869

SCORE Office (East Alabama)
601 Ave. A
Opelika, AL 36801
(334)745-4861
E-mail: score636@hotmail.com
Website: http://www.angelfire.com/sc/
score636/

SCORE Office (Tuscaloosa)
2200 University Blvd.
Tuscaloosa, AL 35402
(205)758-7588

Alaska

SCORE Office (Anchorage)
510 L St., Ste. 310
Anchorage, AK 99501
(907)271-4022
Fax: (907)271-4545

Arizona

SCORE Office (Lake Havasu)
10 S. Acoma Blvd.
Lake Havasu City, AZ 86403
(520)453-5951
E-mail: SCORE@ctaz.com
Website: http://www.scorearizona.org/
lake_havasu/

SCORE Office (East Valley)
Federal Bldg., Rm. 104
26 N. MacDonald St.
Mesa, AZ 85201
(602)379-3100
Fax: (602)379-3143
E-mail: 402@aol.com
Website: http://www.scorearizona.
org/mesa/

SCORE Office (Phoenix)
2828 N. Central Ave., Ste. 800
Central & One Thomas
Phoenix, AZ 85004
(602)640-2329
Fax: (602)640-2360
E-mail: e-mail@SCORE-phoenix.org
Website: http://www.score-phoenix.org/

SCORE Office (Prescott Arizona)
1228 Willow Creek Rd., Ste. 2
Prescott, AZ 86301
(520)778-7438
Fax: (520)778-0812
E-mail: score@northlink.com
Website: http://www.scorearizona.org/
prescott/

SCORE Office (Tucson)
110 E. Pennington St.
Tucson, AZ 85702
(520)670-5008
Fax: (520)670-5011
E-mail: score@azstarnet.com
Website: http://www.scorearizona.org/
tucson/

SCORE Office (Yuma)
281 W. 24th St., Ste. 116
Yuma, AZ 85364
(520)314-0480
E-mail: score@C2i2.com
Website: http://www.scorearizona.org/
yuma

Arkansas

SCORE Office (South Central)
201 N. Jackson Ave.
El Dorado, AR 71730-5803
(870)863-6113
Fax: (870)863-6115

SCORE Office (Ozark)
Fayetteville, AR 72701
(501)442-7619

SCORE Office (Northwest Arkansas)
Glenn Haven Dr., No. 4
Ft. Smith, AR 72901
(501)783-3556

SCORE Office (Garland County)
Grand & Ouachita
PO Box 6012
Hot Springs Village, AR 71902
(501)321-1700

SCORE Office (Little Rock)
2120 Riverfront Dr., Rm. 100
Little Rock, AR 72202-1747
(501)324-5893
Fax: (501)324-5199

SCORE Office (Southeast Arkansas)
121 W. 6th
Pine Bluff, AR 71601
(870)535-7189
Fax: (870)535-1643

California

SCORE Office (Golden Empire)
1706 Chester Ave., No. 200
Bakersfield, CA 93301
(805)322-5881
Fax: (805)322-5663

SCORE Office (Greater Chico Area)
1324 Mangrove St., Ste. 114
Chico, CA 95926
(916)342-8932
Fax: (916)342-8932

SCORE Office (Concord)
2151-A Salvio St., Ste. B
Concord, CA 94520
(510)685-1181
Fax: (510)685-5623

SCORE Office (Covina)
935 W. Badillo St.
Covina, CA 91723
(818)967-4191
Fax: (818)966-9660

SCORE Office (Rancho Cucamonga)
8280 Utica, Ste. 160
Cucamonga, CA 91730
(909)987-1012
Fax: (909)987-5917

SCORE Office (Culver City)
PO Box 707
Culver City, CA 90232-0707
(310)287-3850
Fax: (310)287-1350

SCORE Office (Danville)
380 Diablo Rd., Ste. 103
Danville, CA 94526
(510)837-4400

SCORE Office (Downey)
11131 Brookshire Ave.
Downey, CA 90241
(310)923-2191
Fax: (310)864-0461

SCORE Office (El Cajon)
109 Rea Ave.
El Cajon, CA 92020
(619)444-1327
Fax: (619)440-6164

SCORE Office (El Centro)
1100 Main St.
El Centro, CA 92243
(619)352-3681
Fax: (619)352-3246

SCORE Office (Escondido)
720 N. Broadway
Escondido, CA 92025
(619)745-2125
Fax: (619)745-1183

SCORE Office (Fairfield)
1111 Webster St.
Fairfield, CA 94533
(707)425-4625
Fax: (707)425-0826

SCORE Office (Fontana)
17009 Valley Blvd., Ste. B
Fontana, CA 92335
(909)822-4433
Fax: (909)822-6238

SCORE Office (Foster City)
1125 E. Hillsdale Blvd.
Foster City, CA 94404
(415)573-7600
Fax: (415)573-5201

SCORE Office (Fremont)
2201 Walnut Ave., Ste. 110
Fremont, CA 94538
(510)795-2244
Fax: (510)795-2240

SCORE Office (Central California)
2719 N. Air Fresno Dr., Ste. 200
Fresno, CA 93727-1547
(559)487-5605
Fax: (559)487-5636

SCORE Office (Gardena)
1204 W. Gardena Blvd.
Gardena, CA 90247
(310)532-9905
Fax: (310)515-4893

SCORE Office (Lompoc)
330 N. Brand Blvd., Ste. 190
Glendale, CA 91203-2304

(818)552-3206
Fax: (818)552-3323

SCORE Office (Los Angeles)
330 N. Brand Blvd., Ste. 190
Glendale, CA 91203-2304
(818)552-3206
Fax: (818)552-3323

SCORE Office (Glendora)
131 E. Foothill Blvd.
Glendora, CA 91740
(818)963-4128
Fax: (818)914-4822

SCORE Office (Grover Beach)
177 S. 8th St.
Grover Beach, CA 93433
(805)489-9091
Fax: (805)489-9091

SCORE Office (Hawthorne)
12477 Hawthorne Blvd.
Hawthorne, CA 90250
(310)676-1163
Fax: (310)676-7661

SCORE Office (Hayward)
22300 Foothill Blvd., Ste. 303
Hayward, CA 94541
(510)537-2424

SCORE Office (Hemet)
1700 E. Florida Ave.
Hemet, CA 92544-4679
(909)652-4390
Fax: (909)929-8543

SCORE Office (Hesperia)
16367 Main St.
PO Box 403656
Hesperia, CA 92340
(619)244-2135

SCORE Office (Holloster)
321 San Felipe Rd., No. 11
Hollister, CA 95023

SCORE Office (Hollywood)
7018 Hollywood Blvd.
Hollywood, CA 90028
(213)469-8311
Fax: (213)469-2805

SCORE Office (Indio)
82503 Hwy. 111
PO Drawer TTT
Indio, CA 92202
(619)347-0676

SCORE Office (Inglewood)
330 Queen St.

Inglewood, CA 90301
(818)552-3206

SCORE Office (La Puente)
218 N. Grendanda St. D.
La Puente, CA 91744
(818)330-3216
Fax: (818)330-9524

SCORE Office (La Verne)
2078 Bonita Ave.
La Verne, CA 91750
(909)593-5265
Fax: (714)929-8475

SCORE Office (Lake Elsinore)
132 W. Graham Ave.
Lake Elsinore, CA 92530
(909)674-2577

SCORE Office (Lakeport)
PO Box 295
Lakeport, CA 95453
(707)263-5092

SCORE Office (Lakewood)
5445 E. Del Amo Blvd., Ste. 2
Lakewood, CA 90714
(213)920-7737

SCORE Office (Long Beach)
1 World Trade Center
Long Beach, CA 90831

SCORE Office (Los Alamitos)
901 W. Civic Center Dr., Ste. 160
Los Alamitos, CA 90720

SCORE Office (Los Altos)
321 University Ave.
Los Altos, CA 94022
(415)948-1455

SCORE Office (Manhattan Beach)
PO Box 3007
Manhattan Beach, CA 90266
(310)545-5313
Fax: (310)545-7203

SCORE Office (Merced)
1632 N. St.
Merced, CA 95340
(209)725-3800
Fax: (209)383-4959

SCORE Office (Milpitas)
75 S. Milpitas Blvd., Ste. 205
Milpitas, CA 95035
(408)262-2613
Fax: (408)262-2823

SCORE Office (Yosemite)
1012 11th St., Ste. 300
Modesto, CA 95354
(209)521-9333

SCORE Office (Montclair)
5220 Benito Ave.
Montclair, CA 91763

SCORE Office (Monterey Bay)
380 Alvarado St.
PO Box 1770
Monterey, CA 93940-1770
(408)649-1770

SCORE Office (Moreno Valley)
25480 Alessandro
Moreno Valley, CA 92553

SCORE Office (Morgan Hill)
25 W. 1st St.
PO Box 786
Morgan Hill, CA 95038
(408)779-9444
Fax: (408)778-1786

SCORE Office (Morro Bay)
880 Main St.
Morro Bay, CA 93442
(805)772-4467

SCORE Office (Mountain View)
580 Castro St.
Mountain View, CA 94041
(415)968-8378
Fax: (415)968-5668

SCORE Office (Napa)
1556 1st St.
Napa, CA 94559
(707)226-7455
Fax: (707)226-1171

SCORE Office (North Hollywood)
5019 Lankershim Blvd.
North Hollywood, CA 91601
(818)552-3206

SCORE Office (Northridge)
8801 Reseda Blvd.
Northridge, CA 91324
(818)349-5676

SCORE Office (Novato)
807 De Long Ave.
Novato, CA 94945
(415)897-1164
Fax: (415)898-9097

SCORE Office (East Bay)
519 17th St.
Oakland, CA 94612

(510)273-6611
Fax: (510)273-6015
E-mail: webmaster@eastbayscore.org
Website: http://www.eastbayscore.org

SCORE Office (Oceanside)
928 N. Coast Hwy.
Oceanside, CA 92054
(619)722-1534

SCORE Office (Ontario)
121 West B. St.
Ontario, CA 91762
Fax: (714)984-6439

SCORE Office (Oxnard)
PO Box 867
Oxnard, CA 93032
(805)385-8860
Fax: (805)487-1763

SCORE Office (Pacifica)
450 Dundee Way, Ste. 2
Pacifica, CA 94044
(415)355-4122

SCORE Office (Palm Desert)
72990 Hwy. 111
Palm Desert, CA 92260
(619)346-6111
Fax: (619)346-3463

SCORE Office (Palm Springs)
650 E. Tahquitz Canyon Way Ste. D
Palm Springs, CA 92262-6706
(760)320-6682
Fax: (760)323-9426

SCORE Office (Lakeside)
2150 Low Tree
Palmdale, CA 93551
(805)948-4518
Fax: (805)949-1212

SCORE Office (Palo Alto)
325 Forest Ave.
Palo Alto, CA 94301
(415)324-3121
Fax: (415)324-1215

SCORE Office (Pasadena)
117 E. Colorado Blvd., Ste. 100
Pasadena, CA 91105
(818)795-3355
Fax: (818)795-5663

SCORE Office (Paso Robles)
1225 Park St.
Paso Robles, CA 93446-2234
(805)238-0506
Fax: (805)238-0527

SCORE Office (Petaluma)
799 Baywood Dr., Ste. 3
Petaluma, CA 94954
(707)762-2785
Fax: (707)762-4721

SCORE Office (Pico Rivera)
9122 E. Washington Blvd.
Pico Rivera, CA 90660

SCORE Office (Pittsburg)
2700 E. Leland Rd.
Pittsburg, CA 94565
(510)439-2181
Fax: (510)427-1599

SCORE Office (Pleasanton)
777 Peters Ave.
Pleasanton, CA 94566
(510)846-9697

SCORE Office (Monterey Park)
485 N. Garey
Pomona, CA 91769

SCORE Office (Pomona)
485 N. Garey Ave.
Pomona, CA 91766
(909)622-1256

SCORE Office (Antelope Valley)
4511 West Ave. M-4
Quartz Hill, CA 93536
(805)272-0087
E-mail: avscore@ptw.com
Website: http://www.score.av.org/

SCORE Office (Shasta)
737 Auditorium Dr.
Redding, CA 96099
(916)225-2770

SCORE Office (Redwood City)
1675 Broadway
Redwood City, CA 94063
(415)364-1722
Fax: (415)364-1729

SCORE Office (Richmond)
3925 MacDonald Ave.
Richmond, CA 94805

SCORE Office (Ridgecrest)
PO Box 771
Ridgecrest, CA 93555
(619)375-8331
Fax: (619)375-0365

SCORE Office (Riverside)
3685 Main St., Ste. 350
Riverside, CA 92501
(909)683-7100

SCORE Office (Sacramento)
9845 Horn Rd., 260-B
Sacramento, CA 95827
(916)361-2322
Fax: (916)361-2164
E-mail: sacchapter@directcon.net

SCORE Office (Salinas)
PO Box 1170
Salinas, CA 93902
(408)424-7611
Fax: (408)424-8639

SCORE Office (Inland Empire)
777 E. Rialto Ave.
Purchasing
San Bernardino, CA 92415-0760
(909)386-8278

SCORE Office (San Carlos)
San Carlos Chamber of Commerce
PO Box 1086
San Carlos, CA 94070
(415)593-1068
Fax: (415)593-9108

SCORE Office (Encinitas)
550 W. C St., Ste. 550
San Diego, CA 92101-3540
(619)557-7272
Fax: (619)557-5894

SCORE Office (San Diego)
550 West C. St., Ste. 550
San Diego, CA 92101-3540
(619)557-7272
Fax: (619)557-5894
Website: http://www.score-sandiego.org

SCORE Office (Menlo Park)
1100 Merrill St.
San Francisco, CA 94105
(415)325-2818
Fax: (415)325-0920

SCORE Office (San Francisco)
455 Market St., 6th Fl.
San Francisco, CA 94105
(415)744-6827
Fax: (415)744-6750
E-mail: sfscore@sfscore.
Website: http://www.sfscore.com

SCORE Office (San Gabriel)
401 W. Las Tunas Dr.
San Gabriel, CA 91776
(818)576-2525
Fax: (818)289-2901

SCORE Office (San Jose)
Deanza College
208 S. 1st. St., Ste. 137
San Jose, CA 95113
(408)288-8479
Fax: (408)535-5541

SCORE Office (Silicon Valley)
84 W. Santa Clara St., Ste. 100
San Jose, CA 95113
(408)288-8479
Fax: (408)535-5541
E-mail: info@svscore.org
Website: http://www.svscore.org

SCORE Office (San Luis Obispo)
3566 S. Hiquera, No. 104
San Luis Obispo, CA 93401
(805)547-0779

SCORE Office (San Mateo)
1021 S. El Camino, 2nd Fl.
San Mateo, CA 94402
(415)341-5679

SCORE Office (San Pedro)
390 W. 7th St.
San Pedro, CA 90731
(310)832-7272

SCORE Office (Orange County)
200 W. Santa Anna Blvd., Ste. 700
Santa Ana, CA 92701
(714)550-7369
Fax: (714)550 0191
Website: http://www.score114.org

SCORE Office (Santa Barbara)
3227 State St.
Santa Barbara, CA 93130
(805)563-0084

SCORE Office (Central Coast)
509 W. Morrison Ave.
Santa Maria, CA 93454
(805)347-7755

SCORE Office (Santa Maria)
614 S. Broadway
Santa Maria, CA 93454-5111
(805)925-2403
Fax: (805)928-7559

SCORE Office (Santa Monica)
501 Colorado, Ste. 150
Santa Monica, CA 90401
(310)393-9825
Fax: (310)394-1868

SCORE Office (Santa Rosa)
777 Sonoma Ave., Rm. 115E
Santa Rosa, CA 95404

(707)571-8342
Fax: (707)541-0331
Website: http://www.pressdemo.com/community/score/score.html

SCORE Office (Scotts Valley)
4 Camp Evers Ln.
Scotts Valley, CA 95066
(408)438-1010
Fax: (408)438-6544

SCORE Office (Simi Valley)
40 W. Cochran St., Ste. 100
Simi Valley, CA 93065
(805)526-3900
Fax: (805)526-6234

SCORE Office (Sonoma)
453 1st St. E
Sonoma, CA 95476
(707)996-1033

SCORE Office (Los Banos)
222 S. Shepard St.
Sonora, CA 95370
(209)532-4212

SCORE Office (Tuolumne County)
39 North Washington St.
Sonora, CA 95370
(209)588-0128
E-mail: score@mlode.com

SCORE Office (South San Francisco)
445 Market St., Ste. 6th Fl.
South San Francisco, CA 94105
(415)744-6827
Fax: (415)744-6812

SCORE Office (Stockton)
401 N. San Joaquin St., Rm. 215
Stockton, CA 95202
(209)946-6293

SCORE Office (Taft)
314 4th St.
Taft, CA 93268
(805)765-2165
Fax: (805)765-6639

SCORE Office (Conejo Valley)
625 W. Hillcrest Dr.
Thousand Oaks, CA 91360
(805)499-1993
Fax: (805)498-7264

SCORE Office (Torrance)
3400 Torrance Blvd., Ste. 100
Torrance, CA 90503
(310)540-5858
Fax: (310)540-7662

SCORE Office (Truckee)
PO Box 2757
Truckee, CA 96160
(916)587-2757
Fax: (916)587-2439

SCORE Office (Visalia)
113 S. M St,
Tulare, CA 93274
(209)627-0766
Fax: (209)627-8149

SCORE Office (Upland)
433 N. 2nd Ave.
Upland, CA 91786
(909)931-4108

SCORE Office (Vallejo)
2 Florida St.
Vallejo, CA 94590
(707)644-5551
Fax: (707)644-5590

SCORE Office (Van Nuys)
14540 Victory Blvd.
Van Nuys, CA 91411
(818)989-0300
Fax: (818)989-3836

SCORE Office (Ventura)
5700 Ralston St., Ste. 310
Ventura, CA 93001
(805)658-2688
Fax: (805)658-2252
E-mail: scoreven@jps.net
Website: http://www.jps.net/scoreven

SCORE Office (Vista)
201 E. Washington St.
Vista, CA 92084
(619)726-1122
Fax: (619)226-8654

SCORE Office (Watsonville)
PO Box 1748
Watsonville, CA 95077
(408)724-3849
Fax: (408)728-5300

SCORE Office (West Covina)
811 S. Sunset Ave.
West Covina, CA 91790
(818)338-8496
Fax: (818)960-0511

SCORE Office (Westlake)
30893 Thousand Oaks Blvd.
Westlake Village, CA 91362
(805)496-5630
Fax: (818)991-1754

Colorado

SCORE Office (Colorado Springs)
2 N. Cascade Ave., Ste. 110
Colorado Springs, CO 80903
(719)636-3074
Website: http://www.cscc.org/score02/
index.html

SCORE Office (Denver)
US Custom's House, 4th Fl.
721 19th St.
Denver, CO 80201-0660
(303)844-3985
Fax: (303)844-6490
E-mail: score62@csn.net
Website: http://www.sni.net/score62

SCORE Office (Tri-River)
1102 Grand Ave.
Glenwood Springs, CO 81601
(970)945-6589

SCORE Office (Grand Junction)
2591 B & 3/4 Rd.
Grand Junction, CO 81503
(970)243-5242

SCORE Office (Gunnison)
608 N. 11th
Gunnison, CO 81230
(303)641-4422

SCORE Office (Montrose)
1214 Peppertree Dr.
Montrose, CO 81401
(970)249-6080

SCORE Office (Pagosa Springs)
PO Box 4381
Pagosa Springs, CO 81157
(970)731-4890

SCORE Office (Rifle)
0854 W. Battlement Pky., Apt. C106
Parachute, CO 81635
(970)285-9390

SCORE Office (Pueblo)
302 N. Santa Fe
Pueblo, CO 81003
(719)542-1704
Fax: (719)542-1624
E-mail: mackey@iex.net
Website: http://www.pueblo.org/score

SCORE Office (Ridgway)
143 Poplar Pl.
Ridgway, CO 81432

SCORE Office (Silverton)
PO Box 480

Silverton, CO 81433
(303)387-5430

SCORE Office (Minturn)
PO Box 2066
Vail, CO 81658
(970)476-1224

Connecticut

SCORE Office (Greater Bridgeport)
230 Park Ave.
Bridgeport, CT 06601-0999
(203)576-4369
Fax: (203)576-4388

SCORE Office (Bristol)
10 Main St. 1st. Fl.
Bristol, CT 06010
(203)584-4718
Fax: (203)584-4722

SCORE office (Greater Danbury)
246 Federal Rd.
Unit LL2, Ste. 7
Brookfield, CT 06804
(203)775-1151

SCORE Office (Greater Danbury)
246 Federal Rd., Unit LL2, Ste. 7
Brookfield, CT 06804
(203)775-1151

SCORE Office (Eastern Connecticut)
Administration Bldg., Rm. 313
PO 625
61 Main St. (Chapter 579)
Groton, CT 06475
(203)388-9508

SCORE Office (Greater Hartford County)
330 Main St.
Hartford, CT 06106
(860)548-1749
Fax: (860)240-4659
Website: http://www.score56.org

SCORE Office (Manchester)
20 Hartford Rd.
Manchester, CT 06040
(203)646-2223
Fax: (203)646-5871

SCORE Office (New Britain)
185 Main St., Ste. 431
New Britain, CT 06051
(203)827-4492
Fax: (203)827-4480

SCORE Office (New Haven)
25 Science Pk., Bldg. 25, Rm. 366

New Haven, CT 06511
(203)865-7645

SCORE Office (Fairfield County)
24 Beldon Ave., 5th Fl.
Norwalk, CT 06850
(203)847-7348
Fax: (203)849-9308

SCORE Office (Old Saybrook)
146 Main St.
Old Saybrook, CT 06475
(860)388-9508

SCORE Office (Simsbury)
Box 244
Simsbury, CT 06070
(203)651-7307
Fax: (203)651-1933

SCORE Office (Torrington)
23 North Rd.
Torrington, CT 06791
(203)482-6586

Delaware

SCORE Office (Dover)
Treadway Towers
PO Box 576
Dover, DE 19903
(302)678-0892
Fax: (302)678-0189

SCORE Office (Lewes)
PO Box 1
Lewes, DE 19958
(302)645-8073
Fax: (302)645-8412

SCORE Office (Milford)
204 NE Front St.
Milford, DE 19963
(302)422-3301

SCORE Office (Wilmington)
824 Market St., Ste. 610
Wilmington, DE 19801
(302)573-6652
Fax: (302)573-6092
Website: http://www.scoredelaware.com

District of Columbia

SCORE Office (George Mason University)
409 3rd St. SW, 4th Fl.
Washington, DC 20024
800-634-0245

SCORE Office (Washington DC)
1110 Vermont Ave. NW, 9th Fl.

Washington, DC 20043
(202)606-4000
Fax: (202)606-4225
E-mail: dcscore@hotmail.com
Website: http://www.scoredc.org/

Florida

SCORE Office (Desota County Chamber of Commerce)
16 South Velucia Ave.
Arcadia, FL 34266
(941)494-4033

SCORE Office (Suncoast/Pinellas)
Airport Business Ctr.
4707 - 140th Ave. N, No. 311
Clearwater, FL 33755
(813)532-6800
Fax: (813)532-6800

SCORE Office (DeLand)
336 N. Woodland Blvd.
DeLand, FL 32720
(904)734-4331
Fax: (904)734-4333

SCORE Office (South Palm Beach)
1050 S. Federal Hwy., Ste. 132
Delray Beach, FL 33483
(561)278-7752
Fax: (561)278-0288

SCORE Office (Ft. Lauderdale)
Federal Bldg., Ste. 123
299 E. Broward Blvd.
Ft. Lauderdale, FL 33301
(954)356-7263
Fax: (954)356-7145

SCORE Office (Southwest Florida)
The Renaissance
8695 College Pky., Ste. 345 & 346
Ft. Myers, FL 33919
(941)489-2935
Fax: (941)489-1170

SCORE Office (Treasure Coast)
Professional Center, Ste. 2
3220 S. US, No. 1
Ft. Pierce, FL 34982
(561)489-0548

SCORE Office (Gainesville)
101 SE 2nd Pl., Ste. 104
Gainesville, FL 32601
(904)375-8278

SCORE Office (Hialeah Dade Chamber)
59 W. 5th St.
Hialeah, FL 33010

(305)887-1515
Fax: (305)887-2453

SCORE Office (Daytona Beach)
921 Nova Rd., Ste. A
Holly Hills, FL 32117
(904)255-6889
Fax: (904)255-0229
E-mail: score87@dbeach.com

SCORE Office (South Broward)
3475 Sheridian St., Ste. 203
Hollywood, FL 33021
(305)966-8415

SCORE Office (Citrus County)
5 Poplar Ct.
Homosassa, FL 34446
(352)382-1037

SCORE Office (Jacksonville)
7825 Baymeadows Way, Ste. 100 B
Jacksonville, FL 32256
(904)443-1911
Fax: (904)443-1980
E-mail: scorejax@juno.com
Website: http://www.scorejax.org/

SCORE Office (Jacksonville Satellite)
3 Independent Dr.
Jacksonville, FL 32256
(904)366-6600
Fax: (904)632-0617

SCORE Office (Central Florida)
5410 S. Florida Ave., No. 3
Lakeland, FL 33801
(941)687-5783
Fax: (941)687-6225

SCORE Office (Lakeland)
100 Lake Morton Dr.
Lakeland, FL 33801
(941)686-2168

SCORE Office (St. Petersburg)
800 W. Bay Dr., Ste. 505
Largo, FL 33712
(813)585-4571

SCORE Office (Leesburg)
9501 US Hwy. 441
Leesburg, FL 34788-8751
(352)365-3556
Fax: (352)365-3501

SCORE Office (Cocoa)
1600 Farno Rd., Unit 205
Melbourne, FL 32935
(407)254-2288

SCORE Office (Melbourne)
Melbourne Professional Complex
1600 Sarno, Ste. 205
Melbourne, FL 32935
(407)254-2288
Fax: (407)245-2288

SCORE Office (Merritt Island)
1600 Sarno Rd., Ste. 205
Melbourne, FL 32935
(407)254-2288
Fax: (407)254-2288

SCORE Office (Space Coast)
Melbourn Professional Complex
1600 Sarno, Ste. 205
Melbourne, FL 32935
(407)254-2288
Fax: (407)254-2288

SCORE Office (Dade)
49 NW 5th St.
Miami, FL 33128
(305)371-6889
Fax: (305)374-1882
E-mail: score@netrox.net
Website: http://www.netrox.net/~score/

SCORE Office (Naples of Collier)
International College
2654 Tamiami Trl. E
Naples, FL 34112
(941)417-1280
Fax: (941)417-1281
E-mail: score@naples.net
Website: http://www.naples.net/clubs/
score/index.htm

SCORE Office (Pasco County)
6014 US Hwy. 19, Ste. 302
New Port Richey, FL 34652
(813)842-4638

SCORE Office (Southeast Volusia)
115 Canal St.
New Smyrna Beach, FL 32168
(904)428-2449
Fax: (904)423-3512

SCORE Office (Ocala)
110 E. Silver Springs Blvd.
Ocala, FL 34470
(352)629-5959

Clay County SCORE Office
Clay County Chamber of Commerce
1734 Kingsdey Ave.
PO Box 1441
Orange Park, FL 32073
(904)264-2651
Fax: (904)269-0363

SCORE Office (Orlando)
80 N. Hughey Ave.
Rm. 445 Federal Bldg.
Orlando, FL 32801
(407)648-6476
Fax: (407)648-6425

SCORE Office (Emerald Coast)
19 W. Garden St., No. 325
Pensacola, FL 32501
(904)444-2060
Fax: (904)444-2070

SCORE Office (Charlotte County)
201 W. Marion Ave., Ste. 211
Punta Gorda, FL 33950
(941)575-1818
E-mail: score@gls3c.com
Website: http://www.charlotte-
florida.com/business/scorepg01.htm

SCORE Office (St. Augustine)
1 Riberia St.
St. Augustine, FL 32084
(904)829-5681
Fax: (904)829-6477

SCORE Office (Bradenton)
2801 Fruitville, Ste. 280
Sarasota, FL 34237
(813)955-1029

SCORE Office (Manasota)
2801 Fruitville Rd., Ste. 280
Sarasota, FL 34237
(941)955-1029
Fax: (941)955-5581
E-mail: score116@gte.net
Website: http://www.score-suncoast.org/

SCORE Office (Tallahassee)
200 W. Park Ave.
Tallahassee, FL 32302
(850)487-2665

SCORE Office (Hillsborough)
4732 Dale Mabry Hwy. N, Ste. 400
Tampa, FL 33614-6509
(813)870-0125

SCORE Office (Lake Sumter)
122 E. Main St.
Tavares, FL 32778-3810
(352)365-3556

SCORE Office (Titusville)
2000 S. Washington Ave.
Titusville, FL 32780
(407)267-3036
Fax: (407)264-0127

SCORE Office (Venice)
257 N. Tamiami Trl.
Venice, FL 34285
(941)488-2236
Fax: (941)484-5903

SCORE Office (Palm Beach)
500 Australian Ave. S, Ste. 100
West Palm Beach, FL 33401
(561)833-1672
Fax: (561)833-1712

SCORE Office (Wildwood)
103 N. Webster St.
Wildwood, FL 34785

Georgia

SCORE Office (Atlanta)
Harris Tower, Suite 1900
233 Peachtree Rd., NE
Atlanta, GA 30309
(404)347-2442
Fax: (404)347-1227

SCORE Office (Augusta)
3126 Oxford Rd.
Augusta, GA 30909
(706)869-9100

SCORE Office (Columbus)
School Bldg.
PO Box 40
Columbus, GA 31901
(706)327-3654

SCORE Office (Dalton-Whitfield)
305 S. Thorton Ave.
Dalton, GA 30720
(706)279-3383

SCORE Office (Gainesville)
PO Box 374
Gainesville, GA 30503
(770)532-6206
Fax: (770)535-8419

SCORE Office (Macon)
711 Grand Bldg.
Macon, GA 31201
(912)751-6160

SCORE Office (Brunswick)
4 Glen Ave.
St. Simons Island, GA 31520
(912)265-0620
Fax: (912)265-0629

SCORE Office (Savannah)
111 E. Liberty St., Ste. 103
Savannah, GA 31401
(912)652-4335

Fax: (912)652-4184
E-mail: info@scoresav.org
Website: http://www.coastalempire.com/
score/index.htm

Guam

SCORE Office (Guam)
Pacific News Bldg., Rm. 103
238 Archbishop Flores St.
Agana, GU 96910-5100
(671)472-7308

Hawaii

SCORE Office (Hawaii, Inc.)
1111 Bishop St., Ste. 204
PO Box 50207
Honolulu, HI 96813
(808)522-8132
Fax: (808)522-8135
E-mail: hnlscore@juno.com

SCORE Office (Kahului)
250 Alamaha, Unit N16A
Kahului, HI 96732
(808)871-7711

SCORE Office (Maui, Inc.)
590 E. Lipoa Pkwy., Ste. 227
Kihei, HI 96753
(808)875-2380

Idaho

SCORE Office (Treasure Valley)
1020 Main St., No. 290
Boise, ID 83702
(208)334-1696
Fax: (208)334-9353

SCORE Office (Eastern Idaho)
2300 N. Yellowstone, Ste. 119
Idaho Falls, ID 83401
(208)523-1022
Fax: (208)528-7127

Illinois

SCORE Office (Fox Valley)
40 W. Downer Pl.
PO Box 277
Aurora, IL 60506
(630)897-9214
Fax: (630)897-7002

SCORE Office (Greater Belvidere)
419 S. State St.
Belvidere, IL 61008
(815)544-4357
Fax: (815)547-7654

SCORE Office (Bensenville)
1050 Busse Hwy. Suite 100
Bensenville, IL 60106
(708)350-2944
Fax: (708)350-2979

SCORE Office (Central Illinois)
402 N. Hershey Rd.
Bloomington, IL 61704
(309)644-0549
Fax: (309)663-8270
E-mail: webmaster@central-illinois-
score.org
Website: http://www.central-illinois-
score.org/

SCORE Office (Southern Illinois)
150 E. Pleasant Hill Rd.
Box 1
Carbondale, IL 62901
(618)453-6654
Fax: (618)453-5040

SCORE Office (Chicago)
Northwest Atrium Ctr.
500 W. Madison St., No. 1250
Chicago, IL 60661
(312)353-7724
Fax: (312)886-5688
Website: http://www.mcs.net/~bic/

SCORE Office (Chicago–Oliver Harvey College)
Pullman Bldg.
1000 E. 11th St., 7th Fl.
Chicago, IL 60628
Fax: (312)468-8086

SCORE Office (Danville)
28 W. N. Street
Danville, IL 61832
(217)442-7232
Fax: (217)442-6228

SCORE Office (Decatur)
Milliken University
1184 W. Main St.
Decatur, IL 62522
(217)424-6297
Fax: (217)424-3993
E-mail: charding@mail.millikin.edu
Website: http://www.millikin.edu/
academics/Tabor/score.html

SCORE Office (Downers Grove)
925 Curtis
Downers Grove, IL 60515
(708)968-4050
Fax: (708)968-8368

SCORE Office (Elgin)
24 E. Chicago, 3rd Fl.
PO Box 648
Elgin, IL 60120
(847)741-5660
Fax: (847)741-5677

SCORE Office (Freeport Area)
26 S. Galena Ave.
Freeport, IL 61032
(815)233-1350
Fax: (815)235-4038

SCORE Office (Galesburg)
292 E. Simmons St.
PO Box 749
Galesburg, IL 61401
(309)343-1194
Fax: (309)343-1195

SCORE Office (Glen Ellyn)
500 Pennsylvania
Glen Ellyn, IL 60137
(708)469-0907
Fax: (708)469-0426

SCORE Office (Greater Alton)
Alden Hall
5800 Godfrey Rd.
Godfrey, IL 62035-2466
(618)467-2280
Fax: (618)466-8289
Website: http://www.altonweb.com/
score/

SCORE Office (Grayslake)
19351 W. Washington St.
Grayslake, IL 60030
(708)223-3633
Fax: (708)223-9371

SCORE Office (Harrisburg)
303 S. Commercial
Harrisburg, IL 62946-1528
(618)252-8528
Fax: (618)252-0210

SCORE Office (Joliet)
100 N. Chicago
Joliet, IL 60432
(815)727-5371
Fax: (815)727-5374

SCORE Office (Kankakee)
101 S. Schuyler Ave.
Kankakee, IL 60901
(815)933-0376
Fax: (815)933-0380

SCORE Office (Macomb)
216 Seal Hall, Rm. 214

Macomb, IL 61455
(309)298-1128
Fax: (309)298-2520

SCORE Office (Matteson)
210 Lincoln Mall
Matteson, IL 60443
(708)709-3750
Fax: (708)503-9322

SCORE Office (Mattoon)
1701 Wabash Ave.
Mattoon, IL 61938
(217)235-5661
Fax: (217)234-6544

SCORE Office (Quad Cities)
622 19th St.
Moline, IL 61265
(309)797-0082
Fax: (309)757-5435
E-mail: score@qconline.com
Website: http://www.qconline.com/
business/score/

SCORE Office (Naperville)
131 W. Jefferson Ave.
Naperville, IL 60540
(708)355-4141
Fax: (708)355-8355

SCORE Office (Northbrook)
2002 Walters Ave.
Northbrook, IL 60062
(847)498-5555
Fax: (847)498-5510

SCORE Office (Palos Hills)
10900 S. 88th Ave.
Palos Hills, IL 60465
(847)974-5468
Fax: (847)974-0078

SCORE Office (Peoria)
124 SW Adams, Ste. 300
Peoria, IL 61602
(309)676-0755
Fax: (309)676-7534

SCORE Office (Prospect Heights)
1375 Wolf Rd.
Prospect Heights, IL 60070
(847)537-8660
Fax: (847)537-7138

SCORE Office (Quincy Tri-State)
300 Civic Center Plz., Ste. 245
Quincy, IL 62301
(217)222-8093
Fax: (217)222-3033

SCORE Office (River Grove)
2000 5th Ave.
River Grove, IL 60171
(708)456-0300
Fax: (708)583-3121

SCORE Office (Northern Illinois)
515 N. Court St.
Rockford, IL 61103
(815)962-0122
Fax: (815)962-0122

SCORE Office (St. Charles)
103 N. 1st Ave.
St. Charles, IL 60174-1982
(847)584-8384
Fax: (847)584-6065

SCORE Office (Springfield)
511 W. Capitol Ave., Ste. 302
Springfield, IL 62704
(217)492-4416
Fax: (217)492-4867

SCORE Office (Sycamore)
112 Somunak St.
Sycamore, IL 60178
(815)895-3456
Fax: (815)895-0125

SCORE Office (University)
Hwy. 50 & Stuenkel Rd. Ste. C3305
University Park, IL 60466
(708)534-5000
Fax: (708)534-8457

Indiana

SCORE Office (Anderson)
205 W. 11th St.
Anderson, IN 46015
(317)642-0264

SCORE Office (Bloomington)
Star Center
216 W. Allen
Bloomington, IN 47403
(812)335-7334
E-mail: wtfische@indiana.edu
Website: http://www.brainfreezemedia.
com/score527/

SCORE Office (South East Indiana)
500 Franklin St.
Box 29
Columbus, IN 47201
(812)379-4457

SCORE Office (Corydon)
310 N. Elm St.
Corydon, IN 47112

(812)738-2137
Fax: (812)738-6438

SCORE Office (Crown Point)
Old Courthouse Sq. Ste. 206
PO Box 43
Crown Point, IN 46307
(219)663-1800

SCORE Office (Elkhart)
418 S. Main St.
Elkhart, IN 46515
(219)293-1531
Fax: (219)294-1859

SCORE Office (Evansville)
1100 W. Lloyd Expy., Ste. 105
Evansville, IN 47708
(812)426-6144

SCORE Office (Fort Wayne)
1300 S. Harrison St.
Ft. Wayne, IN 46802
(219)422-2601
Fax: (219)422-2601

SCORE Office (Gary)
973 W. 6th Ave., Rm. 326
Gary, IN 46402
(219)882-3918

SCORE Office (Hammond)
7034 Indianapolis Blvd.
Hammond, IN 46324
(219)931-1000
Fax: (219)845-9548

SCORE Office (Indianapolis)
429 N. Pennsylvania St., Ste. 100
Indianapolis, IN 46204-1873
(317)226-7264
Fax: (317)226-7259
E-mail: inscore@indy.net
Website: http://www.score-
indianapolis.org/

SCORE Office (Jasper)
PO Box 307
Jasper, IN 47547-0307
(812)482-6866

**SCORE Office (Kokomo/Howard
Counties)**
106 N. Washington St.
Kokomo, IN 46901
(765)457-5301
Fax: (765)452-4564

SCORE Office (Logansport)
300 E. Broadway, Ste. 103
Logansport, IN 46947
(219)753-6388

SCORE Office (Madison)
301 E. Main St.
Madison, IN 47250
(812)265-3135
Fax: (812)265-2923

SCORE Office (Marengo)
Rt. 1 Box 224D
Marengo, IN 47140
Fax: (812)365-2793

SCORE Office (Marion/Grant Counties)
215 S. Adams
Marion, IN 46952
(765)664-5107

SCORE Office (Merrillville)
255 W. 80th Pl.
Merrillville, IN 46410
(219)769-8180
Fax: (219)736-6223

SCORE Office (Michigan City)
200 E. Michigan Blvd.
Michigan City, IN 46360
(219)874-6221
Fax: (219)873-1204

SCORE Office (South Central Indiana)
4100 Charleston Rd.
New Albany, IN 47150-9538
(812)945-0066

SCORE Office (Rensselaer)
104 W. Washington
Rensselaer, IN 47978

SCORE Office (Salem)
210 N. Main St.
Salem, IN 47167
(812)883-4303
Fax: (812)883-1467

SCORE Office (South Bend)
300 N. Michigan St.
South Bend, IN 46601
(219)282-4350
E-mail: chair@southbend-score.org
Website: http://www.southbend-score.org/

SCORE Office (Valparaiso)
150 Lincolnway
Valparaiso, IN 46383
(219)462-1105
Fax: (219)469-5710

SCORE Office (Vincennes)
27 N. 3rd
PO Box 553
Vincennes, IN 47591
(812)882-6440
Fax: (812)882-6441

SCORE Office (Wabash)
PO Box 371
Wabash, IN 46992
(219)563-1168
Fax: (219)563-6920

Iowa

SCORE Office (Burlington)
Federal Bldg.
300 N. Main St.
Burlington, IA 52601
(319)752-2967

SCORE Office (Cedar Rapids)
2750 1st Ave. NE, Ste 350
Cedar Rapids, IA 52401-1806
(319)362-6405
Fax: (319)362-7861
E:mail: score@scorecr.org
Website: http://www.scorecr.org

SCORE Office (Illowa)
333 4th Ave. S
Clinton, IA 52732
(319)242-5702

SCORE Office (Council Bluffs)
7 N. 6th St.
Council Bluffs, IA 51502
(712)325-1000

SCORE Office (Northeast Iowa)
3404 285th St.
Cresco, IA 52136
(319)547-3377

SCORE Office (Des Moines)
Federal Bldg., Rm. 749
210 Walnut St.
Des Moines, IA 50309-2186
(515)284-4760

SCORE Office (Ft. Dodge)
Federal Bldg., Rm. 436
205 S. 8th St.
Ft. Dodge, IA 50501
(515)955-2622

SCORE Office (Independence)
110 1st. St. east
Independence, IA 50644
(319)334-7178
Fax: (319)334-7179

SCORE Office (Iowa City)
210 Federal Bldg.
PO Box 1853
Iowa City, IA 52240-1853
(319)338-1662

SCORE Office (Keokuk)
401 Main St.
Pierce Bldg., No. 1
Keokuk, IA 52632
(319)524-5055

SCORE Office (Central Iowa)
Fisher Community College
709 S. Center
Marshalltown, IA 50158
(515)753-6645

SCORE Office (River City)
15 West State St.
Mason City, IA 50401
(515)423-5724

SCORE Office (South Central)
SBDC, Indian Hills Community College
525 Grandview Ave.
Ottumwa, IA 52501
(515)683-5127
Fax: (515)683-5263

SCORE Office (Dubuque)
10250 Sundown Rd.
Peosta, IA 52068
(319)556-5110

SCORE Office (Southwest Iowa)
614 W. Sheridan
Shenandoah, IA 51601
(712)246-3260

SCORE Office (Sioux City)
Federal Bldg.
320 6th St.
Sioux City, IA 51101
(712)277-2324
Fax: (712)277-2325

SCORE Office (Iowa Lakes)
122 W. 5th St.
Spencer, IA 51301
(712)262-3059

SCORE Office (Vista)
119 W. 6th St.
Storm Lake, IA 50588
(712)732-3780

SCORE Office (Waterloo)
215 E. 4th
Waterloo, IA 50703
(319)233-8431

Kansas

SCORE Office (Southwest Kansas)
501 W. Spruce
Dodge City, KS 67801
(316)227-3119

SCORE Office (Emporia)
811 Homewood
Emporia, KS 66801
(316)342-1600

SCORE Office (Golden Belt)
1307 Williams
Great Bend, KS 67530
(316)792-2401

SCORE Office (Hays)
PO Box 400
Hays, KS 67601
(913)625-6595

SCORE Office (Hutchinson)
1 E. 9th St.
Hutchinson, KS 67501
(316)665-8468
Fax: (316)665-7619

SCORE Office (Southeast Kansas)
404 Westminster Pl.
PO Box 886
Independence, KS 67301
(316)331-4741

SCORE Office (McPherson)
306 N. Main
PO Box 616
McPherson, KS 67460
(316)241-3303

SCORE Office (Salina)
120 Ash St.
Salina, KS 67401
(785)243-4290
Fax: (785)243-1833

SCORE Office (Topeka)
1700 College
Topeka, KS 66621
(785)231-1010

SCORE Office (Wichita)
100 E. English, Ste. 510
Wichita, KS 67202
(316)269-6273
Fax: (316)269-6499

SCORE Office (Ark Valley)
205 E. 9th St.
Winfield, KS 67156
(316)221-1617

Kentucky

SCORE Office (Ashland)
PO Box 830
Ashland, KY 41105
(606)329-8011
Fax: (606)325-4607

SCORE Office (Bowling Green)
812 State St.
PO Box 51
Bowling Green, KY 42101
(502)781-3200
Fax: (502)843-0458

SCORE Office (Tri-Lakes)
508 Barbee Way
Danville, KY 40422-1548
(606)231-9902

SCORE Office (Glasgow)
301 W. Main St.
Glasgow, KY 42141
(502)651-3161
Fax: (502)651-3122

SCORE Office (Hazard)
B & I Technical Center
100 Airport Gardens Rd.
Hazard, KY 41701
(606)439-5856
Fax: (606)439-1808

SCORE Office (Lexington)
410 W. Vine St., Ste. 290, Civic C
Lexington, KY 40507
(606)231-9902
Fax: (606)253-3190
E-mail: scorelex@uky.campus.mci.net

SCORE Office (Louisville)
188 Federal Office Bldg.
600 Dr. Martin L. King Jr. Pl.
Louisville, KY 40202
(502)582-5976

SCORE Office (Madisonville)
257 N. Main
Madisonville, KY 42431
(502)825-1399
Fax: (502)825-1396

SCORE Office (Paducah)
Federal Office Bldg.
501 Broadway, Rm. B-36
Paducah, KY 42001
(502)442-5685

Louisiana

SCORE Office (Central Louisiana)
802 3rd St.
Alexandria, LA 71309
(318)442-6671

SCORE Office (Baton Rouge)
564 Laurel St.
PO Box 3217
Baton Rouge, LA 70801

(504)381-7130
Fax: (504)336-4306

SCORE Office (North Shore)
2 W. Thomas
Hammond, LA 70401
(504)345-4457
Fax: (504)345-4749

SCORE Office (Lafayette)
804 St. Mary Blvd.
Lafayette, LA 70505-1307
(318)233-2705
Fax: (318)234-8671
E-mail: score302@aol.com

SCORE Office (Lake Charles)
120 W. Pujo St.
Lake Charles, LA 70601
(318)433-3632

SCORE Office (New Orleans)
365 Canal St., Ste. 3100
New Orleans, LA 70130
(504)589-2356
Fax: (504)589-2339

SCORE Office (Shreveport)
400 Edwards St.
Shreveport, LA 71101
(318)677-2536
Fax: (318)677-2541

Maine

SCORE Office (Augusta)
40 Western Ave.
Augusta, ME 04330
(207)622-8509

SCORE Office (Bangor)
Peabody Hall, Rm. 229
One College Cir.
Bangor, ME 04401
(207)941-9707

SCORE Office (Central & Northern Arroostock)
111 High St.
Caribou, ME 04736
(207)492-8010
Fax: (207)492-8010

SCORE Office (Penquis)
South St.
Dover Foxcroft, ME 04426
(207)564-7021

SCORE Office (Maine Coastal)
Mill Mall
Box 1105
Ellsworth, ME 04605-1105

(207)667-5800

E-mail: score@arcadia.net

SCORE Office (Lewiston-Auburn)

BIC of Maine-Bates Mill Complex

35 Canal St.

Lewiston, ME 04240-7764

(207)782-3708

Fax: (207)783-7745

SCORE Office (Portland)

66 Pearl St., Rm. 210

Portland, ME 04101

(207)772-1147

Fax: (207)772-5581

E-mail: Score53@score.maine.org

Website: http://www.score.maine.org/
chapter53/

SCORE Office (Western Mountains)

255 River St.

PO Box 252

Rumford, ME 04257-0252

(207)369-9976

SCORE Office (Oxford Hills)

166 Main St.

South Paris, ME 04281

(207)743-0499

Maryland

SCORE Office (Southern Maryland)

2525 Riva Rd., Ste. 110

Annapolis, MD 21401

(410)266-9553

Fax: (410)573-0981

E-mail: score390@aol.com

Website: http://members.aol.com/
score390/index.htm

SCORE Office (Baltimore)

The City Crescent Bldg., 6th Fl.

10 S. Howard St.

Baltimore, MD 21201

(410)962-2233

Fax: (410)962-1805

SCORE Office (Bel Air)

108 S. Bond St.

Bel Air, MD 21014

(410)838-2020

Fax: (410)893-4715

SCORE Office (Bethesda)

7910 Woodmont Ave., Ste. 1204

Bethesda, MD 20814

(301)652-4900

Fax: (301)657-1973

SCORE Office (Bowie)

6670 Race Track Rd.

Bowie, MD 20715

(301)262-0920

Fax: (301)262-0921

SCORE Office (Dorchester County)

203 Sunburst Hwy.

Cambridge, MD 21613

(410)228-3575

SCORE Office (Upper Shore)

210 Marlboro Ave.

Easton, MD 21601

(410)822-4606

Fax: (410)822-7922

SCORE Office (Frederick County)

43A S. Market St.

Frederick, MD 21701

(301)662-8723

Fax: (301)846-4427

SCORE Office (Gaithersburg)

9 Park Ave.

Gaithersburg, MD 20877

(301)840-1400

Fax: (301)963-3918

SCORE Office (Glen Burnie)

103 Crain Hwy. SE

Glen Burnie, MD 21061

(410)766-8282

Fax: (410)766-9722

SCORE Office (Hagerstown)

111 W. Washington St.

Hagerstown, MD 21740

(301)739-2015

Fax: (301)739-1278

SCORE Office (Laurel)

7901 Sandy Spring Rd. Ste. 501

Laurel, MD 20707

(301)725-4000

Fax: (301)725-0776

SCORE Office (Salisbury)

300 E. Main St.

Salisbury, MD 21801

(410)749-0185

Fax: (410)860-9925

Massachusetts

SCORE Office (NE Massachusetts)

100 Cummings Ctr., Ste. 101 K

Beverly, MA 01923

(978)922-9441

Website: http://www1.shore.net/~score/

SCORE Office (Boston)

10 Causeway St., Rm. 265

Boston, MA 02222-1093

(617)565-5591

Fax: (617)565-5598

E-mail: boston-score-20@worldnet.att.net

Website: http://www.scoreboston.org/

SCORE office (Bristol/Plymouth County)

53 N. 6th St., Federal Bldg.

Bristol, MA 02740

(508)994-5093

SCORE Office (SE Massachusetts)

60 School St.

Brockton, MA 02401

(508)587-2673

Fax: (508)587-1340

Website: http://www.metrosouth
chamber.com/score.html

SCORE Office (North Adams)

820 N. State Rd.

Cheshire, MA 01225

(413)743-5100

SCORE Office (Clinton Satellite)

1 Green St.

Clinton, MA 01510

Fax: (508)368-7689

SCORE Office (Greenfield)

PO Box 898

Greenfield, MA 01302

(413)773-5463

Fax: (413)773-7008

SCORE Office (Haverhill)

87 Winter St.

Haverhill, MA 01830

(508)373-5663

Fax: (508)373-8060

SCORE Office (Hudson Satellite)

PO Box 578

Hudson, MA 01749

(508)568-0360

Fax: (508)568-0360

SCORE Office (Cape Cod)

Independence Pk., Ste. 5B

270 Communications Way

Hyannis, MA 02601

(508)775-4884

Fax: (508)790-2540

SCORE Office (Lawrence)

264 Essex St.

Lawrence, MA 01840

(508)686-0900

Fax: (508)794-9953

SCORE Office (Leominster Satellite)
110 Erdman Way
Leominster, MA 01453
(508)840-4300
Fax: (508)840-4896

SCORE Office (Bristol/Plymouth Counties)
53 N. 6th St., Federal Bldg.
New Bedford, MA 02740
(508)994-5093

SCORE Office (Newburyport)
29 State St.
Newburyport, MA 01950
(617)462-6680

SCORE Office (Pittsfield)
66 West St.
Pittsfield, MA 01201
(413)499-2485

SCORE Office (Haverhill-Salem)
32 Derby Sq.
Salem, MA 01970
(508)745-0330
Fax: (508)745-3855

SCORE Office (Springfield)
1350 Main St.
Federal Bldg.
Springfield, MA 01103
(413)785-0314

SCORE Office (Carver)
12 Taunton Green, Ste. 201
Taunton, MA 02780
(508)824-4068
Fax: (508)824-4069

SCORE Office (Worcester)
33 Waldo St.
Worcester, MA 01608
(508)753-2929
Fax: (508)754-8560

Michigan

SCORE Office (Allegan)
PO Box 338
Allegan, MI 49010
(616)673-2479

SCORE Office (Ann Arbor)
425 S. Main St., Ste. 103
Ann Arbor, MI 48104
(313)665-4433

SCORE Office (Battle Creek)
34 W. Jackson Ste. 4A
Battle Creek, MI 49017-3505

(616)962-4076
Fax: (616)962-6309

SCORE Office (Cadillac)
222 Lake St.
Cadillac, MI 49601
(616)775-9776
Fax: (616)768-4255

SCORE Office (Detroit)
477 Michigan Ave., Rm. 515
Detroit, MI 48226
(313)226-7947
Fax: (313)226-3448

SCORE Office (Flint)
708 Root Rd., Rm. 308
Flint, MI 48503
(810)233-6846

SCORE Office (Grand Rapids)
111 Pearl St. NW
Grand Rapids, MI 49503-2831
(616)771-0305
Fax: (616)771-0328
E-mail: scoreone@iserv.net
Website: http://www.iserv.net/
~scoreone/

SCORE Office (Holland)
480 State St.
Holland, MI 49423
(616)396-9472

SCORE Office (Jackson)
209 East Washington
PO Box 80
Jackson, MI 49204
(517)782-8221
Fax: (517)782-0061

SCORE Office (Kalamazoo)
345 W. Michigan Ave.
Kalamazoo, MI 49007
(616)381-5382
Fax: (616)384-0096
E-mail: score@nucleus.net

SCORE Office (Lansing)
117 E. Allegan
PO Box 14030
Lansing, MI 48901
(517)487-6340
Fax: (517)484-6910

SCORE Office (Livonia)
15401 Farmington Rd.
Livonia, MI 48154
(313)427-2122
Fax: (313)427-6055

SCORE Office (Madison Heights)
26345 John R
Madison Heights, MI 48071
(810)542-5010
Fax: (810)542-6821

SCORE Office (Monroe)
111 E. 1st
Monroe, MI 48161
(313)242-3366
Fax: (313)242-7253

SCORE Office (Mt. Clemens)
58 S/B Gratiot
Mt. Clemens, MI 48043
(810)463-1528
Fax: (810)463-6541

SCORE Office (Muskegon)
PO Box 1087
230 Terrace Plz.
Muskegon, MI 49443
(616)722-3751
Fax: (616)728-7251

SCORE Office (Petoskey)
401 E. Mitchell St.
Petoskey, MI 49770
(616)347-4150

SCORE Office (Pontiac)
Executive Office Bldg.
1200 N. Telegraph Rd.
Pontiac, MI 48341
(810)975-9555

SCORE Office (Pontiac)
PO Box 430025
Pontiac, MI 48343
(810)335-9600

SCORE Office (Port Huron)
920 Pinegrove Ave.
Port Huron, MI 48060
(810)985-7101

SCORE Office (Rochester)
71 Walnut Ste. 110
Rochester, MI 48307
(810)651-6700
Fax: (810)651-5270

SCORE Office (Saginaw)
901 S. Washington Ave.
Saginaw, MI 48601
(517)752-7161
Fax: (517)752-9055

SCORE Office (Upper Peninsula)
2581 I-75 Business Spur
Sault Ste. Marie, MI 49783
(906)632-3301

SCORE Office (Southfield)
21000 W. 10 Mile Rd.
Southfield, MI 48075
(810)204-3050
Fax: (810)204-3099

SCORE Office (Traverse City)
202 E. Grandview Pkwy.
PO Box 387
Traverse City, MI 49685
(616)947-5075
Fax: (616)946-2565

SCORE Office (Warren)
30500 Van Dyke, Ste. 118
Warren, MI 48093
(810)751-3939

Minnesota

SCORE Office (Aitkin)
Aitkin, MN 56431
(218)741-3906

SCORE Office (Albert Lea)
202 N. Broadway Ave.
Albert Lea, MN 56007
(507)373-7487

SCORE Office (Austin)
PO Box 864
Austin, MN 55912
(507)437-4561
Fax: (507)437-4869

SCORE Office (South Metro)
Ames Business Ctr.
2500 W. County Rd., No. 42
Burnsville, MN 55337
(612)898-5645
Fax: (612)435-6972
E-mail: southmetro@scoreminn.org
Website: http://www.scoreminn.org/
southmetro/

SCORE Office (Duluth)
1717 Minnesota Ave.
Duluth, MN 55802
(218)727-8286
Fax: (218)727-3113
E-mail: duluth@scoreminn.org
Website: http://www.scoreminn.org

SCORE Office (Fairmont)
PO Box 826
Fairmont, MN 56031
(507)235-5547
Fax: (507)235-8411

SCORE Office (Southwest Minnesota)
112 Riverfront St.

Box 999
Mankato, MN 56001
(507)345-4519
Fax: (507)345-4451
Website: http://www.scoreminn.org/

SCORE Office (Minneapolis)
North Plaza Bldg., Ste. 51
5217 Wayzata Blvd.
Minneapolis, MN 55416
(612)591-0539
Fax: (612)544-0436
Website: http://www.scoreminn.org/

SCORE Office (Owatonna)
PO Box 331
Owatonna, MN 55060
(507)451-7970
Fax: (507)451-7972

SCORE Office (Red Wing)
2000 W. Main St., Ste. 324
Red Wing, MN 55066
(612)388-4079

SCORE Office (Southeastern Minnesota)
220 S. Broadway, Ste. 100
Rochester, MN 55901
(507)288-1122
Fax: (507)282-8960
Website: http://www.scoreminn.org/

SCORE Office (Brainerd)
St. Cloud, MN 56301

SCORE Office (Central Area)
1527 Northway Dr.
St. Cloud, MN 56301
(320)240-1332
Fax: (320)255-9050
Website: http://www.scoreminn.org/

SCORE Office (St. Paul)
350 St. Peter St., No. 295
Lowry Professional Bldg.
St. Paul, MN 55102
(651)223-5010
Fax: (651)223-5048
Website: http://www.scoreminn.org/

SCORE Office (Winona)
Box 870
Winona, MN 55987
(507)452-2272
Fax: (507)454-8814

SCORE Office (Worthington)
1121 3rd Ave.
Worthington, MN 56187
(507)372-2919
Fax: (507)372-2827

Mississippi

SCORE Office (Delta)
915 Washington Ave.
PO Box 933
Greenville, MS 38701
(601)378-3141

SCORE Office (Gulfcoast)
1 Government Plaza
2909 13th St., Ste. 203
Gulfport, MS 39501
(228)863-0054

SCORE Office (Jackson)
1st Jackson Center, Ste. 400
101 W. Capitol St.
Jackson, MS 39201
(601)965-5533

SCORE Office (Meridian)
5220 16th Ave.
Meridian, MS 39305
(601)482-4412

Missouri

SCORE Office (Lake of the Ozark)
University Extension
113 Kansas St.
PO Box 1405
Camdenton, MO 65020
(573)346-2644
Fax: (573)346-2694
E-mail: score@cdoc.net
Website: http://sites.cdoc.net/score/

Chamber of Commerce (Cape Girardeau)
PO Box 98
Cape Girardeau, MO 63702-0098
(314)335-3312

SCORE Office (Mid-Missouri)
1705 Halstead Ct.
Columbia, MO 65203
(573)874-1132

SCORE Office (Ozark-Gateway)
1486 Glassy Rd.
Cuba, MO 65453-1640
(573)885-4954

SCORE Office (Kansas City)
323 W. 8th St., Ste. 104
Kansas City, MO 64105
(816)374-6675
Fax: (816)374-6692
E-mail: SCOREBIC@AOL.COM
Website: http://www.crn.org/score/

SCORE Office (Sedalia)
Lucas Place
323 W. 8th St., Ste.104
Kansas City, MO 64105
(816)374-6675

SCORE office (Tri-Lakes)
PO Box 1148
Kimberling, MO 65686
(417)739-3041

SCORE Office (Tri-Lakes)
HCRI Box 85
Lampe, MO 65681
(417)858-6798

SCORE Office (Mexico)
111 N. Washington St.
Mexico, MO 65265
(314)581-2765

SCORE Office (Southeast Missouri)
Rte. 1, Box 280
Neelyville, MO 63954
(573)989-3577

SCORE office (Poplar Bluff Area)
806 Emma St.
Poplar Bluff, MO 63901
(573)686-8892

SCORE Office (St. Joseph)
3003 Frederick Ave.
St. Joseph, MO 64506
(816)232-4461

SCORE Office (St. Louis)
815 Olive St., Rm. 242
St. Louis, MO 63101-1569
(314)539-6970
Fax: (314)539-3785
E-mail: info@stlscore.org
Website: http://www.stlscore.org/

SCORE Office (Lewis & Clark)
425 Spencer Rd.
St. Peters, MO 63376
(314)928-2900
Fax: (314)928-2900
E-mail: score01@mail.win.org

SCORE Office (Springfield)
620 S. Glenstone, Ste. 110
Springfield, MO 65802-3200
(417)864-7670
Fax: (417)864-4108

SCORE office (Southeast Kansas)
1206 W. First St.
Webb City, MO 64870
(417)673-3984

Montana

SCORE Office (Billings)
815 S. 27th St.
Billings, MT 59101
(406)245-4111

SCORE Office (Bozeman)
1205 E. Main St.
Bozeman, MT 59715
(406)586-5421

SCORE Office (Butte)
1000 George St.
Butte, MT 59701
(406)723-3177

SCORE Office (Great Falls)
710 First Ave. N
Great Falls, MT 59401
(406)761-4434
E-mail: scoregtf@in.tch.com

SCORE Office (Havre, Montana)
518 First St.
Havre, MT 59501
(406)265-4383

SCORE Office (Helena)
Federal Bldg.
301 S. Park
Helena, MT 59626-0054
(406)441-1081

SCORE Office (Kalispell)
2 Main St.
Kalispell, MT 59901
(406)756-5271
Fax: (406)752-6665

SCORE Office (Missoula)
723 Ronan
Missoula, MT 59806
(406)327-8806
E-mail: score@safeshop.com
Website: http://missoula.bigsky.net/
score/

Nebraska

SCORE Office (Columbus)
Columbus, NE 68601
(402)564-2769

SCORE Office (Fremont)
92 W. 5th St.
Fremont, NE 68025
(402)721-2641

SCORE Office (Hastings)
Hastings, NE 68901
(402)463-3447

SCORE Office (Lincoln)
8800 O St.
Lincoln, NE 68520
(402)437-2409

SCORE Office (Panhandle)
150549 CR 30
Minatare, NE 69356
(308)632-2133
Website: http://www.tandt.com/
SCORE

SCORE Office (Norfolk)
3209 S. 48th Ave.
Norfolk, NE 68106
(402)564-2769

SCORE Office (North Platte)
3301 W. 2nd St.
North Platte, NE 69101
(308)532-4466

SCORE Office (Omaha)
11145 Mill Valley Rd.
Omaha, NE 68154
(402)221-3606
Fax: (402)221-3680
E-mail: infoctr@ne.uswest.net
Website: http://www.tandt.com/score/

Nevada

SCORE Office (Incline Village)
969 Tahoe Blvd.
Incline Village, NV 89451
(702)831-7327
Fax: (702)832-1605

SCORE Office (Carson City)
301 E. Stewart
PO Box 7527
Las Vegas, NV 89125
(702)388-6104

SCORE Office (Las Vegas)
300 Las Vegas Blvd. S, Ste. 1100
Las Vegas, NV 89101
(702)388-6104

SCORE Office (Northern Nevada)
SBDC, College of Business
Administration
Univ. of Nevada
Reno, NV 89557-0100
(702)784-4436
Fax: (702)784-4337

New Hampshire

SCORE Office (North Country)
PO Box 34

Berlin, NH 03570
(603)752-1090

SCORE Office (Concord)
143 N. Main St., Rm. 202A
PO Box 1258
Concord, NH 03301
(603)225-1400
Fax: (603)225-1409

SCORE Office (Dover)
299 Central Ave.
Dover, NH 03820
(603)742-2218
Fax: (603)749-6317

SCORE Office (Monadnock)
34 Mechanic St.
Keene, NH 03431-3421
(603)352-0320

SCORE Office (Lakes Region)
67 Water St., Ste. 105
Laconia, NH 03246
(603)524-9168

SCORE Office (Upper Valley)
Citizens Bank Bldg., Rm. 310
20 W. Park St.
Lebanon, NH 03766
(603)448-3491
Fax: (603)448-1908
E-mail: billt@valley.net
Website: http://www.valley.net/~score/

SCORE Office (Merrimack Valley)
275 Chestnut St., Rm. 618
Manchester, NH 03103
(603)666-7561
Fax: (603)666-7925

SCORE Office (Mt. Washington Valley)
PO Box 1066
North Conway, NH 03818
(603)383-0800

SCORE Office (Seacoast)
195 Commerce Way, Unit-A
Portsmouth, NH 03801-3251
(603)433-0575

New Jersey

SCORE Office (Somerset)
Paritan Valley Community College,
Rte. 28
Branchburg, NJ 08807
(908)218-8874
E-mail: nj-score@grizbiz.com.
Website: http://www.nj-score.org/

SCORE Office (Chester)
5 Old Mill Rd.
Chester, NJ 07930
(908)879-7080

SCORE Office (Greater Princeton)
4 A George Washington Dr.
Cranbury, NJ 08512
(609)520-1776

SCORE Office (Freehold)
36 W. Main St.
Freehold, NJ 07728
(908)462-3030
Fax: (908)462-2123

SCORE Office (North West)
Picantinny Innovation Ctr.
3159 Schrader Rd.
Hamburg, NJ 07419
(973)209-8525
Fax: (973)209-7252
E-mail: nj-score@grizbiz.com
Website: http://www.nj-score.org/

SCORE Office (Monmouth)
765 Newman Springs Rd.
Lincroft, NJ 07738
(908)224-2573
E-mail: nj-score@grizbiz.com
Website: http://www.nj-score.org/

SCORE Office (Manalapan)
125 Symmes Dr.
Manalapan, NJ 07726
(908)431-7220

SCORE Office (Jersey City)
2 Gateway Ctr., 4th Fl.
Newark, NJ 07102
(973)645-3982
Fax: (973)645-2375

SCORE Office (Newark)
2 Gateway Center, 15th Fl.
Newark, NJ 07102-5553
(973)645-3982
Fax: (973)645-2375
E-mail: nj-score@grizbiz.com
Website: http://www.nj-score.org

SCORE Office (Bergen County)
327 E. Ridgewood Ave.
Paramus, NJ 07652
(201)599-6090
E-mail: nj-score@grizbiz.com
Website: http://www.nj-score.org/

SCORE Office (Pennsauken)
4900 Rte. 70

Pennsauken, NJ 08109
(609)486-3421

SCORE Office (Southern New Jersey)
4900 Rte. 70
Pennsauken, NJ 08109
(609)486-3421
E-mail: nj-score@grizbiz.com
Website: http://www.nj-score.org/

SCORE Office (Greater Princeton)
216 Rockingham Row
Princeton Forrestal Village
Princeton, NJ 08540
(609)520-1776
Fax: (609)520-9107
E-mail: nj-score@grizbiz.com
Website: http://www.nj-score.org/

SCORE Office (Shrewsbury)
Hwy. 35
Shrewsbury, NJ 07702
(908)842-5995
Fax: (908)219-6140

SCORE Office (Ocean County)
33 Washington St.
Toms River, NJ 08754
(732)505-6033
E-mail: nj-score@grizbiz.com
Website: http://www.nj-score.org/

SCORE Office (Wall)
2700 Allaire Rd.
Wall, NJ 07719
(908)449-8877

SCORE Office (Wayne)
2055 Hamburg Tpke.
Wayne, NJ 07470
(201)831-7788
Fax: (201)831-9112

New Mexico

SCORE Office (Albuquerque)
525 Buena Vista, SE
Albuquerque, NM 87106
(505)272-7999
Fax: (505)272-7963

SCORE Office (Las Cruces)
Loretto Towne Center
505 S. Main St., Ste. 125
Las Cruces, NM 88001
(505)523-5627
Fax: (505)524-2101
E-mail: score.397@zianet.com

SCORE Office (Roswell)
Federal Bldg., Rm. 237

Roswell, NM 88201
(505)625-2112
Fax: (505)623-2545

SCORE Office (Santa Fe)
Montoya Federal Bldg.
120 Federal Place, Rm. 307
Santa Fe, NM 87501
(505)988-6302
Fax: (505)988-6300

New York

SCORE Office (Northeast)
1 Computer Dr. S
Albany, NY 12205
(518)446-1118
Fax: (518)446-1228

SCORE Office (Auburn)
30 South St.
PO Box 675
Auburn, NY 13021
(315)252-7291

SCORE Office (South Tier Binghamton)
Metro Center, 2nd Fl.
49 Court St.
PO Box 995
Binghamton, NY 13902
(607)772-8860

SCORE Office (Queens County City)
12055 Queens Blvd., Rm. 333
Borough Hall, NY 11424
(718)263-8961

SCORE Office (Buffalo)
Federal Bldg., Rm. 1311
111 W. Huron St.
Buffalo, NY 14202
(716)551-4301
Website: http://www2.pcom.net/score/buf45.html

SCORE Office (Canandaigua)
Chamber of Commerce Bldg.
113 S. Main St.
Canandaigua, NY 14424
(716)394-4400
Fax: (716)394-4546

SCORE Office (Chemung)
333 E. Water St., 4th Fl.
Elmira, NY 14901
(607)734-3358

SCORE Office (Geneva)
Chamber of Commerce Bldg.
PO Box 587

Geneva, NY 14456
(315)789-1776
Fax: (315)789-3993

SCORE Office (Glens Falls)
84 Broad St.
Glens Falls, NY 12801
(518)798-8463
Fax: (518)745-1433

SCORE Office (Orange County)
40 Matthews St.
Goshen, NY 10924
(914)294-8080
Fax: (914)294-6121

SCORE Office (Huntington Area)
151 W. Carver St.
Huntington, NY 11743
(516)423-6100

SCORE Office (Tompkins County)
904 E. Shore Dr.
Ithaca, NY 14850
(607)273-7080

SCORE Office (Long Island City)
120-55 Queens Blvd.
Jamaica, NY 11424
(718)263-8961
Fax: (718)263-9032

SCORE Office (Chatauqua)
101 W. 5th St.
Jamestown, NY 14701
(716)484-1103

SCORE Office (Westchester)
2 Caradon Ln.
Katonah, NY 10536
(914)948-3907
Fax: (914)948-4645
E-mail: score@w-w-w.com
Website: http://w-w-w.com/score/

SCORE Office (Queens County)
Queens Borough Hall
120-55 Queens Blvd. Rm. 333
Kew Gardens, NY 11424
(718)263-8961
Fax: (718)263-9032

SCORE Office (Brookhaven)
3233 Rte. 112
Medford, NY 11763
(516)451-6563
Fax: (516)451-6925

SCORE Office (Melville)
35 Pinelawn Rd., Rm. 207-W
Melville, NY 11747
(516)454-0771

SCORE Office (Nassau County)
400 County Seat Dr., No. 140
Mineola, NY 11501
(516)571-3303
E-mail: Counse1998@aol.com
Website: http://members.aol.com/Counse1998/Default.htm

SCORE Office (Mt. Vernon)
4 N. 7th Ave.
Mt. Vernon, NY 10550
(914)667-7500

SCORE Office (New York)
26 Federal Plz., Rm. 3100
New York, NY 10278
(212)264-4507
Fax: (212)264-4963
E-mail: score1000@erols.com
Website: http://users.erols.com/score-nyc/

SCORE Office (Newburgh)
47 Grand St.
Newburgh, NY 12550
(914)562-5100

SCORE Office (Owego)
188 Front St.
Owego, NY 13827
(607)687-2020

SCORE Office (Peekskill)
1 S. Division St.
Peekskill, NY 10566
(914)737-3600
Fax: (914)737-0541

SCORE Office (Penn Yan)
2375 Rte. 14A
Penn Yan, NY 14527
(315)536-3111

SCORE Office (Dutchess)
110 Main St.
Poughkeepsie, NY 12601
(914)454-1700

SCORE Office (Rochester)
601 Keating Federal Bldg., Rm. 410
100 State St.
Rochester, NY 14614
(716)263-6473
Fax: (716)263-3146
Website: http://www.ggw.org/score/

SCORE Office (Saranac Lake)
30 Main St.
Saranac Lake, NY 12983
(315)448-0415

SCORE Office (Suffolk)
286 Main St.
Setauket, NY 11733
(516)751-3886

SCORE Office (Staten Island)
130 Bay St.
Staten Island, NY 10301
(718)727-1221

SCORE Office (Ulster)
Clinton Bldg., Rm. 107
Stone Ridge, NY 12484
(914)687-5035
Fax: (914)687-5015
Website: http://www.scoreulster.org/

SCORE Office (Syracuse)
401 S. Salina, 5th Fl.
Syracuse, NY 13202
(315)471-9393

SCORE Office (Utica)
SUNY Institute of Technology, Route 12
Utica, NY 13504-3050
(315)792-7553

SCORE Office (Watertown)
518 Davidson St.
Watertown, NY 13601
(315)788-1200
Fax: (315)788-8251

North Carolina

SCORE office (Asheboro)
317 E. Dixie Dr.
Asheboro, NC 27203
(336)626-2626
Fax: (336)626-7077

SCORE Office (Asheville)
Federal Bldg., Rm. 259
151 Patton
Asheville, NC 28801-5770
(828)271-4786
Fax: (828)271-4009

SCORE Office (Chapel Hill)
104 S. Estes Dr.
PO Box 2897
Chapel Hill, NC 27514
(919)967-7075

SCORE Office (Coastal Plains)
PO Box 2897
Chapel Hill, NC 27515
(919)967-7075
Fax: (919)968-6874

SCORE Office (Charlotte)
200 N. College St., Ste. A-2015

Charlotte, NC 28202
(704)344-6576
Fax: (704)344-6769
E-mail: CharlotteSCORE47@AOL.com
Website: http://www.charweb.org/
business/score/

SCORE Office (Durham)
411 W. Chapel Hill St.
Durham, NC 27707
(919)541-2171

SCORE Office (Gastonia)
PO Box 2168
Gastonia, NC 28053
(704)864-2621
Fax: (704)854-8723

SCORE Office (Greensboro)
400 W. Market St., Ste. 103
Greensboro, NC 27401-2241
(910)333-5399

SCORE Office (Henderson)
PO Box 917
Henderson, NC 27536
(919)492-2061
Fax: (919)430-0460

SCORE Office (Hendersonville)
Federal Bldg., Rm. 108
W. 4th Ave. & Church St.
Hendersonville, NC 28792
(828)693-8702
E-mail: score@circle.net
Website: http://www.wncguide.com/
score/Welcome.html

SCORE Office (Unifour)
PO Box 1828
Hickory, NC 28603
(704)328-6111

SCORE Office (High Point)
1101 N. Main St.
High Point, NC 27262
(336)882-8625
Fax: (336)889-9499

SCORE Office (Outer Banks)
Collington Rd. and Mustain
Kill Devil Hills, NC 27948
(252)441-8144

SCORE Office (Down East)
312 S. Front St., Ste. 6
New Bern, NC 28560
(252)633-6688
Fax: (252)633-9608

SCORE Office (Kinston)
PO Box 95

New Bern, NC 28561
(919)633-6688

SCORE Office (Raleigh)
Century Post Office Bldg., Ste. 306
300 Federal St. Mall
Raleigh, NC 27601
(919)856-4739
E-mail: jendres@ibm.net
Website: http://www.intrex.net/score96/
score96.htm

SCORE Office (Sanford)
1801 Nash St.
Sanford, NC 27330
(919)774-6442
Fax: (919)776-8739

SCORE Office (Sandhills Area)
1480 Hwy. 15-501
PO Box 458
Southern Pines, NC 28387
(910)692-3926

SCORE Office (Wilmington)
Corps of Engineers Bldg.
96 Darlington Ave., Ste. 207
Wilmington, NC 28403
(910)815-4576
Fax: (910)815-4658

North Dakota

**SCORE Office
(Bismarck-Mandan)**
700 E. Main Ave., 2nd Fl.
PO Box 5509
Bismarck, ND 58506-5509
(701)250-4303

SCORE Office (Fargo)
657 2nd Ave., Rm. 225
Fargo, ND 58108-3083
(701)239-5677

SCORE Office (Upper Red River)
4275 Technology Dr., Rm. 156
Grand Forks, ND 58202-8372
(701)777-3051

SCORE Office (Minot)
100 1st St. SW
Minot, ND 58701-3846
(701)852-6883
Fax: (701)852-6905

Ohio

SCORE Office (Akron)
1 Cascade Plz., 7th Fl.
Akron, OH 44308

(330)379-3163
Fax: (330)379-3164

SCORE Office (Ashland)
Gill Center
47 W. Main St.
Ashland, OH 44805
(419)281-4584

SCORE Office (Canton)
116 Cleveland Ave. NW, Ste. 601
Canton, OH 44702-1720
(330)453-6047

SCORE Office (Chillicothe)
165 S. Paint St.
Chillicothe, OH 45601
(614)772-4530

SCORE Office (Cincinnati)
Ameritrust Bldg., Rm. 850
525 Vine St.
Cincinnati, OH 45202
(513)684-2812
Fax: (513)684-3251
Website: http://www.score.
chapter34.org/

SCORE Office (Cleveland)
Eaton Center, Ste. 620
1100 Superior Ave.
Cleveland, OH 44114-2507
(216)522-4194
Fax: (216)522-4844

SCORE Office (Columbus)
2 Nationwide Plz., Ste. 1400
Columbus, OH 43215-2542
(614)469-2357
Fax: (614)469-2391
E-mail: info@scorecolumbus.org
Website: http://www.scorecolumbus.org/

SCORE Office (Dayton)
Dayton Federal Bldg., Rm. 505
200 W. Second St.
Dayton, OH 45402-1430
(513)225-2887
Fax: (513)225-7667

SCORE Office (Defiance)
615 W. 3rd St.
PO Box 130
Defiance, OH 43512
(419)782-7946

SCORE Office (Findlay)
123 E. Main Cross St.
PO Box 923
Findlay, OH 45840
(419)422-3314

SCORE Office (Lima)
147 N. Main St.
Lima, OH 45801
(419)222-6045
Fax: (419)229-0266

SCORE Office (Mansfield)
55 N. Mulberry St.
Mansfield, OH 44902
(419)522-3211

SCORE Office (Marietta)
Thomas Hall
Marietta, OH 45750
(614)373-0268

SCORE Office (Medina)
County Administrative Bldg.
144 N. Broadway
Medina, OH 44256
(216)764-8650

SCORE Office (Licking County)
50 W. Locust St.
Newark, OH 43055
(614)345-7458

SCORE Office (Salem)
2491 State Rte. 45 S
Salem, OH 44460
(216)332-0361

SCORE Office (Tiffin)
62 S. Washington St.
Tiffin, OH 44883
(419)447-4141
Fax: (419)447-5141

SCORE Office (Toledo)
608 Madison Ave, Ste. 910
Toledo, OH 43624
(419)259-7598
Fax: (419)259-6460

SCORE Office (Heart of Ohio)
377 W. Liberty St.
Wooster, OH 44691
(330)262-5735
Fax: (330)262-5745

SCORE Office (Youngstown)
306 Williamson Hall
Youngstown, OH 44555
(330)746-2687

Oklahoma

SCORE Office (Anadarko)
PO Box 366
Anadarko, OK 73005
(405)247-6651

SCORE Office (Ardmore)
410 W. Main
Ardmore, OK 73401
(580)226-2620

SCORE Office (Northeast Oklahoma)
210 S. Main
Grove, OK 74344
(918)787-2796
Fax: (918)787-2796
E-mail: Score595@greencis.net

SCORE Office (Lawton)
4500 W. Lee Blvd., Bldg. 100, Ste. 107
Lawton, OK 73505
(580)353-8727
Fax: (580)250-5677

SCORE Office (Oklahoma City)
210 Park Ave., No. 1300
Oklahoma City, OK 73102
(405)231-5163
Fax: (405)231-4876
E-mail: score212@usa.net

SCORE Office (Stillwater)
439 S. Main
Stillwater, OK 74074
(405)372-5573
Fax: (405)372-4316

SCORE Office (Tulsa)
616 S. Boston, Ste. 406
Tulsa, OK 74119
(918)581-7462
Fax: (918)581-6908
Website: http://www.ionet.net/~tulscore/

Oregon

SCORE Office (Bend)
63085 N. Hwy. 97
Bend, OR 97701
(541)923-2849
Fax: (541)330-6900

SCORE Office (Willamette)
1401 Willamette St.
PO Box 1107
Eugene, OR 97401-4003
(541)465-6600
Fax: (541)484-4942

SCORE Office (Florence)
3149 Oak St.
Florence, OR 97439
(503)997-8444
Fax: (503)997-8448

SCORE Office (Southern Oregon)
33 N. Central Ave., Ste. 216

Medford, OR 97501
(541)776-4220
E-mail: pgr134f@prodigy.com

SCORE Office (Portland)
1515 SW 5th Ave., Ste. 1050
Portland, OR 97201
(503)326-3441
Fax: (503)326-2808
E-mail: gr134@prodigy.com

SCORE Office (Salem)
416 State St. (corner of Liberty)
Salem, OR 97301
(503)370-2896

Pennsylvania

SCORE Office (Altoona Blair)
1212 12th Ave.
Altoona, PA 16601-3493
(814)943-8151

SCORE Office (Lehigh Valley)
Rauch Bldg. 37
Lehigh University
621 Taylor St.
Bethlehem, PA 18015
(610)758-4496
Fax: (610)758-5205

SCORE Office (Butler County)
100 N. Main St.
PO Box 1082
Butler, PA 16003
(412)283-2222
Fax: (412)283-0224

SCORE Office (Harrisburg)
4211 Trindle Rd.
Camp Hill, PA 17011
(717)761-4304
Fax: (717)761-4315

SCORE Office (Cumberland Valley)
75 S. 2nd St.
Chambersburg, PA 17201
(717)264-2935

SCORE Office (Monroe County-Stroudsburg)
556 Main St.
East Stroudsburg, PA 18301
(717)421-4433

SCORE Office (Erie)
120 W. 9th St.
Erie, PA 16501
(814)871-5650
Fax: (814)871-7530

SCORE Office (Bucks County)
409 Hood Blvd.
Fairless Hills, PA 19030
(215)943-8850
Fax: (215)943-7404

SCORE Office (Hanover)
146 Broadway
Hanover, PA 17331
(717)637-6130
Fax: (717)637-9127

SCORE Office (Harrisburg)
100 Chestnut, Ste. 309
Harrisburg, PA 17101
(717)782-3874

SCORE Office (East Montgomery County)
Baederwood Shopping Center
1653 The Fairways, Ste. 204
Jenkintown, PA 19046
(215)885-3027

SCORE Office (Kittanning)
2 Butler Rd.
Kittanning, PA 16201
(412)543-1305
Fax: (412)543-6206

SCORE Office (Lancaster)
118 W. Chestnut St.
Lancaster, PA 17603
(717)397-3092

SCORE Office (Westmoreland County)
300 Fraser Purchase Rd.
Latrobe, PA 15650-2690
(412)539-7505
Fax: (412)539-1850

SCORE Office (Lebanon)
252 N. 8th St.
PO Box 899
Lebanon, PA 17042-0899
(717)273-3727
Fax: (717)273-7940

SCORE Office (Lewistown)
3 W. Monument Sq., Ste. 204
Lewistown, PA 17044
(717)248-6713
Fax: (717)248-6714

SCORE Office (Delaware County)
602 E. Baltimore Pike
Media, PA 19063
(610)565-3677
Fax: (610)565-1606

SCORE Office (Milton Area)
112 S. Front St.
Milton, PA 17847

(717)742-7341
Fax: (717)792-2008

SCORE Office (Mon-Valley)
435 Donner Ave.
Monessen, PA 15062
(412)684-4277
Fax: (412)684-7688

SCORE Office (Monroeville)
William Penn Plaza
2790 Mosside Blvd., Ste. 295
Monroeville, PA 15146
(412)856-0622
Fax: (412)856-1030

SCORE Office (Airport Area)
986 Brodhead Rd.
Moon Township, PA 15108-2398
(412)264-6270
Fax: (412)264-1575

SCORE Office (Northeast)
8601 E. Roosevelt Blvd.
Philadelphia, PA 19152
(215)332-3400
Fax: (215)332-6050

SCORE Office (Philadelphia)
1315 Walnut St., Ste. 500
Philadelphia, PA 19107
(215)790-5050
Fax: (215)790-5057
E-mail: score46@bellatlantic.net
Website: http://www.pgweb.net/score46/

SCORE Office (Pittsburgh)
1000 Liberty Ave., Rm. 1122
Pittsburgh, PA 15222
(412)395-6560
Fax: (412)395-6562

SCORE Office (Tri-County)
801 N. Charlotte St.
Pottstown, PA 19464
(610)327-2673

SCORE Office (Reading)
601 Penn St.
Reading, PA 19601
(610)376-3497

SCORE Office (Scranton)
Oppenheim Bldg.
116 N. Washington Ave., Ste. 650
Scranton, PA 18503
(717)347-4611
Fax: (717)347-4611

SCORE Office (Central Pennsylvania)
200 Innovation Blvd., Ste. 242-B
State College, PA 16803

(814)234-9415
Fax: (814)238-9686
Website: http://countrystore.org/
business/score.htm

SCORE Office (Monroe-Stroudsburg)
556 Main St.
Stroudsburg, PA 18360
(717)421-4433

SCORE Office (Uniontown)
Federal Bldg.
Pittsburg St.
PO Box 2065 DTS
Uniontown, PA 15401
(412)437-4222
E-mail: uniontownscore@lcsys.net

SCORE Office (Warren County)
315 2nd Ave.
Warren, PA 16365
(814)723-9017

SCORE Office (Waynesboro)
323 E. Main St.
Waynesboro, PA 17268
(717)762-7123
Fax: (717)962-7124

SCORE Office (Chester County)
Government Service Center, Ste. 281
601 Westtown Rd.
West Chester, PA 19382-4538
(610)344-6910
Fax: (610)344-6919
E-mail: score@locke.ccil.org

SCORE Office (Wilkes-Barre)
7 N. Wilkes-Barre Blvd.
Wilkes Barre, PA 18702-5241
(717)826-6502
Fax: (717)826-6287

SCORE Office (North Central Pennsylvania)
240 W. 3rd St., Rm. 227
PO Box 725
Williamsport, PA 17703
(717)322-3720
Fax: (717)322-1607
E-mail: score234@mail.csrlink.net
Website: http://www.lycoming.org/
score/

SCORE Office (York)
Cyber Center
2101 Pennsylvania Ave.
York, PA 17404
(717)845-8830
Fax: (717)854-9333

Puerto Rico

SCORE Office (Puerto Rico & Virgin Islands)
PO Box 12383-96
San Juan, PR 00914-0383
(787)726-8040
Fax: (787)726-8135

Rhode Island

SCORE Office (Barrington)
281 County Rd.
Barrington, RI 02806
(401)247-1920
Fax: (401)247-3763

SCORE Office (Woonsocket)
640 Washington Hwy.
Lincoln, RI 02865
(401)334-1000
Fax: (401)334-1009

SCORE Office (Wickford)
8045 Post Rd.
North Kingstown, RI 02852
(401)295-5566
Fax: (401)295-8987

SCORE Office (J.G.E. Knight)
380 Westminster St.
Providence, RI 02903
(401)528-4571
Fax: (401)528-4539
Website: http://www.riscore.org

SCORE Office (Warwick)
3288 Post Rd.
Warwick, RI 02886
(401)732-1100
Fax: (401)732-1101

SCORE Office (Westerly)
74 Post Rd.
Westerly, RI 02891
(401)596-7761
800-732-7636
Fax: (401)596-2190

South Carolina

SCORE Office (Aiken)
PO Box 892
Aiken, SC 29802
(803)641-1111
800-542-4536
Fax: (803)641-4174

SCORE Office (Anderson)
Anderson Mall
3130 N. Main St.

Anderson, SC 29621
(864)224-0453

SCORE Office (Coastal)
284 King St.
Charleston, SC 29401
(803)727-4778
Fax: (803)853-2529

SCORE Office (Midlands)
Strom Thurmond Bldg., Rm. 358
1835 Assembly St., Rm 358
Columbia, SC 29201
(803)765-5131
Fax: (803)765-5962
Website: http://www.scoremid
lands.org/

SCORE Office (Piedmont)
Federal Bldg., Rm. B-02
300 E. Washington St.
Greenville, SC 29601
(864)271-3638

SCORE Office (Greenwood)
PO Drawer 1467
Greenwood, SC 29648
(864)223-8357

SCORE Office (Hilton Head Island)
52 Savannah Trail
Hilton Head, SC 29926
(803)785-7107
Fax: (803)785-7110

SCORE Office (Grand Strand)
937 Broadway
Myrtle Beach, SC 29577
(803)918-1079
Fax: (803)918-1083
E-mail: score381@aol.com

SCORE Office (Spartanburg)
PO Box 1636
Spartanburg, SC 29304
(864)594-5000
Fax: (864)594-5055

South Dakota

SCORE Office (West River)
Rushmore Plz. Civic Ctr.
444 Mount Rushmore Rd., No. 209
Rapid City, SD 57701
(605)394-5311
E-mail: score@gwtc.net

SCORE Office (Sioux Falls)
First Financial Center
110 S. Phillips Ave., Ste. 200
Sioux Falls, SD 57104-6727

(605)330-4231
Fax: (605)330-4231

Tennessee

SCORE Office (Chattanooga)
Federal Bldg., Rm. 26
900 Georgia Ave.
Chattanooga, TN 37402
(423)752-5190
Fax: (423)752-5335

SCORE Office (Cleveland)
PO Box 2275
Cleveland, TN 37320
(423)472-6587
Fax: (423)472-2019

SCORE Office (Upper Cumberland Center)
1225 S. Willow Ave.
Cookeville, TN 38501
(615)432-4111
Fax: (615)432-6010

SCORE Office (Unicoi County)
PO Box 713
Erwin, TN 37650
(423)743-3000
Fax: (423)743-0942

SCORE Office (Greeneville)
115 Academy St.
Greeneville, TN 37743
(423)638-4111
Fax: (423)638-5345

SCORE Office (Jackson)
194 Auditorium St.
Jackson, TN 38301
(901)423-2200

SCORE Office (Northeast Tennessee)
1st Tennessee Bank Bldg.
2710 S. Roan St., Ste. 584
Johnson City, TN 37601
(423)929-7686
Fax: (423)461-8052

SCORE Office (Kingsport)
151 E. Main St.
Kingsport, TN 37662
(423)392-8805

SCORE Office (Greater Knoxville)
Farragot Bldg., Ste. 224
530 S. Gay St.
Knoxville, TN 37902
(423)545-4203
E-mail: scoreknox@ntown.com
Website: http://www.scoreknox.org/

SCORE Office (Maryville)
201 S. Washington St.
Maryville, TN 37804-5728
(423)983-2241
800-525-6834
Fax: (423)984-1386

SCORE Office (Memphis)
Federal Bldg., Ste. 390
167 N. Main St.
Memphis, TN 38103
(901)544-3588

SCORE Office (Nashville)
50 Vantage Way, Ste. 201
Nashville, TN 37228-1500
(615)736-7621

Texas

SCORE Office (Abilene)
2106 Federal Post Office and Court Bldg.
Abilene, TX 79601
(915)677-1857

SCORE Office (Austin)
2501 S. Congress
Austin, TX 78701
(512)442-7235
Fax: (512)442-7528

SCORE Office (Golden Triangle)
450 Boyd St.
Beaumont, TX 77704
(409)838-6581
Fax: (409)833-6718

SCORE Office (Brownsville)
3505 Boca Chica Blvd., Ste. 305
Brownsville, TX 78521
(210)541-4508

SCORE Office (Brazos Valley)
3000 Briarcrest, Ste. 302
Bryan, TX 77802
(409)776-8876
E-mail: 102633.2612@compuserve.com

SCORE Office (Cleburne)
Watergarden Pl., 9th Fl., Ste. 400
Cleburne, TX 76031
(817)871-6002

SCORE Office (Corpus Christi)
651 Upper North Broadway, Ste. 654
Corpus Christi, TX 78477
(512)888-4322
Fax: (512)888-3418

SCORE Office (Dallas)
6260 E. Mockingbird
Dallas, TX 75214-2619

(214)828-2471
Fax: (214)821-8033

SCORE Office (El Paso)
10 Civic Center Plaza
El Paso, TX 79901
(915)534-0541
Fax: (915)534-0513

SCORE Office (Bedford)
100 E. 15th St., Ste. 400
Ft. Worth, TX 76102
(817)871-6002

SCORE Office (Ft. Worth)
100 E. 15th St., No. 24
Ft. Worth, TX 76102
(817)871-6002
Fax: (817)871-6031
E-mail: fwbac@onramp.net

SCORE Office (Garland)
2734 W. Kingsley Rd.
Garland, TX 75041
(214)271-9224

SCORE Office (Granbury Chamber of Commerce)
416 S. Morgan
Granbury, TX 76048
(817)573-1622
Fax: (817)573-0805

SCORE Office (Lower Rio Grande Valley)
222 E. Van Buren, Ste. 500
Harlingen, TX 78550
(956)427-8533
Fax: (956)427-8537

SCORE Office (Houston)
9301 Southwest Fwy., Ste. 550
Houston, TX 77074
(713)773-6565
Fax: (713)773-6550

SCORE Office (Irving)
3333 N. MacArthur Blvd., Ste. 100
Irving, TX 75062
(214)252-8484
Fax: (214)252-6710

SCORE Office (Lubbock)
1205 Texas Ave., Rm. 411D
Lubbock, TX 79401
(806)472-7462
Fax: (806)472-7487

SCORE Office (Midland)
Post Office Annex
200 E. Wall St., Rm. P121
Midland, TX 79701
(915)687-2649

SCORE Office (Orange)
1012 Green Ave.
Orange, TX 77630-5620
(409)883-3536
800-528-4906
Fax: (409)886-3247

SCORE Office (Plano)
1200 E. 15th St.
PO Drawer 940287
Plano, TX 75094-0287
(214)424-7547
Fax: (214)422-5182

SCORE Office (Port Arthur)
4749 Twin City Hwy., Ste. 300
Port Arthur, TX 77642
(409)963-1107
Fax: (409)963-3322

SCORE Office (Richardson)
411 Belle Grove
Richardson, TX 75080
(214)234-4141
800-777-8001
Fax: (214)680-9103

SCORE Office (San Antonio)
Federal Bldg., Rm. A527
727 E. Durango
San Antonio, TX 78206
(210)472-5931
Fax: (210)472-5935

SCORE Office (Texarkana State College)
819 State Line Ave.
Texarkana, TX 75501
(903)792-7191
Fax: (903)793-4304

SCORE Office (East Texas)
RTDC
1530 SSW Loop 323, Ste. 100
Tyler, TX 75701
(903)510-2975
Fax: (903)510-2978

SCORE Office (Waco)
401 Franklin Ave.
Waco, TX 76701
(817)754-8898
Fax: (817)756-0776
Website: http://www.brc-waco.com/

SCORE Office (Wichita Falls)
Hamilton Bldg.
900 8th St.
Wichita Falls, TX 76307
(940)723-2741
Fax: (940)723-8773

Utah

SCORE Office (Northern Utah)
160 N. Main
Logan, UT 84321
(435)746-2269

SCORE Office (Ogden)
1701 E. Windsor Dr.
Ogden, UT 84604
(801)629-8613
E-mail: score158@netscape.net

SCORE Office (Central Utah)
1071 E. Windsor Dr.
Provo, UT 84604
(801)373-8660

SCORE Office (Southern Utah)
225 South 700 East
St. George, UT 84770
(435)652-7751

SCORE Office (Salt Lake)
310 S Main St.
Salt Lake City, UT 84101
(801)746-2269
Fax: (801)746-2273

Vermont

SCORE Office (Champlain Valley)
Winston Prouty Federal Bldg.
11 Lincoln St., Rm. 106
Essex Junction, VT 05452
(802)951-6762

SCORE Office (Montpelier)
87 State St., Rm. 205
PO Box 605
Montpelier, VT 05601
(802)828-4422
Fax: (802)828-4485

SCORE Office (Marble Valley)
256 N. Main St.
Rutland, VT 05701-2413
(802)773-9147

SCORE Office (Northeast Kingdom)
20 Main St.
PO Box 904
St. Johnsbury, VT 05819
(802)748-5101

Virgin Islands

SCORE Office (St. Croix)
United Plaza Shopping Center
PO Box 4010, Christiansted
St. Croix, VI 00822
(809)778-5380

SCORE Office (St. Thomas-St. John)
Federal Bldg., Rm. 21
Veterans Dr.
St. Thomas, VI 00801
(809)774-8530

Virginia

SCORE Office (Arlington)
2009 N. 14th St., Ste. 111
Arlington, VA 22201
(703)525-2400

SCORE Office (Blacksburg)
141 Jackson St.
Blacksburg, VA 24060
(540)552-4061

SCORE Office (Bristol)
20 Volunteer Pkwy.
Bristol, VA 24203
(540)989-4850

SCORE Office (Central Virginia)
1001 E. Market St., Ste. 101
Charlottesville, VA 22902
(804)295-6712
Fax: (804)295-7066

SCORE Office (Alleghany Satellite)
241 W. Main St.
Covington, VA 24426
(540)962-2178
Fax: (540)962-2179

SCORE Office (Central Fairfax)
3975 University Dr., Ste. 350
Fairfax, VA 22030
(703)591-2450

SCORE Office (Falls Church)
PO Box 491
Falls Church, VA 22040
(703)532-1050
Fax: (703)237-7904

SCORE Office (Glenns)
Glenns Campus
Box 287
Glenns, VA 23149
(804)693-9650

SCORE Office (Peninsula)
6 Manhattan Sq.
PO Box 7269
Hampton, VA 23666
(757)766-2000
Fax: (757)865-0339
E-mail: score100@seva.net

SCORE Office (Tri-Cities)
108 N. Main St.

Hopewell, VA 23860
(804)458-5536

SCORE Office (Lynchburg)
Federal Bldg.
1100 Main St.
Lynchburg, VA 24504-1714
(804)846-3235

SCORE Office (Greater Prince William)
8963 Center St
Manassas, VA 20110
(703)368-4813
Fax: (703)368-4733

SCORE Office (Martinsville)
115 Broad St.
Martinsville, VA 24112-0709
(540)632-6401
Fax: (540)632-5059

SCORE Officc (Hampton Roads)
Federal Bldg., Rm. 737
200 Grandby St.
Norfolk, VA 23510
(757)441-3733
Fax: (757)441-3733
E-mail: scorehr60@juno.com

SCORE Office (Norfolk)
Federal Bldg., Rm. 737
200 Granby St.
Norfolk, VA 23510
(757)441-3733
Fax: (757)441-3733

SCORE Office (Virginia Beach)
Chamber of Commerce
200 Grandby St., Rm 737
Norfolk, VA 23510
(804)441-3733

SCORE Office (Radford)
1126 Norwood St.
Radford, VA 24141
(540)639-2202

SCORE Office (Richmond)
Federal Bldg.
400 N. 8th St., Ste. 1150
PO Box 10126
Richmond, VA 23240-0126
(804)771-2400
Fax: (804)771-8018
E-mail: scorechapter12@yahoo.com
Website: http://www.cvco.org/score/

SCORE Office (Roanoke)
Federal Bldg., Rm. 716
250 Franklin Rd.
Roanoke, VA 24011

(540)857-2834
Fax: (540)857-2043
E-mail: scorerva@juno.com
Website: http://hometown.aol.com/
scorerv/Index.html

SCORE Office (Fairfax)
8391 Old Courthouse Rd., Ste. 300
Vienna, VA 22182
(703)749-0400

SCORE Office (Greater Vienna)
513 Maple Ave. West
Vienna, VA 22180
(703)281-1333
Fax: (703)242-1482

SCORE Office (Shenandoah Valley)
301 W. Main St.
Waynesboro, VA 22980
(540)949-8203
Fax: (540)949-7740
E-mail: score427@intelos.net

SCORE Office (Williamsburg)
201 Penniman Rd.
Williamsburg, VA 23185
(757)229-6511
E-mail: wacc@williamsburgcc.com

SCORE Office (Northern Virginia)
1360 S. Pleasant Valley Rd.
Winchester, VA 22601
(540)662-4118

Washington

SCORE Office (Gray's Harbor)
506 Duffy St.
Aberdeen, WA 98520
(360)532-1924
Fax: (360)533-7945

SCORE Office (Bellingham)
101 E. Holly St.
Bellingham, WA 98225
(360)676-3307

SCORE Office (Everett)
2702 Hoyt Ave.
Everett, WA 98201-3556
(206)259-8000

SCORE Office (Gig Harbor)
3125 Judson St.
Gig Harbor, WA 98335
(206)851-6865

SCORE Office (Kennewick)
PO Box 6986
Kennewick, WA 99336
(509)736-0510

SCORE Office (Puyallup)
322 2nd St. SW
PO Box 1298
Puyallup, WA 98371
(206)845-6755
Fax: (206)848-6164

SCORE Office (Seattle)
1200 6th Ave., Ste. 1700
Seattle, WA 98101
(206)553-7320
Fax: (206)553-7044
E-mail: score55@aol.com
Website: http://www.scn.org/civic/score-online/index55.html

SCORE Office (Spokane)
801 W. Riverside Ave., No. 240
Spokane, WA 99201
(509)353-2820
Fax: (509)353-2600
E-mail: scorc@dmi.net
Website: http://www.dmi.net/score/

SCORE Office (Clover Park)
PO Box 1933
Tacoma, WA 98401-1933
(206)627-2175

SCORE Office (Tacoma)
1101 Pacific Ave.
Tacoma, WA 98402
(253)274-1288
Fax: (253)274-1289

SCORE Office (Fort Vancouver)
1701 Broadway, S-1
Vancouver, WA 98663
(360)699-1079

SCORE Office (Walla Walla)
500 Tausick Way
Walla Walla, WA 99362
(509)527-4681

SCORE Office (Mid-Columbia)
1113 S. 14th Ave.
Yakima, WA 98907
(509)574-4944
Fax: (509)574-2943
Website: http://www.ellensburg.com/
~score/

West Virginia

SCORE Office (Charleston)
1116 Smith St.
Charleston, WV 25301
(304)347-5463
E-mail: score256@juno.com

SCORE Office (Virginia Street)
1116 Smith St., Ste. 302
Charleston, WV 25301
(304)347-5463

SCORE Office (Marion County)
PO Box 208
Fairmont, WV 26555-0208
(304)363-0486

SCORE Office (Upper Monongahela Valley)
1000 Technology Dr., Ste. 1111
Fairmont, WV 26555
(304)363-0486
E-mail: score537@hotmail.com

SCORE Office (Huntington)
1101 6th Ave., Ste. 220
Huntington, WV 25701-2309
(304)523-4092

SCORE Office (Wheeling)
1310 Market St.
Wheeling, WV 26003
(304)233-2575
Fax: (304)233-1320

Wisconsin

SCORE Office (Fox Cities)
227 S. Walnut St.
Appleton, WI 54913
(920)734-7101
Fax: (920)734-7161

SCORE Office (Beloit)
136 W. Grand Ave., Ste. 100
PO Box 717
Beloit, WI 53511
(608)365-8835
Fax: (608)365-9170

SCORE Office (Eau Claire)
Federal Bldg., Rm. B11
510 S. Barstow St.
Eau Claire, WI 54701
(715)834-1573
E-mail: score@ecol.net
Website: http://www.ecol.net/~score/

SCORE Office (Fond du Lac)
207 N. Main St.
Fond du Lac, WI 54935
(414)921-9500
Fax: (414)921-9559

SCORE Office (Green Bay)
835 Potts Ave.
Green Bay, WI 54304
(414)496-8930
Fax: (414)496-6009

SCORE Office (Janesville)
20 S. Main St., Ste. 11
PO Box 8008
Janesville, WI 53547
(608)757-3160
Fax: (608)757-3170

SCORE Office (La Crosse)
712 Main St.
La Crosse, WI 54602-0219
(608)784-4880

SCORE Office (Madison)
505 S. Rosa Rd.
Madison, WI 53719
(608)441-2820

SCORE Office (Manitowoc)
1515 Memorial Dr.
PO Box 903
Manitowoc, WI 54221-0903
(414)684-5575
Fax: (414)684-1915

SCORE Office (Milwaukee)
310 W. Wisconsin Ave., Ste. 425
Milwaukee, WI 53203
(414)297-3942
Fax: (414)297-1377

SCORE Office (Central Wisconsin)
1224 Lindbergh Ave.
Stevens Point, WI 54481
(715)344-7729

SCORE Office (Superior)
Superior Business Center Inc.
1423 N. 8th St.
Superior, WI 54880
(715)394-7388
Fax: (715)393-7414

SCORE Office (Waukesha)
223 Wisconsin Ave.
Waukesha, WI 53186-4926
(414)542-4249

SCORE Office (Wausau)
300 3rd St., Ste. 200
Wausau, WI 54402-6190
(715)845-6231

SCORE Office (Wisconsin Rapids)
2240 Kingston Rd.
Wisconsin Rapids, WI 54494
(715)423-1830

Wyoming

SCORE Office (Casper)
Federal Bldg., No. 2215
100 East B St.

Casper, WY 82602
(307)261-6529
Fax: (307)261-6530

Venture capital & financing companies

This section contains a listing of financing and loan companies in the United States and Canada. These listing are arranged alphabetically by country, then by state or province, then by city, then by organization name.

Canada

Alberta

Launchworks Inc.
1902J 11th St., S.E.
Calgary, AB, Canada T2G 3G2
(403)269-1119
Fax: (403)269-1141
Website: http://www.launchworks.com

Native Venture Capital Company, Inc.
21 Artist View Point, Box 7
Site 25, RR 12
Calgary, AB, Canada T3E 6W3
(903)208-5380

Miralta Capital Inc.
4445 Calgary Trail South
888 Terrace Plaza Alberta
Edmonton, AB, Canada T6H 5R7
(780)438-3535
Fax: (780)438-3129

Vencap Equities Alberta Ltd.
10180-101st St., Ste. 1980
Edmonton, AB, Canada T5J 3S4
(403)420-1171
Fax: (403)429-2541

British Columbia

Discovery Capital
5th Fl., 1199 West Hastings
Vancouver, BC, Canada V6E 3T5
(604)683-3000
Fax: (604)662-3457
E-mail: info@discoverycapital.com
Website: http://www.discoverycapital.com

Greenstone Venture Partners
1177 West Hastings St.
Ste. 400
Vancouver, BC, Canada V6E 2K3
(604)717-1977
Fax: (604)717-1976
Website: http://www.greenstonevc.com

Growthworks Capital
2600-1055 West Georgia St.
Box 11170 Royal Centre
Vancouver, BC, Canada V6E 3R5
(604)895-7259
Fax: (604)669-7605
Website: http://www.wofund.com

MDS Discovery Venture Management, Inc.
555 W. Eighth Ave., Ste. 305
Vancouver, BC, Canada V5Z 1C6
(604)872-8464
Fax: (604)872-2977
E-mail: info@mds-ventures.com

Ventures West Management Inc.
1285 W. Pender St., Ste. 280
Vancouver, BC, Canada V6E 4B1
(604)688-9495
Fax: (604)687-2145
Website: http://www.ventureswest.com

Nova Scotia

ACF Equity Atlantic Inc.
Purdy's Wharf Tower 11
Ste. 2106
Halifax, NS, Canada B3J 3R7
(902)421-1965
Fax: (902)421-1808

Montgomerie, Huck & Co.
146 Bluenose Dr.
PO Box 538
Lunenburg, NS, Canada B0J 2C0
(902)634-7125
Fax: (902)634-7130

Ontario

IPS Industrial Promotion Services Ltd.
60 Columbia Way, Ste. 720
Markham, ON, Canada L3R 0C9
(905)475-9400
Fax: (905)475-5003

Betwin Investments Inc.
Box 23110
Sault Ste. Marie, ON, Canada P6A 6W6
(705)253-0744
Fax: (705)253-0744

Bailey & Company, Inc.
594 Spadina Ave.
Toronto, ON, Canada M5S 2H4
(416)921-6930
Fax: (416)925-4670

BCE Capital
200 Bay St.

South Tower, Ste. 3120
Toronto, ON, Canada M5J 2J2
(416)815-0078
Fax: (416)941-1073
Website: http://www.bcecapital.com

Castlehill Ventures
55 University Ave., Ste. 500
Toronto, ON, Canada M5J 2H7
(416)862-8574
Fax: (416)862-8875

CCFL Mezzanine Partners of Canada
70 University Ave.
Ste. 1450
Toronto, ON, Canada M5J 2M4
(416)977-1450
Fax: (416)977-6764
E-mail: info@ccfl.com
Website: http://www.ccfl.com

Celtic House International
100 Simcoe St., Ste. 100
Toronto, ON, Canada M5H 3G2
(416)542-2436
Fax: (416)542-2435
Website: http://www.celtic house.com

Clairvest Group Inc.
22 St. Clair Ave. East
Ste. 1700
Toronto, ON, Canada M4T 2S3
(416)925-9270
Fax: (416)925-5753

Crosbie & Co., Inc.
One First Canadian Place
9th Fl.
PO Box 116
Toronto, ON, Canada M5X 1A4
(416)362-7726
Fax: (416)362-3447
E-mail: info@crosbieco.com
Website: http://www.crosbieco.com

Drug Royalty Corp.
Eight King St. East
Ste. 202
Toronto, ON, Canada M5C 1B5
(416)863-1865
Fax: (416)863-5161

Grieve, Horner, Brown & Asculai
8 King St. E, Ste. 1704
Toronto, ON, Canada M5C 1B5
(416)362-7668
Fax: (416)362-7660

Jefferson Partners
77 King St. West
Ste. 4010

PO Box 136
Toronto, ON, Canada M5K 1H1
(416)367-1533
Fax: (416)367-5827
Website: http://www.jefferson.com

J.L. Albright Venture Partners
Canada Trust Tower, 161 Bay St.
Ste. 4440
PO Box 215
Toronto, ON, Canada M5J 2S1
(416)367-2440
Fax: (416)367-4604
Website: http://www.jlaventures.com

McLean Watson Capital Inc.
One First Canadian Place
Ste. 1410
PO Box 129
Toronto, ON, Canada M5X 1A4
(416)363-2000
Fax: (416)363-2010
Website: http://www.mcleanwatson.com

Middlefield Capital Fund
One First Canadian Place
85th Fl.
PO Box 192
Toronto, ON, Canada M5X 1A6
(416)362-0714
Fax: (416)362-7925
Website: http://www.middlefield.com

Mosaic Venture Partners
24 Duncan St.
Ste. 300
Toronto, ON, Canada M5V 3M6
(416)597-8889
Fax: (416)597-2345

Onex Corp.
161 Bay St.
PO Box 700
Toronto, ON, Canada M5J 2S1
(416)362-7711
Fax: (416)362-5765

Penfund Partners Inc.
145 King St. West
Ste. 1920
Toronto, ON, Canada M5H 1J8
(416)865-0300
Fax: (416)364-6912
Website: http://www.penfund.com

Primaxis Technology Ventures Inc.
1 Richmond St. West, 8th Fl.
Toronto, ON, Canada M5H 3W4
(416)313-5210
Fax: (416)313-5218
Website: http://www.primaxis.com

Priveq Capital Funds
240 Duncan Mill Rd., Ste. 602
Toronto, ON, Canada M3B 3P1
(416)447-3330
Fax: (416)447-3331
E-mail: priveq@sympatico.ca

Roynat Ventures
40 King St. West, 26th Fl.
Toronto, ON, Canada M5H 1H1
(416)933-2667
Fax: (416)933-2783
Website: http://www.roynatcapital.com

Tera Capital Corp.
366 Adelaide St. East, Ste. 337
Toronto, ON, Canada M5A 3X9
(416)368-1024
Fax: (416)368-1427

Working Ventures Canadian Fund Inc.
250 Bloor St. East, Ste. 1600
Toronto, ON, Canada M4W 1E6
(416)934-7718
Fax: (416)929-0901
Website: http://www.workingventures.ca

Quebec

Altamira Capital Corp.
202 University
Niveau de Maisoneuve, Bur. 201
Montreal, QC, Canada H3A 2A5
(514)499-1656
Fax: (514)499-9570

Federal Business Development Bank
Venture Capital Division
Five Place Ville Marie, Ste. 600
Montreal, QC, Canada H3B 5E7
(514)283-1896
Fax: (514)283-5455

Hydro-Quebec Capitech Inc.
75 Boul, Rene Levesque Quest
Montreal, QC, Canada H2Z 1A4
(514)289-4783
Fax: (514)289-5420
Website: http://www.hqcapitech.com

Investissement Desjardins
2 complexe Desjardins
C.P. 760
Montreal, QC, Canada H5B 1B8
(514)281-7131
Fax: (514)281-7808
Website: http://www.desjardins.com/id

Marleau Lemire Inc.
One Place Ville-Marie, Ste. 3601
Montreal, QC, Canada H3B 3P2

(514)877-3800
Fax: (514)875-6415

Speirs Consultants Inc.
365 Stanstead
Montreal, QC, Canada H3R 1X5
(514)342-3858
Fax: (514)342-1977

Tecnocap Inc.
4028 Marlowe
Montreal, QC, Canada H4A 3M2
(514)483-6009
Fax: (514)483-6045
Website: http://www.technocap.com

Telsoft Ventures
1000, Rue de la Gauchetiere
Quest, 25eme Etage
Montreal, QC, Canada H3B 4W5
(514)397-8450
Fax: (514)397-8451

Saskatchewan

Saskatchewan Government Growth Fund
1801 Hamilton St., Ste. 1210
Canada Trust Tower
Regina, SK, Canada S4P 4B4
(306)787-2994
Fax: (306)787-2086

United states

Alabama

FHL Capital Corp.
600 20th Street North
Suite 350
Birmingham, AL 35203
(205)328-3098
Fax: (205)323-0001

Harbert Management Corp.
One Riverchase Pkwy. South
Birmingham, AL 35244
(205)987-5500
Fax: (205)987-5707
Website: http://www.harbert.net

Jefferson Capital Fund
PO Box 13129
Birmingham, AL 35213
(205)324-7709

Private Capital Corp.
100 Brookwood Pl., 4th Fl.
Birmingham, AL 35209
(205)879-2722
Fax: (205)879-5121

21st Century Health Ventures
One Health South Pkwy.
Birmingham, AL 35243
(256)268-6250
Fax: (256)970-8928

FJC Growth Capital Corp.
200 W. Side Sq., Ste. 340
Huntsville, AL 35801
(256)922-2918
Fax: (256)922-2909

Hickory Venture Capital Corp.
301 Washington St. NW
Suite 301
Huntsville, AL 35801
(256)539-1931
Fax: (256)539-5130
E-mail: hvcc@hvcc.com
Website: http://www.hvcc.com

Southeastern Technology Fund
7910 South Memorial Pkwy., Ste. F
Huntsville, AL 35802
(256)883-8711
Fax: (256)883-8558

Cordova Ventures
4121 Carmichael Rd., Ste. 301
Montgomery, AL 36106
(334)271-6011
Fax: (334)260-0120
Website: http://www.cordova
ventures.com

**Small Business Clinic of Alabama/AG
Bartholomew & Associates**
PO Box 231074
Montgomery, AL 36123-1074
(334)284-3640

Arizona

Miller Capital Corp.
4909 E. McDowell Rd.
Phoenix, AZ 85008
(602)225-0504
Fax: (602)225-9024
Website: http://www.themiller
group.com

The Columbine Venture Funds
9449 North 90th St., Ste. 200
Scottsdale, AZ 85258
(602)661-9222
Fax: (602)661-6262

Koch Ventures
17767 N. Perimeter Dr., Ste. 101
Scottsdale, AZ 85255
(480)419-3600

Fax: (480)419-3606
Website: http://www.kochventures.com

McKee & Co.
7702 E. Doubletree Ranch Rd.
Suite 230
Scottsdale, AZ 85258
(480)368-0333
Fax: (480)607-7446

Merita Capital Ltd.
7350 E. Stetson Dr., Ste. 108-A
Scottsdale, AZ 85251
(480)947-8700
Fax: (480)947-8766

Valley Ventures / Arizona Growth Partners L.P.
6720 N. Scottsdale Rd., Ste. 208
Scottsdale, AZ 85253
(480)661-6600
Fax: (480)661-6262

Estreetcapital.com
660 South Mill Ave., Ste. 315
Tempe, AZ 85281
(480)968-8400
Fax: (480)968-8480
Website: http://www.estreetcapital.com

Coronado Venture Fund
PO Box 65420
Tucson, AZ 85728-5420
(520)577-3764
Fax: (520)299-8491

Arkansas

Arkansas Capital Corp.
225 South Pulaski St.
Little Rock, AR 72201
(501)374-9247
Fax: (501)374-9425
Website: http://www.arcapital.com

California

Sundance Venture Partners, L.P.
100 Clocktower Place, Ste. 130
Carmel, CA 93923
(831)625-6500
Fax: (831)625-6590

Westar Capital (Costa Mesa)
949 South Coast Dr., Ste. 650
Costa Mesa, CA 92626
(714)481-5160
Fax: (714)481-5166
E-mail: mailbox@westarcapital.com
Website: http://www.westarcapital.com

Alpine Technology Ventures
20300 Stevens Creek Boulevard, Ste. 495
Cupertino, CA 95014
(408)725-1810
Fax: (408)725-1207
Website: http://www.alpineventures.com

Bay Partners
10600 N. De Anza Blvd.
Cupertino, CA 95014-2031
(408)725-2444
Fax: (408)446-4502
Website: http://www.baypartners.com

Novus Ventures
20111 Stevens Creek Blvd., Ste. 130
Cupertino, CA 95014
(408)252-3900
Fax: (408)252-1713
Website: http://www.novusventures.com

Triune Capital
19925 Stevens Creek Blvd., Ste. 200
Cupertino, CA 95014
(310)284-6800
Fax: (310)284-3290

Acorn Ventures
268 Bush St., Ste. 2829
Daly City, CA 94014
(650)994-7801
Fax: (650)994-3305
Website: http://www.acornventures.com

Digital Media Campus
2221 Park Place
El Segundo, CA 90245
(310)426-8000
Fax: (310)426-8010
E-mail: info@thecampus.com
Website: http://www.digital
mediacampus.com

BankAmerica Ventures / BA Venture Partners
950 Tower Ln., Ste. 700
Foster City, CA 94404
(650)378-6000
Fax: (650)378-6040
Website: http://
www.baventurepartners.com

Starting Point Partners
666 Portofino Lane
Foster City, CA 94404
(650)722-1035
Website: http://www.startingpoint
partners.com

Opportunity Capital Partners
2201 Walnut Ave., Ste. 210

Fremont, CA 94538
(510)795-7000
Fax: (510)494-5439
Website: http://www.ocpcapital.com

Imperial Ventures Inc.
9920 S. La Cienega Boulevar, 14th Fl.
Inglewood, CA 90301
(310)417-5409
Fax: (310)338-6115

Ventana Global (Irvine)
18881 Von Karman Ave., Ste. 1150
Irvine, CA 92612
(949)476-2204
Fax: (949)752-0223
Website: http://www.ventanaglobal.com

Integrated Consortium Inc.
50 Ridgecrest Rd.
Kentfield, CA 94904
(415)925-0386
Fax: (415)461-2726

Enterprise Partners
979 Ivanhoe Ave., Ste. 550
La Jolla, CA 92037
(858)454-8833
Fax: (858)454-2489
Website: http://www.epvc.com

Domain Associates
28202 Cabot Rd., Ste. 200
Laguna Niguel, CA 92677
(949)347-2446
Fax: (949)347-9720
Website: http://www.domainvc.com

Cascade Communications Ventures
60 E. Sir Francis Drake Blvd., Ste. 300
Larkspur, CA 94939
(415)925-6500
Fax: (415)925-6501

Allegis Capital
One First St., Ste. Two
Los Altos, CA 94022
(650)917-5900
Fax: (650)917-5901
Website: http://www.allegiscapital.com

Aspen Ventures
1000 Fremont Ave., Ste. 200
Los Altos, CA 94024
(650)917-5670
Fax: (650)917-5677
Website: http://www.aspenventures.com

AVI Capital L.P.
1 First St., Ste. 2
Los Altos, CA 94022

(650)949-9862
Fax: (650)949-8510
Website: http://www.avicapital.com

Bastion Capital Corp.
1999 Avenue of the Stars, Ste. 2960
Los Angeles, CA 90067
(310)788-5700
Fax: (310)277-7582
E-mail: ga@bastioncapital.com
Website: http://www.bastioncapital.com

Davis Group
PO Box 69953
Los Angeles, CA 90069-0953
(310)659-6327
Fax: (310)659-6337

Developers Equity Corp.
1880 Century Park East, Ste. 211
Los Angeles, CA 90067
(213)277-0300

Far East Capital Corp.
350 S. Grand Ave., Ste. 4100
Los Angeles, CA 90071
(213)687-1361
Fax: (213)617-7939
E-mail: free@fareastnationalbank.com

Kline Hawkes & Co.
11726 San Vicente Blvd., Ste. 300
Los Angeles, CA 90049
(310)442-4700
Fax: (310)442-4707
Website: http://www.klinehawkes.com

Lawrence Financial Group
701 Teakwood
PO Box 491773
Los Angeles, CA 90049
(310)471-4060
Fax: (310)472-3155

Riordan Lewis & Haden
300 S. Grand Ave., 29th Fl.
Los Angeles, CA 90071
(213)229-8500
Fax: (213)229-8597

Union Venture Corp.
445 S. Figueroa St., 9th Fl.
Los Angeles, CA 90071
(213)236-4092
Fax: (213)236-6329

Wedbush Capital Partners
1000 Wilshire Blvd.
Los Angeles, CA 90017
(213)688-4545
Fax: (213)688-6642
Website: http://www.wedbush.com

Advent International Corp.
2180 Sand Hill Rd., Ste. 420
Menlo Park, CA 94025
(650)233-7500
Fax: (650)233-7515
Website: http://www.adventinter
national.com

Altos Ventures
2882 Sand Hill Rd., Ste. 100
Menlo Park, CA 94025
(650)234-9771
Fax: (650)233-9821
Website: http://www.altosvc.com

Applied Technology
1010 El Camino Real, Ste. 300
Menlo Park, CA 94025
(415)326-8622
Fax: (415)326-8163

APV Technology Partners
535 Middlefield, Ste. 150
Menlo Park, CA 94025
(650)327-7871
Fax: (650)327-7631
Website: http://www.apvtp.com

August Capital Management
2480 Sand Hill Rd., Ste. 101
Menlo Park, CA 94025
(650)234-9900
Fax: (650)234-9910
Website: http://www.augustcap.com

Baccharis Capital Inc.
2420 Sand Hill Rd., Ste. 100
Menlo Park, CA 94025
(650)324-6844
Fax: (650)854-3025

Benchmark Capital
2480 Sand Hill Rd., Ste. 200
Menlo Park, CA 94025
(650)854-8180
Fax: (650)854-8183
E-mail: info@benchmark.com
Website: http://www.benchmark.com

Bessemer Venture Partners (Menlo Park)
535 Middlefield Rd., Ste. 245
Menlo Park, CA 94025
(650)853-7000
Fax: (650)853-7001
Website: http://www.bvp.com

The Cambria Group
1600 El Camino Real Rd., Ste. 155
Menlo Park, CA 94025
(650)329-8600

Fax: (650)329-8601
Website: http://www.cambriagroup.com

Canaan Partners
2884 Sand Hill Rd., Ste. 115
Menlo Park, CA 94025
(650)854-8092
Fax: (650)854-8127
Website: http://www.canaan.com

Capstone Ventures
3000 Sand Hill Rd., Bldg. One, Ste. 290
Menlo Park, CA 94025
(650)854-2523
Fax: (650)854-9010
Website: http://www.capstonevc.com

Comdisco Venture Group (Silicon Valley)
3000 Sand Hill Rd., Bldg. 1, Ste. 155
Menlo Park, CA 94025
(650)854-9484
Fax: (650)854-4026

Commtech International
535 Middlefield Rd., Ste. 200
Menlo Park, CA 94025
(650)328-0190
Fax: (650)328-6442

Compass Technology Partners
1550 El Camino Real, Ste. 275
Menlo Park, CA 94025-4111
(650)322-7595
Fax: (650)322-0588
Website: http://www.compass
techpartners.com

Convergence Partners
3000 Sand Hill Rd., Ste. 235
Menlo Park, CA 94025
(650)854-3010
Fax: (650)854-3015
Website: http://www.conver
gencepartners.com

The Dakota Group
PO Box 1025
Menlo Park, CA 94025
(650)853-0600
Fax: (650)851-4899
E-mail: info@dakota.com

Delphi Ventures
3000 Sand Hill Rd.
Bldg. One, Ste. 135
Menlo Park, CA 94025
(650)854-9650
Fax: (650)854-2961
Website: http://www.delphiventures.com

El Dorado Ventures
2884 Sand Hill Rd., Ste. 121
Menlo Park, CA 94025
(650)854-1200
Fax: (650)854-1202
Website: http://www.eldorado
ventures.com

Glynn Ventures
3000 Sand Hill Rd., Bldg. 4, Ste. 235
Menlo Park, CA 94025
(650)854-2215

Indosuez Ventures
2180 Sand Hill Rd., Ste. 450
Menlo Park, CA 94025
(650)854-0587
Fax: (650)323-5561
Website: http://www.indosuez
ventures.com

Institutional Venture Partners
3000 Sand Hill Rd., Bldg. 2, Ste. 290
Menlo Park, CA 94025
(650)854-0132
Fax: (650)854-5762
Website: http://www.ivp.com

Interwest Partners (Menlo Park)
3000 Sand Hill Rd., Bldg. 3, Ste. 255
Menlo Park, CA 94025-7112
(650)854-8585
Fax: (650)854-4706
Website: http://www.interwest.com

**Kleiner Perkins Caufield & Byers
(Menlo Park)**
2750 Sand Hill Rd.
Menlo Park, CA 94025
(650)233-2750
Fax: (650)233-0300
Website: http://www.kpcb.com

Magic Venture Capital LLC
1010 El Camino Real, Ste. 300
Menlo Park, CA 94025
(650)325-4149

Matrix Partners
2500 Sand Hill Rd., Ste. 113
Menlo Park, CA 94025
(650)854-3131
Fax: (650)854-3296
Website: http://www.matrixpartners.com

Mayfield Fund
2800 Sand Hill Rd.
Menlo Park, CA 94025
(650)854-5560
Fax: (650)854-5712
Website: http://www.mayfield.com

**McCown De Leeuw and Co. (Menlo
Park)**
3000 Sand Hill Rd., Bldg. 3, Ste. 290
Menlo Park, CA 94025-7111
(650)854-6000
Fax: (650)854-0853
Website: http://www.mdcpartners.com

Menlo Ventures
3000 Sand Hill Rd., Bldg. 4, Ste. 100
Menlo Park, CA 94025
(650)854-8540
Fax: (650)854-7059
Website: http://www.menloventures.com

Merrill Pickard Anderson & Eyre
2480 Sand Hill Rd., Ste. 200
Menlo Park, CA 94025
(650)854-8600
Fax: (650)854-0345

**New Enterprise Associates (Menlo
Park)**
2490 Sand Hill Rd.
Menlo Park, CA 94025
(650)854-9499
Fax: (650)854-9397
Website: http://www.nea.com

Onset Ventures
2400 Sand Hill Rd., Ste. 150
Menlo Park, CA 94025
(650)529-0700
Fax: (650)529-0777
Website: http://www.onset.com

Paragon Venture Partners
3000 Sand Hill Rd., Bldg. 1, Ste. 275
Menlo Park, CA 94025
(650)854-8000
Fax: (650)854-7260

**Pathfinder Venture Capital Funds
(Menlo Park)**
3000 Sand Hill Rd., Bldg. 3, Ste. 255
Menlo Park, CA 94025
(650)854-0650
Fax: (650)854-4706

Rocket Ventures
3000 Sandhill Rd., Bldg. 1, Ste. 170
Menlo Park, CA 94025
(650)561-9100
Fax: (650)561-9183
Website: http://www.rocketventures.com

Sequoia Capital
3000 Sand Hill Rd., Bldg. 4, Ste. 280
Menlo Park, CA 94025
(650)854-3927
Fax: (650)854-2977

E-mail: sequoia@sequoiacap.com
Website: http://www.sequoiacap.com

Sierra Ventures
3000 Sand Hill Rd., Bldg. 4, Ste. 210
Menlo Park, CA 94025
(650)854-1000
Fax: (650)854-5593
Website: http://www.sierraventures.com

Sigma Partners
2884 Sand Hill Rd., Ste. 121
Menlo Park, CA 94025-7022
(650)853-1700
Fax: (650)853-1717
E-mail: info@sigmapartners.com
Website: http://www.sigmapartners.com

Sprout Group (Menlo Park)
3000 Sand Hill Rd.
Bldg. 3, Ste. 170
Menlo Park, CA 94025
(650)234-2700
Fax: (650)234-2779
Website: http://www.sproutgroup.com

TA Associates (Menlo Park)
70 Willow Rd., Ste. 100
Menlo Park, CA 94025
(650)328-1210
Fax: (650)326-4933
Website: http://www.ta.com

Thompson Clive & Partners Ltd.
3000 Sand Hill Rd., Bldg. 1, Ste. 185
Menlo Park, CA 94025-7102
(650)854-0314
Fax: (650)854-0670
E-mail: mail@tcvc.com
Website: http://www.tcvc.com

Trinity Ventures Ltd.
3000 Sand Hill Rd., Bldg. 1, Ste. 240
Menlo Park, CA 94025
(650)854-9500
Fax: (650)854-9501
Website: http://www.trinityventures.com

U.S. Venture Partners
2180 Sand Hill Rd., Ste. 300
Menlo Park, CA 94025
(650)854-9080
Fax: (650)854-3018
Website: http://www.usvp.com

USVP-Schlein Marketing Fund
2180 Sand Hill Rd., Ste. 300
Menlo Park, CA 94025
(415)854-9080
Fax: (415)854-3018
Website: http://www.usvp.com

Venrock Associates
2494 Sand Hill Rd., Ste. 200
Menlo Park, CA 94025
(650)561-9580
Fax: (650)561-9180
Website: http://www.venrock.com

Brad Peery Capital Inc.
145 Chapel Pkwy.
Mill Valley, CA 94941
(415)389-0625
Fax: (415)389-1336

Dot Edu Ventures
650 Castro St., Ste. 270
Mountain View, CA 94041
(650)575-5638
Fax: (650)325-5247
Website: http://www.dotedu
ventures.com

Forrest, Binkley & Brown
840 Newport Ctr. Dr., Ste. 480
Newport Beach, CA 92660
(949)729-3222
Fax: (949)729-3226
Website: http://www.fbbvc.com

Marwit Capital LLC
180 Newport Center Dr., Ste. 200
Newport Beach, CA 92660
(949)640-6234
Fax: (949)720-8077
Website: http://www.marwit.com

Kaiser Permanente / National Venture Development
1800 Harrison St., 22nd Fl.
Oakland, CA 94612
(510)267-4010
Fax: (510)267-4036
Website: http://www.kpventures.com

Nu Capital Access Group, Ltd.
7677 Oakport St., Ste. 105
Oakland, CA 94621
(510)635-7345
Fax: (510)635-7068

Inman and Bowman
4 Orinda Way, Bldg. D, Ste. 150
Orinda, CA 94563
(510)253-1611
Fax: (510)253-9037

Accel Partners (San Francisco)
428 University Ave.
Palo Alto, CA 94301
(650)614-4800
Fax: (650)614-4880
Website: http://www.accel.com

Advanced Technology Ventures
485 Ramona St., Ste. 200
Palo Alto, CA 94301
(650)321-8601
Fax: (650)321-0934
Website: http://www.atvcapital.com

Anila Fund
400 Channing Ave.
Palo Alto, CA 94301
(650)833-5790
Fax: (650)833-0590
Website: http://www.anila.com

Asset Management Company Venture Capital
2275 E. Bayshore, Ste. 150
Palo Alto, CA 94303
(650)494-7400
Fax: (650)856-1826
E-mail: postmaster@assetman.com
Website: http://www.assetman.com

BancBoston Capital / BancBoston Ventures
435 Tasso St., Ste. 250
Palo Alto, CA 94305
(650)470-4100
Fax: (650)853-1425
Website: http://www.bancboston
capital.com

Charter Ventures
525 University Ave., Ste. 1400
Palo Alto, CA 94301
(650)325-6953
Fax: (650)325-4762
Website: http://www.charterventures.com

Communications Ventures
505 Hamilton Avenue, Ste. 305
Palo Alto, CA 94301
(650)325-9600
Fax: (650)325-9608
Website: http://www.comven.com

HMS Group
2468 Embarcadero Way
Palo Alto, CA 94303-3313
(650)856-9862
Fax: (650)856-9864

Jafco America Ventures, Inc.
505 Hamilton Ste. 310
Palto Alto, CA 94301
(650)463-8800
Fax: (650)463-8801
Website: http://www.jafco.com

New Vista Capital
540 Cowper St., Ste. 200

Palo Alto, CA 94301
(650)329-9333
Fax: (650)328-9434
E-mail: fgreene@nvcap.com
Website: http://www.nvcap.com

Norwest Equity Partners (Palo Alto)
245 Lytton Ave., Ste. 250
Palo Alto, CA 94301-1426
(650)321-8000
Fax: (650)321-8010
Website: http://www.norwestvp.com

Oak Investment Partners
525 University Ave., Ste. 1300
Palo Alto, CA 94301
(650)614-3700
Fax: (650)328-6345
Website: http://www.oakinv.com

Patricof & Co. Ventures, Inc. (Palo Alto)
2100 Geng Rd., Ste. 150
Palo Alto, CA 94303
(650)494-9944
Fax: (650)494-6751
Website: http://www.patricof.com

RWI Group
835 Page Mill Rd.
Palo Alto, CA 94304
(650)251-1800
Fax: (650)213-8660
Website: http://www.rwigroup.com

Summit Partners (Palo Alto)
499 Hamilton Ave., Ste. 200
Palo Alto, CA 94301
(650)321-1166
Fax: (650)321-1188
Website: http://www.summit
partners.com

Sutter Hill Ventures
755 Page Mill Rd., Ste. A-200
Palo Alto, CA 94304
(650)493-5600
Fax: (650)858-1854
E-mail: shv@shv.com

Vanguard Venture Partners
525 University Ave., Ste. 600
Palo Alto, CA 94301
(650)321-2900
Fax: (650)321-2902
Website: http://www.vanguard
ventures.com

Venture Growth Associates
2479 East Bayshore St., Ste. 710
Palo Alto, CA 94303

(650)855-9100
Fax: (650)855-9104

Worldview Technology Partners
435 Tasso St., Ste. 120
Palo Alto, CA 94301
(650)322-3800
Fax: (650)322-3880
Website: http://www.worldview.com

Draper, Fisher, Jurvetson / Draper Associates
400 Seaport Ct., Ste.250
Redwood City, CA 94063
(415)599-9000
Fax: (415)599-9726
Website: http://www.dfj.com

Gabriel Venture Partners
350 Marine Pkwy., Ste. 200
Redwood Shores, CA 94065
(650)551-5000
Fax: (650)551-5001
Website: http://www.gabrielvp.com

Hallador Venture Partners, L.L.C.
740 University Ave., Ste. 110
Sacramento, CA 95825-6710
(916)920-0191
Fax: (916)920-5188
E-mail: chris@hallador.com

Emerald Venture Group
12396 World Trade Dr., Ste. 116
San Diego, CA 92128
(858)451-1001
Fax: (858)451-1003
Website: http://www.emerald
venture.com

Forward Ventures
9255 Towne Centre Dr.
San Diego, CA 92121
(858)677-6077
Fax: (858)452-8799
E-mail: info@forwardventure.com
Website: http://www.forward
venture.com

Idanta Partners Ltd.
4660 La Jolla Village Dr., Ste. 850
San Diego, CA 92122
(619)452-9690
Fax: (619)452-2013
Website: http://www.idanta.com

Kingsbury Associates
3655 Nobel Dr., Ste. 490
San Diego, CA 92122
(858)677-0600
Fax: (858)677-0800

Kyocera International Inc.
Corporate Development
8611 Balboa Ave.
San Diego, CA 92123
(858)576-2600
Fax: (858)492-1456

Sorrento Associates, Inc.
4370 LaJolla Village Dr., Ste. 1040
San Diego, CA 92122
(619)452-3100
Fax: (619)452-7607
Website: http://www.sorrento
ventures.com

Western States Investment Group
9191 Towne Ctr. Dr., Ste. 310
San Diego, CA 92122
(619)678-0800
Fax: (619)678-0900

Aberdare Ventures
One Embarcadero Center, Ste. 4000
San Francisco, CA 94111
(415)392-7442
Fax: (415)392-4264
Website: http://www.aberdare.com

Acacia Venture Partners
101 California St., Ste. 3160
San Francisco, CA 94111
(415)433-4200
Fax: (415)433-4250
Website: http://www.acaciavp.com

Access Venture Partners
319 Laidley St.
San Francisco, CA 94131
(415)586-0132
Fax: (415)392-6310
Website: http://www.access
venturepartners.com

Alta Partners
One Embarcadero Center, Ste. 4050
San Francisco, CA 94111
(415)362-4022
Fax: (415)362-6178
E-mail: alta@altapartners.com
Website: http://www.altapartners.com

Bangert Dawes Reade Davis & Thom
220 Montgomery St., Ste. 424
San Francisco, CA 94104
(415)954-9900
Fax: (415)954-9901
E-mail: bdrdt@pacbell.net

Berkeley International Capital Corp.
650 California St., Ste. 2800
San Francisco, CA 94108-2609

(415)249-0450
Fax: (415)392-3929
Website: http://www.berkeleyvc.com

Blueprint Ventures LLC
456 Montgomery St., 22nd Fl.
San Francisco, CA 94104
(415)901-4000
Fax: (415)901-4035
Website: http://www.blue
printventures.com

Blumberg Capital Ventures
580 Howard St., Ste. 401
San Francisco, CA 94105
(415)905-5007
Fax: (415)357-5027
Website: http://www.blumberg-
capital.com

Burr, Egan, Deleage, and Co. (San Francisco)
1 Embarcadero Center, Ste. 4050
San Francisco, CA 94111
(415)362-4022
Fax: (415)362-6178

Burrill & Company
120 Montgomery St., Ste. 1370
San Francisco, CA 94104
(415)743-3160
Fax: (415)743-3161
Website: http://www.burrillandco.com

CMEA Ventures
235 Montgomery St., Ste. 920
San Francisco, CA 94401
(415)352-1520
Fax: (415)352-1524
Website: http://www.cmeaventures.com

Crocker Capital
1 Post St., Ste. 2500
San Francisco, CA 94101
(415)956-5250
Fax: (415)959-5710

Dominion Ventures, Inc.
44 Montgomery St., Ste. 4200
San Francisco, CA 94104
(415)362-4890
Fax: (415)394-9245

Dorset Capital
Pier 1
Bay 2
San Francisco, CA 94111
(415)398-7101
Fax: (415)398-7141
Website: http://www.dorsetcapital.com

Gatx Capital
Four Embarcadero Center, Ste. 2200
San Francisco, CA 94904
(415)955-3200
Fax: (415)955-3449

IMinds
135 Main St., Ste. 1350
San Francisco, CA 94105
(415)547-0000
Fax: (415)227-0300
Website: http://www.iminds.com

LF International Inc.
360 Post St., Ste. 705
San Francisco, CA 94108
(415)399-0110
Fax: (415)399-9222
Website: http://www.lfvc.com

Newbury Ventures
535 Pacific Ave., 2nd Fl.
San Francisco, CA 94133
(415)296-7408
Fax: (415)296-7416
Website: http://www.newburyven.com

Quest Ventures (San Francisco)
333 Bush St., Ste. 1750
San Francisco, CA 94104
(415)782-1414
Fax: (415)782-1415

Robertson-Stephens Co.
555 California St., Ste. 2600
San Francisco, CA 94104
(415)781-9700
Fax: (415)781-2556
Website: http://www.omegaad
ventures.com

Rosewood Capital, L.P.
One Maritime Plaza, Ste. 1330
San Francisco, CA 94111-3503
(415)362-5526
Fax: (415)362-1192
Website: http://www.rosewoodvc.com

Ticonderoga Capital Inc.
555 California St., No. 4950
San Francisco, CA 94104
(415)296-7900
Fax: (415)296-8956

21st Century Internet Venture Partners
Two South Park
2nd Floor
San Francisco, CA 94107
(415)512-1221
Fax: (415)512-2650
Website: http://www.21vc.com

VK Ventures
600 California St., Ste.1700
San Francisco, CA 94111
(415)391-5600
Fax: (415)397-2744

Walden Group of Venture Capital Funds
750 Battery St., Seventh Floor
San Francisco, CA 94111
(415)391-7225
Fax: (415)391-7262

Acer Technology Ventures
2641 Orchard Pkwy.
San Jose, CA 95134
(408)433-4945
Fax: (408)433-5230

Authosis
226 Airport Pkwy., Ste. 405
San Jose, CA 95110
(650)814-3603
Website: http://www.authosis.com

Western Technology Investment
2010 N. First St., Ste. 310
San Jose, CA 95131
(408)436-8577
Fax: (408)436-8625
E-mail: mktg@westerntech.com

Drysdale Enterprises
177 Bovet Rd., Ste. 600
San Mateo, CA 94402
(650)341-6336
Fax: (650)341-1329
E-mail: drysdale@aol.com

Greylock
2929 Campus Dr., Ste. 400
San Mateo, CA 94401
(650)493-5525
Fax: (650)493-5575
Website: http://www.greylock.com

Technology Funding
2000 Alameda de las Pulgas, Ste. 250
San Mateo, CA 94403
(415)345-2200
Fax: (415)345-1797

2M Invest Inc.
1875 S. Grant St.
Suite 750
San Mateo, CA 94402
(650)655-3765
Fax: (650)372-9107
E-mail: 2minfo@2minvest.com
Website: http://www.2minvest.com

Phoenix Growth Capital Corp.
2401 Kerner Blvd.
San Rafael, CA 94901
(415)485-4569
Fax: (415)485-4663

NextGen Partners LLC
1705 East Valley Rd.
Santa Barbara, CA 93108
(805)969-8540
Fax: (805)969-8542
Website: http://www.nextgen
partners.com

Denali Venture Capital
1925 Woodland Ave.
Santa Clara, CA 95050
(408)690-4838
Fax: (408)247-6979
E-mail: wael@denaliventurecapital.com
Website: http://www.denali
venturecapital.com

Dotcom Ventures LP
3945 Freedom Circle, Ste. 740
Santa Clara, CA 95045
(408)919-9855
Fax: (408)919-9857
Website: http://www.dotcom
venturesatl.com

Silicon Valley Bank
3003 Tasman
Santa Clara, CA 95054
(408)654-7400
Fax: (408)727-8728

Al Shugart International
920 41st Ave.
Santa Cruz, CA 95062
(831)479-7852
Fax: (831)479-7852
Website: http://www.alshugart.com

Leonard Mautner Associates
1434 Sixth St.
Santa Monica, CA 90401
(213)393-9788
Fax: (310)459-9918

Palomar Ventures
100 Wilshire Blvd., Ste. 450
Santa Monica, CA 90401
(310)260-6050
Fax: (310)656-4150
Website: http://www.palomar
ventures.com

Medicus Venture Partners
12930 Saratoga Ave., Ste. D8
Saratoga, CA 95070

(408)447-8600
Fax: (408)447-8599
Website: http://www.medicusvc.com

Redleaf Venture Management
14395 Saratoga Ave., Ste. 130
Saratoga, CA 95070
(408)868-0800
Fax: (408)868-0810
E-mail: nancy@redleaf.com
Website: http://www.redleaf.com

Artemis Ventures
207 Second St., Ste. E
3rd Fl.
Sausalito, CA 94965
(415)289-2500
Fax: (415)289-1789
Website: http://www.artemisventures.com

Deucalion Venture Partners
19501 Brooklime
Sonoma, CA 95476
(707)938-4974
Fax: (707)938-8921

Windward Ventures
PO Box 7688
Thousand Oaks, CA 91359-7688
(805)497-3332
Fax: (805)497-9331

National Investment Management, Inc.
2601 Airport Dr., Ste.210
Torrance, CA 90505
(310)784-7600
Fax: (310)784-7605

Southern California Ventures
406 Amapola Ave. Ste. 125
Torrance, CA 90501
(310)787-4381
Fax: (310)787-4382

Sandton Financial Group
21550 Oxnard St., Ste. 300
Woodland Hills, CA 91367
(818)702-9283

Woodside Fund
850 Woodside Dr.
Woodside, CA 94062
(650)368-5545
Fax: (650)368-2416
Website: http://www.woodsidefund.com

Colorado

Colorado Venture Management
Ste. 300
Boulder, CO 80301

(303)440-4055
Fax: (303)440-4636

Dean & Associates
4362 Apple Way
Boulder, CO 80301
Fax: (303)473-9900

Roser Ventures LLC
1105 Spruce St.
Boulder, CO 80302
(303)443-6436
Fax: (303)443-1885
Website: http://www.roserventures.com

Sequel Venture Partners
4430 Arapahoe Ave., Ste. 220
Boulder, CO 80303
(303)546-0400
Fax: (303)546-9728
E-mail: tom@sequelvc.com
Website: http://www.sequelvc.com

New Venture Resources
445C E. Cheyenne Mtn. Blvd.
Colorado Springs, CO 80906-4570
(719)598-9272
Fax: (719)598-9272

The Centennial Funds
1428 15th St.
Denver, CO 80202-1318
(303)405-7500
Fax: (303)405-7575
Website: http://www.centennial.com

Rocky Mountain Capital Partners
1125 17th St., Ste. 2260
Denver, CO 80202
(303)291-5200
Fax: (303)291-5327

Sandlot Capital LLC
600 South Cherry St., Ste. 525
Denver, CO 80246
(303)893-3400
Fax: (303)893-3403
Website: http://www.sandlotcapital.com

Wolf Ventures
50 South Steele St., Ste. 777
Denver, CO 80209
(303)321-4800
Fax: (303)321-4848
E-mail: businessplan@wolf
ventures.com
Website: http://www.wolfventures.com

The Columbine Venture Funds
5460 S. Quebec St., Ste. 270
Englewood, CO 80111

(303)694-3222
Fax: (303)694-9007

Investment Securities of Colorado, Inc.
4605 Denice Dr.
Englewood, CO 80111
(303)796-9192

Kinship Partners
6300 S. Syracuse Way, Ste. 484
Englewood, CO 80111
(303)694-0268
Fax: (303)694-1707
E-mail: block@vailsys.com

Boranco Management, L.L.C.
1528 Hillside Dr.
Fort Collins, CO 80524-1969
(970)221-2297
Fax: (970)221-4787

Aweida Ventures
890 West Cherry St., Ste. 220
Louisville, CO 80027
(303)664-9520
Fax: (303)664-9530
Website: http://www.aweida.com

Access Venture Partners
8787 Turnpike Dr., Ste. 260
Westminster, CO 80030
(303)426-8899
Fax: (303)426-8828

Medmax Ventures LP
1 Northwestern Dr., Ste. 203
Bloomfield, CT 06002
(860)286-2960
Fax: (860)286-9960

James B. Kobak & Co.
Four Mansfield Place
Darien, CT 06820
(203)656-3471
Fax: (203)655-2905

Orien Ventures
1 Post Rd.
Fairfield, CT 06430
(203)259-9933
Fax: (203)259-5288

ABP Acquisition Corporation
115 Maple Ave.
Greenwich, CT 06830
(203)625-8287
Fax: (203)447-6187

Catterton Partners
9 Greenwich Office Park
Greenwich, CT 06830
(203)629-4901

Fax: (203)629-4903
Website: http://www.cpequity.com

Consumer Venture Partners
3 Pickwick Plz.
Greenwich, CT 06830
(203)629-8800
Fax: (203)629-2019

Insurance Venture Partners
31 Brookside Dr., Ste. 211
Greenwich, CT 06830
(203)861-0030
Fax: (203)861-2745

The NTC Group
Three Pickwick Plaza
Ste. 200
Greenwich, CT 06830
(203)862-2800
Fax: (203)622-6538

Regulus International Capital Co., Inc.
140 Greenwich Ave.
Greenwich, CT 06830
(203)625-9700
Fax: (203)625-9706

Axiom Venture Partners
City Place II
185 Asylum St., 17th Fl.
Hartford, CT 06103
(860)548-7799
Fax: (860)548-7797
Website: http://www.axiomventures.com

Conning Capital Partners
City Place II
185 Asylum St.
Hartford, CT 06103-4105
(860)520-1289
Fax: (860)520-1299
E-mail: pe@conning.com
Website: http://www.conning.com

First New England Capital L.P.
100 Pearl St.
Hartford, CT 06103
(860)293-3333
Fax: (860)293-3338
E-mail: info@firstnewenglandcapital.com
Website: http://www.firstnewengland
capital.com

Northeast Ventures
One State St., Ste. 1720
Hartford, CT 06103
(860)547-1414
Fax: (860)246-8755

Windward Holdings
38 Sylvan Rd.
Madison, CT 06443
(203)245-6870
Fax: (203)245-6865

Advanced Materials Partners, Inc.
45 Pine St.
PO Box 1022
New Canaan, CT 06840
(203)966-6415
Fax: (203)966-8448
E-mail: wkb@amplink.com

RFE Investment Partners
36 Grove St.
New Canaan, CT 06840
(203)966-2800
Fax: (203)966-3109
Website: http://www.rfeip.com

Connecticut Innovations, Inc.
999 West St.
Rocky Hill, CT 06067
(860)563-5851
Fax: (860)563-4877
E-mail: pamela.hartley@ctin
novations.com
Website: http://www.ctinnovations.com

Canaan Partners
105 Rowayton Ave.
Rowayton, CT 06853
(203)855-0400
Fax: (203)854-9117
Website: http://www.canaan.com

Landmark Partners, Inc.
10 Mill Pond Ln.
Simsbury, CT 06070
(860)651-9760
Fax: (860)651-8890
Website: http://
www.landmarkpartners.com

Sweeney & Company
PO Box 567
Southport, CT 06490
(203)255-0220
Fax: (203)255-0220
E-mail: sweeney@connix.com

Baxter Associates, Inc.
PO Box 1333
Stamford, CT 06904
(203)323-3143
Fax: (203)348-0622

Beacon Partners Inc.
6 Landmark Sq., 4th Fl.
Stamford, CT 06901-2792

(203)359-5776
Fax: (203)359-5876

Collinson, Howe, and Lennox, LLC
1055 Washington Blvd., 5th Fl.
Stamford, CT 06901
(203)324-7700
Fax: (203)324-3636
E-mail: info@chlmedical.com
Website: http://www.chlmedical.com

Prime Capital Management Co.
550 West Ave.
Stamford, CT 06902
(203)964-0642
Fax: (203)964-0862

Saugatuck Capital Co.
1 Canterbury Green
Stamford, CT 06901
(203)348-6669
Fax: (203)324-6995
Website: http://www.sauga
tuckcapital.com

Soundview Financial Group Inc.
22 Gatehouse Rd.
Stamford, CT 06902
(203)462-7200
Fax: (203)462-7350
Website: http://www.sndv.com

TSG Ventures, L.L.C.
177 Broad St., 12th Fl.
Stamford, CT 06901
(203)406-1500
Fax: (203)406-1590

Whitney & Company
177 Broad St.
Stamford, CT 06901
(203)973-1400
Fax: (203)973-1422
Website: http://www.jhwhitney.com

Cullinane & Donnelly Venture Partners L.P.
970 Farmington Ave.
West Hartford, CT 06107
(860)521-7811

The Crestview Investment and Financial Group
431 Post Rd. E, Ste. 1
Westport, CT 06880-4403
(203)222-0333
Fax: (203)222-0000

Marketcorp Venture Associates, L.P. (MCV)
274 Riverside Ave.
Westport, CT 06880

(203)222-3030
Fax: (203)222-3033

Oak Investment Partners (Westport)
1 Gorham Island
Westport, CT 06880
(203)226-8346
Fax: (203)227-0372
Website: http://www.oakinv.com

Oxford Bioscience Partners
315 Post Rd. W
Westport, CT 06880-5200
(203)341-3300
Fax: (203)341-3309
Website: http://www.oxbio.com

Prince Ventures (Westport)
25 Ford Rd.
Westport, CT 06880
(203)227-8332
Fax: (203)226-5302

LTI Venture Leasing Corp.
221 Danbury Rd.
Wilton, CT 06897
(203)563-1100
Fax: (203)563-1111
Website: http://www.ltileasing.com

Delaware

Blue Rock Capital
5803 Kennett Pike, Ste. A
Wilmington, DE 19807
(302)426-0981
Fax: (302)426-0982
Website: http://www.bluerockcapital.com

District of Columbia

Allied Capital Corp.
1919 Pennsylvania Ave. NW
Washington, DC 20006-3434
(202)331-2444
Fax: (202)659-2053
Website: http://www.alliedcapital.com

Atlantic Coastal Ventures, L.P.
3101 South St. NW
Washington, DC 20007
(202)293-1166
Fax: (202)293-1181
Website: http://www.atlanticcv.com

Columbia Capital Group, Inc.
1660 L St. NW, Ste. 308
Washington, DC 20036
(202)775-8815
Fax: (202)223-0544

Core Capital Partners
901 15th St., NW
9th Fl.
Washington, DC 20005
(202)589-0090
Fax: (202)589-0091
Website: http://www.core-capital.com

Next Point Partners
701 Pennsylvania Ave. NW, Ste. 900
Washington, DC 20004
(202)661-8703
Fax: (202)434-7400
E-mail: mf@nextpoint.vc
Website: http://www.nextpointvc.com

Telecommunications Development Fund
2020 K. St. NW
Ste. 375
Washington, DC 20006
(202)293-8840
Fax: (202)293-8850
Website: http://www.tdfund.com

Wachtel & Co., Inc.
1101 4th St. NW
Washington, DC 20005-5680
(202)898-1144

Winslow Partners LLC
1300 Connecticut Ave. NW
Washington, DC 20036-1703
(202)530-5000
Fax: (202)530-5010
E-mail: winslow@winslowpartners.com

Women's Growth Capital Fund
1054 31st St., NW
Ste. 110
Washington, DC 20007
(202)342-1431
Fax: (202)341-1203
Website: http://www.wgcf.com

Sigma Capital Corp.
22668 Caravelle Circle
Boca Raton, FL 33433
(561)368-9783

North American Business Development Co., L.L.C.
111 East Las Olas Blvd.
Ft. Lauderdale, FL 33301
(305)463-0681
Fax: (305)527-0904
Website: http://
www.northamericanfund.com

Chartwell Capital Management Co. Inc.
1 Independent Dr., Ste. 3120

Jacksonville, FL 32202
(904)355-3519
Fax: (904)353-5833
E-mail: info@chartwellcap.com

CEO Advisors
1061 Maitland Center Commons
Ste. 209
Maitland, FL 32751
(407)660-9327
Fax: (407)660-2109

Henry & Co.
8201 Peters Rd., Ste. 1000
Plantation, FL 33324
(954)797-7400

Avery Business Development Services
2506 St. Michel Ct.
Ponte Vedra, FL 32082
(904)285-6033

New South Ventures
5053 Ocean Blvd.
Sarasota, FL 34242
(941)358-6000
Fax: (941)358-6078
Website: http://www.newsouth
ventures.com

Venture Capital Management Corp.
PO Box 2626
Satellite Beach, FL 32937
(407)777-1969

Florida Capital Venture Ltd.
325 Florida Bank Plaza
100 W. Kennedy Blvd.
Tampa, FL 33602
(813)229-2294
Fax: (813)229-2028

Quantum Capital Partners
339 South Plant Ave.
Tampa, FL 33606
(813)250-1999
Fax: (813)250-1998
Website: http://www.quantum
capitalpartners.com

South Atlantic Venture Fund
614 W. Bay St.
Tampa, FL 33606-2704
(813)253-2500
Fax: (813)253-2360
E-mail: venture@southatlantic.com
Website: http://www.southatlantic.com

LM Capital Corp.
120 S. Olive, Ste. 400
West Palm Beach, FL 33401

(561)833-9700
Fax: (561)655-6587
Website: http://www.lmcapital
securities.com

Georgia

Venture First Associates
4811 Thornwood Dr.
Acworth, GA 30102
(770)928-3733
Fax: (770)928-6455

Alliance Technology Ventures
8995 Westside Pkwy., Ste. 200
Alpharetta, GA 30004
(678)336-2000
Fax: (678)336-2001
E-mail: info@atv.com
Website: http://www.atv.com

Cordova Ventures
2500 North Winds Pkwy., Ste. 475
Alpharetta, GA 30004
(678)942-0300
Fax: (678)942-0301
Website: http://www.cordovaventures.
com

Advanced Technology Development Fund
1000 Abernathy, Ste. 1420
Atlanta, GA 30328-5614
(404)668-2333
Fax: (404)668-2333

CGW Southeast Partners
12 Piedmont Center, Ste. 210
Atlanta, GA 30305
(404)816-3255
Fax: (404)816-3258
Website: http://www.cgwlp.com

Cyberstarts
1900 Emery St., NW
3rd Fl.
Atlanta, GA 30318
(404)267-5000
Fax: (404)267-5200
Website: http://www.cyberstarts.com

EGL Holdings, Inc.
10 Piedmont Center, Ste. 412
Atlanta, GA 30305
(404)949-8300
Fax: (404)949-8311

Equity South
1790 The Lenox Bldg.
3399 Peachtree Rd. NE
Atlanta, GA 30326

(404)237-6222
Fax: (404)261-1578

Five Paces
3400 Peachtree Rd., Ste. 200
Atlanta, GA 30326
(404)439-8300
Fax: (404)439-8301
Website: http://www.fivepaces.com

Frontline Capital, Inc.
3475 Lenox Rd., Ste. 400
Atlanta, GA 30326
(404)240-7280
Fax: (404)240-7281

Fuqua Ventures LLC
1201 W. Peachtree St. NW, Ste. 5000
Atlanta, GA 30309
(404)815-4500
Fax: (404)815-4528
Website: http://www.fuquaventures.com

Noro-Moseley Partners
4200 Northside Pkwy., Bldg. 9
Atlanta, GA 30327
(404)233-1966
Fax: (404)239-9280
Website: http://www.noro-moseley.com

Renaissance Capital Corp.
34 Peachtree St. NW, Ste. 2230
Atlanta, GA 30303
(404)658-9061
Fax: (404)658-9064

River Capital, Inc.
Two Midtown Plaza
1360 Peachtree St. NE, Ste. 1430
Atlanta, GA 30309
(404)873-2166
Fax: (404)873-2158

State Street Bank & Trust Co.
3414 Peachtree Rd. NE, Ste. 1010
Atlanta, GA 30326
(404)364-9500
Fax: (404)261-4469

UPS Strategic Enterprise Fund
55 Glenlake Pkwy. NE
Atlanta, GA 30328
(404)828-8814
Fax: (404)828-8088
E-mail: jcacyce@ups.com
Website: http://www.ups.com/sef/
sef_home

Wachovia
191 Peachtree St. NE, 26th Fl.
Atlanta, GA 30303

(404)332-1000
Fax: (404)332-1392
Website: http://www.wachovia.com/wca

Brainworks Ventures
4243 Dunwoody Club Dr.
Chamblee, GA 30341
(770)239-7447

First Growth Capital Inc.
Best Western Plaza, Ste. 105
PO Box 815
Forsyth, GA 31029
(912)781-7131

Financial Capital Resources, Inc.
21 Eastbrook Bend, Ste. 116
Peachtree City, GA 30269
(404)487-6650

Hawaii

HMS Hawaii Management Partners
Davies Pacific Center
841 Bishop St., Ste. 860
Honolulu, HI 96813
(808)545-3755
Fax: (808)531-2611

Idaho

Sun Valley Ventures
160 Second St.
Ketchum, ID 83340
(208)726-5005
Fax: (208)726-5094

Illinois

Open Prairie Ventures
115 N. Neil St., Ste. 209
Champaign, IL 61820
(217)351-7000
Fax: (217)351-7051
E-mail: inquire@openprairie.com
Website: http://www.openprairie.com

ABN AMRO Private Equity
208 S. La Salle St., 10th Fl.
Chicago, IL 60604
(312)855-7079
Fax: (312)553-6648
Website: http://www.abnequity.com

Alpha Capital Partners, Ltd.
122 S. Michigan Ave., Ste. 1700
Chicago, IL 60603
(312)322-9800
Fax: (312)322-9808
E-mail: acp@alphacapital.com

Ameritech Development Corp.
30 S. Wacker Dr., 37th Fl.
Chicago, IL 60606
(312)750-5083
Fax: (312)609-0244

Apex Investment Partners
225 W. Washington, Ste. 1450
Chicago, IL 60606
(312)857-2800
Fax: (312)857-1800
E-mail: apex@apexvc.com
Website: http://www.apexvc.com

Arch Venture Partners
8725 W. Higgins Rd., Ste. 290
Chicago, IL 60631
(773)380-6600
Fax: (773)380-6606
Website: http://www.archventure.com

The Bank Funds
208 South LaSalle St., Ste. 1680
Chicago, IL 60604
(312)855-6020
Fax: (312)855-8910

Batterson Venture Partners
303 W. Madison St., Ste. 1110
Chicago, IL 60606-3309
(312)269-0300
Fax: (312)269-0021
Website: http://www.battersonvp.com

William Blair Capital Partners, L.L.C.
222 W. Adams St., Ste. 1300
Chicago, IL 60606
(312)364-8250
Fax: (312)236-1042
E-mail: privateequity@wmblair.com
Website: http://www.wmblair.com

Bluestar Ventures
208 South LaSalle St., Ste. 1020
Chicago, IL 60604
(312)384-5000
Fax: (312)384-5005
Website: http://www.bluestarventures.com

The Capital Strategy Management Co.
233 S. Wacker Dr.
Box 06334
Chicago, IL 60606
(312)444-1170

DN Partners
77 West Wacker Dr., Ste. 4550
Chicago, IL 60601
(312)332-7960
Fax: (312)332-7979

Dresner Capital Inc.
29 South LaSalle St., Ste. 310
Chicago, IL 60603
(312)726-3600
Fax: (312)726-7448

Eblast Ventures LLC
11 South LaSalle St., 5th Fl.
Chicago, IL 60603
(312)372-2600
Fax: (312)372-5621
Website: http://www.eblastventures.com

Essex Woodlands Health Ventures, L.P.
190 S. LaSalle St., Ste. 2800
Chicago, IL 60603
(312)444-6040
Fax: (312)444-6034
Website: http://www.essexwood
lands.com

First Analysis Venture Capital
233 S. Wacker Dr., Ste. 9500
Chicago, IL 60606
(312)258-1400
Fax: (312)258-0334
Website: http://www.firstanalysis.com

Frontenac Co.
135 S. LaSalle St., Ste.3800
Chicago, IL 60603
(312)368-0044
Fax: (312)368-9520
Website: http://www.frontenac.com

GTCR Golder Rauner, LLC
6100 Sears Tower
Chicago, IL 60606
(312)382-2200
Fax: (312)382-2201
Website: http://www.gtcr.com

High Street Capital LLC
311 South Wacker Dr., Ste. 4550
Chicago, IL 60606
(312)697-4990
Fax: (312)697-4994
Website: http://www.highstr.com

IEG Venture Management, Inc.
70 West Madison
Chicago, IL 60602
(312)644-0890
Fax: (312)454-0369
Website: http://www.iegventure.com

JK&B Capital
180 North Stetson, Ste. 4500
Chicago, IL 60601
(312)946-1200
Fax: (312)946-1103

E-mail: gspencer@jkbcapital.com
Website: http://www.jkbcapital.com

Kettle Partners L.P.
350 W. Hubbard, Ste. 350
Chicago, IL 60610
(312)329-9300
Fax: (312)527-4519
Website: http://www.kettlevc.com

Lake Shore Capital Partners
20 N. Wacker Dr., Ste. 2807
Chicago, IL 60606
(312)803-3536
Fax: (312)803-3534

LaSalle Capital Group Inc.
70 W. Madison St., Ste. 5710
Chicago, IL 60602
(312)236-7041
Fax: (312)236-0720

Linc Capital, Inc.
303 E. Wacker Pkwy., Ste. 1000
Chicago, IL 60601
(312)946-2670
Fax: (312)938-4290
E-mail: bdemars@linccap.com

Madison Dearborn Partners, Inc.
3 First National Plz., Ste. 3800
Chicago, IL 60602
(312)895-1000
Fax: (312)895-1001
E-mail: invest@mdcp.com
Website: http://www.mdcp.com

Mesirow Private Equity Investments Inc.
350 N. Clark St.
Chicago, IL 60610
(312)595-6950
Fax: (312)595-6211
Website: http://www.meisrow
financial.com

Mosaix Ventures LLC
1822 North Mohawk
Chicago, IL 60614
(312)274-0988
Fax: (312)274-0989
Website: http://www.mosaix
ventures.com

Nesbitt Burns
111 West Monroe St.
Chicago, IL 60603
(312)416-3855
Fax: (312)765-8000
Website: http://www.harrisbank.com

Polestar Capital, Inc.
180 N. Michigan Ave., Ste. 1905
Chicago, IL 60601
(312)984-9090
Fax: (312)984-9877
E-mail: wl@polestarvc.com
Website: http://www.polestarvc.com

Prince Ventures (Chicago)
10 S. Wacker Dr., Ste. 2575
Chicago, IL 60606-7407
(312)454-1408
Fax: (312)454-9125

Prism Capital
444 N. Michigan Ave.
Chicago, IL 60611
(312)464-7900
Fax: (312)464-7915
Website: http://www.prismfund.com

Third Coast Capital
900 N. Franklin St., Ste. 700
Chicago, IL 60610
(312)337-3303
Fax: (312)337-2567
E-mail: manic@earthlink.com
Website: http://www.third
coastcapital.com

Thoma Cressey Equity Partners
4460 Sears Tower, 92nd Fl.
233 S. Wacker Dr.
Chicago, IL 60606
(312)777-4444
Fax: (312)777-4445
Website: http://www.thomacressey.com

Tribune Ventures
435 N. Michigan Ave., Ste. 600
Chicago, IL 60611
(312)527-8797
Fax: (312)222-5993
Website: http://www.tribuneventures.com

Wind Point Partners (Chicago)
676 N. Michigan Ave., Ste. 330
Chicago, IL 60611
(312)649-4000
Website: http://www.wppartners.com

Marquette Venture Partners
520 Lake Cook Rd., Ste. 450
Deerfield, IL 60015
(847)940-1700
Fax: (847)940-1724
Website: http://www.marquette
ventures.com

Duchossois Investments Limited, LLC
845 Larch Ave.
Elmhurst, IL 60126

(630)530-6105
Fax: (630)993-8644
Website: http://www.duchtec.com

Evanston Business Investment Corp.
1840 Oak Ave.
Evanston, IL 60201
(847)866-1840
Fax: (847)866-1808
E-mail: t-parkinson@nwu.com
Website: http://www.ebic.com

Inroads Capital Partners L.P.
1603 Orrington Ave., Ste. 2050
Evanston, IL 60201-3841
(847)864-2000
Fax: (847)864-9692

The Cerulean Fund/WGC Enterprises
1701 E. Lake Ave., Ste. 170
Glenview, IL 60025
(847)657-8002
Fax: (847)657-8168

Ventana Financial Resources, Inc.
249 Market Sq.
Lake Forest, IL 60045
(847)234-3434

Beecken, Petty & Co.
901 Warrenville Rd., Ste. 205
Lisle, IL 60532
(630)435-0300
Fax: (630)435-0370
E-mail: hep@bpcompany.com
Website: http://www.bpcompany.com

Allstate Private Equity
3075 Sanders Rd., Ste. G5D
Northbrook, IL 60062-7127
(847)402-8247
Fax: (847)402-0880

KB Partners
1101 Skokie Blvd., Ste. 260
Northbrook, IL 60062-2856
(847)714-0444
Fax: (847)714-0445
E-mail: keith@kbpartners.com
Website: http://www.kbpartners.com

Transcap Associates Inc.
900 Skokie Blvd., Ste. 210
Northbrook, IL 60062
(847)753-9600
Fax: (847)753-9090

**Graystone Venture Partners, L.L.C. /
Portage Venture Partners**
One Northfield Plaza, Ste. 530
Northfield, IL 60093

(847)446-9460
Fax: (847)446-9470
Website: http://www.portage
ventures.com

Motorola Inc.
1303 E. Algonquin Rd.
Schaumburg, IL 60196-1065
(847)576-4929
Fax: (847)538-2250
Website: http://www.mot.com/mne

Indiana

Irwin Ventures LLC
500 Washington St.
Columbus, IN 47202
(812)373-1434
Fax: (812)376-1709
Website: http://www.irwinventures.com

Cambridge Venture Partners
4181 East 96th St., Ste. 200
Indianapolis, IN 46240
(317)814-6192
Fax: (317)944-9815

CID Equity Partners
One American Square, Ste. 2850
Box 82074
Indianapolis, IN 46282
(317)269-2350
Fax: (317)269-2355
Website: http://www.cidequity.com

Gazelle Techventures
6325 Digital Way, Ste. 460
Indianapolis, IN 46278
(317)275-6800
Fax: (317)275-1101
Website: http://www.gazellevc.com

Monument Advisors Inc.
Bank One Center/Circle
111 Monument Circle, Ste. 600
Indianapolis, IN 46204-5172
(317)656-5065
Fax: (317)656-5060
Website: http://www.monumentadv.com

MWV Capital Partners
201 N. Illinois St., Ste. 300
Indianapolis, IN 46204
(317)237-2323
Fax: (317)237-2325
Website: http://www.mwvcapital.com

First Source Capital Corp.
100 North Michigan St.
PO Box 1602
South Bend, IN 46601

(219)235-2180
Fax: (219)235-2227

Iowa

Allsop Venture Partners
118 Third Ave. SE, Ste. 837
Cedar Rapids, IA 52401
(319)368-6675
Fax: (319)363-9515

InvestAmerica Investment Advisors, Inc.
101 2nd St. SE, Ste. 800
Cedar Rapids, IA 52401
(319)363-8249
Fax: (319)363-9683

Pappajohn Capital Resources
2116 Financial Center
Des Moines, IA 50309
(515)244-5746
Fax: (515)244-2346
Website: http://www.pappajohn.com

Berthel Fisher & Company Planning Inc.
701 Tama St.
PO Box 609
Marion, IA 52302
(319)497-5700
Fax: (319)497-4244

Kansas

Enterprise Merchant Bank
7400 West 110th St., Ste. 560
Overland Park, KS 66210
(913)327-8500
Fax: (913)327-8505

Kansas Venture Capital, Inc. (Overland Park)
6700 Antioch Plz., Ste. 460
Overland Park, KS 66204
(913)262-7117
Fax: (913)262-3509
E-mail: jdalton@kvci.com

Child Health Investment Corp.
6803 W. 64th St., Ste. 208
Shawnee Mission, KS 66202
(913)262-1436
Fax: (913)262-1575
Website: http://www.chca.com

Kansas Technology Enterprise Corp.
214 SW 6th, 1st Fl.
Topeka, KS 66603-3719
(785)296-5272
Fax: (785)296-1160

E-mail: ktec@ktec.com
Website: http://www.ktec.com

Kentucky

Kentucky Highlands Investment Corp.
362 Old Whitley Rd.
London, KY 40741
(606)864-5175
Fax: (606)864-5194
Website: http://www.khic.org

Chrysalis Ventures, L.L.C.
1850 National City Tower
Louisville, KY 40202
(502)583-7644
Fax: (502)583-7648
E-mail: bobsany@chrysalisventures.com
Website: http://www.chrysalis
ventures.com

Humana Venture Capital
500 West Main St.
Louisville, KY 40202
(502)580-3922
Fax: (502)580-2051
E-mail: gemont@humana.com
George Emont, Director

Summit Capital Group, Inc.
6510 Glenridge Park Pl., Ste. 8
Louisville, KY 40222
(502)332-2700

Louisiana

Bank One Equity Investors, Inc.
451 Florida St.
Baton Rouge, LA 70801
(504)332-4421
Fax: (504)332-7377

Advantage Capital Partners
LLE Tower
909 Poydras St., Ste. 2230
New Orleans, LA 70112
(504)522-4850
Fax: (504)522-4950
Website: http://www.advantagecap.com

Maine

CEI Ventures / Coastal Ventures LP
2 Portland Fish Pier, Ste. 201
Portland, ME 04101
(207)772-5356
Fax: (207)772-5503
Website: http://www.ceiventures.com

Commwealth Bioventures, Inc.
4 Milk St.
Portland, ME 04101

(207)780-0904
Fax: (207)780-0913

Maryland

Annapolis Ventures LLC
151 West St., Ste. 302
Annapolis, MD 21401
(443)482-9555
Fax: (443)482-9565
Website: http://www.annapolis
ventures.com

Delmag Ventures
220 Wardour Dr.
Annapolis, MD 21401
(410)267-8196
Fax: (410)267-8017
Website: http://www.delmag
ventures.com

Abell Venture Fund
111 S. Calvert St., Ste. 2300
Baltimore, MD 21202
(410)547-1300
Fax: (410)539-6579
Website: http://www.abell.org

ABS Ventures (Baltimore)
1 South St., Ste. 2150
Baltimore, MD 21202
(410)895-3895
Fax: (410)895-3899
Website: http://www.absventures.com

Anthem Capital, L.P.
16 S. Calvert St., Ste. 800
Baltimore, MD 21202-1305
(410)625-1510
Fax: (410)625-1735
Website: http://www.anthemcapital.com

Catalyst Ventures
1119 St. Paul St.
Baltimore, MD 21202
(410)244-0123
Fax: (410)752-7721

Maryland Venture Capital Trust
217 E. Redwood St., Ste. 2200
Baltimore, MD 21202
(410)767-6361
Fax: (410)333-6931

New Enterprise Associates (Baltimore)
1119 St. Paul St.
Baltimore, MD 21202
(410)244-0115
Fax: (410)752-7721
Website: http://www.nea.com

T. Rowe Price Threshold Partnerships
100 E. Pratt St., 8th Fl.
Baltimore, MD 21202
(410)345-2000
Fax: (410)345-2800

Spring Capital Partners
16 W. Madison St.
Baltimore, MD 21201
(410)685-8000
Fax: (410)727-1436
E-mail: mailbox@springcap.com

Arete Corporation
3 Bethesda Metro Ctr., Ste. 770
Bethesda, MD 20814
(301)657-6268
Fax: (301)657-6254
Website: http://www.arete-microgen.com

Embryon Capital
7903 Sleaford Place
Bethesda, MD 20814
(301)656-6837
Fax: (301)656-8056

Potomac Ventures
7920 Norfolk Ave., Ste. 1100
Bethesda, MD 20814
(301)215-9240
Website: http://www.potomac
ventures.com

Toucan Capital Corp.
3 Bethesda Metro Center, Ste. 700
Bethesda, MD 20814
(301)961-1970
Fax: (301)961-1969
Website: http://www.toucancapital.com

Kinetic Ventures LLC
2 Wisconsin Cir., Ste. 620
Chevy Chase, MD 20815
(301)652-8066
Fax: (301)652-8310
Website: http://www.kineticventures.com

Boulder Ventures Ltd.
4750 Owings Mills Blvd.
Owings Mills, MD 21117
(410)998-3114
Fax: (410)356-5492
Website: http://www.boulderventures.com

Grotech Capital Group
9690 Deereco Rd., Ste. 800
Timonium, MD 21093
(410)560-2000
Fax: (410)560-1910
Website: http://www.grotech.com

Massachusetts

Adams, Harkness & Hill, Inc.
60 State St.
Boston, MA 02109
(617)371-3900

Advent International
75 State St., 29th Fl.
Boston, MA 02109
(617)951-9400
Fax: (617)951-0566
Website: http://www.adventiner
national.com

American Research and Development
30 Federal St.
Boston, MA 02110-2508
(617)423-7500
Fax: (617)423-9655

Ascent Venture Partners
255 State St., 5th Fl.
Boston, MA 02109
(617)270-9400
Fax: (617)270-9401
E-mail: info@ascentvp.com
Website: http://www.ascentvp.com

Atlas Venture
222 Berkeley St.
Boston, MA 02116
(617)488-2200
Fax: (617)859-9292
Website: http://www.atlasventure.com

Axxon Capital
28 State St., 37th Fl.
Boston, MA 02109
(617)722-0980
Fax: (617)557-6014
Website: http://www.axxoncapital.com

BancBoston Capital/BancBoston Ventures
175 Federal St., 10th Fl.
Boston, MA 02110
(617)434-2509
Fax: (617)434-6175
Website: http://
www.bancbostoncapital.com

Boston Capital Ventures
Old City Hall
45 School St.
Boston, MA 02108
(617)227-6550
Fax: (617)227-3847
E-mail: info@bcv.com
Website: http://www.bcv.com

Boston Financial & Equity Corp.
20 Overland St.
PO Box 15071
Boston, MA 02215
(617)267-2900
Fax: (617)437-7601
E-mail: debbie@bfec.com

Boston Millennia Partners
30 Rowes Wharf
Boston, MA 02110
(617)428-5150
Fax: (617)428-5160
Website: http://www.millennia
partners.com

Bristol Investment Trust
842A Beacon St.
Boston, MA 02215-3199
(617)566-5212
Fax: (617)267-0932

Brook Venture Management LLC
50 Federal St., 5th Fl.
Boston, MA 02110
(617)451-8989
Fax: (617)451-2369
Website: http://www.brookventure.com

Burr, Egan, Deleage, and Co. (Boston)
200 Clarendon St., Ste. 3800
Boston, MA 02116
(617)262-7770
Fax: (617)262-9779

Cambridge/Samsung Partners
One Exeter Plaza
Ninth Fl.
Boston, MA 02116
(617)262-4440
Fax: (617)262-5562

Chestnut Street Partners, Inc.
75 State St., Ste. 2500
Boston, MA 02109
(617)345-7220
Fax: (617)345-7201
E-mail: chestnut@chestnutp.com

Claflin Capital Management, Inc.
10 Liberty Sq., Ste. 300
Boston, MA 02109
(617)426-6505
Fax: (617)482-0016
Website: http://www.claflincapital.com

Copley Venture Partners
99 Summer St., Ste. 1720
Boston, MA 02110
(617)737-1253
Fax: (617)439-0699

Corning Capital / Corning Technology Ventures
121 High Street, Ste. 400
Boston, MA 02110
(617)338-2656
Fax: (617)261-3864
Website: http://www.corningventures.com

Downer & Co.
211 Congress St.
Boston, MA 02110
(617)482-6200
Fax: (617)482-6201
E-mail: cdowner@downer.com
Website: http://www.downer.com

Fidelity Ventures
82 Devonshire St.
Boston, MA 02109
(617)563-6370
Fax: (617)476-9023
Website: http://www.fidelityventures.com

Greylock Management Corp. (Boston)
1 Federal St.
Boston, MA 02110-2065
(617)423-5525
Fax: (617)482-0059

Gryphon Ventures
222 Berkeley St., Ste.1600
Boston, MA 02116
(617)267-9191
Fax: (617)267-4293
E-mail: all@gryphoninc.com

Halpern, Denny & Co.
500 Boylston St.
Boston, MA 02116
(617)536-6602
Fax: (617)536-8535

Harbourvest Partners, LLC
1 Financial Center, 44th Fl.
Boston, MA 02111
(617)348-3707
Fax: (617)350-0305
Website: http://www.hvpllc.com

Highland Capital Partners
2 International Pl.
Boston, MA 02110
(617)981-1500
Fax: (617)531-1550
E-mail: info@hcp.com
Website: http://www.hcp.com

Lee Munder Venture Partners
John Hancock Tower T-53
200 Clarendon St.
Boston, MA 02103

(617)380-5600
Fax: (617)380-5601
Website: http://www.leemunder.com

M/C Venture Partners
75 State St., Ste. 2500
Boston, MA 02109
(617)345-7200
Fax: (617)345-7201
Website: http://www.mcventure
partners.com

Massachusetts Capital Resources Co.
420 Boylston St.
Boston, MA 02116
(617)536-3900
Fax: (617)536-7930

Massachusetts Technology Development Corp. (MTDC)
148 State St.
Boston, MA 02109
(617)723-4920
Fax: (617)723-5983
E-mail: jhodgman@mtdc.com
Website: http://www.mtdc.com

New England Partners
One Boston Place, Ste. 2100
Boston, MA 02108
(617)624-8400
Fax: (617)624-8999
Website: http://www.nepartners.com

North Hill Ventures
Ten Post Office Square
11th Fl.
Boston, MA 02109
(617)788-2112
Fax: (617)788-2152
Website: http://www.northhill
ventures.com

OneLiberty Ventures
150 Cambridge Park Dr.
Boston, MA 02140
(617)492-7280
Fax: (617)492-7290
Website: http://www.oneliberty.com

Schroder Ventures
Life Sciences
60 State St., Ste. 3650
Boston, MA 02109
(617)367-8100
Fax: (617)367-1590
Website: http://www.shroderventures.com

Shawmut Capital Partners
75 Federal St., 18th Fl.
Boston, MA 02110

(617)368-4900
Fax: (617)368-4910
Website: http://www.shawmutcapital.com

Solstice Capital LLC
15 Broad St., 3rd Fl.
Boston, MA 02109
(617)523-7733
Fax: (617)523-5827
E-mail: solticecapital@solcap.com

Spectrum Equity Investors
One International Pl., 29th Fl.
Boston, MA 02110
(617)464-4600
Fax: (617)464-4601
Website: http://www.spectrumequity.com

Spray Venture Partners
One Walnut St.
Boston, MA 02108
(617)305-4140
Fax: (617)305-4144
Website: http://www.sprayventure.com

The Still River Fund
100 Federal St., 29th Fl.
Boston, MA 02110
(617)348-2327
Fax: (617)348-2371
Website: http://www.stillriverfund.com

Summit Partners
600 Atlantic Ave., Ste. 2800
Boston, MA 02210-2227
(617)824-1000
Fax: (617)824-1159
Website: http://www.summitpartners.com

TA Associates, Inc. (Boston)
High Street Tower
125 High St., Ste. 2500
Boston, MA 02110
(617)574-6700
Fax: (617)574-6728
Website: http://www.ta.com

TVM Techno Venture Management
101 Arch St., Ste. 1950
Boston, MA 02110
(617)345-9320
Fax: (617)345-9377
E-mail: info@tvmvc.com
Website: http://www.tvmvc.com

UNC Ventures
64 Burough St.
Boston, MA 02130-4017
(617)482-7070
Fax: (617)522-2176

Venture Investment Management Company (VIMAC)
177 Milk St.
Boston, MA 02190-3410
(617)292-3300
Fax: (617)292-7979
E-mail: bzeisig@vimac.com
Website: http://www.vimac.com

MDT Advisers, Inc.
125 Cambridge Park Dr.
Cambridge, MA 02140-2314
(617)234-2200
Fax: (617)234-2210
Website: http://www.mdtai.com

TTC Ventures
One Main St., 6th Fl.
Cambridge, MA 02142
(617)528-3137
Fax: (617)577-1715
E-mail: info@ttcventures.com

Zero Stage Capital Co. Inc.
101 Main St., 17th Fl.
Cambridge, MA 02142
(617)876-5355
Fax: (617)876-1248
Website: http://www.zerostage.com

Atlantic Capital
164 Cushing Hwy.
Cohasset, MA 02025
(617)383-9449
Fax: (617)383-6040
E-mail: info@atlanticcap.com
Website: http://www.atlanticcap.com

Seacoast Capital Partners
55 Ferncroft Rd.
Danvers, MA 01923
(978)750-1300
Fax: (978)750-1301
E-mail: gdeli@seacoastcapital.com
Website: http://www.seacoast
capital.com

Sage Management Group
44 South Street
PO Box 2026
East Dennis, MA 02641
(508)385-7172
Fax: (508)385-7272
E-mail: sagemgt@capecod.net

Applied Technology
1 Cranberry Hill
Lexington, MA 02421-7397
(617)862-8622
Fax: (617)862-8367

Royalty Capital Management
5 Downing Rd.
Lexington, MA 02421-6918
(781)861-8490

Argo Global Capital
210 Broadway, Ste. 101
Lynnfield, MA 01940
(781)592-5250
Fax: (781)592-5230
Website: http://www.gsmcapital.com

Industry Ventures
6 Bayne Lane
Newburyport, MA 01950
(978)499-7606
Fax: (978)499-0686
Website: http://
www.industryventures.com

Softbank Capital Partners
10 Langley Rd., Ste. 202
Newton Center, MA 02459
(617)928-9300
Fax: (617)928-9305
E-mail: clax@bvc.com

Advanced Technology Ventures (Boston)
281 Winter St., Ste. 350
Waltham, MA 02451
(781)290-0707
Fax: (781)684-0045
E-mail: info@atvcapital.com
Website: http://www.atvcapital.com

Castile Ventures
890 Winter St., Ste. 140
Waltham, MA 02451
(781)890-0060
Fax: (781)890-0065
Website: http://www.castileventures.com

Charles River Ventures
1000 Winter St., Ste. 3300
Waltham, MA 02451
(781)487-7060
Fax: (781)487-7065
Website: http://www.crv.com

Comdisco Venture Group (Waltham)
Totton Pond Office Center
400-1 Totten Pond Rd.
Waltham, MA 02451
(617)672-0250
Fax: (617)398-8099

Marconi Ventures
890 Winter St., Ste. 310
Waltham, MA 02451
(781)839-7177

Fax: (781)522-7477
Website: http://www.marconi.com

Matrix Partners
Bay Colony Corporate Center
1000 Winter St., Ste.4500
Waltham, MA 02451
(781)890-2244
Fax: (781)890-2288
Website: http://www.matrix
partners.com

North Bridge Venture Partners
950 Winter St. Ste. 4600
Waltham, MA 02451
(781)290-0004
Fax: (781)290-0999
E-mail: eta@nbvp.com

Polaris Venture Partners
Bay Colony Corporate Ctr.
1000 Winter St., Ste. 3500
Waltham, MA 02451
(781)290-0770
Fax: (781)290-0880
E-mail: partners@polarisventures.com
Website: http://www.polar
isventures.com

Seaflower Ventures
Bay Colony Corporate Ctr.
1000 Winter St. Ste. 1000
Waltham, MA 02451
(781)466-9552
Fax: (781)466-9553
E-mail: moot@seaflower.com
Website: http://www.seaflower.com

Ampersand Ventures
55 William St., Ste. 240
Wellesley, MA 02481
(617)239-0700
Fax: (617)239-0824
E-mail: info@ampersandventures.com
Website: http://www.ampersand
ventures.com

Battery Ventures (Boston)
20 William St., Ste. 200
Wellesley, MA 02481
(781)577-1000
Fax: (781)577-1001
Website: http://www.battery.com

Commonwealth Capital Ventures, L.P.
20 William St., Ste.225
Wellesley, MA 02481
(781)237-7373
Fax: (781)235-8627
Website: http://www.ccvlp.com

Fowler, Anthony & Company
20 Walnut St.
Wellesley, MA 02481
(781)237-4201
Fax: (781)237-7718

Gemini Investors
20 William St.
Wellesley, MA 02481
(781)237-7001
Fax: (781)237-7233

Grove Street Advisors Inc.
20 William St., Ste. 230
Wellesley, MA 02481
(781)263-6100
Fax: (781)263-6101
Website: http://www.groves
treetadvisors.com

Mees Pierson Investeringsmaat B.V.
20 William St., Ste. 210
Wellesley, MA 02482
(781)239-7600
Fax: (781)239-0377

Norwest Equity Partners
40 William St., Ste. 305
Wellesley, MA 02481-3902
(781)237-5870
Fax: (781)237-6270
Website: http://www.norwestvp.com

Bessemer Venture Partners (Wellesley Hills)
83 Walnut St.
Wellesley Hills, MA 02481
(781)237-6050
Fax: (781)235-7576
E-mail: travis@bvpny.com
Website: http://www.bvp.com

Venture Capital Fund of New England
20 Walnut St., Ste. 120
Wellesley Hills, MA 02481-2175
(781)239-8262
Fax: (781)239-8263

Prism Venture Partners
100 Lowder Brook Dr., Ste. 2500
Westwood, MA 02090
(781)302-4000
Fax: (781)302-4040
E-mail: dwbaum@prismventure.com

Palmer Partners LP
200 Unicorn Park Dr.
Woburn, MA 01801
(781)933-5445
Fax: (781)933-0698

Michigan

Arbor Partners, L.L.C.
130 South First St.
Ann Arbor, MI 48104
(734)668-9000
Fax: (734)669-4195
Website: http://www.arborpartners.com

EDF Ventures
425 N. Main St.
Ann Arbor, MI 48104
(734)663-3213
Fax: (734)663-7358
E-mail: edf@edfvc.com
Website: http://www.edfvc.com

White Pines Management, L.L.C.
2401 Plymouth Rd., Ste. B
Ann Arbor, MI 48105
(734)747-9401
Fax: (734)747-9704
E-mail: ibund@whitepines.com
Website: http://www.whitepines.com

Wellmax, Inc.
3541 Bendway Blvd., Ste. 100
Bloomfield Hills, MI 48301
(248)646-3554
Fax: (248)646-6220

Venture Funding, Ltd.
Fisher Bldg.
3011 West Grand Blvd., Ste. 321
Detroit, MI 48202
(313)871-3606
Fax: (313)873-4935

Investcare Partners L.P. / GMA Capital LLC
32330 W. Twelve Mile Rd.
Farmington Hills, MI 48334
(248)489-9000
Fax: (248)489-8819
E-mail: gma@gmacapital.com
Website: http://www.gmacapital.com

Liberty Bidco Investment Corp.
30833 Northwestern Highway, Ste. 211
Farmington Hills, MI 48334
(248)626-6070
Fax: (248)626-6072

Seaflower Ventures
5170 Nicholson Rd.
PO Box 474
Fowlerville, MI 48836
(517)223-3335
Fax: (517)223-3337
E-mail: gibbons@seaflower.com
Website: http://www.seaflower.com

Ralph Wilson Equity Fund LLC
15400 E. Jefferson Ave.
Gross Pointe Park, MI 48230
(313)821-9122
Fax: (313)821-9101
Website: http://www.Ralph
WilsonEquityFund.com
J. Skip Simms, President

Minnesota

Development Corp. of Austin
1900 Eighth Ave., NW
Austin, MN 55912
(507)433-0346
Fax: (507)433-0361
E mail: dca@smig.net
Website: http://www.spamtownusa.com

Northeast Ventures Corp.
802 Alworth Bldg.
Duluth, MN 55802
(218)722-9915
Fax: (218)722-9871

Medical Innovation Partners, Inc.
6450 City West Pkwy.
Eden Prairie, MN 55344-3245
(612)828-9616
Fax: (612)828-9596

St. Paul Venture Capital, Inc.
10400 Vicking Dr., Ste. 550
Eden Prairie, MN 55344
(612)995-7474
Fax: (612)995-7475
Website: http://www.stpaulvc.com

Cherry Tree Investments, Inc.
7601 France Ave. S, Ste. 150
Edina, MN 55435
(612)893-9012
Fax: (612)893-9036
Website: http://www.cherrytree.com

Shared Ventures, Inc.
6550 York Ave. S
Edina, MN 55435
(612)925-3411

Sherpa Partners LLC
5050 Lincoln Dr., Ste. 490
Edina, MN 55436
(952)942-1070
Fax: (952)942-1071
Website: http://www.sherpapartners.com

Affinity Capital Management
901 Marquette Ave., Ste. 1810
Minneapolis, MN 55402
(612)252-9900

Fax: (612)252-9911
Website: http://www.affinitycapital.com

Artesian Capital
1700 Foshay Tower
821 Marquette Ave.
Minneapolis, MN 55402
(612)334-5600
Fax: (612)334-5601
E-mail: artesian@artesian.com

Coral Ventures
60 S. 6th St., Ste. 3510
Minneapolis, MN 55402
(612)335-8666
Fax: (612)335-8668
Website: http://www.coralventures.com

Crescendo Venture Management, L.L.C.
800 LaSalle Ave., Ste. 2250
Minneapolis, MN 55402
(612)607-2800
Fax: (612)607-2801
Website: http://www.crescendo
ventures.com

Gideon Hixon Venture
1900 Foshay Tower
821 Marquette Ave.
Minneapolis, MN 55402
(612)904-2314
Fax: (612)204-0913

Norwest Equity Partners
3600 IDS Center
80 S. 8th St.
Minneapolis, MN 55402
(612)215-1600
Fax: (612)215-1601
Website: http://www.norwestvp.com

Oak Investment Partners (Minneapolis)
4550 Norwest Center
90 S. 7th St.
Minneapolis, MN 55402
(612)339-9322
Fax: (612)337-8017
Website: http://www.oakinv.com

Pathfinder Venture Capital Funds (Minneapolis)
7300 Metro Blvd., Ste. 585
Minneapolis, MN 55439
(612)835-1121
Fax: (612)835-8389
E-mail: jahrens620@aol.com

U.S. Bancorp Piper Jaffray Ventures, Inc.
800 Nicollet Mall, Ste. 800
Minneapolis, MN 55402

(612)303-5686
Fax: (612)303-1350
Website: http://www.paperjaffrey
ventures.com

The Food Fund, Ltd. Partnership
5720 Smatana Dr., Ste. 300
Minnetonka, MN 55343
(612)939-3950
Fax: (612)939-8106

Mayo Medical Ventures
200 First St. SW
Rochester, MN 55905
(507)266-4586
Fax: (507)284-5410
Website: http://www.mayo.edu

Missouri

Bankers Capital Corp.
3100 Gillham Rd.
Kansas City, MO 64109
(816)531-1600
Fax: (816)531-1334

Capital for Business, Inc. (Kansas City)
1000 Walnut St., 18th Fl.
Kansas City, MO 64106
(816)234-2357
Fax: (816)234-2952
Website: http://
www.capitalforbusiness.com

De Vries & Co. Inc.
800 West 47th St.
Kansas City, MO 64112
(816)756-0055
Fax: (816)756-0061

InvestAmerica Venture Group Inc. (Kansas City)
Commerce Tower
911 Main St., Ste. 2424
Kansas City, MO 64105
(816)842-0114
Fax: (816)471-7339

Kansas City Equity Partners
233 W. 47th St.
Kansas City, MO 64112
(816)960-1771
Fax: (816)960-1777
Website: http://www.kcep.com

Bome Investors, Inc.
8000 Maryland Ave., Ste. 1190
St. Louis, MO 63105
(314)721-5707
Fax: (314)721-5135

Website: http://www.gateway
ventures.com

Capital for Business, Inc. (St. Louis)
11 S. Meramac St., Ste. 1430
St. Louis, MO 63105
(314)746-7427
Fax: (314)746-8739
Website: http://www.capitalfor
business.com

Crown Capital Corp.
540 Maryville Centre Dr., Ste. 120
Saint Louis, MO 63141
(314)576-1201
Fax: (314)576-1525
Website: http://www.crown-
cap.com

Gateway Associates L.P.
8000 Maryland Ave., Ste. 1190
St. Louis, MO 63105
(314)721-5707
Fax: (314)721-5135

Harbison Corp.
8112 Maryland Ave., Ste. 250
Saint Louis, MO 63105
(314)727-8200
Fax: (314)727-0249

Heartland Capital Fund, Ltd.
PO Box 642117
Omaha, NE 68154
(402)778-5124
Fax: (402)445-2370
Website: http://www.heartland
capitalfund.com

Odin Capital Group
1625 Farnam St., Ste. 700
Omaha, NE 68102
(402)346-6200
Fax: (402)342-9311
Website: http://www.odincapital.com

Nevada

Edge Capital Investment Co. LLC
1350 E. Flamingo Rd., Ste. 3000
Las Vegas, NV 89119
(702)438-3343
E-mail: info@edgecapital.net
Website: http://www.edgecapital.net

The Benefit Capital Companies Inc.
PO Box 542
Logandale, NV 89021
(702)398-3222
Fax: (702)398-3700

Millennium Three Venture Group LLC
6880 South McCarran Blvd., Ste. A-11
Reno, NV 89509
(775)954-2020
Fax: (775)954-2023
Website: http://www.m3vg.com

New Jersey

Alan I. Goldman & Associates
497 Ridgewood Ave.
Glen Ridge, NJ 07028
(973)857-5680
Fax: (973)509-8856

CS Capital Partners LLC
328 Second St., Ste. 200
Lakewood, NJ 08701
(732)901-1111
Fax: (212)202-5071
Website: http://www.cs-capital.com

Edison Venture Fund
1009 Lenox Dr., Ste. 4
Lawrenceville, NJ 08648
(609)896-1900
Fax: (609)896-0066
E-mail: info@edisonventure.com
Website: http://www.edisonventure.com

Tappan Zee Capital Corp. (New Jersey)
201 Lower Notch Rd.
PO Box 416
Little Falls, NJ 07424
(973)256-8280
Fax: (973)256-2841

The CIT Group/Venture Capital, Inc.
650 CIT Dr.
Livingston, NJ 07039
(973)740-5429
Fax: (973)740-5555
Website: http://www.cit.com

Capital Express, L.L.C.
1100 Valleybrook Ave.
Lyndhurst, NJ 07071
(201)438-8228
Fax: (201)438-5131
E-mail: niles@capitalexpress.com
Website: http://www.capitalexpress.com

Westford Technology Ventures, L.P.
17 Academy St.
Newark, NJ 07102
(973)624-2131
Fax: (973)624-2008

Accel Partners
1 Palmer Sq.
Princeton, NJ 08542

(609)683-4500
Fax: (609)683-4880
Website: http://www.accel.com

Cardinal Partners
221 Nassau St.
Princeton, NJ 08542
(609)924-6452
Fax: (609)683-0174
Website: http://www.cardinal
healthpartners.com

Domain Associates L.L.C.
One Palmer Sq., Ste. 515
Princeton, NJ 08542
(609)683-5656
Fax: (609)683-9789
Website: http://www.domainvc.com

Johnston Associates, Inc.
181 Cherry Valley Rd.
Princeton, NJ 08540
(609)924-3131
Fax: (609)683-7524
E-mail: jaincorp@aol.com

Kemper Ventures
Princeton Forrestal Village
155 Village Blvd.
Princeton, NJ 08540
(609)936-3035
Fax: (609)936-3051

Penny Lane Parnters
One Palmer Sq., Ste. 309
Princeton, NJ 08542
(609)497-4646
Fax: (609)497-0611

Early Stage Enterprises L.P.
995 Route 518
Skillman, NJ 08558
(609)921-8896
Fax: (609)921-8703
Website: http://www.esevc.com

MBW Management Inc.
1 Springfield Ave.
Summit, NJ 07901
(908)273-4060
Fax: (908)273-4430

BCI Advisors, Inc.
Glenpointe Center W.
Teaneck, NJ 07666
(201)836-3900
Fax: (201)836-6368
E-mail: info@bciadvisors.com
Website: http://www.bci
partners.com

Demuth, Folger & Wetherill / DFW Capital Partners
Glenpointe Center E., 5th Fl.
300 Frank W. Burr Blvd.
Teaneck, NJ 07666
(201)836-2233
Fax: (201)836-5666
Website: http://www.dfwcapital.com

First Princeton Capital Corp.
189 Berdan Ave., No. 131
Wayne, NJ 07470-3233
(973)278-3233
Fax: (973)278-4290
Website: http://www.lytellcatt.net

Edelson Technology Partners
300 Tice Blvd.
Woodcliff Lake, NJ 07675
(201)930-9898
Fax: (201)930-8899
Website: http://www.edelsontech.com

New Mexico

Bruce F. Glaspell & Associates
10400 Academy Rd. NE, Ste. 313
Albuquerque, NM 87111
(505)292-4505
Fax: (505)292-4258

High Desert Ventures, Inc.
6101 Imparata St. NE, Ste. 1721
Albuquerque, NM 87111
(505)797-3330
Fax: (505)338-5147

New Business Capital Fund, Ltd.
5805 Torreon NE
Albuquerque, NM 87109
(505)822-8445

SBC Ventures
10400 Academy Rd. NE, Ste. 313
Albuquerque, NM 87111
(505)292-4505
Fax: (505)292-4528

Technology Ventures Corp.
1155 University Blvd. SE
Albuquerque, NM 87106
(505)246-2882
Fax: (505)246-2891

New York

New York State Science & Technology Foundation
Small Business Technology Investment Fund
99 Washington Ave., Ste. 1731
Albany, NY 12210

(518)473-9741
Fax: (518)473-6876

Rand Capital Corp.
2200 Rand Bldg.
Buffalo, NY 14203
(716)853-0802
Fax: (716)854-8480
Website: http://www.randcapital.com

Seed Capital Partners
620 Main St.
Buffalo, NY 14202
(716)845-7520
Fax: (716)845-7539
Website: http://www.seedcp.com

Coleman Venture Group
5909 Northern Blvd.
PO Box 224
East Norwich, NY 11732
(516)626-3642
Fax: (516)626-9722

Vega Capital Corp.
45 Knollwood Rd.
Elmsford, NY 10523
(914)345-9500
Fax: (914)345-9505

Herbert Young Securities, Inc.
98 Cuttermill Rd.
Great Neck, NY 11021
(516)487-8300
Fax: (516)487-8319

Sterling/Carl Marks Capital, Inc.
175 Great Neck Rd., Ste. 408
Great Neck, NY 11021
(516)482-7374
Fax: (516)487-0781
E-mail: stercrlmar@aol.com
Website: http://www.serling
carlmarks.com

Impex Venture Management Co.
PO Box 1570
Green Island, NY 12183
(518)271-8008
Fax: (518)271-9101

Corporate Venture Partners L.P.
200 Sunset Park
Ithaca, NY 14850
(607)257-6323
Fax: (607)257-6128

Arthur P. Gould & Co.
One Wilshire Dr.
Lake Success, NY 11020
(516)773-3000
Fax: (516)773-3289

Dauphin Capital Partners
108 Forest Ave.
Locust Valley, NY 11560
(516)759-3339
Fax: (516)759-3322
Website: http://www.dauphincapital.com

550 Digital Media Ventures
555 Madison Ave., 10th Fl.
New York, NY 10022
Website: http://www.550dmv.com

Aberlyn Capital Management Co., Inc.
500 Fifth Ave.
New York, NY 10110
(212)391-7750
Fax: (212)391-7762

Adler & Company
342 Madison Ave., Ste. 807
New York, NY 10173
(212)599-2535
Fax: (212)599-2526

Alimansky Capital Group, Inc.
605 Madison Ave., Ste. 300
New York, NY 10022-1901
(212)832-7300
Fax: (212)832-7338

Allegra Partners
515 Madison Ave., 29th Fl.
New York, NY 10022
(212)826-9080
Fax: (212)759-2561

The Argentum Group
The Chyrsler Bldg.
405 Lexington Ave.
New York, NY 10174
(212)949-6262
Fax: (212)949-8294
Website: http://www.argentum
group.com

Axavision Inc.
14 Wall St., 26th Fl.
New York, NY 10005
(212)619-4000
Fax: (212)619-7202

Bedford Capital Corp.
18 East 48th St., Ste. 1800
New York, NY 10017
(212)688-5700
Fax: (212)754-4699
E-mail: info@bedfordnyc.com
Website: http://www.bedfordnyc.com

Bloom & Co.
950 Third Ave.

New York, NY 10022
(212)838-1858
Fax: (212)838-1843

Bristol Capital Management
300 Park Ave., 17th Fl.
New York, NY 10022
(212)572-6306
Fax: (212)705-4292

**Citicorp Venture Capital Ltd.
(New York City)**
399 Park Ave., 14th Fl.
Zone 4
New York, NY 10043
(212)559-1127
Fax: (212)888-2940

CM Equity Partners
135 E. 57th St.
New York, NY 10022
(212)909-8428
Fax: (212)980-2630

Cohen & Co., L.L.C.
800 Third Ave.
New York, NY 10022
(212)317-2250
Fax: (212)317-2255
E-mail: nlcohen@aol.com

Cornerstone Equity Investors, L.L.C.
717 5th Ave., Ste. 1100
New York, NY 10022
(212)753-0901
Fax: (212)826-6798
Website: http://www.cornerstone-
equity.com

CW Group, Inc.
1041 3rd Ave., 2nd fl.
New York, NY 10021
(212)308-5266
Fax: (212)644-0354
Website: http://www.cwventures.com

DH Blair Investment Banking Corp.
44 Wall St., 2nd Fl.
New York, NY 10005
(212)495-5000
Fax: (212)269-1438

Dresdner Kleinwort Capital
75 Wall St.
New York, NY 10005
(212)429-3131
Fax: (212)429-3139
Website: http://www.dresdnerkb.com

East River Ventures, L.P.
645 Madison Ave., 22nd Fl.

New York, NY 10022
(212)644-2322
Fax: (212)644-5498

Easton Hunt Capital Partners
641 Lexington Ave., 21st Fl.
New York, NY 10017
(212)702-0950
Fax: (212)702-0952
Website: http://www.eastoncapital.com

Elk Associates Funding Corp.
747 3rd Ave., Ste. 4C
New York, NY 10017
(212)355-2449
Fax: (212)759-3338

EOS Partners, L.P.
320 Park Ave., 22nd Fl.
New York, NY 10022
(212)832-5800
Fax: (212)832-5815
E-mail: mfirst@eospartners.com
Website: http://www.eospartners.com

Euclid Partners
45 Rockefeller Plaza, Ste. 3240
New York, NY 10111
(212)218-6880
Fax: (212)218-6877
E-mail: graham@euclidpartners.com
Website: http://www.euclidpartners.com

Evergreen Capital Partners, Inc.
150 East 58th St.
New York, NY 10155
(212)813-0758
Fax: (212)813-0754

Exeter Capital L.P.
10 E. 53rd St.
New York, NY 10022
(212)872-1172
Fax: (212)872-1198
E-mail: exeter@usa.net

Financial Technology Research Corp.
518 Broadway
Penthouse
New York, NY 10012
(212)625-9100
Fax: (212)431-0300
E-mail: fintek@financier.com

4C Ventures
237 Park Ave., Ste. 801
New York, NY 10017
(212)692-3680
Fax: (212)692-3685
Website: http://www.4cventures.com

Fusient Ventures
99 Park Ave., 20th Fl.
New York, NY 10016
(212)972-8999
Fax: (212)972-9876
E-mail: info@fusient.com
Website: http://www.fusient.com

Generation Capital Partners
551 Fifth Ave., Ste. 3100
New York, NY 10176
(212)450-8507
Fax: (212)450-8550
Website: http://www.genpartners.com

Golub Associates, Inc.
555 Madison Ave.
New York, NY 10022
(212)750-6060
Fax: (212)750-5505

Hambro America Biosciences Inc.
650 Madison Ave., 21st Floor
New York, NY 10022
(212)223-7400
Fax: (212)223-0305

Hanover Capital Corp.
505 Park Ave., 15th Fl.
New York, NY 10022
(212)755-1222
Fax: (212)935-1787

Harvest Partners, Inc.
280 Park Ave, 33rd Fl.
New York, NY 10017
(212)559-6300
Fax: (212)812-0100
Website: http://www.harvpart.com

Holding Capital Group, Inc.
10 E. 53rd St., 30th Fl.
New York, NY 10022
(212)486-6670
Fax: (212)486-0843

Hudson Venture Partners
660 Madison Ave., 14th Fl.
New York, NY 10021-8405
(212)644-9797
Fax: (212)644-7430
Website: http://www.hudsonptr.com

IBJS Capital Corp.
1 State St., 9th Fl.
New York, NY 10004
(212)858-2018
Fax: (212)858-2768

InterEquity Capital Partners, L.P.
220 5th Ave.
New York, NY 10001

(212)779-2022
Fax: (212)779-2103
Website: http://www.interequity-capital.com

The Jordan Edmiston Group Inc.
150 East 52nd St., 18th Fl.
New York, NY 10022
(212)754-0710
Fax: (212)754-0337

Josephberg, Grosz and Co., Inc.
633 3rd Ave., 13th Fl.
New York, NY 10017
(212)974-9926
Fax: (212)397-5832

J.P. Morgan Capital Corp.
60 Wall St.
New York, NY 10260-0060
(212)648-9000
Fax: (212)648 5002
Website: http://www.jpmorgan.com

The Lambda Funds
380 Lexington Ave., 54th Fl.
New York, NY 10168
(212)682-3454
Fax: (212)682-9231

Lepercq Capital Management Inc.
1675 Broadway
New York, NY 10019
(212)698-0795
Fax: (212)262-0155

Loeb Partners Corp.
61 Broadway, Ste. 2400
New York, NY 10006
(212)483-7000
Fax: (212)574-2001

Madison Investment Partners
660 Madison Ave.
New York, NY 10021
(212)223-2600
Fax: (212)223-8208

MC Capital Inc.
520 Madison Ave., 16th Fl.
New York, NY 10022
(212)644-0841
Fax: (212)644-2926

McCown, De Leeuw and Co. (New York)
65 E. 55th St., 36th Fl.
New York, NY 10022
(212)355-5500
Fax: (212)355-6283
Website: http://www.mdcpartners.com

Morgan Stanley Venture Partners
1221 Avenue of the Americas, 33rd Fl.
New York, NY 10020
(212)762-7900
Fax: (212)762-8424
E-mail: msventures@ms.com
Website: http://www.msvp.com

Nazem and Co.
645 Madison Ave., 12th Fl.
New York, NY 10022
(212)371-7900
Fax: (212)371-2150

Needham Capital Management, L.L.C.
445 Park Ave.
New York, NY 10022
(212)371-8300
Fax: (212)705-0299
Website: http://www.needhamco.com

Norwood Venture Corp.
1430 Broadway, Ste. 1607
New York, NY 10018
(212)869-5075
Fax: (212)869-5331
E-mail: nvc@mail.idt.net
Website: http://www.norven.com

Noveltek Venture Corp.
521 Fifth Ave., Ste. 1700
New York, NY 10175
(212)286-1963

Paribas Principal, Inc.
787 7th Ave.
New York, NY 10019
(212)841-2005
Fax: (212)841-3558

Patricof & Co. Ventures, Inc.
(New York)
445 Park Ave.
New York, NY 10022
(212)753-6300
Fax: (212)319-6155
Website: http://www.patricof.com

The Platinum Group, Inc.
350 Fifth Ave, Ste. 7113
New York, NY 10118
(212)736-4300
Fax: (212)736-6086
Website: http://www.platinumgroup.com

Pomona Capital
780 Third Ave., 28th Fl.
New York, NY 10017
(212)593-3639
Fax: (212)593-3987
Website: http://www.pomonacapital.com

Prospect Street Ventures
10 East 40th St., 44th Fl.
New York, NY 10016
(212)448-0702
Fax: (212)448-9652
E-mail: wkohler@prospectstreet.com
Website: http://www.prospectstreet.com

Regent Capital Management
505 Park Ave., Ste. 1700
New York, NY 10022
(212)735-9900
Fax: (212)735-9908

Rothschild Ventures, Inc.
1251 Avenue of the Americas, 51st Fl.
New York, NY 10020
(212)403-3500
Fax: (212)403-3652
Website: http://www.nmrothschild.com

Sandler Capital Management
767 Fifth Ave., 45th Fl.
New York, NY 10153
(212)754-8100
Fax: (212)826-0280

Siguler Guff & Company
630 Fifth Ave., 16th Fl.
New York, NY 10111
(212)332-5100
Fax: (212)332-5120

Spencer Trask Ventures Inc.
535 Madison Ave.
New York, NY 10022
(212)355-5565
Fax: (212)751-3362
Website: http://www.spencertrask.com

Sprout Group (New York City)
277 Park Ave.
New York, NY 10172
(212)892-3600
Fax: (212)892-3444
E-mail: info@sproutgroup.com
Website: http://www.sproutgroup.com

US Trust Private Equity
114 W.47th St.
New York, NY 10036
(212)852-3949
Fax: (212)852-3759
Website: http://www.ustrust.com/
privateequity

Vencon Management Inc.
301 West 53rd St., Ste. 10F
New York, NY 10019
(212)581-8787
Fax: (212)397-4126
Website: http://www.venconinc.com

Venrock Associates
30 Rockefeller Plaza, Ste. 5508
New York, NY 10112
(212)649-5600
Fax: (212)649-5788
Website: http://www.venrock.com

Venture Capital Fund of America, Inc.
509 Madison Ave., Ste. 812
New York, NY 10022
(212)838-5577
Fax: (212)838-7614
E-mail: mail@vcfa.com
Website: http://www.vcfa.com

Venture Opportunities Corp.
150 E. 58th St.
New York, NY 10155
(212)832-3737
Fax: (212)980-6603

Warburg Pincus Ventures, Inc.
466 Lexington Ave., 11th Fl.
New York, NY 10017
(212)878-9309
Fax: (212)878-9200
Website: http://www.warburgpincus.com

Wasserstein, Perella & Co. Inc.
31 W. 52nd St., 27th Fl.
New York, NY 10019
(212)702-5691
Fax: (212)969-7879

Welsh, Carson, Anderson, & Stowe
320 Park Ave., Ste. 2500
New York, NY 10022-6815
(212)893-9500
Fax: (212)893-9575

Whitney and Co. (New York)
630 Fifth Ave. Ste. 3225
New York, NY 10111
(212)332-2400
Fax: (212)332-2422
Website: http://www.jhwitney.com

Winthrop Ventures
74 Trinity Place, Ste. 600
New York, NY 10006
(212)422-0100

The Pittsford Group
8 Lodge Pole Rd.
Pittsford, NY 14534
(716)223-3523

Genesee Funding
70 Linden Oaks, 3rd Fl.
Rochester, NY 14625
(716)383-5550
Fax: (716)383-5305

Gabelli Multimedia Partners
One Corporate Center
Rye, NY 10580
(914)921-5395
Fax: (914)921-5031

Stamford Financial
108 Main St.
Stamford, NY 12167
(607)652-3311
Fax: (607)652-6301
Website: http://www.stamford
financial.com

Northwood Ventures LLC
485 Underhill Blvd., Ste. 205
Syosset, NY 11791
(516)364-5544
Fax: (516)364-0879
E-mail: northwood@northwood.com
Website: http://www.north
woodventures.com

Exponential Business Development Co.
216 Walton St.
Syracuse, NY 13202-1227
(315)474-4500
Fax: (315)474-4682
E-mail: dirksonn@aol.com
Website: http://www.exponential-ny.com

Onondaga Venture Capital Fund Inc.
714 State Tower Bldg.
Syracuse, NY 13202
(315)478-0157
Fax: (315)478-0158

Bessemer Venture Partners (Westbury)
1400 Old Country Rd., Ste. 109
Westbury, NY 11590
(516)997-2300
Fax: (516)997-2371
E-mail: bob@bvpny.com
Website: http://www.bvp.com

Ovation Capital Partners
120 Bloomingdale Rd., 4th Fl.
White Plains, NY 10605
(914)258-0011
Fax: (914)684-0848
Website: http://www.ovation
capital.com

North Carolina

Carolinas Capital Investment Corp.
1408 Biltmore Dr.
Charlotte, NC 28207
(704)375-3888
Fax: (704)375-6226

First Union Capital Partners
1st Union Center, 12th Fl.
301 S. College St.
Charlotte, NC 28288-0732
(704)383-0000
Fax: (704)374-6711
Website: http://www.fucp.com

Frontier Capital LLC
525 North Tryon St., Ste. 1700
Charlotte, NC 28202
(704)414-2880
Fax: (704)414-2881
Website: http://www.frontierfunds.com

Kitty Hawk Capital
2700 Coltsgate Rd., Ste. 202
Charlotte, NC 28211
(704)362-3909
Fax: (704)362-2774
Website: http://www.kittyhawk
capital.com

Piedmont Venture Partners
One Morrocroft Centre
6805 Morisson Blvd., Ste. 380
Charlotte, NC 28211
(704)731-5200
Fax: (704)365-9733
Website: http://www.piedmontvp.com

Ruddick Investment Co.
1800 Two First Union Center
Charlotte, NC 28282
(704)372-5404
Fax: (704)372-6409

The Shelton Companies Inc.
3600 One First Union Center
301 S. College St.
Charlotte, NC 28202
(704)348-2200
Fax: (704)348-2260

Wakefield Group
1110 E. Morehead St.
PO Box 36329
Charlotte, NC 28236
(704)372-0355
Fax: (704)372-8216
Website: http://www.wakefiel
dgroup.com

Aurora Funds, Inc.
2525 Meridian Pkwy., Ste. 220
Durham, NC 27713
(919)484-0400
Fax: (919)484-0444
Website: http://www.aurora
funds.com

Intersouth Partners
3211 Shannon Rd., Ste. 610
Durham, NC 27707
(919)493-6640
Fax: (919)493-6649
E-mail: info@intersouth.com
Website: http://www.intersouth.com

Geneva Merchant Banking Partners
PO Box 21962
Greensboro, NC 27420
(336)275-7002
Fax: (336)275-9155
Website: http://www.geneva
merchantbank.com

The North Carolina Enterprise Fund, L.P.
3600 Glenwood Ave., Ste. 107
Raleigh, NC 27612
(919)781-2691
Fax: (919)783-9195
Website: http://www.ncef.com

Ohio

Senmend Medical Ventures
4445 Lake Forest Dr., Ste. 600
Cincinnati, OH 45242
(513)563-3264
Fax: (513)563-3261

The Walnut Group
312 Walnut St., Ste. 1151
Cincinnati, OH 45202
(513)651-3300
Fax: (513)929-4441
Website: http://www.thewal
nutgroup.com

Brantley Venture Partners
20600 Chagrin Blvd., Ste. 1150
Cleveland, OH 44122
(216)283-4800
Fax: (216)283-5324

Clarion Capital Corp.
1801 E. 9th St., Ste. 1120
Cleveland, OH 44114
(216)687-1096
Fax: (216)694-3545

Crystal Internet Venture Fund, L.P.
1120 Chester Ave., Ste. 418
Cleveland, OH 44114
(216)263-5515
Fax: (216)263-5518
E-mail: jf@crystalventure.com
Website: http://www.crystal
venture.com

Key Equity Capital Corp.
127 Public Sq., 28th Fl.
Cleveland, OH 44114
(216)689-3000
Fax: (216)689-3204
Website: http://www.keybank.com

Morgenthaler Ventures
Terminal Tower
50 Public Square, Ste. 2700
Cleveland, OH 44113
(216)416-7500
Fax: (216)416-7501
Website: http://www.morgenthaler.com

National City Equity Partners Inc.
1965 E. 6th St.
Cleveland, OH 44114
(216)575-2491
Fax: (216)575-9965
E-mail: nccap@aol.com
Website: http://www.nccapital.com

Primus Venture Partners, Inc.
5900 LanderBrook Dr., Ste. 2000
Cleveland, OH 44124-4020
(440)684-7300
Fax: (440)684-7342
E-mail: info@primusventure.com
Website: http://www.primusventure.com

Banc One Capital Partners (Columbus)
150 East Gay St., 24th Fl.
Columbus, OH 43215
(614)217-1100
Fax: (614)217-1217

Battelle Venture Partners
505 King Ave.
Columbus, OH 43201
(614)424-7005
Fax: (614)424-4874

Ohio Partners
62 E. Board St., 3rd Fl.
Columbus, OH 43215
(614)621-1210
Fax: (614)621-1240

Capital Technology Group, L.L.C.
400 Metro Place North, Ste. 300
Dublin, OH 43017
(614)792-6066
Fax: (614)792-6036
E-mail: info@capitaltech.com
Website: http://www.capitaltech.com

Northwest Ohio Venture Fund
4159 Holland-Sylvania R., Ste. 202
Toledo, OH 43623
(419)824-8144

Fax: (419)882-2035
E-mail: bwalsh@novf.com

Oklahoma

Moore & Associates
1000 W. Wilshire Blvd., Ste. 370
Oklahoma City, OK 73116
(405)842-3660
Fax: (405)842-3763

Chisholm Private Capital Partners
100 West 5th St., Ste. 805
Tulsa, OK 74103
(918)584-0440
Fax: (918)584-0441
Website: http://www.chisholmvc.com

Davis, Tuttle Venture Partners (Tulsa)
320 S. Boston, Ste. 1000
Tulsa, OK 74103-3703
(918)584-7272
Fax: (918)582-3404
Website: http://www.davistuttle.com

RBC Ventures
2627 E. 21st St.
Tulsa, OK 74114
(918)744-5607
Fax: (918)743-8630

Oregon

Utah Ventures II LP
10700 SW Beaverton-Hillsdale Hwy.,
Ste. 548
Beaverton, OR 97005
(503)574-4125
E-mail: adishlip@uven.com
Website: http://www.uven.com

Orien Ventures
14523 SW Westlake Dr.
Lake Oswego, OR 97035
(503)699-1680
Fax: (503)699-1681

OVP Venture Partners (Lake Oswego)
340 Oswego Pointe Dr., Ste. 200
Lake Oswego, OR 97034
(503)697-8766
Fax: (503)697-8863
E-mail: info@ovp.com
Website: http://www.ovp.com

Oregon Resource and Technology Development Fund
4370 NE Halsey St., Ste. 233
Portland, OR 97213-1566
(503)282-4462
Fax: (503)282-2976

Shaw Venture Partners
400 SW 6th Ave., Ste. 1100
Portland, OR 97204-1636
(503)228-4884
Fax: (503)227-2471
Website: http://www.shawventures.com

Pennsylvania

Mid-Atlantic Venture Funds
125 Goodman Dr.
Bethlehem, PA 18015
(610)865-6550
Fax: (610)865-6427
Website: http://www.mavf.com

Newspring Ventures
100 W. Elm St., Ste. 101
Conshohocken, PA 19428
(610)567-2380
Fax: (610)567-2388
Website: http://www.news
printventures.com

Patricof & Co. Ventures, Inc.
455 S. Gulph Rd., Ste. 410
King of Prussia, PA 19406
(610)265-0286
Fax: (610)265-4959
Website: http://www.patricof.com

Loyalhanna Venture Fund
527 Cedar Way, Ste. 104
Oakmont, PA 15139
(412)820-7035
Fax: (412)820-7036

Innovest Group Inc.
2000 Market St., Ste. 1400
Philadelphia, PA 19103
(215)564-3960
Fax: (215)569-3272

Keystone Venture Capital Management Co.
1601 Market St., Ste. 2500
Philadelphia, PA 19103
(215)241-1200
Fax: (215)241-1211
Website: http://www.keystonevc.com

Liberty Venture Partners
2005 Market St., Ste. 200
Philadelphia, PA 19103
(215)282-4484
Fax: (215)282-4485
E-mail: info@libertyvp.com
Website: http://www.libertyvp.com

Penn Janney Fund, Inc.
1801 Market St., 11th Fl.
Philadelphia, PA 19103

(215)665-4447
Fax: (215)557-0820

Philadelphia Ventures, Inc.
The Bellevue
200 S. Broad St.
Philadelphia, PA 19102
(215)732-4445
Fax: (215)732-4644

Birchmere Ventures Inc.
2000 Technology Dr.
Pittsburgh, PA 15219-3109
(412)803-8000
Fax: (412)687-8139
Website: http://www.birchmerevc.com

CEO Venture Fund
2000 Technology Dr., Ste. 160
Pittsburgh, PA 15219-3109
(412)687-3451
Fax: (412)687-8139
E-mail: ceofund@aol.com
Website: http://www.ceoventure
fund.com

Innovation Works Inc.
2000 Technology Dr., Ste. 250
Pittsburgh, PA 15219
(412)681-1520
Fax: (412)681-2625
Website: http://www.innovation
works.org

Keystone Minority Capital Fund L.P.
1801 Centre Ave., Ste. 201
Williams Sq.
Pittsburgh, PA 15219
(412)338-2230
Fax: (412)338-2224

Mellon Ventures, Inc.
One Mellon Bank Ctr., Rm. 3500
Pittsburgh, PA 15258
(412)236-3594
Fax: (412)236-3593
Website: http://www.mellon
ventures.com

Pennsylvania Growth Fund
5850 Ellsworth Ave., Ste. 303
Pittsburgh, PA 15232
(412)661-1000
Fax: (412)361-0676

Point Venture Partners
The Century Bldg.
130 Seventh St., 7th Fl.
Pittsburgh, PA 15222
(412)261-1966
Fax: (412)261-1718

Cross Atlantic Capital Partners
5 Radnor Corporate Center, Ste. 555
Radnor, PA 19087
(610)995-2650
Fax: (610)971-2062
Website: http://www.xacp.com

Meridian Venture Partners (Radnor)
The Radnor Court Bldg., Ste. 140
259 Radnor-Chester Rd.
Radnor, PA 19087
(610)254-2999
Fax: (610)254-2996
E-mail: mvpart@ix.netcom.com

TDH
919 Conestoga Rd., Bldg. 1, Ste. 301
Rosemont, PA 19010
(610)526-9970
Fax: (610)526-9971

Adams Capital Management
500 Blackburn Ave.
Sewickley, PA 15143
(412)749-9454
Fax: (412)749-9459
Website: http://www.acm.com

S.R. One, Ltd.
Four Tower Bridge
200 Barr Harbor Dr., Ste. 250
W. Conshohocken, PA 19428
(610)567-1000
Fax: (610)567-1039

Greater Philadelphia Venture Capital Corp.
351 East Conestoga Rd.
Wayne, PA 19087
(610)688-6829
Fax: (610)254-8958

PA Early Stage
435 Devon Park Dr., Bldg. 500, Ste. 510
Wayne, PA 19087
(610)293-4075
Fax: (610)254-4240
Website: http://www.paearlystage.com

The Sandhurst Venture Fund, L.P.
351 E. Constoga Rd.
Wayne, PA 19087
(610)254-8900
Fax: (610)254-8958

TL Ventures
700 Bldg.
435 Devon Park Dr.
Wayne, PA 19087-1990
(610)975-3765
Fax: (610)254-4210
Website: http://www.tlventures.com

Rockhill Ventures, Inc.
100 Front St., Ste. 1350
West Conshohocken, PA 19428
(610)940-0300
Fax: (610)940-0301

Puerto Rico

Advent-Morro Equity Partners
Banco Popular Bldg.
206 Tetuan St., Ste. 903
San Juan, PR 00902
(787)725-5285
Fax: (787)721-1735

North America Investment Corp.
Mercantil Plaza, Ste. 813
PO Box 191831
San Juan, PR 00919
(787)754-6178
Fax: (787)754-6181

Rhode Island

Manchester Humphreys, Inc.
40 Westminster St., Ste. 900
Providence, RI 02903
(401)454-0400
Fax: (401)454-0403

Navis Partners
50 Kennedy Plaza, 12th Fl.
Providence, RI 02903
(401)278-6770
Fax: (401)278-6387
Website: http://www.navis
partners.com

South Carolina

Capital Insights, L.L.C.
PO Box 27162
Greenville, SC 29616-2162
(864)242-6832
Fax: (864)242-6755
E-mail: jwarner@capitalinsights.com
Website: http://www.capitalin
sights.com

Transamerica Mezzanine Financing
7 N. Laurens St., Ste. 603
Greenville, SC 29601
(864)232-6198
Fax: (864)241-4444

Tennessee

Valley Capital Corp.
Krystal Bldg.
100 W. Martin Luther King Blvd.,
Ste. 212

Chattanooga, TN 37402
(423)265-1557
Fax: (423)265-1588

Coleman Swenson Booth Inc.
237 2nd Ave. S
Franklin, TN 37064-2649
(615)791-9462
Fax: (615)791-9636
Website: http://
www.colemanswenson.com

Capital Services & Resources, Inc.
5159 Wheelis Dr., Ste. 106
Memphis, TN 38117
(901)761-2156
Fax: (907)767-0060

Paradigm Capital Partners LLC
6410 Poplar Ave., Ste. 395
Memphis, TN 38119
(901)682-6060
Fax: (901)328-3061

SSM Ventures
845 Crossover Ln., Ste. 140
Memphis, TN 38117
(901)767-1131
Fax: (901)767-1135
Website: http://www.ssm
ventures.com

Capital Across America L.P.
501 Union St., Ste. 201
Nashville, TN 37219
(615)254-1414
Fax: (615)254-1856
Website: http://
www.capitalacrossamerica.com

Equitas L.P.
2000 Glen Echo Rd., Ste. 101
PO Box 158838
Nashville, TN 37215-8838
(615)383-8673
Fax: (615)383-8693

Massey Burch Capital Corp.
One Burton Hills Blvd., Ste. 350
Nashville, TN 37215
(615)665-3221
Fax: (615)665-3240
E-mail: tcalton@masseyburch.com
Website: http://www.masseyburch.com

Nelson Capital Corp.
3401 West End Ave., Ste. 300
Nashville, TN 37203
(615)292-8787
Fax: (615)385-3150

Texas

Phillips-Smith Specialty Retail Group
5080 Spectrum Dr., Ste. 805 W
Addison, TX 75001
(972)387-0725
Fax: (972)458-2560
E-mail: pssrg@aol.com
Website: http://www.phillips-smith.com

Austin Ventures, L.P.
701 Brazos St., Ste. 1400
Austin, TX 78701
(512)485-1900
Fax: (512)476-3952
E-mail: info@ausven.com
Website: http://www.austinventures.com

The Capital Network
3925 West Braker Lane, Ste. 406
Austin, TX 78759-5321
(512)305-0826
Fax: (512)305-0836

Techxas Ventures LLC
5000 Plaza on the Lake
Austin, TX 78746
(512)343-0118
Fax: (512)343-1879
E-mail: bruce@techxas.com
Website: http://www.techxas.com

Alliance Financial of Houston
218 Heather Ln.
Conroe, TX 77385-9013
(936)447-3300
Fax: (936)447-4222

Amerimark Capital Corp.
1111 W. Mockingbird, Ste. 1111
Dallas, TX 75247
(214)638-7878
Fax: (214)638-7612
E-mail: amerimark@amcapital.com
Website: http://www.amcapital.com

AMT Venture Partners / AMT Capital Ltd.
5220 Spring Valley Rd., Ste. 600
Dallas, TX 75240
(214)905-9757
Fax: (214)905-9761
Website: http://www.amtcapital.com

Arkoma Venture Partners
5950 Berkshire Lane, Ste. 1400
Dallas, TX 75225
(214)739-3515
Fax: (214)739-3572
E-mail: joelf@arkomavp.com

Capital Southwest Corp.
12900 Preston Rd., Ste. 700
Dallas, TX 75230
(972)233-8242
Fax: (972)233-7362
Website: http://
www.capitalsouthwest.com

Dali, Hook Partners
One Lincoln Center, Ste. 1550
5400 LBJ Freeway
Dallas, TX 75240
(972)991-5457
Fax: (972)991-5458
E-mail: dhook@hookpartners.com
Website: http://www.hookpartners.com

HO2 Partners
Two Galleria Tower
13455 Noel Rd., Ste. 1670
Dallas, TX 75240
(972)702-1144
Fax: (972)702-8234
Website: http://www.ho2.com

Interwest Partners (Dallas)
2 Galleria Tower
13455 Noel Rd., Ste. 1670
Dallas, TX 75240
(972)392-7279
Fax: (972)490-6348
Website: http://www.interwest.com

Kahala Investments, Inc.
8214 Westchester Dr., Ste. 715
Dallas, TX 75225
(214)987-0077
Fax: (214)987-2332

MESBIC Ventures Holding Co.
2435 North Central Expressway, Ste. 200
Dallas, TX 75080
(972)991-1597
Fax: (972)991-4770
Website: http://www.mvhc.com

North Texas MESBIC, Inc.
9500 Forest Lane, Ste. 430
Dallas, TX 75243
(214)221-3565
Fax: (214)221-3566

Richard Jaffe & Company, Inc,
7318 Royal Cir.
Dallas, TX 75230
(214)265-9397
Fax: (214)739-1845

Sevin Rosen Management Co.
13455 Noel Rd., Ste. 1670
Dallas, TX 75240

(972)702-1100
Fax: (972)702-1103
E-mail: info@srfunds.com
Website: http://www.srfunds.com

Stratford Capital Partners, L.P.
300 Crescent Ct., Ste. 500
Dallas, TX 75201
(214)740-7377
Fax: (214)720-7393
E-mail: stratcap@hmtf.com

Sunwestern Investment Group
12221 Merit Dr., Ste. 935
Dallas, TX 75251
(972)239-5650
Fax: (972)701-0024

Wingate Partners
750 N. St. Paul St., Ste. 1200
Dallas, TX 75201
(214)720-1313
Fax: (214)871-8799

Buena Venture Associates
201 Main St., 32nd Fl.
Fort Worth, TX 76102
(817)339-7400
Fax: (817)390-8408
Website: http://www.buenaventure.com

The Catalyst Group
3 Riverway, Ste. 770
Houston, TX 77056
(713)623-8133
Fax: (713)623-0473
E-mail: herman@thecatalystgroup.net
Website: http://www.thecatalyst
group.net

Cureton & Co., Inc.
1100 Louisiana, Ste. 3250
Houston, TX 77002
(713)658-9806
Fax: (713)658-0476

Davis, Tuttle Venture Partners (Dallas)
8 Greenway Plaza, Ste. 1020
Houston, TX 77046
(713)993-0440
Fax: (713)621-2297
Website: http://www.davistuttle.com

Houston Partners
401 Louisiana, 8th Fl.
Houston, TX 77002
(713)222-8600
Fax: (713)222-8932

Southwest Venture Group
10878 Westheimer, Ste. 178

Houston, TX 77042
(713)827-8947
(713)461-1470

AM Fund
4600 Post Oak Place, Ste. 100
Houston, TX 77027
(713)627-9111
Fax: (713)627-9119

Ventex Management, Inc.
3417 Milam St.
Houston, TX 77002-9531
(713)659-7870
Fax: (713)659-7855

MBA Venture Group
1004 Olde Town Rd., Ste. 102
Irving, TX 75061
(972)986-6703

First Capital Group Management Co.
750 East Mulberry St., Ste. 305
PO Box 15616
San Antonio, TX 78212
(210)736-4233
Fax: (210)736-5449

The Southwest Venture Partnerships
16414 San Pedro, Ste. 345
San Antonio, TX 78232
(210)402-1200
Fax: (210)402-1221
E-mail: swvp@aol.com

Medtech International Inc.
1742 Carriageway
Sugarland, TX 77478
(713)980-8474
Fax: (713)980-6343

Utah

First Security Business Investment Corp.
15 East 100 South, Ste. 100
Salt Lake City, UT 84111
(801)246-5737
Fax: (801)246-5740

Utah Ventures II, L.P.
423 Wakara Way, Ste. 206
Salt Lake City, UT 84108
(801)583-5922
Fax: (801)583-4105
Website: http://www.uven.com

Wasatch Venture Corp.
1 S. Main St., Ste. 1400
Salt Lake City, UT 84133
(801)524-8939

Fax: (801)524-8941
E-mail: mail@wasatchvc.com

Vermont

North Atlantic Capital Corp.
76 Saint Paul St., Ste. 600
Burlington, VT 05401
(802)658-7820
Fax: (802)658-5757
Website: http://www.north
atlanticcapital.com

Green Mountain Advisors Inc.
PO Box 1230
Quechee, VT 05059
(802)296-7800
Fax: (802)296-6012
Website: http://www.gmtcap.com

Virginia

Oxford Financial Services Corp.
Alexandria, VA 22314
(703)519-4900
Fax: (703)519-4910
E-mail: oxford133@aol.com

Continental SBIC
4141 N. Henderson Rd.
Arlington, VA 22203
(703)527-5200
Fax: (703)527-3700

Novak Biddle Venture Partners
1750 Tysons Blvd., Ste. 1190
McLean, VA 22102
(703)847-3770
Fax: (703)847-3771
E-mail: roger@novakbiddle.com
Website: http://www.novakbiddle.com

Spacevest
11911 Freedom Dr., Ste. 500
Reston, VA 20190
(703)904-9800
Fax: (703)904-0571
E-mail: spacevest@spacevest.com
Website: http://www.spacevest.com

Virginia Capital
1801 Libbie Ave., Ste. 201
Richmond, VA 23226
(804)648-4802
Fax: (804)648-4809
E-mail: webmaster@vacapital.com
Website: http://www.vacapital.com

Calvert Social Venture Partners
402 Maple Ave. W
Vienna, VA 22180

(703)255-4930
Fax: (703)255-4931
E-mail: calven2000@aol.com

Fairfax Partners
8000 Towers Crescent Dr., Ste. 940
Vienna, VA 22182
(703)847-9486
Fax: (703)847-0911

Global Internet Ventures
8150 Leesburg Pike, Ste. 1210
Vienna, VA 22182
(703)442-3300
Fax: (703)442-3388
Website: http://www.givinc.com

Walnut Capital Corp. (Vienna)
8000 Towers Crescent Dr., Ste. 1070
Vienna, VA 22182
(703)448-3771
Fax: (703)448-7751

Washington

Encompass Ventures
777 108th Ave. NE, Ste. 2300
Bellevue, WA 98004
(425)486-3900
Fax: (425)486-3901
E-mail: info@evpartners.com
Website: http://www.encom
passventures.com

Fluke Venture Partners
11400 SE Sixth St., Ste. 230
Bellevue, WA 98004
(425)453-4590
Fax: (425)453-4675
E-mail: gabelein@flukeventures.com
Website: http://www.flukeventures.com

Pacific Northwest Partners SBIC, L.P.
15352 SE 53rd St.
Bellevue, WA 98006
(425)455-9967
Fax: (425)455-9404

Materia Venture Associates, L.P.
3435 Carillon Pointe
Kirkland, WA 98033-7354
(425)822-4100
Fax: (425)827-4086

OVP Venture Partners (Kirkland)
2420 Carillon Pt.
Kirkland, WA 98033
(425)889-9192
Fax: (425)889-0152
E-mail: info@ovp.com
Website: http://www.ovp.com

Digital Partners
999 3rd Ave., Ste. 1610
Seattle, WA 98104
(206)405-3607
Fax: (206)405-3617
Website: http://www.digitalpartners.com

Frazier & Company
601 Union St., Ste. 3300
Seattle, WA 98101
(206)621-7200
Fax: (206)621-1848
E-mail: jon@frazierco.com

Kirlan Venture Capital, Inc.
221 First Ave. W, Ste. 108
Seattle, WA 98119-4223
(206)281-8610
Fax: (206)285-3451
Website: http://www.kirlanventure.com

Phoenix Partners
1000 2nd Ave., Ste. 3600
Seattle, WA 98104
(206)624-8968
Fax: (206)624-1907

Voyager Capital
800 5th St., Ste. 4100
Seattle, WA 98103
(206)470-1180
Fax: (206)470-1185
E-mail: info@voyagercap.com
Website: http://www.voyagercap.com

Northwest Venture Associates
221 N. Wall St., Ste. 628
Spokane, WA 99201
(509)747-0728
Fax: (509)747-0758
Website: http://www.nwva.com

Wisconsin

Venture Investors Management, L.L.C.
University Research Park
505 S. Rosa Rd.
Madison, WI 53719
(608)441-2700
Fax: (608)441-2727
E-mail: roger@ventureinvestors.com
Website: http://www.venture
investers.com

Capital Investments, Inc.
1009 West Glen Oaks Lane, Ste. 103
Mequon, WI 53092
(414)241-0303
Fax: (414)241-8451
Website: http://
www.capitalinvestmentsinc.com

Future Value Venture, Inc.
2745 N. Martin Luther King
Dr., Ste. 204
Milwaukee, WI 53212-2300
(414)264-2252
Fax: (414)264-2253
E-mail: fvvventures@aol.com
William Beckett, President

Lubar and Co., Inc.
700 N. Water St., Ste. 1200
Milwaukee, WI 53202
(414)291-9000
Fax: (414)291-9061

GCI
20875 Crossroads Cir., Ste. 100
Waukesha, WI 53186
(262)798-5080
Fax: (262)798-5087

Glossary of Small Business Terms

Absolute liability
Liability that is incurred due to product defects or negligent actions. Manufacturers or retail establishments are held responsible, even though the defect or action may not have been intentional or negligent.

ACE
See Active Corps of Executives

Accident and health benefits
Benefits offered to employees and their families in order to offset the costs associated with accidental death, accidental injury, or sickness.

Account statement
A record of transactions, including payments, new debt, and deposits, incurred during a defined period of time.

Accounting system
System capturing the costs of all employees and/or machinery included in business expenses.

Accounts payable
See Trade credit

Accounts receivable
Unpaid accounts which arise from unsettled claims and transactions from the sale of a company's products or services to its customers.

Active Corps of Executives (ACE)
A group of volunteers for a management assistance program of the U.S. Small Business Administration; volunteers provide one-on-one counseling and teach workshops and seminars for small firms.

ADA
See Americans with Disabilities Act

Adaptation
The process whereby an invention is modified to meet the needs of users.

Adaptive engineering
The process whereby an invention is modified to meet the manufacturing and commercial requirements of a targeted market.

Adverse selection
The tendency for higher-risk individuals to purchase health care and more comprehensive plans, resulting in increased costs.

Advertising
A marketing tool used to capture public attention and influence purchasing decisions for a product or service. Utilizes various forms of media to generate consumer response, such as flyers, magazines, newspapers, radio, and television.

Age discrimination
The denial of the rights and privileges of employment based solely on the age of an individual.

Agency costs
Costs incurred to insure that the lender or investor maintains control over assets while allowing the borrower or entrepreneur to use them. Monitoring and information costs are the two major types of agency costs.

Agribusiness
The production and sale of commodities and products from the commercial farming industry.

America Online
An online service which is accessible by computer modem. The service features Internet access, bulletin boards, online periodicals, electronic mail, and other services for subscribers.

Americans with Disabilities Act (ADA)
Law designed to ensure equal access and opportunity to handicapped persons.

Annual report
Yearly financial report prepared by a business that adheres to the requirements set forth by the Securities and Exchange Commission (SEC).

Antitrust immunity
Exemption from prosecution under antitrust laws. In the transportation industry, firms with antitrust immunity are permitted under certain conditions to set schedules and sometimes prices for the public benefit.

Applied research
Scientific study targeted for use in a product or process.

Asians
A minority category used by the U.S. Bureau of the Census to represent a diverse group that includes Aleuts, Eskimos, American Indians, Asian Indians, Chinese, Japanese, Koreans, Vietnamese, Filipinos, Hawaiians, and other Pacific Islanders.

Assets
Anything of value owned by a company.

Audit
The verification of accounting records and business procedures conducted by an outside accounting service.

Average cost
Total production costs divided by the quantity produced.

Balance Sheet
A financial statement listing the total assets and liabilities of a company at a given time.

Bankruptcy
The condition in which a business cannot meet its debt obligations and petitions a federal district court either for reorganization of its debts (Chapter 11) or for liquidation of its assets (Chapter 7).

Basic research
Theoretical scientific exploration not targeted to application.

Basket clause
A provision specifying the amount of public pension funds that may be placed in investments not included on a state's legal list (see separate citation).

BBS
See Bulletin Board Service

BDC
See Business development corporation

Benefit
Various services, such as health care, flextime, day care, insurance, and vacation, offered to employees as part of a hiring package. Typically subsidized in whole or in part by the business.

BIDCO
See Business and industrial development company

Billing cycle
A system designed to evenly distribute customer billing throughout the month, preventing clerical backlogs.

Birth
See Business birth

Blue chip security
A low-risk, low-yield security representing an interest in a very stable company.

Blue sky laws
A general term that denotes various states' laws regulating securities.

Bond
A written instrument executed by a bidder or contractor (the principal) and a second party (the surety or sureties) to assure fulfillment of the principal's obligations to a third party (the obligee or government) identified in the bond. If the principal's obligations are not met, the bond assures payment to the extent stipulated of any loss sustained by the obligee.

Bonding requirements
Terms contained in a bond (see separate citation).

Bonus
An amount of money paid to an employee as a reward for achieving certain business goals or objectives.

Brainstorming
A group session where employees contribute their ideas for solving a problem or meeting a company objective without fear of retribution or ridicule.

Brand name
The part of a brand, trademark, or service mark that can be spoken. It can be a word, letter, or group of words or letters.

Bridge financing
A short-term loan made in expectation of intermediateterm or long-term financing. Can be used when a company plans to go public in the near future.

Broker
One who matches resources available for innovation with those who need them.

Budget
An estimate of the spending necessary to complete a project or offer a service in comparison to cash-on-hand and expected earnings for the coming year, with an emphasis on cost control.

Bulletin Board Service (BBS)
An online service enabling users to communicate with each other about specific topics.

Business and industrial development company (BIDCO)
A private, for-profit financing corporation chartered by the state to provide both equity and long-term debt capital to small business owners (see separate citations for equity and debt capital).

Business birth
The formation of a new establishment or enterprise. The appearance of a new establishment or enterprise in the Small Business Data Base (see separate citation).

Business conditions
Outside factors that can affect the financial performance of a business.

Business contractions
The number of establishments that have decreased in employment during a specified time.

Business cycle
A period of economic recession and recovery. These cycles vary in duration.

Business death
The voluntary or involuntary closure of a firm or establishment. The disappearance of an establishment or enterprise from the Small Business Data Base (see separate citation).

Business development corporation (BDC)
A business financing agency, usually composed of the financial institutions in an area or state, organized to assist in financing businesses unable to obtain assistance through normal channels; the risk is spread among various members of the business development corporation, and interest rates may vary somewhat from those charged by member institutions. A venture capital firm in which shares of ownership are publicly held and to which the Investment Act of 1940 applics.

Business dissolution
For enumeration purposes, the absence of a business that was present in the prior time period from any current record.

Business entry
See Business birth

Business ethics
Moral values and principles espoused by members of the business community as a guide to fair and honest business practices.

Business exit
See Business death

Business expansions
The number of establishments that added employees during a specified time.

Business failure
Closure of a business causing a loss to at least one creditor.

Business format franchising
The purchase of the name, trademark, and an ongoing business plan of the parent corporation or franchisor by the franchisee.

Business license
A legal authorization issued by municipal and state governments and required for business operations.

Business name
Enterprises must register their business names with local governments usually on a "doing business as" (DBA) form. (This name is sometimes referred to as a

"fictional name.") The procedure is part of the business licensing process and prevents any other business from using that same name for a similar business in the same locality.

Business norms
See Financial ratios

Business permit
See Business license

Business plan
A document that spells out a company's expected course of action for a specified period, usually including a detailed listing and analysis of risks and uncertainties. For the small business, it should examine the proposed products, the market, the industry, the management policies, the marketing policies, production needs, and financial needs. Frequently, it is used as a prospectus for potential investors and lenders.

Business proposal
See Business plan

Business service firm
An establishment primarily engaged in rendering services to other business organizations on a fee or contract basis.

Business start
For enumeration purposes, a business with a name or similar designation that did not exist in a prior time period.

Cafeteria plan
See Flexible benefit plan

Capacity
Level of a firm's, industry's, or nation's output corresponding to full practical utilization of available resources.

Capital
Assets less liabilities, representing the ownership interest in a business. A stock of accumulated goods, especially at a specified time and in contrast to income received during a specified time period. Accumulated goods devoted to production. Accumulated possessions calculated to bring income.

Capital expenditure
Expenses incurred by a business for improvements that will depreciate over time.

Capital gain
The monetary difference between the purchase price and the selling price of capital. Capital gains are taxed at a rate of 28% by the federal government.

Capital intensity
The relative importance of capital in the production process, usually expressed as the ratio of capital to labor but also sometimes as the ratio of capital to output.

Capital resource
The equipment, facilities and labor used to create products and services.

Caribbean Basin Initiative
An interdisciplinary program to support commerce among the businesses in the nations of the Caribbean Basin and the United States. Agencies involved include: the Agency for International Development, the U.S. Small Business Administration, the International Trade Administration of the U.S. Department of Commerce, and various private sector groups.

Catastrophic care
Medical and other services for acute and long-term illnesses that cost more than insurance coverage limits or that cost the amount most families may be expected to pay with their own resources.

CDC
See Certified development corporation

CD-ROM
Compact disc with read-only memory used to store large amounts of digitized data.

Certified development corporation (CDC)
A local area or statewide corporation or authority (for profit or nonprofit) that packages U.S. Small Business Administration (SBA), bank, state, and/or private money into financial assistance for existing business capital improvements. The SBA holds the second lien on its maximum share of 40 percent involvement. Each state has at least one certified development corporation. This program is called the SBA 504 Program.

Certified lenders

Banks that participate in the SBA guaranteed loan program (see separate citation). Such banks must have a good track record with the U.S. Small Business Administration (SBA) and must agree to certain conditions set forth by the agency. In return, the SBA agrees to process any guaranteed loan application within three business days.

Champion

An advocate for the development of an innovation.

Channel of distribution

The means used to transport merchandise from the manufacturer to the consumer.

Chapter 7 of the 1978 Bankruptcy Act

Provides for a court-appointed trustee who is responsible for liquidating a company's assets in order to settle outstanding debts.

Chapter 11 of the 1978 Bankruptcy Act

Allows the business owners to retain control of the company while working with their creditors to reorganize their finances and establish better business practices to prevent liquidation of assets.

Closely held corporation

A corporation in which the shares are held by a few persons, usually officers, employees, or others close to the management; these shares are rarely offered to the public.

Code of Federal Regulations

Codification of general and permanent rules of the federal government published in the Federal Register.

Code sharing

See Computer code sharing

Coinsurance

Upon meeting the deductible payment, health insurance participants may be required to make additional health care cost-sharing payments. Coinsurance is a payment of a fixed percentage of the cost of each service; copayment is usually a fixed amount to be paid with each service.

Collateral

Securities, evidence of deposit, or other property pledged by a borrower to secure repayment of a loan.

Collective ratemaking

The establishment of uniform charges for services by a group of businesses in the same industry.

Commercial insurance plan

See Underwriting

Commercial loans

Short-term renewable loans used to finance specific capital needs of a business.

Commercialization

The final stage of the innovation process, including production and distribution.

Common stock

The most frequently used instrument for purchasing ownership in private or public companies. Common stock generally carries the right to vote on certain corporate actions and may pay dividends, although it rarely does in venture investments. In liquidation, common stockholders are the last to share in the proceeds from the sale of a corporation's assets; bondholders and preferred shareholders have priority. Common stock is often used in firstround start-up financing.

Community development corporation

A corporation established to develop economic programs for a community and, in most cases, to provide financial support for such development.

Competitor

A business whose product or service is marketed for the same purpose/use and to the same consumer group as the product or service of another.

Computer code sharing

An arrangement whereby flights of a regional airline are identified by the two-letter code of a major carrier in the computer reservation system to help direct passengers to new regional carriers.

Consignment

A merchandising agreement, usually referring to secondhand shops, where the dealer pays the owner of an item a percentage of the profit when the item is sold.

Consortium

A coalition of organizations such as banks and corporations for ventures requiring large capital resources.

Consultant
An individual that is paid by a business to provide advice and expertise in a particular area.

Consumer price index
A measure of the fluctuation in prices between two points in time.

Consumer research
Research conducted by a business to obtain information about existing or potential consumer markets.

Continuation coverage
Health coverage offered for a specified period of time to employees who leave their jobs and to their widows, divorced spouses, or dependents.

Contractions
See Business contractions

Convertible preferred stock
A class of stock that pays a reasonable dividend and is convertible into common stock (see separate citation). Generally the convertible feature may only be exercised after being held for a stated period of time. This arrangement is usually considered second-round financing when a company needs equity to maintain its cash flow.

Convertible securities
A feature of certain bonds, debentures, or preferred stocks that allows them to be exchanged by the owner for another class of securities at a future date and in accordance with any other terms of the issue.

Copayment
See Coinsurance

Copyright
A legal form of protection available to creators and authors to safeguard their works from unlawful use or claim of ownership by others. Copyrights may be acquired for works of art, sculpture, music, and published or unpublished manuscripts. All copyrights should be registered at the Copyright Office of the Library of Congress.

Corporate financial ratios
The relationship between key figures found in a company's financial statement expressed as a numeric value. Used to evaluate risk and company performance. Also known as Financial averages, Operating ratios, and Business ratios.

Corporation
A legal entity, chartered by a state or the federal government, recognized as a separate entity having its own rights, privileges, and liabilities distinct from those of its members.

Cost containment
Actions taken by employers and insurers to curtail rising health care costs; for example, increasing employee cost sharing (see separate citation), requiring second opinions, or preadmission screening.

Cost sharing
The requirement that health care consumers contribute to their own medical care costs through deductibles and coinsurance (see separate citations). Cost sharing does not include the amounts paid in premiums. It is used to control utilization of services; for example, requiring a fixed amount to be paid with each health care service.

Cottage industry
Businesses based in the home in which the family members are the labor force and family-owned equipment is used to process the goods.

Credit Rating
A letter or number calculated by an organization (such as Dun & Bradstreet) to represent the ability and disposition of a business to meet its financial obligations.

Customer service
Various techniques used to ensure the satisfaction of a customer.

Cyclical peak
The upper turning point in a business cycle.

Cyclical trough
The lower turning point in a business cycle.

DBA
See Business name

Death
See Business death

Debenture
A certificate given as acknowledgment of a debt (see separate citation) secured by the general credit of the issuing corporation. A bond, usually without security, issued by a corporation and sometimes convertible to common stock.

Debt
Something owed by one person to another. Financing in which a company receives capital that must be repaid; no ownership is transferred.

Debt capital
Business financing that normally requires periodic interest payments and repayment of the principal within a specified time.

Debt financing
See Debt capital

Debt securities
Loans such as bonds and notes that provide a specified rate of return for a specified period of time.

Deductible
A set amount that an individual must pay before any benefits are received.

Demand shock absorbers
A term used to describe the role that some small firms play by expanding their output levels to accommodate a transient surge in demand.

Demographics
Statistics on various markets, including age, income, and education, used to target specific products or services to appropriate consumer groups.

Demonstration
Showing that a product or process has been modified sufficiently to meet the needs of users.

Deregulation
The lifting of government restrictions; for example, the lifting of government restrictions on the entry of new businesses, the expansion of services, and the setting of prices in particular industries.

Desktop Publishing
Using personal computers and specialized software to produce camera-ready copy for publications.

Disaster loans
Various types of physical and economic assistance available to individuals and businesses through the U.S. Small Business Administration (SBA). This is the only SBA loan program available for residential purposes.

Discrimination
The denial of the rights and privileges of employment based on factors such as age, race, religion, or gender.

Diseconomies of scale
The condition in which the costs of production increase faster than the volume of production.

Dissolution
See Business dissolution

Distribution
Delivering a product or process to the user.

Distributor
One who delivers merchandise to the user.

Diversified company
A company whose products and services are used by several different markets.

Doing business as (DBA)
See Business name

Dow Jones
An information services company that publishes the Wall Street Journal and other sources of financial information.

Dow Jones Industrial Average
An indicator of stock market performance.

Earned income
A tax term that refers to wages and salaries earned by the recipient, as opposed to monies earned through interest and dividends.

Economic efficiency
The use of productive resources to the fullest practical extent in the provision of the set of goods and services that is most preferred by purchasers in the economy.

Economic indicators
Statistics used to express the state of the economy. These include the length of the average work week, the rate of unemployment, and stock prices.

Economically disadvantaged
See Socially and economically disadvantaged

Economies of scale
See Scale economies

EEOC
See Equal Employment Opportunity Commission

8(a) Program
A program authorized by the Small Business Act that directs federal contracts to small businesses owned and operated by socially and economically disadvantaged individuals.

Electronic mail (e-mail)
The electronic transmission of mail via phone lines.

E-mail
See Electronic mail

Employee leasing
A contract by which employers arrange to have their workers hired by a leasing company and then leased back to them for a management fee. The leasing company typically assumes the administrative burden of payroll and provides a benefit package to the workers.

Employee tenure
The length of time an employee works for a particular employer.

Employer identification number
The business equivalent of a social security number. Assigned by the U.S. Internal Revenue Service.

Enterprise
An aggregation of all establishments owned by a parent company. An enterprise may consist of a single, independent establishment or include subsidiaries and other branches under the same ownership and control.

Enterprise zone
A designated area, usually found in inner cities and other areas with significant unemployment, where businesses receive tax credits and other incentives to entice them to establish operations there.

Entrepreneur
A person who takes the risk of organizing and operating a new business venture.

Entry
See Business entry

Equal Employment Opportunity Commission (EEOC)
A federal agency that ensures nondiscrimination in the hiring and firing practices of a business.

Equal opportunity employer
An employer who adheres to the standards set by the Equal Employment Opportunity Commission (see separate citation).

Equity
The ownership interest. Financing in which partial or total ownership of a company is surrendered in exchange for capital. An investor's financial return comes from dividend payments and from growth in the net worth of the business.

Equity capital
See Equity; Equity midrisk venture capital

Equity financing
See Equity; Equity midrisk venture capital

Equity midrisk venture capital
An unsecured investment in a company. Usually a purchase of ownership interest in a company that occurs in the later stages of a company's development.

Equity partnership
A limited partnership arrangement for providing start-up and seed capital to businesses.

Equity securities
See Equity

Equity-type
Debt financing subordinated to conventional debt.

Establishment
A single-location business unit that may be independent (a single-establishment enterprise) or owned by a parent enterprise.

Establishment and Enterprise Microdata File
See U.S. Establishment and Enterprise Microdata File

Establishment birth
See Business birth

Establishment Longitudinal Microdata File
See U.S. Establishment Longitudinal Microdata File

Ethics
See Business ethics

Evaluation
Determining the potential success of translating an invention into a product or process.

Exit
See Business exit

Experience rating
See Underwriting

Export
A product sold outside of the country.

Export license
A general or specific license granted by the U.S. Department of Commerce required of anyone wishing to export goods. Some restricted articles need approval from the U.S. Departments of State, Defense, or Energy.

Failure
See Business failure

Fair share agreement
An agreement reached between a franchisor and a minority business organization to extend business ownership to minorities by either reducing the amount of capital required or by setting aside certain marketing areas for minority business owners.

Feasibility study
A study to determine the likelihood that a proposed product or development will fulfill the objectives of a particular investor.

Federal Trade Commission (FTC)
Federal agency that promotes free enterprise and competition within the U.S.

Federal Trade Mark Act of 1946
See Lanham Act

Fictional name
See Business name

Fiduciary
An individual or group that hold assets in trust for a beneficiary.

Financial analysis
The techniques used to determine money needs in a business. Techniques include ratio analysis, calculation of return on investment, guides for measuring profitability, and break-even analysis to determine ultimate success.

Financial intermediary
A financial institution that acts as the intermediary between borrowers and lenders. Banks, savings and loan associations, finance companies, and venture capital companies are major financial intermediaries in the United States.

Financial ratios
See Corporate financial ratios; Industry financial ratios

Financial statement
A written record of business finances, including balance sheets and profit and loss statements.

Financing
See First-stage financing; Second-stage financing; Thirdstage financing

First-stage financing
Financing provided to companies that have expended their initial capital, and require funds to start full-scale manufacturing and sales. Also known as First-round financing.

Fiscal year
Any twelve-month period used by businesses for accounting purposes.

504 Program
See Certified development corporation

Flexible benefit plan
A plan that offers a choice among cash and/or qualified benefits such as group term life insurance, accident and health insurance, group legal services, dependent care assistance, and vacations.

FOB
See Free on board

Format franchising
See Business format franchising; Franchising

401(k) plan
A financial plan where employees contribute a percentage of their earnings to a fund that is invested in stocks, bonds, or money markets for the purpose of saving money for retirement.

Four Ps
Marketing terms referring to Product, Price, Place, and Promotion.

Franchising
A form of licensing by which the owner-the franchisor- distributes or markets a product, method, or service through affiliated dealers called franchisees. The product, method, or service being marketed is identified by a brand name, and the franchisor maintains control over the marketing methods employed. The franchisee is often given exclusive access to a defined geographic area.

Free on board (FOB)
A pricing term indicating that the quoted price includes the cost of loading goods into transport vessels at a specified place.

Frictional unemployment
See Unemployment

FTC
See Federal Trade Commission

Fulfillment
The systems necessary for accurate delivery of an ordered item, including subscriptions and direct marketing.

Full-time workers
Generally, those who work a regular schedule of more than 35 hours per week.

Garment registration number
A number that must appear on every garment sold in the U.S. to indicate the manufacturer of the garment, which may or may not be the same as the label under which the garment is sold. The U.S. Federal Trade Commission assigns and regulates garment registration numbers.

Gatekeeper
A key contact point for entry into a network.

GDP
See Gross domestic product

General obligation bond
A municipal bond secured by the taxing power of the municipality. The Tax Reform Act of 1986 limits the purposes for which such bonds may be issued and establishes volume limits on the extent of their issuance.

GNP
See Gross national product

Good Housekeeping Seal
Seal appearing on products that signifies the fulfillment of the standards set by the Good Housekeeping Institute to protect consumer interests.

Goods sector
All businesses producing tangible goods, including agriculture, mining, construction, and manufacturing businesses.

GPO
See Gross product originating

Gross domestic product (GDP)
The part of the nation's gross national product (see separate citation) generated by private business using resources from within the country.

Gross national product (GNP)
The most comprehensive single measure of aggregate economic output. Represents the market value of the total output of goods and services produced by a nation's economy.

Gross product originating (GPO)
A measure of business output estimated from the income or production side using employee compensation, profit income, net interest, capital consumption, and indirect business taxes.

HAL
See Handicapped assistance loan program

Handicapped assistance loan program (HAL)
Low-interest direct loan program through the U.S. Small Business Administration (SBA) for handicapped persons. The SBA requires that these persons demonstrate that their disability is such that it is impossible for them to secure employment, thus making it necessary to go into their own business to make a living.

Health maintenance organization (HMO)
Organization of physicians and other health care professionals that provides health services to subscribers and their dependents on a prepaid basis.

Health provider
An individual or institution that gives medical care. Under Medicare, an institutional provider is a hospital, skilled nursing facility, home health agency, or provider of certain physical therapy services.

Hispanic
A person of Cuban, Mexican, Puerto Rican, Latin American (Central or South American), European Spanish, or other Spanish-speaking origin or ancestry.

HMO
See Health maintenance organization

Home-based business
A business with an operating address that is also a residential address (usually the residential address of the proprietor).

Hub-and-spoke system
A system in which flights of an airline from many different cities (the spokes) converge at a single airport (the hub). After allowing passengers sufficient time to make connections, planes then depart for different cities.

Human Resources Management
A business program designed to oversee recruiting, pay, benefits, and other issues related to the company's work force, including planning to determine the optimal use of labor to increase production, thereby increasing profit.

Idea
An original concept for a new product or process.

Import
Products produced outside the country in which they are consumed.

Income
Money or its equivalent, earned or accrued, resulting from the sale of goods and services.

Income statement
A financial statement that lists the profits and losses of a company at a given time.

Incorporation
The filing of a certificate of incorporation with a state's secretary of state, thereby limiting the business owner's liability.

Incubator
A facility designed to encourage entrepreneurship and minimize obstacles to new business formation and growth, particularly for high-technology firms, by housing a number of fledgling enterprises that share an array of services, such as meeting areas, secretarial services, accounting, research library, on-site financial and management counseling, and word processing facilities.

Independent contractor
An individual considered self-employed (see separate citation) and responsible for paying Social Security taxes and income taxes on earnings.

Indirect health coverage
Health insurance obtained through another individual's health care plan; for example, a spouse's employersponsored plan.

Industrial development authority
The financial arm of a state or other political subdivision established for the purpose of financing economic development in an area, usually through loans to nonprofit organizations, which in turn provide facilities for manufacturing and other industrial operations.

Industry financial ratios
Corporate financial ratios averaged for a specified industry. These are used for comparison purposes and reveal industry trends and identify differences between the performance of a specific company and the performance of its industry. Also known as Industrial averages, Industry ratios, Financial averages, and Business or Industrial norms.

Inflation
Increases in volume of currency and credit, generally resulting in a sharp and continuing rise in price levels.

Informal capital
Financing from informal, unorganized sources; includes informal debt capital such as trade credit or loans from friends and relatives and equity capital from informal investors.

Initial public offering (IPO)
A corporation's first offering of stock to the public.

Innovation
The introduction of a new idea into the marketplace in the form of a new product or service or an improvement in organization or process.

Intellectual property
Any idea or work that can be considered proprietary in nature and is thus protected from infringement by others.

Internal capital
Debt or equity financing obtained from the owner or through retained business earnings.

Internet
A government-designed computer network that contains large amounts of information and is accessible through various vendors for a fee.

Intrapreneurship
The state of employing entrepreneurial principles to nonentrepreneurial situations.

Invention
The tangible form of a technological idea, which could include a laboratory prototype, drawings, formulas, etc.

IPO
See Initial public offering

Job description
The duties and responsibilities required in a particular position.

Job tenure
A period of time during which an individual is continuously employed in the same job.

Joint marketing agreements
Agreements between regional and major airlines, often involving the coordination of flight schedules, fares, and baggage transfer. These agreements help regional carriers operate at lower cost.

Joint venture
Venture in which two or more people combine efforts in a particular business enterprise, usually a single transaction or a limited activity, and agree to share the profits and losses jointly or in proportion to their contributions.

Keogh plan
Designed for self-employed persons and unincorporated businesses as a tax-deferred pension account.

Labor force
Civilians considered eligible for employment who are also willing and able to work.

Labor force participation rate
The civilian labor force as a percentage of the civilian population.

Labor intensity
The relative importance of labor in the production process, usually measured as the capital-labor ratio; i.e., the ratio of units of capital (typically, dollars of tangible assets) to the number of employees. The higher the capital-labor ratio exhibited by a firm or industry, the lower the capital intensity of that firm or industry is said to be.

Labor surplus area
An area in which there exists a high unemployment rate. In procurement (see separate citation), extra points are given to firms in counties that are designated a labor surplus area; this information is requested on procurement bid sheets.

Labor union
An organization of similarly-skilled workers who collectively bargain with management over the conditions of employment.

Laboratory prototype
See Prototype

LAN
See Local Area Network

Lanham Act
Refers to the Federal Trade Mark Act of 1946. Protects registered trademarks, trade names, and other service marks used in commerce.

Large business-dominated industry
Industry in which a minimum of 60 percent of employment or sales is in firms with more than 500 workers.

LBO
See Leveraged buy-out

Leader pricing
A reduction in the price of a good or service in order to generate more sales of that good or service.

Legal list
A list of securities selected by a state in which certain institutions and fiduciaries (such as pension funds, insurance companies, and banks) may invest. Securities not on the list are not eligible for investment. Legal lists typically restrict investments to high quality securities meeting certain specifications. Generally, investment is limited to U.S. securities and investment-grade blue chip securities (see separate citation).

Leveraged buy-out (LBO)
The purchase of a business or a division of a corporation through a highly leveraged financing package.

Liability
An obligation or duty to perform a service or an act. Also defined as money owed.

License
A legal agreement granting to another the right to use a technological innovation.

Limited partnerships
See Venture capital limited partnerships

Liquidity
The ability to convert a security into cash promptly.

Loans
See Commercial loans; Disaster loans; SBA direct loans; SBA guaranteed loans; SBA special lending institution categories Local Area Network (LAN) Computer networks contained within a single building or small area; used to facilitate the sharing of information.

Local development corporation
An organization, usually made up of local citizens of a community, designed to improve the economy of the area by inducing business and industry to locate and expand there. A local development corporation establishes a capability to finance local growth.

Long-haul rates
Rates charged by a transporter in which the distance traveled is more than 800 miles.

Long-term debt
An obligation that matures in a period that exceeds five years.

Low-grade bond
A corporate bond that is rated below investment grade by the major rating agencies (Standard and Poor's, Moody's).

Macro-efficiency
Efficiency as it pertains to the operation of markets and market systems.

Managed care
A cost-effective health care program initiated by employers whereby low-cost health care is made available to the employees in return for exclusive patronage to program doctors.

Management Assistance Programs
See SBA Management Assistance Programs

Management and technical assistance
A term used by many programs to mean business (as opposed to technological) assistance.

Mandated benefits
Specific treatments, providers, or individuals required by law to be included in commercial health plans.

Market evaluation
The use of market information to determine the sales potential of a specific product or process.

Market failure
The situation in which the workings of a competitive market do not produce the best results from the point of view of the entire society.

Market information
Data of any type that can be used for market evaluation, which could include demographic data, technology forecasting, regulatory changes, etc.

Market research
A systematic collection, analysis, and reporting of data about the market and its preferences, opinions, trends, and plans; used for corporate decision-making.

Glossary

Market share
In a particular market, the percentage of sales of a specific product.

Marketing
Promotion of goods or services through various media.

Master Establishment List (MEL)
A list of firms in the United States developed by the U.S. Small Business Administration; firms can be selected by industry, region, state, standard metropolitan statistical area (see separate citation), county, and zip code.

Maturity
The date upon which the principal or stated value of a bond or other indebtedness becomes due and payable.

Medicaid (Title XIX)
A federally aided, state-operated and administered program that provides medical benefits for certain low income persons in need of health and medical care who are eligible for one of the government's welfare cash payment programs, including the aged, the blind, the disabled, and members of families with dependent children where one parent is absent, incapacitated, or unemployed.

Medicare (Title XVIII)
A nationwide health insurance program for disabled and aged persons. Health insurance is available to insured persons without regard to income. Monies from payroll taxes cover hospital insurance and monies from general revenues and beneficiary premiums pay for supplementary medical insurance.

MEL
See Master Establishment List

MESBIC
See Minority enterprise small business investment corporation

MET
See Multiple employer trust

Metropolitan statistical area (MSA)
A means used by the government to define large population centers that may transverse different governmental jurisdictions. For example, the Washington, D.C. MSA includes the District of Columbia and contiguous parts of Maryland and Virginia because all of these geopolitical areas comprise one population and economic operating unit.

Mezzanine financing
See Third-stage financing

Micro-efficiency
Efficiency as it pertains to the operation of individual firms.

Microdata
Information on the characteristics of an individual business firm.

Mid-term debt
An obligation that matures within one to five years.

Midrisk venture capital
See Equity midrisk venture capital

Minimum premium plan
A combination approach to funding an insurance plan aimed primarily at premium tax savings. The employer self-funds a fixed percentage of estimated monthly claims and the insurance company insures the excess.

Minimum wage
The lowest hourly wage allowed by the federal government.

Minority Business Development Agency
Contracts with private firms throughout the nation to sponsor Minority Business Development Centers which provide minority firms with advice and technical assistance on a fee basis.

Minority Enterprise Small Business Investment Corporation (MESBIC)
A federally funded private venture capital firm licensed by the U.S. Small Business Administration to provide capital to minority-owned businesses (see separate citation).

Minority-owned business
Businesses owned by those who are socially or economically disadvantaged (see separate citation).

Mom and Pop business
A small store or enterprise having limited capital, principally employing family members.

Moonlighter
A wage-and-salary worker with a side business.

MSA
See Metropolitan statistical area

Multi-employer plan
A health plan to which more than one employer is required to contribute and that may be maintained through a collective bargaining agreement and required to meet standards prescribed by the U.S. Department of Labor.

Multi-level marketing
A system of selling in which you sign up other people to assist you and they, in turn, recruit others to help them. Some entrepreneurs have built successful companies on this concept because the main focus of their activities is their product and product sales.

Multimedia
The use of several types of media to promote a product or service. Also, refers to the use of several different types of media (sight, sound, pictures, text) in a CD-ROM (see separate citation) product.

Multiple employer trust (MET)
A self-funded benefit plan generally geared toward small employers sharing a common interest.

NAFTA
See North American Free Trade Agreement

NASDAQ
See National Association of Securities Dealers Automated Quotations

National Association of Securities Dealers Automated Quotations
Provides price quotes on over-the-counter securities as well as securities listed on the New York Stock Exchange.

National income
Aggregate earnings of labor and property arising from the production of goods and services in a nation's economy.

Net assets
See Net worth

Net income
The amount remaining from earnings and profits after all expenses and costs have been met or deducted. Also known as Net earnings.

Net profit
Money earned after production and overhead expenses (see separate citations) have been deducted.

Net worth
The difference between a company's total assets and its total liabilities.

Network
A chain of interconnected individuals or organizations sharing information and/or services.

New York Stock Exchange (NYSE)
The oldest stock exchange in the U.S. Allows for trading in stocks, bonds, warrants, options, and rights that meet listing requirements.

Niche
A career or business for which a person is well-suited. Also, a product which fulfills one need of a particular market segment, often with little or no competition.

Nodes
One workstation in a network, either local area or wide area (see separate citations).

Nonbank bank
A bank that either accepts deposits or makes loans, but not both. Used to create many new branch banks.

Noncompetitive awards
A method of contracting whereby the federal government negotiates with only one contractor to supply a product or service.

Nonmember bank
A state-regulated bank that does not belong to the federal bank system.

Nonprofit
An organization that has no shareholders, does not distribute profits, and is without federal and state tax liabilities.

Norms
See Financial ratios

Glossary

North American Free Trade Agreement (NAFTA)
Passed in 1993, NAFTA eliminates trade barriers among businesses in the U.S., Canada, and Mexico.

NYSE
See New York Stock Exchange

Occupational Safety & Health Administration (OSHA)
Federal agency that regulates health and safety standards within the workplace.

Optimal firm size
The business size at which the production cost per unit of output (average cost) is, in the long run, at its minimum.

Organizational chart
A hierarchical chart tracking the chain of command within an organization.

OSHA
See Occupational Safety & Health Administration

Overhead
Expenses, such as employee benefits and building utilities, incurred by a business that are unrelated to the actual product or service sold.

Owner's capital
Debt or equity funds provided by the owner(s) of a business; sources of owner's capital are personal savings, sales of assets, or loans from financial institutions.

P & L
See Profit and loss statement

Part-time workers
Normally, those who work less than 35 hours per week. The Tax Reform Act indicated that part-time workers who work less than 17.5 hours per week may be excluded from health plans for purposes of complying with federal nondiscrimination rules.

Part-year workers
Those who work less than 50 weeks per year.

Partnership
Two or more parties who enter into a legal relationship to conduct business for profit. Defined by the U.S. Internal Revenue Code as joint ventures, syndicates, groups, pools, and other associations of two or more persons organized for profit that are not specifically classified in the IRS code as corporations or proprietorships.

Patent
A grant made by the government assuring an inventor the sole right to make, use, and sell an invention for a period of 17 years.

PC
See Professional corporation

Peak
See Cyclical peak

Pension
A series of payments made monthly, semiannually, annually, or at other specified intervals during the lifetime of the pensioner for distribution upon retirement. The term is sometimes used to denote the portion of the retirement allowance financed by the employer's contributions.

Pension fund
A fund established to provide for the payment of pension benefits; the collective contributions made by all of the parties to the pension plan.

Performance appraisal
An established set of objective criteria, based on job description and requirements, that is used to evaluate the performance of an employee in a specific job.

Permit
See Business license

Plan
See Business plan

Pooling
An arrangement for employers to achieve efficiencies and lower health costs by joining together to purchase group health insurance or self-insurance.

PPO
See Preferred provider organization

Preferred lenders program
See SBA special lending institution categories

Preferred provider organization (PPO)
A contractual arrangement with a health care services organization that agrees to discount its health care rates in return for faster payment and/or a patient base.

Premiums
The amount of money paid to an insurer for health insurance under a policy. The premium is generally paid periodically (e.g., monthly), and often is split between the employer and the employee. Unlike deductibles and coinsurance or copayments, premiums arc paid for coverage whether or not benefits are actually used.

Prime-age workers
Employees 25 to 54 years of age.

Prime contract
A contract awarded directly by the U.S. Federal Government.

Private company
See Closely held corporation

Private placement
A method of raising capital by offering for sale an investment or business to a small group of investors (generally avoiding registration with the Securities and Exchange Commission or state securities registration agencies). Also known as Private financing or Private offering.

Pro forma
The use of hypothetical figures in financial statements to represent future expenditures, debts, and other potential financial expenses.

Proactive
Taking the initiative to solve problems and anticipate future events before they happen, instead of reacting to an already existing problem or waiting for a difficult situation to occur.

Procurement
A contract from an agency of the federal government for goods or services from a small business.

Prodigy
An online service which is accessible by computer modem. The service features Internet access, bulletin boards, online periodicals, electronic mail, and other services for subscribers.

Product development
The stage of the innovation process where research is translated into a product or process through evaluation, adaptation, and demonstration.

Product franchising
An arrangement for a franchisee to use the name and to produce the product line of the franchisor or parent corporation.

Production
The manufacture of a product.

Production prototype
See Prototype

Productivity
A measurement of the number of goods produced during a specific amount of time.

Professional corporation (PC)
Organized by members of a profession such as medicine, dentistry, or law for the purpose of conducting their professional activities as a corporation. Liability of a member or shareholder is limited in the same manner as in a business corporation.

Profit and loss statement (P & L)
The summary of the incomes (total revenues) and costs of a company's operation during a specific period of time. Also known as Income and expense statement.

Proposal
See Business plan

Proprietorship
The most common legal form of business ownership; about 85 percent of all small businesses are proprietorships. The liability of the owner is unlimited in this form of ownership.

Prospective payment system
A cost-containment measure included in the Social Security Amendments of 1983 whereby Medicare payments to hospitals are based on established prices, rather than on cost reimbursement.

Prototype
A model that demonstrates the validity of the concept of an invention (laboratory prototype); a model that meets the needs of the manufacturing process and the user (production prototype).

Prudent investor rule or standard
A legal doctrine that requires fiduciaries to make investments using the prudence, diligence, and intelligence that would be used by a prudent person in making similar investments. Because fiduciaries make investments on behalf of third-party beneficiaries, the standard results in very conservative investments. Until recently, most state regulations required the fiduciary to apply this standard to each investment. Newer, more progressive regulations permit fiduciaries to apply this standard to the portfolio taken as a whole, thereby allowing a fiduciary to balance a portfolio with higher-yield, higher-risk investments. In states with more progressive regulations, practically every type of security is eligible for inclusion in the portfolio of investments made by a fiduciary, provided that the portfolio investments, in their totality, are those of a prudent person.

Public equity markets
Organized markets for trading in equity shares such as common stocks, preferred stocks, and warrants. Includes markets for both regularly traded and nonregularly traded securities.

Public offering
General solicitation for participation in an investment opportunity. Interstate public offerings are supervised by the U.S. Securities and Exchange Commission (see separate citation).

Quality control
The process by which a product is checked and tested to ensure consistent standards of high quality.

Rate of return
The yield obtained on a security or other investment based on its purchase price or its current market price. The total rate of return is current income plus or minus capital appreciation or depreciation.

Real property
Includes the land and all that is contained on it.

Realignment
See Resource realignment

Recession
Contraction of economic activity occurring between the peak and trough (see separate citations) of a business cycle.

Regulated market
A market in which the government controls the forces of supply and demand, such as who may enter and what price may be charged.

Regulation D
A vehicle by which small businesses make small offerings and private placements of securities with limited disclosure requirements. It was designed to ease the burdens imposed on small businesses utilizing this method of capital formation.

Regulatory Flexibility Act
An act requiring federal agencies to evaluate the impact of their regulations on small businesses before the regulations are issued and to consider less burdensome alternatives.

Research
The initial stage of the innovation process, which includes idea generation and invention.

Research and development financing
A tax-advantaged partnership set up to finance product development for start-ups as well as more mature companies.

Resource mobility
The ease with which labor and capital move from firm to firm or from industry to industry.

Resource realignment
The adjustment of productive resources to interindustry changes in demand.

Resources
The sources of support or help in the innovation process, including sources of financing, technical evaluation, market evaluation, management and business assistance, etc.

Retained business earnings
Business profits that are retained by the business rather than being distributed to the shareholders as dividends.

Revolving credit
An agreement with a lending institution for an amount of money, which cannot exceed a set maximum, over a specified period of time. Each time the borrower repays a portion of the loan, the amount of the repayment may be borrowed yet again.

Risk capital
See Venture capital

Risk management
The act of identifying potential sources of financial loss and taking action to minimize their negative impact.

Routing
The sequence of steps necessary to complete a product during production.

S corporations
See Sub chapter S corporations

SBA
See Small Business Administration

SBA direct loans
Loans made directly by the U.S. Small Business Administration (SBA); monies come from funds appropriated specifically for this purpose. In general, SBA direct loans carry interest rates slightly lower than those in the private financial markets and are available only to applicants unable to secure private financing or an SBA guaranteed loan.

SBA 504 Program
See Certified development corporation

SBA guaranteed loans
Loans made by lending institutions in which the U.S. Small Business Administration (SBA) will pay a prior agreed-upon percentage of the outstanding principal in the event the borrower of the loan defaults. The terms of the loan and the interest rate are negotiated between theborrower and the lending institution, within set parameters.

SBA loans
See Disaster loans; SBA direct loans; SBA guaranteed loans; SBA special lending institution categories

SBA Management Assistance Programs
Classes, workshops, counseling, and publications offered by the U.S. Small Business Administration.

SBA special lending institution categories
U.S. Small Business Administration (SBA) loan program in which the SBA promises certified banks a 72-hour turnaround period in giving its approval for a loan, and in which preferred lenders in a pilot program are allowed to write SBA loans without seeking prior SBA approval.

SBDB
See Small Business Data Base

SBDC
See Small business development centers

SBI
See Small business institutes program

SBIC
See Small business investment corporation

SBIR Program
See Small Business Innovation Development Act of 1982

Scale economies
The decline of the production cost per unit of output (average cost) as the volume of output increases.

Scale efficiency
The reduction in unit cost available to a firm when producing at a higher output volume.

SCORE
See Service Corps of Retired Executives

SEC
See Securities and Exchange Commission

SECA
See Self-Employment Contributions Act

Second-stage financing
Working capital for the initial expansion of a company that is producing, shipping, and has growing accounts receivable and inventories. Also known as Second-round financing.

Secondary market
A market established for the purchase and sale of outstanding securities following their initial distribution.

Secondary worker
Any worker in a family other than the person who is the primary source of income for the family.

Secondhand capital
Previously used and subsequently resold capital equipment (e.g., buildings and machinery).

Securities and Exchange Commission (SEC)
Federal agency charged with regulating the trade of securities to prevent unethical practices in the investor market.

Securitized debt
A marketing technique that converts long-term loans to marketable securities.

Seed capital
Venture financing provided in the early stages of the innovation process, usually during product development.

Self-employed person
One who works for a profit or fees in his or her own business, profession, or trade, or who operates a farm.

Self-Employment Contributions Act (SECA)
Federal law that governs the self-employment tax (see separate citation).

Self-employment income
Income covered by Social Security if a business earns a net income of at least $400.00 during the year. Taxes are paid on earnings that exceed $400.00.

Self-employment retirement plan
See Keogh plan

Self-employment tax
Required tax imposed on self-employed individuals for the provision of Social Security and Medicare. The tax must be paid quarterly with estimated income tax statements.

Self-funding
A health benefit plan in which a firm uses its own funds to pay claims, rather than transferring the financial risks of paying claims to an outside insurer in exchange for premium payments.

Service Corps of Retired Executives (SCORE)
Volunteers for the SBA Management Assistance Program who provide one-on-one counseling and teach workshops and seminars for small firms.

Service firm
See Business service firm

Service sector
Broadly defined, all U.S. industries that produce intangibles, including the five major industry divisions of transportation, communications, and utilities; wholesale trade; retail trade; finance, insurance, and real estate; and services.

Set asides
See Small business set asides

Short-haul service
A type of transportation service in which the transporter supplies service between cities where the maximum distance is no more than 200 miles.

Short-term debt
An obligation that matures in one year.

SIC codes
See Standard Industrial Classification codes

Single-establishment enterprise
See Establishment

Small business
An enterprise that is independently owned and operated, is not dominant in its field, and employs fewer than 500 people. For SBA purposes, the U.S. Small Business Administration (SBA) considers various other factors (such as gross annual sales) in determining size of a business.

Small Business Administration (SBA)
An independent federal agency that provides assistance with loans, management, and advocating interests before other federal agencies.

Small Business Data Base
A collection of microdata (see separate citation) files on individual firms developed and maintained by the U.S. Small Business Administration.

Small business development centers (SBDC)
Centers that provide support services to small businesses, such as individual counseling, SBA advice, seminars and conferences, and other learning center activities. Most services are free of charge, or available at minimal cost.

Small business development corporation
See Certified development corporation

Small business-dominated industry
Industry in which a minimum of 60 percent of employment or sales is in firms with fewer than 500 employees.

Small Business Innovation Development Act of 1982
Federal statute requiring federal agencies with large extramural research and development budgets to allocate a certain percentage of these funds to small research and development firms. The program, called the Small Business Innovation Research (SBIR) Program, is designed to stimulate technological innovation and make greater use of small businesses in meeting national innovation needs.

Small business institutes (SBI) program
Cooperative arrangements made by U.S. Small Business Administration district offices and local colleges and universities to provide small business firms with graduate students to counsel them without charge.

Small business investment corporation (SBIC)
A privately owned company licensed and funded through the U.S. Small Business Administration and private sector sources to provide equity or debt capital to small businesses.

Small business set asides
Procurement (see separate citation) opportunities required by law to be on all contracts under $10,000 or a certain percentage of an agency's total procurement expenditure.

Smaller firms
For U.S. Department of Commerce purposes, those firms not included in the Fortune 1000.

SMSA
See Metropolitan statistical area

Socially and economically disadvantaged
Individuals who have been subjected to racial or ethnic prejudice or cultural bias without regard to their qualities as individuals, and whose abilities to compete are impaired because of diminished opportunities to obtain capital and credit.

Sole proprietorship
An unincorporated, one-owner business, farm, or professional practice.

Special lending institution categories
See SBA special lending institution categories

Standard Industrial Classification (SIC) codes
Four-digit codes established by the U.S. Federal Government to categorize businesses by type of economic activity; the first two digits correspond to major groups such as construction and manufacturing, while the last two digits correspond to subgroups such as home construction or highway construction.

Standard metropolitan statistical area (SMSA)
See Metropolitan statistical area

Start-up
A new business, at the earliest stages of development and financing.

Start-up costs
Costs incurred before a business can commence operations.

Start-up financing
Financing provided to companies that have either completed product development and initial marketing or have been in business for less than one year but have not yet sold their product commercially.

Stock
A certificate of equity ownership in a business.

Stop-loss coverage
Insurance for a self-insured plan that reimburses the company for any losses it might incur in its health claims beyond a specified amount.

Strategic planning
Projected growth and development of a business to establish a guiding direction for the future. Also used

to determine which market segments to explore for optimal sales of products or services.

Structural unemployment
See Unemployment

Sub chapter S corporations
Corporations that are considered noncorporate for tax purposes but legally remain corporations.

Subcontract
A contract between a prime contractor and a subcontractor, or between subcontractors, to furnish supplies or services for performance of a prime contract (see separate citation) or a subcontract.

Surety bonds
Bonds providing reimbursement to an individual, company, or the government if a firm fails to complete a contract. The U.S. Small Business Administration guarantees surety bonds in a program much like the SBA guaranteed loan program (see separate citation).

Swing loan
See Bridge financing

Target market
The clients or customers sought for a business' product or service.

Targeted Jobs Tax Credit
Federal legislation enacted in 1978 that provides a tax credit to an employer who hires structurally unemployed individuals.

Tax number
A number assigned to a business by a state revenue department that enables the business to buy goods without paying sales tax.

Taxable bonds
An interest-bearing certificate of public or private indebtedness. Bonds are issued by public agencies to finance economic development.

Technical assistance
See Management and technical assistance

Technical evaluation
Assessment of technological feasibility.

Technology
The method in which a firm combines and utilizes labor and capital resources to produce goods or services; the application of science for commercial or industrial purposes.

Technology transfer
The movement of information about a technology or intellectual property from one party to another for use.

Tenure
See Employee tenure

Term
The length of time for which a loan is made.

Terms of a note
The conditions or limits of a note; includes the interest rate per annum, the due date, and transferability and convertibility features, if any.

Third-party administrator
An outside company responsible for handling claims and performing administrative tasks associated with health insurance plan maintenance.

Third-stage financing
Financing provided for the major expansion of a company whose sales volume is increasing and that is breaking even or profitable. These funds are used for further plant expansion, marketing, working capital, or development of an improved product. Also known as Third-round or Mezzanine financing.

Time deposit
A bank deposit that cannot be withdrawn before a specified future time.

Time management
Skills and scheduling techniques used to maximize productivity.

Trade credit
Credit extended by suppliers of raw materials or finished products. In an accounting statement, trade credit is referred to as "accounts payable."

Trade name
The name under which a company conducts business, or by which its business, goods, or services are identified. It may or may not be registered as a trademark.

Trade periodical
A publication with a specific focus on one or more aspects of business and industry.

Trade secret
Competitive advantage gained by a business through the use of a unique manufacturing process or formula.

Trade show
An exhibition of goods or services used in a particular industry. Typically held in exhibition centers where exhibitors rent space to display their merchandise.

Trademark
A graphic symbol, device, or slogan that identifies a business. A business has property rights to its trademark from the inception of its use, but it is still prudent to register all trademarks with the Trademark Office of the U.S. Department of Commerce.

Translation
See Product development

Treasury bills
Investment tender issued by the Federal Reserve Bank in amounts of $10,000 that mature in 91 to 182 days.

Treasury bonds
Long-term notes with maturity dates of not less than seven and not more than twenty-five years.

Treasury notes
Short-term notes maturing in less than seven years.

Trend
A statistical measurement used to track changes that occur over time.

Trough
See Cyclical trough

UCC
See Uniform Commercial Code

UL
See Underwriters Laboratories

Underwriters Laboratories (UL)
One of several private firms that tests products and processes to determine their safety. Although various firms can provide this kind of testing service, many local and insurance codes specify UL certification.

Underwriting
A process by which an insurer determines whether or not and on what basis it will accept an application for insurance. In an experience-rated plan, premiums are based on a firm's or group's past claims; factors other than prior claims are used for community-rated or manually rated plans.

Unfair competition
Refers to business practices, usually unethical, such as using unlicensed products, pirating merchandise, or misleading the public through false advertising, which give the offending business an unequitable advantage over others.

Unfunded accrued liability
The excess of total liabilities, both present and prospective, over present and prospective assets.

Unemployment
The joblessness of individuals who are willing to work, who are legally and physically able to work, and who are seeking work. Unemployment may represent the temporary joblessness of a worker between jobs (frictional unemployment) or the joblessness of a worker whose skills are not suitable for jobs available in the labor market (structural unemployment).

Uniform Commercial Code (UCC)
A code of laws governing commercial transactions across the U.S., except Louisiana. Their purpose is to bring uniformity to financial transactions.

Uniform product code (UPC symbol)
A computer-readable label comprised of ten digits and stripes that encodes what a product is and how much it costs. The first five digits are assigned by the Uniform Product Code Council, and the last five digits by the individual manufacturer.

Unit cost
See Average cost

UPC symbol
See Uniform product code

U.S. Establishment and Enterprise Microdata (USEEM) File
A cross-sectional database containing information on employment, sales, and location for individual

enterprises and establishments with employees that have a Dun & Bradstreet credit rating.

U.S. Establishment Longitudinal Microdata (USELM) File
A database containing longitudinally linked sample microdata on establishments drawn from the U.S. Establishment and Enterprise Microdata file (see separate citation).

U.S. Small Business Administration 504 Program
See Certified development corporation

USEEM
See U.S. Establishment and Enterprise Microdata File

USELM
See U.S. Establishment Longitudinal Microdata File

VCN
See Venture capital network

Venture capital
Money used to support new or unusual business ventures that exhibit above-average growth rates, significant potential for market expansion, and are in need of additional financing to sustain growth or further research and development; equity or equity-type financing traditionally provided at the commercialization stage, increasingly available prior to commercialization.

Venture capital company
A company organized to provide seed capital to a business in its formation stage, or in its first or second stage of expansion. Funding is obtained through public or private pension funds, commercial banks and bank holding companies, small business investment corporations licensed by the U.S. Small Business Administration, private venture capital firms, insurance companies, investment management companies, bank trust departments, industrial companies seeking to diversify their investment, and investment bankers acting as intermediaries for other investors or directly investing on their own behalf.

Venture capital limited partnerships
Designed for business development, these partnerships are an institutional mechanism for providing capital for young, technology-oriented businesses. The

investors' money is pooled and invested in money market assets until venture investments have been selected. The general partners are experienced investment managers who select and invest the equity and debt securities of firms with high growth potential and the ability to go public in the near future.

Venture capital network (VCN)
A computer database that matches investors with entrepreneurs.

WAN
See Wide Area Network

Wide Area Network (WAN)
Computer networks linking systems throughout a state or around the world in order to facilitate the sharing of information.

Withholding
Federal, state, social security, and unemployment taxes withheld by the employer from employees' wages; employers are liable for these taxes and the corporate umbrella and bankruptcy will not exonerate an employer from paying back payroll withholding. Employers should escrow these funds in a separate account and disperse them quarterly to withholding authorities.

Workers' compensation
A state-mandated form of insurance covering workers injured in job-related accidents. In some states, the state is the insurer; in other states, insurance must be acquired from commercial insurance firms. Insurance rates are based on a number of factors, including salaries, firm history, and risk of occupation.

Working capital
Refers to a firm's short-term investment of current assets, including cash, short-term securities, accounts receivable, and inventories.

Yield
The rate of income returned on an investment, expressed as a percentage. Income yield is obtained by dividing the current dollar income by the current market price of the security. Net yield or yield to maturity is the current income yield minus any premium above par or plus any discount from par in purchase price, with the adjustment spread over the period from the date of purchase to the date of maturity.

Index

Listings in this index are arranged alphabetically by business plan type, then alphabetically by business plan name. Users are provided with the volume number in which the plan appears.

Index